T0221232

Cyberactivism on the Participatory Web

Cyberactivism already has a rich history, but over the past decade the participatory web—with its decentralized information/media sharing, portability, storage capacity, and user-generated content—has reshaped political and social change. *Cyberactivism on the Participatory Web* examines the impact of these new technologies on political organizing and protest across the political spectrum, from the Arab Spring to artists to far-right groups. Linking new information and communication technologies to possibilities for solidarity and action—as well as surveillance and control—in a context of global capital flow, war, and environmental crisis, the contributors to this volume provide nuanced analyses of the dramatic transformations in media, citizenship, and social movements taking place today.

Martha McCaughey is Professor of Sociology at Appalachian State University, U.S. She is the editor, with Michael D. Ayers, of *Cyberactivism: Online Activism in Theory and Practice* (Routledge, 2003).

Routledge Studies in New Media and Cyberculture

Cyberactivism on the Participatory Web

Edited by Martha McCaughey

Routledge
Taylor & Francis Group

NEW YORK AND LONDON

First published 2014
by Routledge
711 Third Avenue, New York, NY 10017

and by Routledge
2 Park Square, Milton Park, Abingdon, Oxon OX14 4RN

*Routledge is an imprint of the Taylor & Francis Group,
an informa business*

Library of Congress Cataloging-in-Publication Data

Cyberactivism on the participatory web / edited by Martha McCaughey.
       pages cm. — (Routledge studies in new media and cyberculture ; 18)
    Includes bibliographical references and index.
   1. Internet—Social aspects.   2. Internet—Political aspects.   3. Social action.
4. Social media.   5. Social change.   I. McCaughey, Martha, 1966–
    HM851.C928 2014
    302.23'1—dc23
    2013045143

ISBN: 978-0-415-70903-3 (hbk)
ISBN: 978-1-315-88579-7 (ebk)

Typeset in Sabon
by Apex CoVantage, LLC

Contents

Figures and Tables

Figures

Tables

Introduction
Cyberactivism 2.0: Studying Cyberactivism a Decade into the Participatory Web

Martha McCaughey

Ten years ago, I wanted to assemble the chapters in *Cyberactivism: Online Activism in Theory and Practice* to highlight the exciting noncommercial, activist uses of the Internet. Much of the scholarly work published back then had dealt with online communities and online identities, but not political and social change online. In 2003, *Cyberactivism* brought together essays that discussed the nature and significance of Internet use by activists, social-movement organizations, and grassroots groups seeking various forms of social transformation.

Much has changed since then, and *Cyberactivism on the Participatory Web* captures these recent changes. First, in the last decade a great deal more scholarship has been published about social-change efforts online. Second, the new technological developments themselves necessitate new studies of social and political action: Twitter, Facebook, BuzzFeed, and other social networking systems; wikis, YouTube, and other user-generated content; podcasting, blogging, vlogging, and e-books; geospatial technologies; artistic practices in digital media; the convergence of old and new media; mobile devices and their apps; and the intense battles over who should have what sorts of control over which technologies and which information. Third, new information and communication technologies offer scholars a wealth of new opportunities to study movement structures, participants, and tactics. Finally, the web itself is populated with far more people and thus more diverse opinions, languages, and approaches to the web than in the 1990s and early 2000s.

Today, the decentralized information/media sharing, portability, storage capacity, collaboration, and user-generated content we've come to expect from the web are not restricted to the die-hard computer nerds. As Ethan Zuckerman puts it, "Web 1.0 was invented to allow physicists to share research papers. Web 2.0 was created to allow people to share pictures of cute cats."[1] As Zuckerman notes, the tools used for "cute cat" purposes are being used by a smaller number of people for activist purposes. The developments and possibilities of Web 2.0 have also been exploited for commercial purposes because consumers help build a business online by "liking" or "pinning" something they find online, making promotional videos go viral, and receiving advertisements targeted to their individual web-browsing activity. Yet, as in every era, activists are using whatever communication technologies exist to share their grievances with as many people as possible and to mobilize as many people as possible around those grievances.

Web 2.0 has facilitated the creation and spread of content, changing social-movement activism and organizing. That activism may be focused on digital rights themselves, on broad social issues such as economic inequality or identity-based rights, or on a very specific, local matter of concern. Whether they are Americans organizing the Occupy Wall Street protests or Egyptians tweeting in the streets during the revolution that same year, movement participants are recognizing and expressing grievances, and organizing resistance, through the information and communication technologies that are now widely available, portable, and participatory.

The essays in this volume show that the web is a standard tool for organizers, not a substitute for "real" action. Cyberactivism is typically combined with many forms of movement organizing and protest from the analog era, including donating time and money, talking to people, showing up to courts, demonstrating on the streets, clashing with police, and otherwise putting one's body on the line. A decade ago, people were asking if online participation "led to" showing up to protest. It's clear now that movements are hybrids of online and offline activity, and one does not cause, or prevent, the other. We therefore can no longer simply ask whether or not Web 2.0 impacts protesting or people's likelihood to end up in a face-to-face protest. As the chapters here show, new social media impact social and political change by presenting new ways to make change and new ways to protest. They also show that the political environment in which digital activists find themselves shapes how activists will use digital technologies. Further, digital activism can be intensely specific, personal, and single-issue; yet it is also distinctly transnational. The theoretically nuanced studies in *Cyberactivism on the Participatory Web* capture changes in, and question outmoded assumptions about, activism, consumption, identity, and social change.

The chapters collected here also serve as excellent models of how cyberactivism is researched, theorized, and assessed. Whereas some of the contributors to the 2003 *Cyberactivism* volume who continue to work in this area have brand new chapters here, this volume includes chapters on topics that could not possibly have been covered a decade ago: the role of new social media in the recent democratic movements in the Middle East, the role of new media technologies in the global environmental justice movement, and the hybrid style of activism (face-to-face and digital) that now characterizes social movements. The studies in this volume also cover a variety of political perspectives from the radical right to the left wing.

Few would question the claim that activism is now just as tied up with participatory social media as activism in the 1960s was with print media and television. Still debated, though, are questions about whether some single-issue or single-purpose digital activism misses the solidarity, mass-protest, and sense of interconnectedness that typified activism in the 1960s; questions about the role of linkages between activist groups; and questions about what makes a group a serious, effective political force. Each contributor to this volume speaks to such debates by pursuing a specific question and offering research to answer it. In doing so, together they raise new questions about trust, place, pluralistic movement structures, transnational connections and collaboration, and the governmental policies that open or control the communications.

The volume opens with Laura J. Gurak's chapter, "Trust and Internet Activism: From Email to Social Networks." Gurak examines the use of Facebook during and after the 2010 tornado touchdown in Minneapolis and the 2012 campaign to defeat a proposed constitutional amendment banning same-sex marriage in Minnesota, demonstrating some important differences between the text-based online activism of the 1990s and today's organizing over new social media. At the same time, Gurak shows that the sense of trust among participants that needed to be established in order for the action to be effective 20 years ago remains an important element of digital activism today. Gurak also points out that, because the web is no longer occupied by a relatively elite group (mostly academics who shared common values about computer privacy), trust must be established differently and amidst (mis)information overload.

John Logie's chapter, "Dark Days: Understanding the Historical Context and the Visual Rhetorics of the SOPA/PIPA Blackout," examines the visual strategies employed in the 2012 SOPA/PIPA online protests, which successfully blocked overreaching U.S. legislation that could have shut down websites for alleged copyright violations. Major sites like Wikipedia used foreboding visuals to spark protest of web censorship. Importantly, Logie situates this web blackout in the context of early online protests, namely the 1996 Black World Wide Web protest and the 1999 Haunting of Geocities. A key component in all of these online movements for digital rights was the harnessing of visual opportunities that helped spread the message virally.

In addition to exploring what makes social-movement participants trust movement leaders they've not encountered in person, this volume raises related questions about *place*. Do movement activists identify or project themselves onto a particular place? Do online organizers need one specific online "place," or are they multimodal, and multi-placed? Jennifer Terrell's chapter, "The Harry Potter Alliance: Sociotechnical Contexts of Digitally Mediated Activism," argues that a new identity based in a sense of placeless online community can create a successful activist campaign. The young fans of Harry Potter novels come together in a virtual community for a variety of social actions. Terrell shows how new social media make the Harry Potter Alliance distinct from previous types of fan activism, as the technology combined with the culture enable fans to identify with people and causes in distant communities of grievance.

In his chapter, "Dangerous Places: Social Media at the Convergence of Peoples, Labor, and Environmental Movements," Richard Widick argues that place is still a central motivator for digitally mediated activism. Suggesting that new media make new identifications possible, Widick develops a theory of the importance of digital media for creating a social imaginary around dangerous places—places into which people project themselves and organize for change. Activists, he argues, now reach through new social media to create a social imaginary that makes sense of climate justice, abuses on Wall Street, and local struggles like deforestation. Like Gurak, Widick situates contemporary movement activism in a historical context to show similarities and shifts across media technology platforms.

The so-called "Twitter revolution" is as young as 2009. But Twitter earned the reputation as a key player in democratic movements before we knew exactly what role it played in on-the-ground organizing, creating solidarity among geographically dispersed groups, or connecting people across language barriers. "The Arab Spring and Its Social Media Audiences: English and Arabic Twitter Users and Their Networks" by Axel Bruns, Tim Highfield, and Jean Burgess addresses these questions through an analysis of Arabic, English, and mixed-language tweeting activity focused on Libya and Egypt in 2011. This study shows who was tweeting during the uprisings, from which locations, and in which language(s)—offering a nuanced picture of the roles Twitter played in the Arab Spring. Notably, the relative lack of local tweets from inside Libya compared to those in Egypt during the uprisings shows how regional and national conditions influence the role new social media will play in and during protest activity.

Alexander Halavais and Maria Garrido's chapter, "Twitter as the People's Microphone: Emergence of Authorities during Protest Tweeting," examines the impact that microblogging had during the G20 protests in Pittsburgh, Pennsylvania, offering a method for studying tweets to determine which organizations' and individuals' tweets have the most influence in a social movement context. Like Widick's chapter, this chapter shows us how new communication technologies help shape the meaning of a political event or social issue. And like the chapter by Bruns, Highfield, and Burgess, this chapter also offers keen insights into new methods for the analysis of large-scale Twitter data. Moreover, Halavais and Garrido's study concerns itself with authority, credibility, trust, and influence over new social media platforms.

The chapter by Jessie Daniels, "From Crisis Pregnancy Centers to Teen-Breaks.com: Anti-Abortion Activism's Use of Cloaked Websites," also concerns credibility and trust in online activism. Daniels examines the cloaked websites of anti-abortion activist groups. While conservative groups are not the only ones to use cloaked websites, Daniels shows the ways in which the political agenda is hidden behind websites laid out to appear moderate and informative so as to deceive and misdirect women seeking abortions. In doing so, she shows the parallels to the deceptive practices of the brick-and-mortar Crisis Pregnancy Center movement. Further, like Gurak's contribution, Daniels' chapter highlights the extent to which struggles over facts, truth, and trust are fundamental to both digital activism and critical Internet literacy.

Digital activism can also demand, and be, business savvy. Constance Kampf's chapter, "Art Interrupting Business, Business Interrupting Art: Re(de)fining the Interface between Business and Society," shows how digital artists' activism can effectively create change because they create projects with media reach and actual financial consequences. Offering as context an explication of 1990s art-activist groups like etoy, ®ᴛᴍ ark, Yes Men, and UBERMORGEN, Kampf shows how ToyWar, Vote-Auction, and Google Will Eat Itself disrupted business as usual through strategies that are at once business-savvy and media-savvy, creatively questioning, for instance, Internet domain ownership, the role of big corporations in elections, and the negative effects of Google's AdSense model. Similar to Daniels' contribution, Kampf's chapter makes the case for critical Internet literacy by showing how digital artist activism exposes deceptive business practices to public scrutiny.

Manuela Caiani and Rossella Borri's chapter, "Cyberactivism of the Radical Right in Europe and the USA: What, Who, and Why?", examines the online activism of extreme right-wing groups in seven Western democracies. Interviewing 45 people in extreme-right political parties, political movements, and subcultural youth groups, as well as doing a content analysis of right-wing websites, Caiani and Borri show how far-right groups use the Internet to foster a group's identity, raise money, stage web-based events, and avoid government infiltration. Although both resources and features of an organization influence the specific approach to online activism, radical right-wing groups are using online communication tools to produce political information and, potentially, link transnationally.

As the cases of far-right activism and the global environmental justice movements demonstrate, a vast number of social movements connect and grow through digital media. Solidarity can quickly become transnational, not just because the issues are more clearly related to one another than ever before but because capital flows, war, and environmental destruction are global. Just as computer-mediated communications enable our awareness of these issues, they enable people to make the connections with those around the world variously impacted by violence, environmental disaster, and repression. Our awareness, identification, and organizing can be transnational—and instantaneously so.

Dorothy Kidd's chapter, "Young Chinese Workers, Contentious Politics, and Cyberactivism in the Global Factory," offers an analysis of the activism of young migrant workers in China, revealing a sporadic and localized set of protests with no clear leadership or unified political direction. Although such movements have been deemed failures by some, Kidd's chapter reveals the urgent need to reassess what counts as movement success and how movement goals are articulated and achieved in the shifting climate of the participatory Web.

Megan Boler and Christina Nitsou's chapter, "Women Activists of Occupy Wall Street: Consciousness-Raising and Connective Action in Hybrid Social Movements," similarly argues that the recent hybrid activism can be effective. This study of the women in the Occupy movement shows that new social media are shaping political organizing and changing how the movements are led—and, significantly, which people end up empowered through the organizing process. The hybrid social movements that typify collective action today are horizontal and therefore relatively "leaderless." The structure of these new hybrid movements thus demands a rethinking of movement leadership and movement success.

Just as the newest technologies enable the passionate pursuit of a single issue, while also enabling people to symbolically and strategically link issues together globally, the technological accessibility and portability that make participation possible also make new forms of surveillance possible. What is the line between participation and surveillance? If Web 1.0 blurred lines between community and commerce, purpose and profit, Web 2.0 blurs the line between participation and control. The volume concludes on a cautionary note with Lee Salter's chapter, "Emergent Social Movements in Online Media and States of Crisis: Analyzing the Potential for Resistance and Repression Online," on state repression through new social media. Drawing on a range of examples from both the Arab Spring as well as protests in liberal states, Salter shows how social media have in some cases become dragnets through which activists can be monitored and pursued.

NOTE

1. Ethan Zuckerman, "The Cute Cat Theory Talk at E-Tech" (2008), last modified October 20, 2013, www.ethanzuckerman.com/blog/2008/03/08/the-cute-cat-theory-talk-at-etech/.

1 Trust and Internet Activism

From Email to Social Networks

Laura J. Gurak

In the time of the first edition of *Cyberactivism*, the use of the Internet for protest, activism, and organizing had only just begun. Technology was changing at a rapid pace, shifting from text-based to web-based, with the coming dominance of Facebook and Twitter still far off on the digital horizon. The earliest documented online protest, the case of Lotus MarketPlace,[1] was effective but limited to the text-only environments of email and Usenet newsgroups, where participants tended to be part of a small, elite group of computer users that shared similar values and were to some extent part of established online communities. In later cases, such as the Yahoo/Geocities protest,[2] the use of web pages that combined textual as well as visual information was fast becoming the norm.

Today, social media in all of its ubiquity and simplicity is the standard approach for online activism. Gone are the days when organizers needed to understand how to code in HTML or run a listserv. A few simple keystrokes, and organizers are able to create blogs, Twitter feeds, or Facebook pages, which are easy to use and require no special technical knowledge either for the organizer or users who want to participate. These platforms combine text, visuals, sound, video, and other content in ways hard to imagine even 10 years ago. In addition, online spaces today typically blend the virtual and the physical, supporting, for example, a movement with a strong physical presence such as the Occupy movement,[3] the so-called "Arab spring,"[4] or the peace movement.[5] While email still plays a role, especially in targeting particular groups of constituents for fund-raising purposes, the prevalence of social media has changed the face of cyberactivism.

This chapter presents three micro-cases: Lotus Marketplace (1992), a tornado touchdown in Minneapolis and the use of Facebook during disaster recovery (2010), and the campaign to defeat a proposed constitutional amendment banning same-sex marriage in Minnesota (2012). The two later cases demonstrate some characteristics of early online activism, especially the sense of trust that must exist among participants in order for the action to be effective. But other features, especially ways in which the later situations have sustained and become community resources, in large part due to the use of social media, demonstrate important differences between 1992 and today.

TEXT ONLY: THE CASE OF LOTUS MARKETPLACE

The earliest documented social action on the Internet is the case of Lotus MarketPlace. Described more fully in the previous edition of *Cyberactivism*[6] and elsewhere,[7,8] the case involved the use of email and Usenet newsgroups to protest a commercial product. This protest was successful in that the product was canceled before it was ever released. On April 10, 1990, Lotus Development Corporation announced a product called MarketPlace: Households, a CD that would contain the names, addresses, and spending habits of 120 million U.S. consumers from 80 million different households. (The market for this CD was people who wanted to do direct marketing from home and did not want to pay the high fees that were then charged to work with a direct market mailing house.) In today's low/no privacy environment, where people readily share everything about themselves in high contact settings (e.g., on Facebook), it is hard to recall that in 1990, the idea of providing such information to a potentially vast audience, without user permission, was seen by many as raising serious concerns about personal privacy and large data sets. Privacy advocates were concerned in particular about the ability of someone to crack the CD's encryption scheme and match salaries and names with local addresses. There was also concern about not being able to correct the data once the CDs were released.

The product was discussed in a November *Wall Street Journal* article of that year, and this article generated much discussion on the Internet. Specifically, Usenet news and email, the only two games in town at the time, were at the center of the initial conversations. At that time, the Internet was dominated by academics, particularly computer scientists and other IT specialists. Even at large companies like Lotus, regular employees did not use email. So when the online discussion began advocating for people to contact the CEO of Lotus via email, it took no time at all for the message to spread. Trust was high in this case: Those writing and forwarding the email and Usenet messages were of a common core of like-minded computer privacy advocates. One of the most widely circulated messages is signed by its author, and even though most recipients didn't actually know him, they trusted him because at that time, the Internet was a small club, full of people-like-us, who shared common values about what "cyberspace" should be.

The messages that circulated about Lotus MarketPlace contained some truth and some fiction. Yet the high-trust environment created a powerful environment, and in January 1991, the CEO of Lotus Corporation announced that it would cancel the product before it was even released. Most observers acknowledged the role of the Internet in the demise of Lotus

MarketPlace. To an observer today, the lack of visual media, web pages, smart phones, Twitter, and so forth might make such a case seem impossible. Yet in this case, we see the core of online social activism as trust-based and established through the rhetorical dynamics of the message (especially the role of ethos as a rhetorical appeal), the speed of delivery, and the like-mindedness of the participants. These features are described in detail elsewhere[9] and provide the basis for examining our next case.

SOCIAL MEDIA: THE CASE OF NORTH MINNEAPOLIS POST TORNADO WATCH

Every spring, residents of the U.S. upper Midwest look forward to the end of a long, dark, cold, winter. Yet along with the joy of spring, there can also be a sense of fear and concern. Major spring flooding, due to rapid melting of a deep snowpack, can be devastating to both urban and rural communities. Spring also brings with it a clash of warm air from the south and cold air from the north, as the seasons do battle with each other and the northern hemisphere shifts from winter to spring. This unsettled situation is the perfect breeding ground for strong storms, many of which bring wind damage from hail, lightening, strong winds, or, worse, tornadoes.

People often believe that significant tornadoes do not touch down in urban areas. Yet on May 22, 2011, a tornado touched down in northeast Minneapolis, devastating one of what was the most economically disadvantaged parts of the city. The impact was so severe, so fast, and so unexpected, that initially everyone was in a state of shock. With no electricity and no phone lines, the only technology available for communication was the cell phone, for those who had one. Hearing about the situation on the news and from his friends and family in the area, a man named Peter Kerre who had lived in Minneapolis but was based at that time in New York city, was able to quickly set up a the North Minneapolis Post Tornado Watch Facebook page. The ensuing story offers an interesting comparison about the similarities as well as differences between Lotus MarketPlace and activism in the early stages of social media.[10]

As Sztompka[11] has noted, trust is often established in relation to social proximity, thereby creating "cultures of trust"—in the case of Lotus MarketPlace, what we might call "Internet social proximity"—and a culture of online trust was clearly a reason why like-minded users circulated the messages so heavily. In the case of the tornado relief, Peter's background as a person with strong ties to the neighborhood had the same effect. Although he was not living in the area at that time, Peter was hearing from friends that no one knew where to turn or how to access resources. Recognizing that on each block, there seemed to be at least one person with a smart phone, Peter set up a Facebook page called "North Minneapolis Post Tornado Watch." This page, as the local paper suggested, quickly became "a sort of virtual public square to share tips, dispel rumors, report suspicious characters and, most of all, get help to the people who need it quickly."[12]

As with the Lotus MarketPlace case, in this situation people tended to trust the online information (Facebook page) more than official city and state resources. In part, this feature was due to the high-trust context of a personal connection versus the low-trust context, especially for people in this neighborhood, of dealing with government bureaucracies. Social proximity and trust were not affixed to location but rather to a known individual. Many people did know Peter first-hand, but many did not, trusting instead in the collective belief that comes when others who are like you trust in something. Also, the Facebook platform made the information easy to access: When there is no electricity and your house and computer have been damaged, but your phone still works, Facebook was simply an easier way to find information.

In our current era, state and city governments, federal agencies, and non-profits have gotten better about using social media in situations such as this. (The aftermath of Hurricane Sandy is just one recent example.) Yet in 2011, Facebook was still primarily a platform for individuals, not organizations. According to Kerre, these organizations (government agencies and disaster relief agencies, among others) were curious to know who he was and why he was setting up a Facebook page (and, for that matter, what a Facebook page was).

In addition to the Facebook page, Peter also set up a Google site, where people could add information, links, and other resources. Because of these concerns from formal agencies, the site offers this disclaimer:

> This page does not represent or/and is not part of any emergency or law enforcement agency or organization. It is a 100% charitable cause initiative created by a joe nobody;) and is people driven. Thank you! For immediate attention and emergencies, dial 911 to get to your local law enforcement and emergency responders.[13]

Official concerns were partially justified: Often, after a disaster, victims are targeted by sham contractors and relief agencies. Yet as with the Lotus case, this situation demonstrates again the clash between structured organizational communication, where those in power who rely on more traditional communication structures wish to retain that power and status (even with the best of intentions), contrasted with the nonhierarchical, democratized nature of online communication, which may be messy and unstructured and not as carefully edited for content, but which often has a better chance of reaching more people with greater speed.

Although these issues about trust and organizational structure were similar between these two cases, a major difference is the technological conditions of social media that allow a site such as this to remain a resource for the community. In the Lotus case, once the product was canceled, the discussion all but ended. In the tornado disaster case, the Facebook page still as of this writing is serving as a resource for this community, with 3,453 "likes" and many postings about events, activities, and resources. The site also appears to be more closely connected with government and other organizations; for instance, in spring 2013, after another series of spring storms, the site posted information from the City of Minneapolis and the local power company about estimated wait times for power to be restored.

This feature, of how social media functions not only to support an immediate urgency and types of activism but also to provide a sustained space to become something beyond the immediate exigency, is demonstrated in the next case.

SOCIAL MEDIA PLUS: SAME-SEX MARRIAGE IN MINNESOTA

In May 2011, the Republican majority Minnesota legislature passed a bill proposing an amendment to the state constitution limiting marriage to one man and one woman. Although the Governor, a Democrat, vetoed the bill, his actions were strictly symbolic, since in Minnesota, constitutional amendment legislation cannot be vetoed. Thus, the amendment was slated to appear on the November 2012 ballot, where it was defeated by the voters by just over 52%. The events that took place between the introduction of the amendment and voting day provide a most interesting case for anyone interested in cyberactivism.

As noted at the end of the previous discussion, social media can play a powerful role in the initial set-up and activity for a specific situation or cause. Yet because social media is so well structured, ubiquitous, and broad-reaching, once the initial exigence has come to a conclusion, there is often tremendous value and efficiency in using the existing platform to continue as a community resource; or, in this case, as a powerful mechanism to take up the next leg of the political issue.

During the November 2012 election, the Minnesota House and Senate turned into democratic majorities. With that plus Democratic Governor Mark Dayton, who had vetoed the original legislation, still the Governor, organizers used the tools, data, and resources they had so carefully cultivated—email lists, Twitter feeds, websites, Facebook pages—to press forward and in the end, turn the tables on those who had sent the initial constitutional amendment forward. In June 2013, Minnesota became the 12th U.S. state to approve same sex marriage.

Between the legislation's introduction (May 2011) and election day (November 2012), a group called Minnesotans United for All Families became the primary force in organizing what became a historic campaign to defeat the proposed amendment. In all states where similar constitutional amendments had been put on the ballot, 100% of these had passed to become part of that state's constitution. Minnesotans United learned valuable lessons from those states. In particular, according to a story by Minnesota Public Radio,[14] a report that was written after the passage of Proposition 8 in California was influential in shaping the approach of Minnesotans United.[15] The report[16] makes many key points, but two are of special interest to this discussion of cyberactivism. First, the report's finding #5 provides evidence that the Vote No on 8 campaign did not offer a clear, concise message. This finding is especially important in our digital age, where sound bites, tweets, email, and Facebook postings, as well as streams of information from traditional media, make long or complicated arguments probably the worst possible choice. Our current media environment simply is not conducive to detailed, complicated discussions. The report's author identifies six different arguments made in the Vote No on 8 campaign, whereas he identified only one clear message (about children) in the Vote Yes campaign.

More to the point, however, is the report's Finding #9, which discussed the key importance of fundraising (something the Minnesotans United campaign did extremely well). The report notes that in October of that year,

> [O]nline fundraising was turned over to an entirely new group of former and current experts from Google, Facebook, and Yahoo. Volunteering their considerable talents, they added a substantial functionality to the Web site and drove traffic to the website. They developed easy ways for the campaign to measure the yield of each fundraising appeal and approach. They put the campaign in a position to track the ways in which people were finding their ways to the No on 8 Web site. With this additional information—updated within hours—the campaign could determine which experiments were working and which weren't. Then it could focus on replicating and rolling out more fully the successful experiments. The much quicker ascension of the learning curve that came from this over data-driven approach—iterative learning is the term that best describes it—greatly increased online fundraising productivity.[17]

Minnesotans United for All Families took these ideas to heart, creating a well-focused, concise message. The message was simple: Don't deny people the freedom to marry. The last three words, "freedom to marry," fit nicely on a t-shirt, in a tweet, or in the subject line of an email. They created a theme and were easy to remember. The campaign also asked volunteers to tell their stories, talk with their neighbors, and connect with one another as people, fellow citizens, and neighbors. In a state that has typically prided itself on neighborliness and a live-and-let-live attitude (sometimes called "Minnesota nice"), this one-on-one approach made sense. The campaign referred to this approach—having conversations—as their "secret weapon."[18]

Yet these efforts on their own would not have succeeded without the incredibly effective, sophisticated use of the web, email, Twitter, and Facebook, not only to raise funds but also to zero in on people who might serve as volunteers at public events (such as the Minnesota State Fair), do some phone banking, or volunteer in dozens of other ways. Thus, social media were woven into a fabric that included a physical campaign. As with the tornado recovery example, the Minnesotans United example illustrates the power of using social media to connect to physical events.

I participated in the Minnesotans United campaign, and my observations are from this experience. In 2012, my partner of 22 years and I decided to go to New York to marry. We did so knowing that Minnesota could very well pass a constitutional same-sex marriage ban, yet we still felt it important to have this legal recognition and knew we could always move to a same-sex marriage state if the ban were passed. It was an interesting year, to be married but then return back to a state where legally it meant nothing. Because of my personal interest, during the year as the campaign ramped up, I began making financial contributions. I noticed that with each contribution, the email messages became more targeted. With each visit to the website or with each item I "liked" or shared on Facebook or retweeted, I became part of a more focused data set. Then, I volunteered for an evening of phone banking and for outreach at the Twin Cities Pride festival and later, at the State Fair. I continued to give money, responding in particular to those email messages that had a strong personal appeal.

As a researcher of new media and online social actions, it was interesting to observe my reactions. I knew that the friendly, personal messages signed by the campaign manager, or a famous football player, or another volunteer, or the mother of a gay son, that were directed at me (Hey Laura, Dear Laura) weren't *really* directed at me, one-to-one. But the rhetorical appeal was strong, and the trust factor was high. The campaign's use of techniques garnered from ecommerce and Facebook—data mining, recommender systems, behavior matching, demographic and giving patterns—were at once sophisticated and personal. These systems and their approach to data matching are based on the algorithms originally developed for what are called "recommender systems," most familiar today on sites like Amazon and Netflix that carefully track and analyze you and your habits and match you with other people and products. Recommender systems work in large part based on the development of trust;[19] for example, as these systems continue to match you with ideas, people, and products that fit well with your habits and values, you as the recipient gain more trust in the recommendations. In the case of the emails I was receiving from Minnesotans United, as these messages became more and more personalized to me, my values, and my concerns, the trust factor increased, which in turn increased my financial contributions and my active participation in the campaign.

Numerous other techniques and approaches contributed to the defeat of the constitutional amendment in November 2012, especially the way in which organizers engaged religious and faith community leaders and the focus on individual conversations.[20] But the use of digital communication to engage, raise funds, and circle in on trusted volunteers who in turn placed high trust in the organization's message, was certainly one of the key factors.

This case also illustrates how the digital infrastructure that was so carefully built during the initial event became a platform for a new action. With the wind at their backs, due in no small part to the powerful digital infrastructure already in place, organizers pushed forward to bring a bill to the legislature making same-sex marriage legal in Minnesota. As noted above, the result was that Minnesota became the 12th state in the U.S. to legalize same sex marriage.

Some might argue that this was a political campaign, pure and simple, not "cyberactivism," as illustrated in the grassroots efforts of Lotus MarketPlace and the tornado recovery. Yet indeed, the Minnesotans United campaign was grassroots. The previously mentioned "secret weapon" of "a massive, one-on-one conversation drive"[21] was based on thousands of individuals talking with one another. Digital media played a key role, as noted, initially in creating a common message and location and then in raising funds, finding volunteers, and, importantly, matching volunteers' demographic backgrounds with areas where these people could be most effective. For instance, citizens in the more liberal parts of the cities of Minneapolis and St. Paul could be counted on to vote no in the majority. But I live in one of the northern suburbs right on the dividing line between the cities and the start of the more rural counties. I was contacted numerous times about the importance of doing phone banking in my district, and eventually, the customized emails and calls got me to participate.

SIMILARITIES AND DIFFERENCES

The three cases presented here illustrate a technological progression of cyberactivism, from the text-based Lotus MarketPlace action to the Facebook page of the tornado recovery situation to the full court press of all forms of digital and social media in the Minnesotans United case. It is worth examining both the similarities and the differences in these cases, not only for the sake of understanding the past but also so that we can think about how digital media will continue to be part of the future of social actions, protests, political campaigns, and more.

Elsewhere, I have argued that speed and reach are two of the key concepts of digital communication that span different media and different time periods.[22] The very earliest uses of email, for instance, made plain just how powerful it is to press "enter" and send a message far and wide, at lightning speed. These dynamics are key to understanding all three cases here. Messages, be they email, Facebook postings, or tweets, travel quickly and with amazingly wide reach. These features are a double-edged sword. On the one hand, reaching so many people so quickly can be critical, especially in an emergency. On the other hand, these same features allow for misinformation to spread just as easily; every day, we see countless examples of

Internet scams and hear about people who fall victim to these. Separating truth from fiction can be hard to do in a space where visual elements can look extremely convincing, identities are created out of thin air, and emotional appeals run high.

A concept from classical rhetoric, illustrated in all three cases, helps explain why, in fact, we need to be alert to both the potentials as well as the problems of online activism around this matter. Focusing on the character and credibility of the speaker and message, this concept is called *ethos*. It is one of the three traditional appeals used when making an argument. Although the other two—*logos* and *pathos*—are important, yet as far back as Aristotle it was observed that of these three, *ethos* was the most powerful in moving an audience.[23] A large reason why, of course, is that character and credibility are related to the trust that is placed in the speaker/message.

In his classic treatise on this topic, Luhmann observes that "[t]rust, in the broadest sense of confidence in one's expectations, is a basic fact of social life . . . a complete absence of trust would prevent [a person] from even getting up in the morning."[24] He goes on to describe the complicated relationship of trust to variables such as time, social relationships, past interactions, and so forth. In all three cases, trust plays a key role. In the Lotus case, participants trusted each other far more than they trusted the company. In the case of the tornado recovery, there was high trust placed in a known person, an individual with strong ties to the community. And in the same-sex marriage case, trust evolved quickly among those working to defeat the amendment based on a powerful combination of social media and email, combined with individual in-person conversations. Even though I realized that the "Dear Laura" emails were not written individually just to me, the custom message and tone was an effective technique in developing trust, at least for me, and presumably for the larger, more diverse group of people receiving these messages.

There are also some obvious differences in these cases as well. In the early days, online protests were typically about esoteric technical topics that appealed to a narrow group of sophisticated computer users. In the first edition of *Cyberactivism*, this point is very clear. The Lotus case, and soon thereafter, another technology protest, the Clipper chip case (discussed in conjunction with the Lotus case in Gurak 1999), were both about computer privacy, with Clipper focused on the even narrower and more technical issue of encryption. The GeoCities Yahoo! protest was also about a topic for the technologically informed: websites and copyright.[25] Today, however, with the ubiquity of the Internet, the broader user base, and the simplicity of interfaces for Twitter, Facebook, and even email, cyberactivism has become a part of broader social and political causes. Even when social media is not used as heavily, online petitions have become the *de facto* method of collecting signatures for most highly visible issues. For instance, in May 2013, 1.8 million people signed a petition advocating that the Boy Scouts of America change its policy banning gay youth.[26]

CONCLUSION: INTERNET ACTIVISM GOING FORWARD

Going forward, we will be less and less able to discern "cyberactivism" from regular activism. As digital and social media become a part of our regular ways of learning, doing business, governing, conducting political campaigns, and various other forms of attempting to move people to action, cyberactivism will be more along a continuum than a special category. In some instances, such as the petition against the Boy Scouts of America policy, the power and reach of digital media is an obvious factor. In other cases, such as the same-sex marriage case in Minnesota, cyberactivism will be woven into the larger fabric of an effective campaign that also includes face-to-face contacts and phone calls as well as television and other traditional media ads.

We have moved into a time when all social actions have a digital component and where speed, reach, ease of use, low cost, and other factors will continue to have a democratizing effect, shifting increasingly away from hierarchical forms of communication as the sole source of information. As described in the tornado recovery case, maintaining a gap between official communication and grassroots, citizen-driven communication no longer makes sense. Just as professional journalists have had to learn to collaborate with citizen journalists and bloggers, so to do organizations of all types need to harness the power and potential of bottom-up communication and activism. Of course, each individual case will be different, based on the desired outcome and the topic at hand. Speed and reach remain key. The rise of visual communication, text reduced to small "info-bites," and new trends in social media, will also continue to influence and shape these cases.

Trust, as it is established in these settings, is a major factor in what drives participation. Because people tend to trust what they already believe or trust in people they feel akin to, the nonhierarchical structure and wide reach and speed of digital communication also create numerous possibilities for deception. For example, Daniels, in this collection, describes the use of "cloaked" websites by opponents of abortion as a way to hide the site's true identity (and thus, ideology) from readers. Although deception is not new, as Daniels argues digital media provides the ability to deceive in a way that is both easier and less traceable than previous media.[27] As mentioned previously, misinformation can spread quickly and easily online. Future studies of online activism should look at this issue as well.

It is useful to reflect on trust as expressed by Uslander: "[t]rust," he claims, "is the chicken soup of life. It brings all sorts of good things . . . [y]et, like chicken soup, it appears to work somewhat mysteriously. It might seem that we can only develop trust in people we know. Yet, trust's benefits come when we put our faith in strangers."[28] This is an important statement for studies of trust and cyberactivism, for although I have claimed that the cases presented here illustrate situations where the speaker or message was trusted, this trust was not completely based on first-hand personal knowledge by the reader/participant about the writer/organizer. In fact, to most observers, the person who wrote the email, or signed the email, or created the website, or wrote the Facebook posting or tweet, is unknown. As noted in the tornado recovery case, not everyone knew Peter first-hand, but people trusted in the collective belief that comes when others who are like you trust in something. This feature—how trust is established in digital settings, often very quickly via close networks and associations, with no true sense of who is behind the message—is something to pay close attention to in future instances of cyberactivism, digital campaigning, and so on. In some cases, strangers who remain strangers (such as the group Anonymous or the unknown authors of a Wikileaks-type project or even Wikipedia entries) may have stronger persuasive power than a known person or group.[29]

Finally, who can predict what new hardware and software, still in their infancy, will emerge in two, five, 10 years or more? Twitter and microblogging were not a part of our discussion of cyberactivism a decade ago. The line between everyday citizen and seasoned professional, between mainstream media and small productions, between the television and Twitter, continue to shape-shift. But the establishment of trust will continue to play a key role in successful actions. If we keep our eyes on using these tools to advance knowledge and human potential, balancing the democratizing effects with continued vigilance and education about misinformation, the future for all forms of social action looks bright.

NOTES

1. Laura J. Gurak, *Persuasion and Privacy in Cyberspace: The Online Protests over Lotus MarketPlace and the Clipper Chip* (New Haven: Yale University Press, 1997).
2. Laura J. Gurak and John Logie, "Internet Protests, from Text to Web," in *Cyberactivism: Online Activism in Theory and Practice*, eds. Martha McCaughey and Michael D. Ayers (New York: Routledge, 2003), 25–46.
3. Boler and Nitsou, "Women Activists," this volume.
4. Philip N. Howard and Muzammil M. Hussain, "The Role of Digital Media," *Journal of Democracy* 22, no. 3 (2011): 35–48.
5. Victoria Carty and Jake Onyett, "Protest, Cyberactivism, and the New Social Movements: The Reemergence of the Peace Movement Post 9/11," *Social Movement Studies* 5, no. 3 (2006): 229–249.
6. Gurak and Logie, "Internet Protests."
7. Gurak, *Persuasion and Privacy.*
8. Laura J. Gurak, "The Promise and the Peril of Social Action in Cyberspace," in *Communities in Cyberspace*, eds. Marc A. Smith and Peter Kollock (New York: Routledge, 1999), 241–262.
9. Gurak, *Persuasion and Privacy.*
10. I would like to thank Peter Kerre for our conversation in February 2012, where he provided more context and background about this case. I would also like to thank Peter for reading a draft of this chapter.
11. Piotr Sztompka, *Trust: A Sociological Theory* (Cambridge: Cambridge University Press, 1999), 128.

12. Matt McKinney, "From New York City, with Love," *Minneapolis Star Tribune*, (May 28, 2011), last modified June 1, 2013, www.startribune.com/local/minneapolis/122777379.html.
13. MplsTornado.Info, "Resource Sheet for North Minneapolis Post-Tornado Relief Efforts," last modified June 1, 2013, https://sites.google.com/site/mplstornado/.
14. Eric Ringham and Sasha Aslanian, "Eighteen Months to History: How the Minnesota Marriage Amendment Was Defeated," *MPRnews*, (Nov. 9, 2012), last modified June 1, 2013, http://minnesota.publicradio.org/display/web/2012/11/09/marriage-how.
15. After the California Supreme Court issued a ruling allowing same-sex marriage in June 2008, in November of that year voters approved Proposition 8 to stop any future same-sex marriages. Proposition 8 was subsequently overturned by the U.S. Supreme Court on June 27, 2013.
16. David Fleischer, "The Prop 8 Report: What Defeat in California Can Teach Us about Winning Future Ballot Measures on Same-Sex Marriage" (LGBT Mentoring Project), (August 3, 2010), last modified June 1, 2013, http://prop8report.lgbtmentoring.org/home.
17. Ibid., 118.
18. Ringham and Aslanian, "Eighteen Months to History."
19. Joseph A. Konstan and John Riedl, "Deconstructing Recommender Systems: How Amazon and Netflix Predict Your Preferences and Prod You to Purchase," *IEEE Spectrum*, (September 24, 2009), last modified May 30, 2013, http://spectrum.ieee.org/computing/software/deconstructing-recommender-systems.
20. See Ringham and Aslanian for a compact but thorough description of the campaign.
21. Ringham and Aslanian, "Eighteen Months to History."
22. Laura J. Gurak, *Cyberliteracy: Navigating the Internet with Awareness* (New Haven: Yale University Press, 2001).
23. "[C]haracter is almost, so to speak, the most authoritative form of persuasion." Quoted from Aristotle, *Rhetoric*, in *Aristotle, on Rhetoric: A Theory of Civic Discourse*, George A. Kennedy (New York/Oxford: Oxford University Press, 1991), 1356a, 39 in the translation.
24. Niklas Luhmann, *Trust and Power: Two Works by Niklas Luhmann* (NJ: Wiley & Sons, 1979), 4. Original German published under N. Luhmann, *Vertrauen* © 1973 Ferdinand Enke Verlag, Stuttgart.
25. Discussed in Gurak and Logie, "Internet Protests."
26. Zoe Fox, "How 1.8 Million Online Activists Helped End the Boy Scouts' Gay Youth Ban," *Mashable*, (May 23, 2013), last modified August 1, 2013, http://mashable.com/2013/05/23/boy-scouts-online-activism/.
27. Jessie Daniels, "From Crisis Pregnancy Center to Teenbreaks.Com," this volume.
28. Eric M. Uslaner, *The Moral Foundations of Trust*, (Cambridge: Cambridge University Press, 2002), 1.
29. Laurie Penny, "Cyberactivism from Egypt to Occupy Wall Street," *The Nation*, (October 11, 2011), last modified on August 1, 2013, www.thenation.com/article/163922/cyberactivism-egypt-occupy-wall-street#.

REFERENCES

Boler, Megan, and Christina Nitsou. "Women Activists within the Leaderless Occupy Wall Street: New Forms of Consciousness-Raising in Hybrid and Connective Action Social Movements." In *Cyberactivism on the Participatory Web*, edited by Martha McCaughey (pp. 232–256). New York: Routledge, 2014.

Carty, Victoria, and Jake Onyett. "Protest, Cyberactivism, and the New Social Movements: The Reemergence of the Peace Movement Post 9/11." *Social Movement Studies 5*, no. 3: 229–249.

Daniels, Jessie. "From Crisis Pregnancy Center to TeenBreaks.com: Anti-abortion Activism's Use of Cloaked Websites." In *Cyberactivism on the Participatory Web*, edited by Martha McCaughey (pp. 140–154). New York: Routledge, 2014.

Fleischer, David. *The Prop 8 Report: What Defeat in California Can Teach Us about Winning Future Ballot Measures on Same-Sex Marriage (LGBT Mentoring Project)*. August 3, 2010. http://prop8report.lgbtmentoring.org/home (accessed June 1, 2013).

Fox, Zoe. "How 1.8 Million Online Activists Helped End the Boy Scouts' Gay Youth Ban." *Mashable*. May 23, 2013. http://mashable.com/2013/05/23/boy-scouts-online-activism/ (accessed August 1, 2013).

Gurak, Laura J. *Persuasion and Privacy in Cyberspace: The Online Protests over Lotus MarketPlace and the Clipper Chip*. New Haven: Yale University Press, 1997.

———. "The Promise and the Peril of Social Action in Cyberspace." In *Communities in Cyberspace*, edited by P. Kollock and M. Smith, pp. 241–262. London: Routledge, 1999.

———. *Cyberliteracy: Navigating the Internet with Awareness*. New Haven: Yale University Press, 2001.

Gurak, Laura J., and John Logie. "Internet Protests, from Text to Web," In *Cyberactivism: Online Activism in Theory and Practice*, edited by Martha McCaughey and Michael D. Ayers (pp. 25–46). New York: Routledge, 2003.

Howard, Philip N., and Muzammil M. Hussain. "The Role of Digital Media." *Journal of Democracy 22*, no. 3 (2011): 35–48.

Kennedy, George A. *Aristotle, on Rhetoric: A Theory of Civic Discourse*. New York and Oxford: Oxford University Press, 1991.

Konstan, Joseph A., and John Riedl. "Deconstructing recommender systems: How Amazon and Netflix Predict Your Preferences and Prod You to Purchase." *IEEE Spectrum*, September 24, 2009. http://spectrum.ieee.org/computing/software/deconstructing-recommender-systems (accessed May 30, 2013).

Luhmann, Niklas. *Trust and Power: Two Works by Niklas Luhmann*. NJ: Wiley & Sons, 1979. Original German published under N. Luhmann, *Vertrauen* ©1973 Ferdinand Enke Verlag, Stuttgart.

McKinney, Matt, "From New York City, with Love." *Minneapolis Star Tribune*. May 28, 2011. www.startribune.com/local/minneapolis/122777379.html (accessed June 1, 2013).

MplsTornado.Info. "Resource Sheet for North Minneapolis Post-Tornado Relief Efforts." https://sites.google.com/site/mplstornado/ (accessed June 1, 2013).

Penny, Laurie. "Cyberactivism from Egypt to Occupy Wall Street." *The Nation*. October 11, 2011. www.thenation.com/article/163922/cyberactivism-egypt-occupy-wall-street# (accessed on August 1, 2013).

Ringham, Eric, and Sasha Aslanian, "Eighteen Months to History: How the Minnesota Marriage Amendment Was Defeated." *MPRnews*. November 9, 2012. http://minnesota.publicradio.org/display/web/2012/11/09/marriage-how (accessed June 1, 2013).

Sztompka, Piotr. *Trust: A Sociological Theory*. Cambridge University Press, 1999.

Uslaner, Eric M. *The Moral Foundations of Trust*. Cambridge University Press, 2002.

2 Dark Days

Understanding the Historical Context and the Visual Rhetorics of the SOPA/PIPA Blackout

John Logie

The January 18, 2012, protests against two "anti-piracy" bills then before the U.S. Congress radiated throughout the Internet and—in some cases—into offline spaces as well. The two bills—the "Stop Online Piracy Act" (SOPA) and the "Protect Intellectual Property Act" (PIPA)—were both so broadly and crudely drawn that they prompted an unusual backlash. Whereas both bills announced themselves to be addressing widespread unauthorized downloads of copyrighted materials, the proposed counter-measures were onerous. In addition to dramatic criminal penalties for infringement, SOPA proposed blocking access to entire Internet domains by law enforcement. PIPA proposed stripping allegedly infringing sites from the Domain Name System, effectively rendering them invisible to Internet users. Distaste for the bills united a broad and diverse ad hoc coalition that mobilized against the bills in a range of protest actions. The clear center of these protests was the "SOPA/PIPA Blackout" in which thousands of popular websites either obscured or delayed access to their core content in order to raise awareness about the bills' contents and—in some cases—drive further protest activities.

Leading Internet sites were driven to action by SOPA and PIPA because the laws—in their broadest interpretation—would have expanded the obligations of sites to ensure that no content within their sites was in violation of copyright and also would have established potentially severe penalties for infringement tantamount to "blacklisting" sites and making them unavailable to users.

APPROACHING BLACKOUT STATUS

The "social news" site Reddit was the first to announce a "blackout" in protest of SOPA. On January 10, 2012, the "Reddit team" posted an announcement reading, in part:

> We've seen some amazing activism organized by redditors at /r/sopa and across the reddit community at large. You have made a difference

in this fight; and as we near the next stage, and after much thought, talking with experts, and hearing the overwhelming voices from the reddit community, we have decided that **we will be blacking out reddit on January 18th from 8am–8pm EST (1300–0100 UTC).** (emphasis in original)[1]

But whereas Reddit was the first to *announce* a SOPA/PIPA "blackout" protest, the idea can be traced back to December 10, 2011, when Jimmy Wales posted a "Request for Comment" on his Wikipedia "user talk" pages regarding the possibility of what he then termed a "strike" in opposition to SOPA:

> A few months ago, the Italian Wikipedia community made a decision to blank all of Italian Wikipedia for a short period in order to protest a law which would infringe on their editorial independence. The Italian Parliament backed down immediately. As Wikipedians may or may not be aware, a much worse law going under the misleading title of "Stop Online Piracy Act" is working its way through Congress on a bit of a fast track. I may be attending a meeting at the White House on Monday (pending confirmation on a couple of fronts) along with executives from many other top Internet firms, and I thought this would be a good time to take a quick reading of the community feeling on this issue. My own view is that a community strike was very powerful and successful in Italy and could be even more powerful in this case.[2]

Wales' request prompted a rolling discussion around the potential symbolic and political value of "blanking" Wikipedia. The notion of a "blackout" rather than a "blanking" appears to have been introduced by Wikipedia editor Wnt, who wrote in opposition to Wales' proposal: "I don't support a site-wide blackout, but a teach-in may be useful"[3] a little over seven hours after Wales had inaugurated the topic. Another editor, Coren, responds a little over an hour after Wnt, writing: "Anything we *can* do to raise awareness of that law is a good thing, and even a brief "blackout" of the English Wikipedia is going to not only be directly noticeable, but is going to bring much-needed press attention to the issue."[4] The notion of a "blackout" quickly took root and became so central to the ongoing discussion that the first news reports about these discussions (on December 13, 2011) somewhat inaccurately suggested that Wales was considering a blackout of Wikipedia. Whereas the distinction between "blanking" and "blacking out" pages may seem subtle, it is significant when one considers the visual possibilities attendant to each choice. A protest that "blanks" pages offers little in the way of visual possibilities, over and above the absence of expected content. A "blackout," by contrast, invites capable designers to consider how the visual elements of the existing site can be countered, obscured, or otherwise challenged by the core thematic color associated with the protest. For this reason, it is not surprising that the Wikipedia community coalesced around the notion of a "blackout" and was actively considering optimal visual strategies by December 13, 2011.

BLACKING OUT IN PUBLIC

In the wake of Reddit's announcement, Wikipedia signaled its intention to also black out Wikipedia on January 18, 2012, issuing a formal press release to that effect on January 16. The press release codified a decision that had clearly already been made. From January 14 to 17, the Wikipedia Media Foundation held an open discussion on the specifics of its Blackout page design, on a page titled "SOPA Initiative/Blackout Screen Designs." At the point where the Foundation took the discussion public, they had established a series of guidelines for the page. These guidelines offer insight into the decision processes of one of the more prominent Blackout participants:
The following design requirements were taken into effect:

1. The screen must be *iconic*. This image will be used in screen shots in the media and elsewhere.
2. The screen must be *simple*. While the issues presented are complex, they must be boiled down to easy-to-understand concepts, with room for expansion.
3. The screen must be *symbolic*. This is potentially a historical event.

The following design considerations were taken into effect:

1. The Wikipedia "puzzle globe" image is a "busy" icon, and not appropriate for the type of statement required.
2. Simplicity over complexity.
3. Seriousness over frivolity.
4. The Wikipedia *wordmark* was deemed important to include.[5]

In the attendant discussion, the distinction between "blanking" and "blacking out" the page is thrown into sharper relief. Wikipedia initially considered two candidate versions of what became the final page graphic, one of which featured black text on a white background, presenting them as follows:
Additional comments:

• The "light" version is closer to the current Wikipedia design and would be less shocking.
• The "dark" version is more symbolic (an encroaching darkness), but may be unsettling to community members.[6]

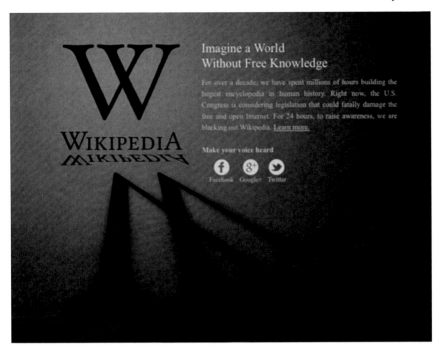

Figure 2.1   Wikipedia's SOPA/PIPA Blackout page

But the participants in the discussion overwhelmingly supported the "dark" version to the point that discussion was promptly closed (on January 15) "so that resources can be better invested into other design aspects."[7] One representative comment came from Wikipedia editor NeilK, who wrote that the dark design was "more powerful" and that "The shadow design is more meaningful when the page is threatened to be engulfed by darkness."[8]

Wikipedia's crowdsourced final Blackout protest page hews very closely to the initial candidate image posted by the Wikipedia Media Foundation on January 14. True to Wikipedia's guidelines, the page foregoes the "busy-ness" of the default home page in favor of austerity, darkness, and—given the *noir*-style shadows stretching into darkness—a sense of foreboding. Wikipedia's Blackout page offers a sharp counter to its typical presentation, in which site visitors are presented with dozens of options (most of them involving choice of language) in order to extract information from the site.

The page offers a single informational option, inviting visitors to "learn more" about SOPA and PIPA, and three links to social media to add their voices to protest-related threads (with #WikipediaBlackout having been solidly established on Twitter prior to the site "going dark"). Whereas Wikipedia's strategy superficially appears to be the outright suppression of the site's core content, the whole of Wikipedia was, in fact, available throughout the

January 18, 2012, protest. Wikipedia left a "backdoor" for users, by maintaining the mobile version of the site. Whereas the site's visual presentation via the mobile site—which is intended primarily for users of smartphones—was clunky, Wikipedia ultimately chose to displace its content and thereby defer access to it. For that day, the price of entry to Wikipedia was at least momentary consideration of Wikipedia's arguments against the proposed laws.

A review of press coverage during and in the immediate wake of the SOPA/PIPA protests strongly suggests that Wikipedia was successful in its overarching goal, the production of an image that would come to be seen as *iconic*. News reports tended to feature one or more screenshots of "blacked out" pages to illustrate their stories. Wikipedia's page appears consistently in these stories, and in cases where a single screenshot is used to illustrate the protest, Wikipedia's page was clearly selected more often than others.

Given that Reddit was the *first* site to announce its planned blackout—almost a full week before Wikipedia—it is fair to ask how and why Reddit's Blackout site failed to achieve levels of acknowledgement and citation commensurate to Wikipedia's. The answer becomes apparent at first glance. Reddit's Blackout site is *busy*. The most prominent design element on the page is a banner reading "SOPA and PIPA damage . . . " and the sentence is concluded by one of a series of rotating examples ranging from "Mozilla" to "Minecraft." Reddit's page also features over two dozen "clickable" elements including links to all manner of information resources, action items, and an informational video.

Reddit's initial strategy of content suppression—denying access to the user-curated torrent of content that is the site's core—is undercut by the

Figure 2.2   Reddit's SOPA/PIPA Blackout page

torrent of options found within the substitute page. True to its nature, Reddit's SOPA/PIPA Blackout page offers a heap of lightly curated information. As such, it was one of the most helpful sites in terms of content, but one of the least "portable" with respect to retransmission by others.

And retransmission was a necessary goal for the SOPA/PIPA Blackout. In addition to pursuing mainstream media coverage, the SOPA/PIPA Blackout was directed at driving publicity via social media. As the SOPA/PIPA protest scaled up, sites consistently encouraged visitors to multiply the impact of the protest by steering others to Blackout sites. The left hand column of Reddit's Blackout page is largely given over to a live, rolling update of tweets featuring the #blackout hashtag. And given that legislators began announcing their opposition to SOPA and PIPA throughout the day of January 18, the ability of tools like Twitter to both track and publicize these announcements (some of which were defections by those who had initially supported the bills) contributed to the sense that the tide was turning against the bills.

Some prominent opponents of SOPA and PIPA made the determination that they were not in a position to pursue full-bore content suppression strategies. Among the sites that successfully executed alternate strategies were Google and Wired, each of which opted to pursue graphic treatments organized around the "black bar" as an icon of censorship (whether used to obscure the eyes of individuals in salacious images, used to cover the mouths of those wishing to speak, or used to "redact" information in documents). Google made a reasonable determination that it could not afford to deny its users access to its core functionality for a day, and opted for a simple black bar covering over its logo.

The site also added a brief, linked injunction to "Tell Congress: Please don't censor the web!" The site's functionality was unimpaired, but because

Figure 2.3   Google's SOPA/PIPA Blackout page

the Google logo has become a space for interaction with site visitors (typically in the form of themed iterations of the logo or animated Google Doodles), the "censorship" of the logo was jarring and rhetorically powerful. WIRED pursued a similar approach on a different scale with dozens of black lines obscuring virtually all of the lines of textual content on its homepage. In these cases of mild content displacement visitors to the sites were not significantly inconvenienced, but iconic representations of censorship in action were employed to encourage readers to consider a post-SOPA/PIPA landscape in which access to their preferred content was no longer certain.

BLACKING OUT CAN BE FUN

The general tenor of most protest sites was sober, but a few SOPA/PIPA Blackout sites opted for satiric approaches. Arguably the most successful of these was Matthew Inman's characteristically and cheerfully obscene animated GIF opposing SOPA and PIPA. The GIF presents an extended argument that somehow weaves together a lustful assignation between a goat and a panda . . . and Oprah Winfrey and Jesus riding a Jetski (in outer space). Inman forcefully underscores shutdowns of websites—without due process—for the clipping and use of images for satiric, parodic, and creative purposes.

The page generally adheres to the graphic baseline for a Blackout page. Other than the animated GIF, the page is austere and features only three links, the first to Inman's own experiences with unauthorized appropriation of his work, and the other two to Wikipedia's information page on the bills and to Wikipedia's page streamlining access to contact information for visitors' Congressional representatives. Cleverly, Inman manages to obscure the regular entertainment offerings of his site, *and* offer a new, protest-specific installment of the type of content his site's visitors appreciate. Inman also underscores the gap between sites like the Oatmeal and current law with a brief P.S. reading "Please pirate the shit out of this animated GIF."[9] The success of Inman's protest strategy is perhaps best expressed in Inman's own words to the Oatmeal's readers the following day:

> [t]he animated GIF received coverage from CNN, Sports Illustrated, Mashable, Business Insider, MSNBC, and a bumload of other mainstream news sources. It was also trending worldwide on Twitter and according to Tweetmeme it was one of the most tweeted links on earth yesterday.
>
> Why am I telling you this? Because I'm fairly certain getting koala lovemaking on CNN is the highlight of my career and I wanted to share the moment with you.
>
> Why else am I telling you this? Because of the combined efforts of some of the internet's biggest players as well as countless awesome underdogs, you could tentatively say that the protests were a success.

Figure 2.4   The Oatmeal.com's SOPA/PIPA Blackout page. The tearful koala is one of many images in an animated GIF and, in this image, not (thankfully) accompanied by a goat.

> 18 senators backed off from the bill, 4.5 million people signed a petition, and anyone who used the internet yesterday for more than five seconds is now well aware of what SOPA is and how to stop it.[10]

As Inman suggests, The SOPA/PIPA protests were strikingly effective. Just two days after the SOPA/PIPA Blackout, both bills were withdrawn from Congressional consideration, ostensibly to address the issues raised in the protests, but more likely because the political climate had shifted to the point where they were no longer viable. Because of this, these protests represent an arguable high-water mark for U.S. cyberprotests in terms of both effectiveness and efficiency.

BLACKOUTS AND MEMORY

Many news reports in the wake of the SOPA/PIPA Blackout described the protests as "unprecedented": the BBC's Steve Kingstone described the blackout as "an unprecedented protest";[11] writing for ArsTechnica, Timothy B. Lee opened an article by stating that "Members of the Senate are rushing for the exits in the wake of the Internet's unprecedented protest of the Protect IP Act (PIPA)";[12] the conservative website Breitbart.com featured Republican Representative Tom McClintlock celebrating the bills' defeat after what he termed "an unprecedented protest across the Internet";[13] and an online opinion piece by Leslie Harris of the Center for Democracy and Technology that appeared on ABCNews.com in early February, 2012, refers to the protests as "an unprecedented online revolt."[14]

But the SOPA/PIPA Blackout was significantly *precedented*. The core elements of the SOPA/PIPA Blackout protest action have clear antecedents in two major protests of the 1990s: the Black World Wide Web protest of 1996 and the Haunting of GeoCities in 1999. Taken together, these 20th-century Internet protest actions offered a rough template for the SOPA/PIPA Blackout in 2012. Further, placing these three protest actions into their proper historical context offers significant insight into how online protest efforts build upon one another, and how online activists revise and refine their strategies over time. Taken together, these protests also call attention to the role visual rhetoric plays in World Wide Web-based protest actions. Whereas recent events have demonstrated that a well-calibrated hashtag can sometimes function as a virtual "gathering place" for activism on the net, the web remains a space where surface look and feel remain critical to the establishment of a functional and viable ethos. Further, when the protest is organized around a flexible and adaptable visual theme, this can produce *memetic protest* in which the spirit of play that facilitates the transmission of Internet memes fuels the expansion of the protest action.

BLACK ROOTS: REVISITING THE FIRST WIDE-SCALE INTERNET-BASED PROTEST

Whereas the Black World Wide Web protest garnered significant mainstream media attention in 1996, it has—for the most part—not been the subject of ongoing analysis or consideration. One of the very few scholarly treatments of the 1996 "Black World Wide Web" protest—Jerry Berman and Dierdre K. Mulligan's 2003 article "Digital Grass Roots: Issue Advocacy in the Age of the Internet"[15]—efficiently summarizes the arc of events as follows:

> As the [Communications Decency Act] was nearing passage in Congress, [the Center for Democracy and Technology] and a tiny group called the Voters Telecommunications Watch (VTW) conceived the Paint the Web

Black campaign as a public education device. VTW and CDT began an e-mail campaign urging webmasters to turn the backgrounds on their pages black on the day that President Clinton signed the bill into law. At 11 a.m. on February 8, 1996, the President signed the bill and thousands of web pages went black for forty-eight hours.

As was the case in the SOPA/PIPA Blackout, the Black World Wide Web was a response to legislative overreach, in this case in the form of The Communications Decency Act (CDA) of 1996, passed as part of an omnibus telecommunications bill in February of that year. Known variously as "Black World Wide Web," "Paint the Web Black," or "Black Thursday," a tiny two-person site/organization called "Voters Telecommunications Watch" (consisting of programmer Shabbir J. Safdar and computer journalist Steven

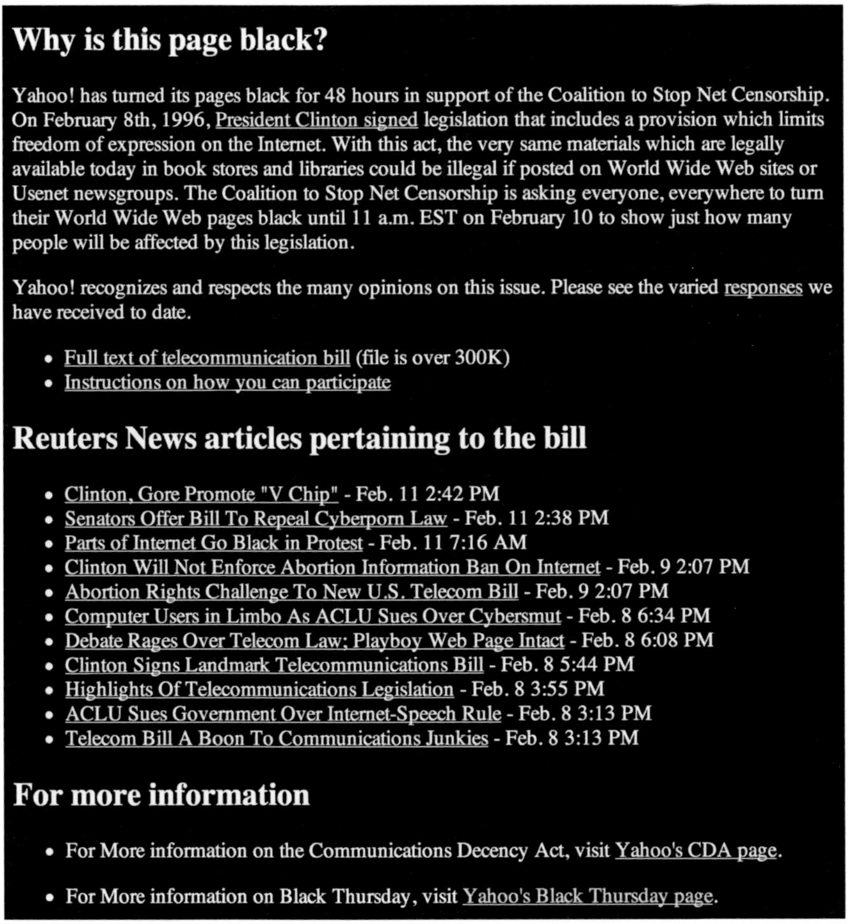

Why is this page black?

Yahoo! has turned its pages black for 48 hours in support of the Coalition to Stop Net Censorship. On February 8th, 1996, President Clinton signed legislation that includes a provision which limits freedom of expression on the Internet. With this act, the very same materials which are legally available today in book stores and libraries could be illegal if posted on World Wide Web sites or Usenet newsgroups. The Coalition to Stop Net Censorship is asking everyone, everywhere to turn their World Wide Web pages black until 11 a.m. EST on February 10 to show just how many people will be affected by this legislation.

Yahoo! recognizes and respects the many opinions on this issue. Please see the varied responses we have received to date.

- Full text of telecommunication bill (file is over 300K)
- Instructions on how you can participate

Reuters News articles pertaining to the bill

- Clinton, Gore Promote "V Chip" - Feb. 11 2:42 PM
- Senators Offer Bill To Repeal Cyberporn Law - Feb. 11 2:38 PM
- Parts of Internet Go Black in Protest - Feb. 11 7:16 AM
- Clinton Will Not Enforce Abortion Information Ban On Internet - Feb. 9 2:07 PM
- Abortion Rights Challenge To New U.S. Telecom Bill - Feb. 9 2:07 PM
- Computer Users in Limbo As ACLU Sues Over Cybersmut - Feb. 8 6:34 PM
- Debate Rages Over Telecom Law; Playboy Web Page Intact - Feb. 8 6:08 PM
- Clinton Signs Landmark Telecommunications Bill - Feb. 8 5:44 PM
- Highlights Of Telecommunications Legislation - Feb. 8 3:55 PM
- ACLU Sues Government Over Internet-Speech Rule - Feb. 8 3:13 PM
- Telecom Bill A Boon To Communications Junkies - Feb. 8 3:13 PM

For more information

- For More information on the Communications Decency Act, visit Yahoo's CDA page.

- For More information on Black Thursday, visit Yahoo's Black Thursday page.

Figure 2.5   Yahoo's home page during the Black World Wide Web protest

Cherry) was the prime mover in persuading tens of thousands of (and per-haps over 100,000) websites to switch to black backgrounds to protest the CDA becoming law. Few archived copies of Black World Wide Web pages exist, but a review of the "Black" version of the Yahoo site at now archived at Xarch[16] offers a striking example of how committed the early Yahoo was to this particular issue. Then less than a year old, Yahoo appears to have participated in the protest by eliminating all recognizable content from its page, including its logo and top-of-page navigational guide.

The surviving traces of the "Black World Wide Web" testify to the limited graphic opportunities that were functionally available at the time. Whereas the World Wide Web offered the promise of text and images working in concert with one another, as a practical matter many 1996 web pages were little more that link-enhanced text. That said, black backgrounds were suf-ficiently rare that the mere presence of such a page was inherently nota-ble. The web of 1996 had settled into an array of crude conventions, links were blue and underlined, sometimes marked by a crude red "sphere," and page backgrounds overwhelmingly tended toward white and battleship grey (with tiled "wallpapers" in mottled patterns also in vogue). In short, given the crudeness of most websites, a black background offered enough of a deviation from the implied norm to serve as a functional interruption to the day-to-day business of the web. And, of course, such interruptions are a standard tactic among many protestors, online and off.

One obvious criticism of the Black World Wide Web protest is that—despite high levels of participation—it was a case of shutting the barn door after the horse had escaped. In a 1996 *Internet World* magazine piece point-edly titled "Too Little, Too Late," Joel Snyder writes:

> [T]he Internet's vision of how to influence legislation looks more like a small child who didn't get a treat than serious lobbyists who know how to play the power game. On the Internet, we're making new rules about how to work, how to act, and how to interact. But the Internet is only a small part of the larger world, and you can't ignore that fact. Just as the Net uses common standardized protocols to let dissimilar systems interact, it has to adapt to the protocols of Washington to be effective.[17]

Snyder's criticism was apt. Though the Communications Decency Act was found unconstitutional by the U.S. Supreme Court in 1997, Snyder rightly argues that a protest staged *after legislation is signed into law by the President* is of questionable value. Though participants in the Black World Wide Web could argue that their efforts set the stage for the law's eventual repeal, theirs seems a modest achievement. Despite the speed with which ideas circulate being one of the distinguishing characteristics of the World Wide Web, the Black World Wide Web was *too late*. As Snyder points out, it would have been better to send the message to where it could have done the most good while there was still a chance of affecting the outcome. Wearing a black armband is not without symbolic meaning, but such signs of grief are best accompanied by real action. Having record numbers of people send e-mail after the Act was signed into law doesn't do nearly as much good as would the same people sending real mail before the bill went to the conference committee.[18]

Nevertheless, the Black World Wide Web served as a functional demonstration of the web's potential for the rapid transmission of a memetic protest concept, and for its rapid adoption and implementation among protest participants. An archived copy of the call for the Black World Wide Web protest suggests that as of February 6, there were only 24 organizations significant enough to be listed as participants. This list is impressive in its range, including: The Center for Democracy and Technology, Computer Professionals for Social Responsibility, The Electronic Frontier Foundation, The Electronic Privacy Information Center, The Libertarian Party, the National Writers Union, People for the American Way, WIRED, the National Gay and Lesbian Task Force, and the Republican Liberty Caucus.[19] Whereas this list speaks to the practical reality that the CDA was objectionable to Internet-engaged citizens from across the political spectrum, something profound appears to have happened between the time that this message was circulated and the inauguration of the Black World Wide Web protest at 11 a.m. February 8, 1996. Using an admittedly limited sample, Georgetown law student Michael Norwick was able to provide a rough estimate that 7% of all U.S. websites participated in the Black World Wide Web protest. Projecting from this number, Norwick estimated that between 35,000 and 105,000 U.S. sites participated in the protest.[20] While these estimates may be high, the consensus from reports at the time makes it clear that thousands of sites participated. Even assuming the lowest estimate, the scaling from what appeared to be dozens of sites to thousands within the space of a week is a striking example of the potential of the web as a platform for messaging during protest actions. This lesson would prove significant in the next major web-based protest.

SPIRITED AWAY—CONTENT AND CONTROL IN THE HAUNTING OF GEOCITIES

The 1999 Haunting of GeoCities remains notable in that this protest action was among the first to leverage the possibilities of the Internet as a visual space. While both the broad outlines of the protest and the protest strategy parallel those of the Black World Wide Web protest, the Haunting's strategies underscore the visual opportunities available within web spaces. Given the selection of "haunting" as a protest theme, the GeoCities homesteaders unleashed an array of quirky, witty, and sometimes absurdist visual presentations incorporating ghosts, gravestones, and the supernatural.

Interestingly, the GeoCities protest involves one of the participants in the Black World Wide Web protest moving into the role of protestee. Between 1996 and 1999, Yahoo had grown exponentially. In January of 1999, after Yahoo's initial public offering left the company flush with cash, Yahoo purchased GeoCities. Since 1994, GeoCities had been offering free web space to anyone who wished to be a "homesteader," with a business model that seemed organized around the notion that thriving Internet neighborhoods would require highways and main streets, and that GeoCities would be in prime position to monetize those arteries (with "billboards" and other commercial developments). At the time of GeoCities' purchase, it was the fifth most popular destination on the Web.

On June 25, 1999, Yahoo circulated an amendment to the GeoCities Terms of Service that strongly suggested that Yahoo would own the content on the GeoCities sites. Five days later, an angry homesteader named Jim Townsend called for a boycott of GeoCities and recommended that homesteaders move their sites to GeoCities' competitors. Notably, Townsend recognized the importance of crafting striking visuals as part of the protest, writing: "If you are a graphics professional, design logos which don't infringe on Yahoo's copyrights but will give viewers the message that [Yahoo is] under boycott (think of the ribbon campaign to defeat the CDA [Communications Decency Act] last year)."[21] The response to Townsend's call for design as a core tactic in the GeoCities protest took a striking turn when many protestors started playfully subverting the real estate framing that had always been front and center in GeoCities' self-representations. If GeoCities had given "homesteaders" virtual "land" on virtual "streets" with the expectation that the homesteaders would develop the land by building "houses" then a protest should logically involve making those houses as unappealing as possible. Whereas the moment the GeoCities protest became a "haunting" is difficult to trace, it is clear that by June 30—five days after the announcement of the new Yahoo terms of service—sites were both haunted and building networks for the transmission of "haunting" content.

In the Haunting, we see the GeoCities homesteaders coalescing around the strategies that would later be used to great effect in the SOPA/PIPA Blackout. The general strategies pursued by Haunting participants can be broken into three core types:

1. *Content displacement*—This strategy involves using a substitute home page or pages as a means of delaying access to the site's core content. In some cases, site visitors are asked to visit alternative sites including information resources, petitions, letter generators, and other protest-related resources.

As of June 30, 1999

Add the official Haunting graphic to your site! Courtesy of supporter Andrew C.

In protest of Section 8 of the Yahoo/Geocities Terms of Service

This page has been visited

626 times

since I joined the

Yahoo Boycott

A list of "GeoSites" turned "Yahoo Boycott" sites

7-5-99 Letter to YAHOO

Sent to: geo-account-replies@yahoo-inc.com geocities@list.geocities.com geo-support@yahoo-inc.com

Figure 2.6   An exemplary page from the Haunting of GeoCities

2. *Content suppression*—In this strategy, access to the site's core content is curtailed altogether. Site visitors are left with *only* the substitute content prepared for the purpose of the protest.
3. *Parodic/Satiric content*—This strategy often involves providing site visitors with a "through a glass darkly" vision of what a site might be like in a dystopian future, or otherwise exploring the comic possibilities of the circumstance that prompted the protest.

Each of these strategies confronted Yahoo with significant challenges. Content displacement meant that visitors to popular sites on GeoCities would be delayed from accessing the materials they sought—always problematic in Internet spaces—or subjected to sustained critiques of Yahoo as they tried to do so. In cases of content removal, GeoCities' streets became the byways of ghost towns, with the significant likelihood that content had migrated to Yahoo's competitors. And in the case of parodic and satiric sites, Yahoo was made to look both out of step with the morés of the Internet, and ridiculously overreaching.

Those who traveled the "neighborhoods" of GeoCities during the protest could not help but notice the strangeness of the "scene." GeoCities homesteaders participating in the Haunting overwhelmingly selected color schemes that mapped onto pop culture representations of ghosts and the supernatural, with black, white, "headstone" greys, and "ectoplasm" greens being especially favored. Given the memetic spread of the protest throughout GeoCities, it is perhaps not surprising that on July 6, 1999, Yahoo abandoned the new terms of service and replaced them with a revision that started by stating "Yahoo does not claim ownership of the Content you place on your Yahoo GeoCities site."[22]

"POTENT" MEMES AND POTENTIAL MEMES

To this day, the Haunting of GeoCities remains a striking example of the potentially viral nature of Internet-based protests. The selection of an engaging theme for the protest prompted GeoCities' homesteaders to participate in a phenomenon that—whereas unfamiliar to many in 1999—is now commonplace: the circulation, appropriation, and revision of a meme. To cite perhaps the most obvious recent example, when a camera caught U.S. gymnast McKayla Maroney appearing underwhelmed by her having been awarded a silver medal at the 2012 London Olympics, thousands of individuals went to work on the "Not Impressed" meme, photoshopping Maroney's scowling stance into a wide range of situations.[23] And whereas "meme" has become almost synonymous with "creatively wasting time on the Internet," we do well to recall how the term was understood at the time of the Haunting of GeoCities.

As it turns out, one of the early definitions of "meme" as a specifically Internet-related phenomenon was published within months of the Haunting of GeoCities in the 1999 book *Culture Jam: How to Reverse America's Suicidal Consumer Binge, and Why We Must* by Kalle Lasn, the founder of *AdBusters*. Lasn writes:

> A meme (rhymes with "dream") is a unit of information (a catchphrase, a concept, a tune, a notion of fashion, philosophy or politics) that leaps from brain to brain to brain. Memes compete with one another for replication, and are passed down through a population much the same way genes pass through a species. Potent memes can change minds, alter behavior, catalyze collective mindshifts and transform cultures. Which

is why meme warfare has become the geopolitical battle of our information age. Whoever has the memes has the power.[24]

After this definition and description, Lasn points the meme toward the Internet in the following terms:

> The next revolution—World War III—will be, as Marshall McLuhan predicted, "a guerilla information war" fought not in the sky or on the streets, not in forests or around international fishing boundaries on the high seas, but in newspapers and magazines, on the radio, on TV and in cyberspace.
>
> We jammers can win this battle for ourselves and Planet Earth. Here's how:
>
> We build our own meme factory, put out a better product and beat the corporations at their own game. We identify the macromemes and the metamemes—the core ideas without which a sustainable future is unthinkable, and deploy them.[25]

Lasn is today best known for his founding (and naming) role in the Occupy Wall Street protests. Lasn remains consistent in presenting memes as ideological weapons. His most recent book, *Meme Wars: The Creative Destruction of Neoclassical Economies*, clearly perpetuates the notion of "meme warfare" as the means toward a more socially just global culture. Whereas Lasn's 1999 definition of the meme no doubt helped to shape how memes were understood among the wave of Internet users who now seem like early adopters (almost all of them used dial-up modems!), today most people are more likely to associate memes with McKayla Maroney than with Lasn's concept of meme warfare. Whereas there are faint traces of cultural criticism in memes like "First World Problems," in which people submit examples of presumably wealthy people complaining about "problems" like substandard Wi-Fi access and minor issues with domestic employees,[26] the satiric touch is light enough that its targets might not even notice that they are being mocked. And for every meme that serves as a point of cultural critique, there are many more that don't. (e.g., "Ermahgerd," which seems directed at nothing more than delighting in the silliness of explosive overstatement).

As Internet memes are currently understood, they seem ill-suited to the kinds of ideological and political action that Lasn foresaw as the 20th century drew to a close. Part of the challenge is the general understanding that one cannot intentionally create a meme. While Lasn would no doubt differ, the popular website KnowYourMeme features a "Meme Research" forum that has had a number of running discussions on the topic. Representative arguments from the forum include "Alex" writing:

> You can't make a meme. It is impossible. You can create a *catalyst* for a meme, but most of the time it is viewed as forced. I remember watching a video of the so called "creator" of that Nigel Thornberry meme, but even then it takes many people to parody/exploit/share this *idea*.[27]

And similarly, "RandomMan" writes:

> DEPENDS ON THE AMOUNT OF CAPS YOU USE FOR THE
> MEME.
> But no, you can't make a meme.
> Memes are created through the popularity and spread they gained
> on the web, along with the various ways they can be used. Basically
> anything that has gained popularity on the web can turn into a meme if
> it grows large enough, but you can't force it to spread. If a meme isn't
> received well by the masses, it won't become a meme and you should
> leave it at that.[28]

These arguments reflect a consensus view among a significant population of
Internet users who likely lack Kalle Lasn's skill-set with respect to concep-
tualizing "potent memes." But these commenters also underscore a practical truth about memes. They earn the name *only because they are widely
embraced*. Indeed, Alex employs not one but *two* hedges to make clear that
he does not view any one individual as the creator of the Nigel Thornberry
meme (using the adjective "so-called" and placing "scare quotes" around
the term "creator"). Thus, while Lasn argues that memes should be mobilized as ideological weapons that are suited to the practical realities of the
Internet era, the "meme community" is skeptical about whether one can
decide to initiate a meme.

My argument here is that *memetic protests* fall into a space between
these poles. What the Black World Wide Web, the Haunting of GeoCities,
and the SOPA/PIPA Blackout have in common—whether by design or good
fortune—is their having settled on flexible and adaptable conceptual and
visual themes that helped their messages spread virally. In these three cases
of *memetic protest* we see increasing levels of creative energy directed at
the question of just *how* a particular site ought to present itself during the
protest. And these answers necessarily vary depending on the site's mission,
role, and relationship to its audience(s). In the SOPA/PIPA Blackouts, we
see a broad array of prominent sites making canny rhetorical choices that
are grounded in their own sense of how best to persuade their audiences to
educate themselves as to the bills' contents and potential consequences.

One of the more striking elements of the SOPA/PIPA protests was the
largely unified approach to protesting the bills on participating sites. The
concept of a "blackout" of core content was interpreted variously, but sites
clearly developed an approach in which visual rhetoric was the central element of their protest actions. We also witnessed sites carefully navigating
a series of choices with respect to their own approaches to "blacking out."
Whereas some sites opted to reinforce their own core content and ethos,
others opted for full interruptions of "business as usual." Many sites chose
to drive others toward other participants in the protest, thereby promoting a
momentary spirit of cooperation and unity among sites that might otherwise

see themselves as competitors. In so doing, the SOPA/PIPA Blackout protesters effectively scaled the protest actions of the 1990s to meet the needs of the complex audiences of the 21st-century Internet, providing ample tools for site visitors to become participants in what became an international outcry against the bills. The SOPA/PIPA Blackouts played a tremendous role in beating back the ill-advised bills, and whereas there are current efforts to resuscitate some or all of the elements of these bills in Congress, legislators do so with a baseline awareness that opponents are capable of mobilizing in a matter of days and producing graphically sophisticated *memetic protests* that call attention to the specifics of the proposed laws.

BLACKOUTS: THEN AND NOW

The SOPA/PIPA Blackout differs from the 20th-century protests because of the positioning of the participants. While both the Black World Wide Web and the Haunting of GeoCities were inaugurated by people who were not especially well known prior to the protests, the SOPA/PIPA Blackout was started by leaders of some of the most popular sites on the Internet. The acknowledged main drivers of the SOPA/PIPA Blackout were Wikipedia's co-founder Jimmy Wales and the social news aggregation site Reddit. Further, whereas both the Black World Wide Web and the Haunting of GeoCities were reactive in nature, responding to changes in law or policy that had already occurred, the SOPA/PIPA Blackout was a preemptive strike, directed at educating Internet users about legislation that was under consideration in the U.S. Congress, but had not yet made it to the floor for votes.

The repeated impulse to describe the SOPA/PIPA Blackout as "unprecedented" despite obvious historical precedents reflects poorly on the media outlets that chose the term. Indeed, Jimmy Wales' initial discussion of the possibility of "blanking out' Wikipedia is framed by his referencing of the successful protest action in Italy against a similarly flawed piece of legislation. A significant portion of mainstream journalists seem largely unaware of the history of protests on the Internet, or unable to successfully process the threaded discussions that are often central to decision-making processes in Internet spaces. (Another example of this is the attribution of the "blackout" to Jimmy Wales when it was clearly the by-product of collective consideration of available possibilities).

The Internet is now *old* enough to have a history. Whereas the Internet's public face dates back to the 1980s, we have had the online packet-switching network since 1969, meaning—somewhat obviously—that we are in the fifth decade of Internet communications. *There are precedents* for current online activities within these decades of human communicative and social interaction. Protests like the SOPA/PIPA Blackout draw upon this history, and, whereas dramatic in terms of scale and scope, they often revive strategies that proved effective on smaller scales in earlier contexts. That said, the Internet is *new* enough that novelty claims constitute one of the most favored rhetorical appeals when journalists, scholars, and critics attempt to underscore the importance of events in Internet spaces. Because "import-ant" and "new" are too often treated as synonyms in Internet spaces, these novelty claims are serving as a functional—but inaccurate—shorthand for claims of significance.

The Internet is mature enough as a medium that novelty claims should no longer be presented as the marker of an event's importance. It is old enough that events can be—and are—substantial and significant even when they are *not* (like the SOPA/PIPA Blackout) "unprecedented." Although there are meaningful precedents to the events of January 18, 2012, that day merits our considered attention because of the striking ways in which a broad *ad hoc* coalition of sites managed to shine a bright spotlight on two poorly crafted pieces of legislation by—momentarily—turning their own lights out.

NOTES

1. The Reddit Team, "What's New on Reddit: Stopped They Must Be; On This All Depends," Reddit.com, last modified January 10, 2012, http://blog. reddit.com/2012/01/stopped-they-must-be-on-this-all.html.
2. Jimmy Wales, "User Talk:Jimbo Wales/Archive 91 Wikipedia, the Free Ency-clopedia," Wikipedia.org, last modified December 10, 2011, https://en.wiki pedia.org/wiki/User_talk:Jimbo_Wales/Archive_91.
3. Wnt, "On the plus side . . .," in "User Talk:Jimbo Wales/Archive 91 Wiki-pedia, the Free Encyclopedia." Wikipedia.org, last modified December 10, 2011, https://en.wikipedia.org/wiki/User_talk:Jimbo_Wales/Archive_91.
4. Coren, "this law is destructive . . .," in "User Talk:Jimbo Wales/Archive 91 Wikipedia, the Free Encyclopedia." Wikipedia.org, last modified December 10, 2011, https://en.wikipedia.org/wiki/User_talk:Jimbo_Wales/Archive_91.
5. Wikipedia community. "Wikipedia:SOPA Initiative/Blackout Screen Designs," Wikipedia, the free encyclopedia, last modified January 17, 2012, http:// en.wikipedia.org/wiki/Wikipedia:SOPA_initiative/Blackout_screen_designs.
6. Ibid.
7. Ibid.
8. Ibid.
9. Matthew Inman, "TheOatmeal.com Blacked Out in Protest of SOPA / PIPA," The Oatmeal, last modified January 18, 2012, http://theoatmeal.com/sopa.
10. Matthew Inman, "The Results of Yesterday's Animated GIF about SOPA," The Oatmeal, last modified January 19, 2012, http://theoatmeal.com/blog/ sopa_results.
11. "Wikipedia Joins Blackout Protest at US Anti-Piracy Moves." BBC News, last modified January 18, 2012, www.bbc.co.uk/news/technology-16590585.
12. Timothy B. Lee, "PIPA Support Collapses, with 13 New Senators Opposed," Ars Technica, last modified January 18, 2012, http://arstechnica.com/ tech-policy/2012/01/pipa-support-collapses-with-13-new-opponents-in-senate/.
13. Tom McClintlock, "Freedom and the Internet: Victorious in SOPA Fight," Breitbart News Network, last modified January 25, 2012, www. breitbart.com/Big-Government/2012/01/25/Freedom-and-the-Internet—Victorious-in-SOPA-Fight.

14. Leslie Harris, "PIPA / SOPA and the Online Tsunami: A First Draft of the Future," ABC News, last modified February 2, 2012, http://abcnews.go.com/ Technology/pipa-sopa-online-tsunami-draft-future/story?id=15500925#. Ua43iZX9OBk.
15. Jerry Berman and Dierdre K. Mulligan, "Digital Grass Roots: Issue Advocacy in the Age of the Internet" in *The Civic Web: Online Politics and Democratic Values*, eds. David M. Anderson and Michael Cornfield (Lanham, MD: Rowman & Littlefield, 2003), 85.
16. Yahoo, "Black Thursday," xarch—experimentelle architekturserver graz, last modified February 10, 1996, http://xarch.tu-graz.ac.at/speech.html.
17. Joel Snyder, "Too Little, Too Late," Internet World, last modified May, 1996, www.opus1.com/www/jms/iw-may96.html.
18. Ibid.
19. Center for Democracy and Technology, "Campaign to Stop the Unconstitutional Communications Decency Act," Internet Archive, last modified February 3, 1996, web.archive.org/web/20080117200241/www.cdt.org/speech/ cda/960203_48hrs_alert.html.
20. Michael A Norwick, "HOW MANY WEB SITES WENT DARK?: An Educated Guess," Internet Archive: Wayback Machine, last modified February, 1996, http://web.archive.org/web/19980121045936/www.bababooey.com/ monkey/study.html.
21. Laura Gurak and John Logie, "Internet Protests, from Text to Web," in *Cyberactivism: Online Activism in Theory and Practice*, eds. Martha McCaughey and Michael D. Ayers (New York: Routledge, 2003), 25–46; the Haunting of Geocities is addressed at significant length in this article, and at still greater length in my article John H. Logie, "Homestead Acts: Rhetoric and Property in the American West, and on the World Wide Web," *Rhetoric Society Quarterly* 32, no. 3 (2002): 33–59. So yes, I have been interested in visually sophisticated online protests for a long, long time.
22. Ibid., 49.
23. If the "Not Impressed" meme somehow escaped your attention, copious examples of the meme in action can be found at: http://mckaylaisnotim pressed.tumblr.com/.
24. Kalle Lasn, *Culture Jam: How to Reverse America's Suicidal Consumer Binge—and Why We Must* (New York: W. Morrow, 1999), 123.
25. Ibid., 123–124.
26. A trove of examples is available at: http://first-world-problems.com.
27. Alex, "Can You Make a Meme if You Want to Make One?" KnowYourMeme. com, last modified June, 2012, knowyourmeme.com/forums/meme-research/ topics/12660-can-you-make-a-meme-if-you-want-to-make-one.
28. RandomMan, "Can You Make a Meme if You Want to Make One?" KnowYourMeme.com, last modified June, 2012, knowyourmeme.com/ forums/meme-research/topics/12660-can-you-make-a-meme-if-you-want-to-make-one.

REFERENCES

Alex. "Can You Make a Meme if You Want to Make One?" KnowYourMeme. com. knowyourmeme.com/forums/meme-research/topics/12660-can-you-make-a-meme-if-you-want-to-make-one (accessed June 6, 2013).
BBC News. "Wikipedia Joins Blackout Protest at US Anti-Piracy Moves." www.bbc. co.uk/news/technology-16590585 (accessed June 6, 2013).
Berman, Jerry, and Dierdre K. Mulligan. "Digital Grass Roots: Issue Advocacy in the Age of the Internet" In *The Civic Web: Online Politics and Democratic Values*,

edited by David M. Anderson and Michael Cornfield (pp. 77–93). Lanham, MD: Rowman & Littlefield, 2003.

Center for Democracy and Technology. "Campaign to Stop the Unconstitutional Communications Decency Act." Internet Archive. web.archive.org/web/20080117200241/www.cdt.org/speech/cda/960203_48hrs_alert.html (accessed June 6, 2013).

Coren. "This Law is Destructive . . . ." In "User talk:Jimbo Wales/Archive 91 Wikipedia, the Free Encyclopedia." Wikipedia.org. https://en.wikipedia.org/wiki/User_talk:Jimbo_Wales/Archive_91 (accessed June 6, 2013).

Gurak, Laura, and John Logie. "Internet Protests, from Text to Web." In *Cyberactivism: Online Activism in Theory and Practice*, edited by Martha McCaughey and Michael D. Ayers (pp. 25–46). New York: Routledge, 2003.

Harris, Leslie. "PIPA/SOPA and the Online Tsunami: A First Draft of the Future." ABC News. http://abcnews.go.com/Technology/pipa-sopa-online-tsunami-draft-future/story?id=15500925#.Ua43iZX9OBk (accessed June 6, 2013).

Inman, Matthew. "TheOatmeal.com Blacked Out in Protest of SOPA/PIPA." The Oatmeal. http://theoatmeal.com/sopa (accessed June 6, 2013).

———. "The Results of Yesterday's Animated GIF about SOPA." The Oatmeal. http://theoatmeal.com/blog/sopa_results (accessed June 6, 2013).

Lasn, Kalle. *Culture Jam: How to Reverse America's Suicidal Consumer Binge—and Why We Must*. New York: W. Morrow, 1999, 123.

———. *Meme Wars: The Creative Destruction of Neoclassical Economics: A Real World Economics Textbook*. New York: Seven Stories Press, 2012.

Lee, Timothy B. "PIPA Support Collapses, with 13 New Senators Opposed." Ars Technica. http://arstechnica.com/tech-policy/2012/01/pipa-support-collapses-with-13-new-opponents-in-senate/ (accessed June 6, 2013).

Logie, John H. "Homestead Acts: Rhetoric and Property in the American West, and on the World Wide Web." *Rhetoric Society Quarterly* 32, no. 3 (2002): 33–59.

McClintlock, Tom. "Freedom and the Internet: Victorious in SOPA Fight." Breitbart News Network. www.breitbart.com/Big-Government/2012/01/25/Freedom-and-the-Internet—Victorious-in-SOPA-Fight (Accessed June 6, 2013).

Norwick, Michael A. "How Many Web Sites Went Dark?: An Educated Guess." Internet Archive: Wayback Machine. http://web.archive.org/web/19980121045936/www.bababooey.com/monkey/study.html (accessed June 6, 2013).

RandomMan. "Can You Make a Meme if You Want to Make One?" KnowYourMeme.com. knowyourmeme.com/forums/meme-research/topics/12660-can-you-make-a-meme-if-you-want-to-make-one (accessed June 6, 2013).

The Reddit Team. "What's New on Reddit: Stopped They Must Be; On This All Depends." Reddit.com. http://blog.reddit.com/2012/01/stopped-they-must-be-on-this-all.html (accessed June 6, 2013).

Snyder, Joel. "Too Little, Too Late." Internet World. www.opus1.com/www/jms/iw-may96.html (accessed June 6, 2013).

Wales, Jimmy. "User talk:Jimbo Wales/Archive 91 Wikipedia, the free encyclopedia." Wikipedia.org (accessed June 6, 2013).

Wikipedia community. "Wikipedia:SOPA Initiative/Blackout Screen Designs." Wikipedia, the Free Encyclopedia. http://en.wikipedia.org/wiki/Wikipedia:SOPA_initiative/Blackout_screen_designs (accessed June 6, 2013).

Wnt. "On the Plus Side . . . ." In "User talk:Jimbo Wales/Archive 91 Wikipedia, the free Encyclopedia." Wikipedia.org. https://en.wikipedia.org/wiki/User_talk:Jimbo_Wales/Archive_91 (accessed June 6, 2013).

Yahoo. "Black Thursday." xarch—experimentelle architekturserver graz. http://xarch.tu-graz.ac.at/speech.html (accessed June 6, 2013).

3 The Harry Potter Alliance
Sociotechnical Contexts of Digitally Mediated Activism

Jennifer Terrell

DUMBLEDORE'S ARMY FOR THE REAL WORLD[1]

In the months following the disastrous earthquake that hit Haiti on January 12, 2010, the Harry Potter Alliance (HPA) sent five cargo planes bearing the names "Harry Potter," "Hermione Granger," "Ron Weasley," "Dumbledore," and "DFTBA" to deliver medical supplies to Port of Prince, Haiti. Funds for these supplies were raised by members of the Harry Potter Alliance, a 501c3 nonprofit collective of fans that use allusions from the Harry Potter series to motivate social change in the real world, and members of other fandoms, such as Nerdfighters and fans of the television shows *LOST* and *Firefly*. Four of the cargo planes were named after characters within the popular Harry Potter series, whereas the plane named "DFTBA" represented the Nerdfighter catchphrase, "Don't Forget to Be Awesome."[2]

People who are unfamiliar with the work of the HPA, especially those unfamiliar with active fans, are often surprised when I tell them the story of these five planes and their cargo. They are surprised that fans of Harry Potter would undertake such serious work in the name of the series they love given that fan behavior is often viewed as frivolous and potentially deviant. They are surprised that an organization comprised of young people, most of whom are not professional fundraisers, could raise such an impressive sum of money. They are surprised that this collection of funds resulted in the directly visible action of the shipment of medical supplies to those in need, for it is often impossible to see how resources donated in disaster relief to large nonprofit organizations such as the American Red Cross are actually used. If cargo planes full of medical supplies bearing the names of fictional characters seem unusual, the means by which the $123,000 that purchased these supplies was raised might seem extraordinary.

The HPA, working with members of other fan groups, organized an event that spanned two weeks to raise money for earthquake relief for Haiti. The event was titled "Help Haiti Heal" and took the form of an Internet telethon of sorts. The HPA organized entertainment to be streamed live over the Internet while fans were able to bid on prizes donated to the effort. Fans were motivated to bid on prizes not just in order to win the prizes, but also because certain entertainment acts would occur once a particular amount of funds had been raised. For instance, a song or dance would be performed if fans donated $500 within a particular time period. Various items, such as a full set of the Harry Potter novels signed by JK Rowling with a limited edition cover artwork signed by Mary Grandpre (the artist for the American versions of the Potter novels); a guitar owned and signed by Tom Felton (the actor portraying Draco Malfoy in the Harry Potter films); and other prizes, such as songs written and performed especially for the prizewinner by various wizard rock bands (a genre of Harry Potter fan music), and popular works by particular fan artists were donated by authors, artists, and prominent fans. Fans could purchase virtual raffle tickets for items they desired, which were then raffled off at the end of the telethon. All proceeds went to purchasing the supplies to be sent to Haiti.

The actual telethon itself took place across the online service livestream. com. Live content that was streamed across the Internet during the telethon ranged from performances by popular podcasters, wizard rockers, YouTube video bloggers, and HPA staff members who explained the purpose of the telethon while giving updates regarding the amount of money raised. Participants were encouraged to tweet using Twitter, a microblogging service, and post Facebook status updates about the telethon in order to spread the word and get others excited about the impressive amount of funds being raised. Although the telethon was initially planned to last only a single day and the original goal was to raise $5,000, the telethon had been so successful by the end of the first day that the organizers of the campaign decided to extend the deadline for participation. They hosted several more live shows and collected more prizes to attract donations.

By the end of two weeks the HPA had raised more than 24 times their original goal. Working with Partners in Health, a local organization within Haiti, the group was able to get medical supplies directly into the hands of those in need. Photographs of the supplies and the cargo planes that carried them were widely circulated among the fans as they became available, and sentiments of pride were expressed. One fan commented on the photo of the plane bearing Harry Potter's name, "This makes me feel proud beyond proudness!"

As I sat in my office logged into the livestream.com chat room observing and participating in the first Help Haiti Heal livestream.com event, I shared the excitement I saw expressed by others present in the livestream.com chat room. I joined over 100 other members in tweeting and updating my Facebook status about the amazing event I was both witnessing and helping to create. I felt *connected, empowered,* and as though even I was helping to change the world. I was not alone in this feeling; many logged into the live stream that afternoon and made statements about the power of a collective of Harry Potter fans. Participants regularly typed one of the HPA's slogans into the chat room, and those performing over the live stream stated again and again, "The weapon we have is love."

Feelings such as these are essential to motivating participation in social movements.[3] This story is a good example of the way that the HPA brings people together from all around the world to organize efforts toward tangible social change. The HPA relies on innovative coupling of storytelling, performance, and digital media to enroll participation within the organization and carry out their various campaigns. As such, it is a valuable site to investigate social movements on the participatory web.

This research on this fan community is part of a broader study examining the role of digitally mediated communication in the construction of human sociality across multiple media forms and channels, especially with regard to organizing social groups, such as fan communities or social movements. The extent to which the adoption of digital media may change the nature of communication, and thus the nature of human relationships, is of interest to many academic fields of study and is a popular topic in public discourse. Research that is engaged in these sorts of questions has often focused on one particular medium.[4] A particular medium can often be thought of as the main place of residence for the social group being studied. Early work that examines "online communities" stresses the need to create a virtual sense of place within whatever medium facilitates the social interaction of the group.[5] This sense of place serves to ground social groups, giving the group a central location to interact, a home base of sorts. However, few groups actually limit their interaction to one particular communications medium. Thus some scholars have begun to explore the construction of social relationships across and through digital media with a more ecological approach, exploring the manner in which people and multiple types of media relate to one another.[6]

As I tried to make ethnographic sense of the HPA and understand communication and media use within wizard rock, I realized that it did not make sense to focus on the use of any one medium and exclude others. Although members of both groups are geographically distributed, and thus the majority of their interactions occur through digital media, neither group has one particular medium through which they primarily interact; neither group has an online "home." The lack of a central virtual place for organization raises other questions regarding the use of digital media in organizing these groups. Without an online home base, how do these groups form social identity? How do they organize events and campaigns?

My ethnographic study took place without a clearly defined *field site*. I conducted participant observation and semi-structured interviews both online through various digital media, and in person. I spent several years engaging with the HPA, participating in their campaigns, and speaking with other members about their experiences within the group. I have identified a pattern of interaction I call "transmediated sociality"[7] to denote notion that, in a digitally mediated world, our social relationships emerge from interactions that happen through a variety of media in different ways.

This chapter will focus on understanding the way that the HPA uses many different digitally networked media to encourage members to participate in campaigns. In doing so, it will examine the way that these networked technologies allow for new types of participation in social movements. I explore several HPA campaigns to examine how fans become involved and consider the ways in which storytelling, culture, and networked digital technology are woven together to construct the organization. After arguing that the HPA must be understood within its sociotechnical context, I suggest implications for further research regarding new types of participation in social movements.

A BRIEF INTRODUCTION TO THE HPA

The HPA is a worthwhile group to examine because it is an organization comprised of young people who are actively involved in civic engagement, using digital media in innovative and interesting ways. The HPA is a rich site for exploration, as it could help us to understand how grassroots social movements work in the digital age. Scholars have examined the social forces behind such movements in general, and the HPA in particular. Scholars have also examined the role of digitally networked technologies in social movements. If we want to truly understand the HPA as an example of successful civic engagement in young people, we must understand it holistically; thus, we must consider both the social forces and the technical means by which the HPA operates.

The HPA was founded in 2005 by a small group of recent college graduates. During the first years of its existence, the HPA engaged primarily in processes of internal organization. They were working to gain members and build chapters around the globe. To do so, the founding members of the HPA had begun to use themes found within the Harry Potter novels to educate young people about human rights issues, advocate for the collection of funds, and recruit new members.

An example of the allusions pulled from the series can be seen in the efforts the HPA made to help refugees from the genocide in Darfur as the conclusion of the Harry Potter series deals with the notion of racial cleansing. Within the story, powerful wizards attempt to cleanse their own world of non-magical folks by demanding that all citizens of the magical world demonstrate their family ties and prove the purity of their magical bloodline. Those with insufficiently pure magical bloodlines are imprisoned and their rights as citizens of the magical world are revoked. The HPA used this plotline to alert fans of the tragedy in Darfur, many of whom expressed ignorance about it prior to their involvement with the HPA.

The group then began working with nongovernment organizations, such as the Genocide Intervention Network and Aegis Trust, in order both to educate young people about and fight against the genocide in Darfur. At the same time, the HPA was raising funds to donate to the Genocide

Intervention Network to protect women in refugee camps in Darfur. Funds were raised through efforts such as the sale of HPA T-shirts at fan events such as symposiums, wizard rock concerts, other social gatherings, and online. Additionally, local-based chapters of the HPA would host various events, such as house parties and bake sales, to raise funds to be donated to the Genocide Intervention Network.

The HPA organization is now made up of a board of directors, paid and volunteer staff members, and over 100,000 members.[8] The HPA's staff coordinates the various campaign efforts carried out by members. Numerous HPA chapters populated by high school students, college students, and community members are located within the United States, although there are a few chapters sprinkled around the world. Chapters may partake in organization-wide campaigns, such as those mentioned below, but they also take on their own local projects. Additionally, some individual members of the HPA may participate in various campaigns without being involved with particular local chapters. Members need not pay dues nor go through any official channels to register their association with the HPA. The very act of engaging with the group in a supportive way constitutes membership within it.

As membership of the HPA grew and the group became more strongly organized, it transitioned into a more substantial campaign-oriented organization. Campaign efforts range from Internet telethons like the one mentioned above to book drives to demanding that Warner Brothers use entirely fair-trade chocolate in their Harry Potter brand candies. Some campaigns occur annually, whereas others are single-run campaigns. For example, every year the HPA holds a campaign entitled "Accio Books" where they collect books to donate to a new library or to a library recovering from a natural disaster, whereas other campaigns, such as the HPA:FTW campaign, discussed below, are single-run campaigns.

Other examples of campaigns include "Wrock 4 Equality" and "Equality FTW," during the 2011 and 2012 voting seasons, respectively. Both of these campaigns were focused on fighting for same-sex marriage rights. These campaigns involved phone-banking efforts to registered voters within states that had bills or propositions on their ballots either banning or legalizing same-sex marriage. Participation in these campaigns included a wide variety of activities ranging in intensity of their engagement. Some members were involved in organizing the events, whereas others showed their support by circulating information about the campaign within their social networks, whereas still others undertook the prescribed tasks of particular campaigns, such as phone banking. These are examples of the ways in which the HPA provides different opportunities for civic engagement for young people.

THE HPA AS FAN ACTIVISTS

Most of the scholarship that examines the HPA has investigated the cultural and social processes present within the HPA. They have asked questions regarding the functioning of the HPA as a fan-based organized, often focusing on the ways that the group uses storytelling to educate young people about issues in our contemporary world. Such work investigates the way that the collective experience of HPA members constructs a particular type of public[9] where fans can participate in civic engagement. Kligler-Vilenchik et al. examine the way that this civic engagement is constructed through personal narratives,[10] whereas Brough and Shresthova theorize about fan activism by investigating a number of tensions involved in participating in the production of politics and culture.[11]

Jenkins[12] analyzes participation in the HPA with respect to social identity. He offers a brief history of fan activism but then discusses the ways in which the HPA embodies fan activism at a level previously unimagined. He explores the way that the HPA maps issues from the novels onto the real-world, arguing that the HPA respects fans' current emotional investments in Harry Potter, thus using them to unite fans. Andrew Slack, cofounder of the HPA, refers to this method of tapping into cultural points of resonance as "cultural acupuncture." According to Jenkins, this approach to social activism makes engaging in social action easier for young people; it makes participation in activism less scary and more accessible because it gives fans the feeling that they really can make a difference just by doing what they are already doing—being fans, being themselves.

Fans engaged in political action are often still hesitant to call themselves activists. Instead, they tend to consider their actions expressions of their fandom. Some fans are hesitant to overtly politicize their fan practices, whereas others are doubtful that their efforts should be considered activism. Whereas many fans expressed pride in their efforts and shared feelings of empowerment, many still feel as though "real activism" is either high risk (such protest where violence is possible) or aims for extreme changes to broader social structures or norms (such as the American civil rights movement). Action undertaken by the HPA tends to be lower risk, although not risk free, and the HPA tends to work toward smaller, more tangible changes within the world. As such, fans who may not feel comfortable with the label of activist can feel more confident framing their efforts as fan behavior.

One of the ways the HPA calls fandom to social action is through the use of rhetoric such as the concept of "breaking the muggle mindset." The muggle[13] mindset as it relates to the Harry Potter novels is the notion of the importance of conformity and compliance with socially accepted norms. Within the novels, muggles are thought to need protection from the knowledge that magic is real. This is because muggles are unable to deal with the foreign otherness of the magical world. Muggles are regularly shown to go to great lengths to maintain their own status quo. If the muggle world represents conformity, compliance, and sameness, the magical world represents a celebration of imagination, innovation, and difference.

Perhaps the clearest symbol of the muggle mindset within the novels can be found in the characters of Harry's muggle aunt and uncle, Petunia and

Vernon Dursley. As Harry's guardians after the death of his parents when he was an infant, the Dursleys are so concerned with living a "normal" lifestyle that they go to great lengths to keep young Harry from accidentally exposing his magical nature. This includes forcing him to live in a closet under the stairs. The HPA uses the notion that Harry was literally closeted for his differences to draw parallels between Harry's world and various oppressions within the real world, such as the denial of marriage rights for same-sex couples.

By urging people to break the muggle mindset, the HPA is encouraging its members to challenge the status quo, to be imaginative, and to celebrate difference. In doing so, the HPA is empowering people who often identify as being marginal to mainstream society. Fans are rarely considered "normal," and, whereas fan studies show all types of fans to be active participants in several facets of social life, they are often popularly conceived as socially ostracized.[14] By calling on fans to help break the muggle mindset of conformity, the HPA is creating a shared identity of otherness around which fans can gather to support each other. At the same time, the HPA is asking for its members to challenge the status quo of our world. Doing so requires people to question the way things are within the world and to think imaginatively of ways the world could be different.

In order to make ethnographic sense of the HPA as a grassroots socially minded collection of young people, one must not only study the culture of the HPA, but the means by which this culture is produced. The social identity of the HPA can be understood through a lens of social theory that denaturalizes, complicates, and challenges taken-for-granted cultural norms. Whereas the literature rooted in fan and media studies presented above exemplifies this, similar lenses can be helpful to understand the role of digital media in the ways the HPA uses technology in an innovative manner to establish a culture that fosters action to challenge the status quo. Theories such as feminist perspectives in human-computer interaction[15] help to challenge taken-for-granted assumptions regarding the design, use, and implementation of technologies. Whereas feminist theories are not applied here to shed light on gender politics within the HPA, the transmediated perspective adopted is intended to explore the use of digital media from a perspective that denaturalizes the normative use of each medium, focuses on the participatory nature of the HPA's engagement with and through the media, and underscores the ecological nature of the relations between HPA members and digital media.

This research adds to the current literature about fan activism and the HPA by exploring more deeply the HPA's innovative use of technology because the HPA could not function in the way that it does without the ways in which they have made use of new digital media. Understanding new forms of activism on the participatory web relies on understanding social movements from cultural and technical points of view. Whereas the HPA could exist without networked digital media, it would not be possible for it to exist on the scale, nor in the manner, it exists without such technology because the culture of the HPA and the media used by the HPA co-shape the development of the organization. Careful consideration of the ways in which the HPA has made innovative use of networked technologies is not meant to diminish the significance of the cultural production of the HPA, but rather to explore further some of the means by which this type of engagement occurs.

Media has played a significant role in the formation of the HPA not only because it allowed the HPA to reach a broader audience, but also because it allowed for new forms of participation. Digital media allows the HPA to reach a broader audience because it allows for communication across any distance. Similarly, it allows for new forms of participation; people can do the work of various social campaigns from their bedrooms, living rooms, or offices. Additionally, new forms of digital media lower the barriers of entry to activities that may have been previously cost prohibitive in terms of investment of finances, time, and effort required.

DIGITAL MEDIA USE IN THE HPA

Participation in each campaign carried out by the HPA requires engagement with multiple forms of digital media through multiple media channels. This section will detail some of the ways that members of the HPA participate in campaigns.

The campaign mentioned in the introduction of this chapter is a good starting point for looking at the nature of participation in the HPA. Participation in Help Haiti Heal took a number of forms: people participated as special entertainment guests for the telethon, organizers of the telethon, audience members, and donors to the telethon. In all four of these types of participatory roles, members of the HPA were encouraged to engage in the event in a couple of ways. Members were encouraged to sign in to the livestream.com channel both to watch the content being streamed and to chat with others in the text-based chat room that appeared in the same window in order to "hang out" with and encourage the other members of the HPA who were also participating. Additionally, members were urged to send tweets and Facebook status updates inviting more participants. Donations were accepted through a website. Some entertainers called into a party line of sorts in order to be broadcast across the livestream. Participation in this event therefore spanned many different types of media: Livestream.com, Twitter, Facebook, websites, phone calls, and more.

One means of creating and reproducing social solidarity during the Help Haiti Heal telethon was through the interactions that took place in the livestream.com service. These interactions took two forms: There was content broadcasted in the form of images and sound through the video feed, and there was a text-based chat room for members to exchange messages.

Although this makes interaction asymmetrical in some cases, it does mean that communication was flowing in a number of different ways. An example of this can been seen in the ways the HPA members present participated in wizard rock performances that were broadcasted through the video feed.

As the popular wizard rock performer The Whomping Willows performed a few of his songs, the audience present in the livestream.com chat room participated virtually by engaging in some of the same rituals they would perform as an audience in a face-to-face concert. Those familiar with the songs being performed would "sing along" by typing the lyrics of the song into the chat room. Some of the most popular songs from The Whomping Willows have grown to include audience participation in the form of patterned clapping and audience callbacks in response to particular moments in the songs. These rituals developed during numerous live performances as The Whomping Willows regularly toured the United States at the time. As the band played these songs over the livestream.com service, people clapped virtually and responded appropriately by typing text into the chat room.

This interaction reproduced a sense of shared identity and culture, as those who were familiar with the cultural norms of audience participation managed to demonstrate their cultural competence as fans of this band. The design of the livestream.com service afforded this type of participation. It is important to note that audience participation in this manner would not be possible if the streaming service offered only a video feed and did not offer the adjacent text chat window. The interactive nature of the medium supports the engaged, participatory nature of the HPA as a social group. However, an understanding of the use of the livestream.com service is insufficient to understand media use during the Help Haiti Heal campaign. We must also understand other media that were used by the group.

An exciting moment during the initial telethon afternoon occurred when HPA members who were interacting through the livestream.com service were able to get the hashtag #HelpHaitiHeal trending on Twitter. The Twitter website offers a list of the most popular topics being discussed on Twitter at any given time. Topics are identified through the use of hashtags, which are similar to keywords and are prepended with the "#" symbol. These tags can be used to search for different topics of conversation on Twitter. A topic is said to be "trending" when it is displayed as a popular topic within the Twitter website. Getting the #HelpHaitiHeal hashtag to trend on Twitter meant that the campaign was receiving quite a bit of attention. In order to achieve this goal, many HPA members had to tweet regularly during the same time frame. This collective action created a sense of solidarity and participation. Members of the HPA were not participating by merely donating money—they were also actively creating the momentum of the event by recruiting others to join in.

The various campaigns advocating for the passage of legislation to legalize same-sex marriage offered different opportunities for participation. In

February 2011, the HPA launched their Wrock4Equality campaign, which included phone banking efforts to advocate for the passage of House Bill 6103 in Rhode Island. Passed in May of 2011, this bill legalized civil unions in Rhode Island.[16] During the Wrock4Equality campaign, participants were once again encouraged to sign into the livestream.com channel to hang out, receive phone banking training, and encourage others. Similar to the Help Haiti Heal campaign, participants were encouraged to invite others by showcasing the campaign on their social media accounts. However, participation in this campaign was different in that HPA members were asked to make phone calls to voters in Rhode Island using the phone banking software, CallFire. Partnering with Marriage Equality Rhode Island and Mass Equality, the HPA offered training to members who wanted to participate in phone banking.

Training involved a visual guide through the CallFire phone banking system and a script to read to those who would be receiving the phone calls. The goal of each phone call was either to convince the voter to sign a digital postcard urging their legislator to vote in favor of the bill or to pass the phone call through to a member of Mass Equality who had advanced training in discussing these issues with voters. The digital postcard was sent to the voter's legislative representative. Members of the HPA could therefore facilitate communication between voters in Rhode Island and their legislators. Representatives from Mass Equality regularly reminded everyone of the reasons the phone calls should be successful: the pool of voters being called had been targeted based on previous voting records and the current state government of Rhode Island seemed to be in favor of passing the legislation. This was meant to be reassuring that the targeted voters would be receptive to the calls being made.

Staff members of the HPA motivated phone bankers by drawing on their identity as Harry Potter fans. The campaign was framed partly as a competition between the Hogwarts houses into which members had self-sorted. Hogwarts, the magical school Harry and his friends attend within the novels, contains four houses in which the students reside. Students are sorted into different houses based on primary characteristics of their personality. For example, Harry is sorted into the house of Gryffindor because of his innate bravery. Fans of the series will often sort themselves into Hogwarts houses based on their perceptions of their own personalities. This is a salient characteristic of identity both in terms of self and in terms of social relationships within fandom, as many fans infer personality traits of others based on self-proclaimed house affiliations.[17] The HPA's framing of the campaign as a competition between different houses therefore both draws on and reinforces fans' identity within the larger fandom.

The notion of competing houses is also carried over from the novels. Within the series, the houses are in competition for the House Cup during the entire school year. Students earn points when they do something especially helpful or clever and are deducted points for misbehaving. Participants in the phone banking campaign received five points for their house for every call made (calls were logged by the CallFire software), five points for every digital postcard signed, and five points for every friend that joined in the campaign. At the end of the campaign, the house with the most points would win. It was possible to keep track of the number of calls made by members of each house, as house identity was part of the information required by the CallFire system when a phone banker registered for his or her account on the system.

The work of phone banking through CallFire was difficult and intimidating for many. The system was complicated to learn, and, even though the HPA provided training, it was hurried and chaotic. Questions from members flew across chat windows constantly. The system made use of one's cell phone number rather than relying solely on voice over IP services. It displayed quite a bit of information about the voters being called: their name, age, gender, address, and legislator. It was unclear whether or not call recipients had access to the caller's cell phone number—something I was not sure I was comfortable with. The system used an automatic dialer that switched between calls very quickly. Most calls were not answered and thus maintaining focus and being ready with one's script in the event that the phone call was answered proved quite difficult. Competence and comfort in the task of phone banking took quite some time to build.

Members of the HPA encouraged each other through the process by sharing stories of their experiences and reminding each other why they were undertaking these tasks in the text chat window within the livestream.com service. One participant shared the following after making a phone call that actually connected with another person: "this guy just told me that I was preaching to the choir and he was like 70-something. He was awesome." Stories of successful phone calls helped others feel at ease.

Participants also encouraged each other by finding support from the themes present in the novels. In response to the intimidating nature of phone banking, another participant stated, "harry potter is about confronting fears, finding inner strength and doing what is right in the eyes of adversity. <3 <3 <3". Sentiments such as these were widely shared in the livestream. com chat windows throughout the phone banking sessions. Such notions were not only words of encouragement, but also help to solidify a shared experience through participating in these campaigns.

The marriage equality campaigns are good examples of the ways that the HPA allows for participation in civic engagement in new ways. Members of the group were able to participate in a very active manner from their locations all around the world because of the affordances of the digital media that was used. Whereas juggling the phone bank and the livestream.com hangout proved difficult for many, participants were actively encouraged to use the livestream.com hangout as a source of support. Phone banking requires a good amount of social skill, and personal energy. It can be intimidating and exhausting, so the livestream.com hangout was an important component of keeping participants motivated. Participation in these campaigns required the participant to be able to juggle several different tasks using several different media with particular social and technical savvy.

Other types of participation can be explored when we examine the HPA:FTW campaign, which ostensibly revolved around Facebook. "FTW" is a popular phrase associated with use on the Internet that means "for the win," so the campaign title can be read as "Harry Potter Alliance for the win!" On a hot, humid afternoon in Orlando, Florida, on July 17th, 2010, Chase Bank presented the HPA with a check for $250,000 before a crowd of well over 500 Harry Potter fans. The fans and members of the HPA were gathered together in Orlando for the Harry Potter fan symposium, Infinitus, which took place that weekend. During the months leading up to Infinitus, the HPA had campaigned to win the grand prize of $250,000 in Chase Community Giving's contest. The campaign took place primarily within social media, such as Facebook and Twitter.

Chase Bank was giving away prize money to the charity that received the most votes within the contest time period. Casting a vote in the contest required participants to access Chase Community Giving's Facebook page. Accessing this page included an agreement to allow for Chase Community Giving to access the participant's Facebook account as well. Voting for the HPA therefore required members to both have a Facebook account and grant Chase Bank access to the member's Facebook account. Every time a person voted for the HPA on the Chase Facebook page, a notification was put onto their Facebook wall and into the newsfeeds of their friends. This was a visual confirmation of support and membership to the HPA.

However, many members participated in ways that went beyond using Facebook to vote for the HPA. Many members participated in heavy campaigning to get others to vote for the HPA as well: They sent tweets, created YouTube videos, branded their avatars and profile pictures with "HPA:FTW," created print media, and staffed the HPA table at the symposium. Tweets and status updates resembled this tweet sent from one participant, "Please help the HPA win $250K to stop genocide, illiteracy, and inequality! Vote at www.hpaftw.com!" Such sentiments were widely circulated. Tweets were retweeted by others, and Facebook statuses were shared. There was quite a bit of social pressure to vote for the HPA in this campaign. These efforts set the tone that membership in the HPA necessitated a vote, and that a lack of voting showed a lack of support for the organization.

Even as voting for the HPA was a signal of belonging and membership, regularly asking others to do the same was an arguably stronger, louder signal. When asked whether or not she felt pressure regarding the HPA:FTW campaign, an informant states, "I recognize pressure. I more feel pressure to look like I support the HPA, which isn't anathema to my beliefs anyhow." Whereas this informant believed in the causes the HPA undertook, she felt uncomfortable with the pressure she felt to demonstrate her support and withdrew her participation in the organization for some time. Few campaigns took on the same tone of strong pressure to support the HPA and as such this is a good example to see the ways in which media use co-constructs social identity.

Another way the HPA motivates participation in campaigns is through weekly email updates. In early May of 2013, I received an email from the HPA with a subject line that read, "This is what 5000 books look like." This email gave a status update regarding Accio Books, the HPA's annual book drive. The email showcased the efforts of the Edmonton chapter of the organization, for they had collected 5,000 books in just over one month. The HPA holds an annual book drive to collect books to donate to various libraries or groups in need each year. Beginning in 2009, the HPA has collected and distributed over 86,000 books to date. In 2013, the book drive was to benefit Read Indeed, a nonprofit organization created by an elementary school student, Maria Keller. The organization aims "to collect and distribute 1 million books to needy kids by the time [Maria's] 18."[18] The email contained a photo of members of the Edmonton chapter sorting stacks of books into boxes. The email was signed with an image of library shelves with the text "Books Turn Muggles into Wizards" imposed over the image.

This image evokes the notion of breaking the muggle mindset through the act of reading and sharing literature. This not only underscores the HPA's tradition of celebrating literacy, but also links the book drive to the broader purpose of the HPA to challenge the status quo and motivate change through education and storytelling. The structure of this email serves to not only celebrate the success of a particular chapter, but also to foster a feeling of shared effort. The photo of the books collected reminds members that others are actively participating and that their efforts result in actual books that will get into the hands of actual people. This can motivate participation in the campaign before the campaign ends.

TRANSMEDIATED SOCIALITY IN THE HPA

The extent to which digital media may shape social movements, either through the presentation of new possibilities or through the distraction from traditional forms of social action, is of interest to many, especially as the adoption of new digital media increases. This broad question is at the foundation of my interest in understanding the role of digital media in the HPA. I have found that adopting a transmediated perspective while examining the HPA's efforts toward social change can shed light on the ways that culture and technology co-construct each other.

The above examples show that sociality—the act of relating to one another, establishing and reproducing social relationships, and cooperating in the organization and execution of campaigns—in the HPA occurs through the weaving together of multiple forms of media. The HPA is founded on social engagement and shared identity of its members as Harry Potter fans.

Each campaign discussed not only involved several different media services, specific social interactions occurring during each campaign often occurred through multiple media. In the cases of Help Haiti Heal and the marriage equality campaign, essential media included livestream.com, Facebook, Twitter, and the HPA website. The marriage equality campaign also relied heavily on CallFire and cell phone service. Even as the HPA:FTW campaign was focused on interactions that occurred through Facebook, other services were still instrumental to the success of the campaign.

Members of the HPA weave multiple media together because there is no particular medium that fits all of their needs. Scholars have shown that people will adopt different media to circumvent the limitations of current media in use in order to accomplish their goals.[19] In the example of the marriage equality campaigns, both livestream.com and CallFire were necessary for carrying out the core tasks involved in the campaign. The technological design of each medium allows for particular kinds of interaction. In the case of livestream.com, the design of the website allows for a single channel broadcast of video and audio data from one particular user to many (the live video feed) and for an exchange of text data (in the chat room) from all users to each other (who are signed into the service). However, livestream.com has limitations: It would not be possible to phone bank using just the livestream.com services. The CallFire software, on the other hand, does make phone banking possible and in doing so handles a number of other interactive tasks, such as call logging and call transfers, but is not interactive amongst members signed in to the service in the manner that livestream.com is. Therefore, both pieces of software are necessary for the HPA to hold an event in which members are capable of simultaneously phone banking and hanging out in a virtual chat room where they can find support. Additional media, such as Facebook and Twitter, were also necessary because of the HPA's focus on involving as many people in the campaign as possible.

Each medium has particular affordances and limitations[20]—some interactions are possible, whereas others are not. What we can see demonstrated here is that groups like the HPA will adopt various media in order to accomplish their tasks at hand. Whereas different media do make particular tasks possible, such as the CallFire system that enables phone banking from one's living room, they do not create the action they facilitate. That is to say, the HPA is not spurred to phone bank because CallFire exists. Instead, we see that whereas new digital media make new forms of participation in social action possible, the weaving together of multiple media shows that no particular medium drives action. Furthermore, the role of any given medium can only be understood within the context of the broader ecology of the HPA.

The media are made meaningful in various ways through their use within the campaigns. When a member of the HPA is using Facebook to vote for the HPA in the HPA:FTW campaign, Facebook becomes simultaneously a vehicle for activism in the task of voting and also a means of both expressing and promoting social identity as a member of the HPA. Facebook means many different things to the various people who interact with and through it on a daily basis, as it does in the context of social movements—it can become a symbol of collective identity as well as individual expression. Similarly, a tweet sent regarding the Help Haiti Heal campaign isn't meaningful only as a message from an individual, but it also represents involvement with a broader group, which also evokes a larger set of beliefs and ideologies. Tweeting about HPA campaigns serves the function of advertising the campaign, but it also conveys membership to the HPA, which, when understood culturally, might express a variety of information. Media are therefore not merely instrumental within the HPA. Engagement with and through media creates different forms of meaning. Such meanings are socially constructed; they do not come from media itself. The role of digital media in the functioning of the HPA is therefore multifaceted, deeply rooted in the culture of the HPA, in the structure of each medium, and in the relations of each medium to the larger constellation of the ecology that makes up the HPA.

Discourse regarding the role of digital media in social movements tends either to credit the media as the impetus of the movement, or places the media as distracting from "real" activism by creating an avenue for "slacktivism." Slacktivism can be defined as political action undertaken through online media that is considered low-risk, low-cost action.[21] Efforts such as changing one's Facebook profile picture to support same-sex marriage rights while the Supreme Court deliberated on California's Proposition 8[22] could be considered slacktivism. Critics of this type of action argue that slacktivism may distract from action that could have impact in the real world,[23] yet some demonstrate that this kind of activity might lead to more meaningful engagement.[24]

Action undertaken by the HPA through digital media cannot be understood in these terms. The efforts of HPA show that real-world change is possible—change accomplished by the HPA is small-scale, yet highly tangible. Whereas members of the HPA are not facing extreme risks for their activist efforts, such as imprisonment or threats to their physical safety, their participation is still costly. Whereas participation in some campaigns such as HPA:FTW could require less effort, some campaigns, such as phone banking in favor of same sex marriage or the collection, sorting, and shipping of books in a book drive, require action that takes significant amounts of time, energy, and devotion. The efforts of active HPA members cannot be considered low-cost. This type of engagement therefore cannot be understood within the framework of slacktivism.

In order to make sense of the HPA as an active organization involved in contemporary social movements, we must understand the ways that the HPA uses digital media to motivate and facilitate participation in social campaigns. We have seen examples of the ways that the HPA uses storytelling to appeal to Harry Potter fans in order to educate young people regarding social issues facing our world and in doing so cultivates a culture that is dedicated to empowering those young people to work towards making a difference. The different media used by the HPA in these processes are significant in shaping the patterns of interaction and communication present within the HPA. However, it is also clear that the HPA adapts different media for their own purposes, therein shaping the role of the media in the construction of the HPA. As current discourse, both public and academic, debates whether digital media detracts from or stimulates social action, the research presented here shows that the role of digital media in social action must be understood within the sociotechnical contexts it exists in order to make sense of the relations between media and social movements.

The HPA functions within a sociotechnical environment that relies on the interweaving of many different types of digital media. The focus of the research presented here therefore is on the relationships between the culture of the HPA, the affordances and limitations of digital media, and the practices embedded within regular participation within the organization. Because the HPA weaves together many different types of media in their campaigns, it would be impossible to understand their efforts and the role of digital media if one were to focus their research on one particular medium. Although livestream.com was an essential component to many of the HPA's campaigns, an attempt to understand the use of media in the HPA through an examination of just livestream.com would be incomplete at best, and potentially full of conclusions drawn from a skewed perspective.

Transmediation is not only useful for describing participation in the HPA and its use of digital media, but it is also a critical analytical perspective to adopt. Not only would it be impossible to describe the ways in which the HPA uses media without describing several different types of media, but it would be impossible to analyze the role of media without this perspective. A transmediated perspective, as opposed to a perspective that focuses on one particular medium, can illuminate different aspects of the role of digital media in social movements. For example, concerns over the notions of agency applied to human and nonhuman actors are often at the heart of discussions regarding recent movements, such as the Arab Spring revolutions, sometimes dubbed the "Twitter revolutions."[25] Claims of Twitter's role as the impetus of the Arab Spring revolutions give quite a bit of agency to Twitter as a medium that is capable of evoking protest behavior. A perspective that focuses only on the role of Twitter in these protests might be prone to giving Twitter significant agency, whereas studies that have examined the situation within the larger context, both in terms of social forces and the other media involved, have not credited Twitter with motivating citizens to action. Through analysis that recognizes the transmediated nature of the HPA, we can see that whereas different media have different technological affordances and limitations that do shape the behavior of HPA participants, HPA members display their agency by developing media practices that circumvent the limitations of any particular medium by adopting additional media that can fulfill their needs.

TRANSMEDIATED STUDIES OF ACTIVIST GROUPS

Not every effort the HPA organizes results in cargo planes carrying medical supplies, a six-figure check from a national bank, or thousands of books shipped to new libraries, but the HPA is nonetheless an example of an active, engaged group of people that constantly tackles new problems faced within our world. Whereas the HPA may seem anomalous in its ability to motivate young people by making social action appear to be less daunting by drawing on existing fandom, other fans have taken on their own social movements.[26] Whereas fans have an active history of initiating social action, networked digital media have in many cases made social action undertaken by fans more visible.[27]

The HPA appeals to young people by giving them the chance to participate differently, to explore their desires to change their world in a manner that might deviate from traditional notions of social action. The HPA creatively constructs a notion of citizenship that appeals to its members through their love of the Harry Potter series by drawing upon notions of citizenship found within the story—ideas such as that youth can fight to make a difference, that everyone has something to contribute, and that one engages in social action because it is his or her responsibility to make the world they live in better. In doing so it also constructs a notion of an actively engaged member of fandom. One supports the HPA because it is what fans that care about their world do.

Uncertain, or even contested, notions of citizenship and civic engagement can be a challenge for organizations that need to appeal to these shifting ideals in order to motivate participation.[28] The HPA is effective at getting young people involved because it makes social action accessible by coupling their conception of civic engagement and innovative uses of digital media. As such, we can understand members' engagement as a result of the HPA's efforts to draw on personalized interests, not only in the novels themselves but also in different social issues,[29] while also drawing on collective social identity[30] as fans of Harry Potter. As participation in social action organized by the HPA is motivated by shared social identity, new digital media provide new arenas for constructing such identities. They provide new ways of raising consciousness toward political causes. The HPA is innovative in its ability to utilize these new arenas to present not only a new framing of civic engagement, but diverse new options for participation in social movements.

Understanding these forms of framing and participation requires one to understand both the ideology expressed by the HPA and the digital media it employs. A key component of ethnographic inquiry into social movements in the digital era is to adopt a perspective that follows movements across all of the media used by the movement. The HPA weaves together multiple digital media in the social interactions that facilitate their organization, communication, and action. The sociality that results in shared identity and the production and reproduction of the group's culture emerges from these interactions spread across many different forms of media. Research that focuses on only one particular medium used within the HPA would be incapable of understanding both the social and technological factors that shape the practices of the HPA. A transmediated perspective is necessary to understand the role of digital media in the HPA.

If the HPA is at all representative of other organizations involved in social movements, a transmediated perspective is helpful for analysis as the discourse surrounding social movements makes space for discussion of forms of social action that are not slacktivism and are not driven by revolutionary media. If we study the sociotechnical context of the HPA, we can see that technology is not deterministic of social movements in that it neither entirely distracts from nor creates the desire for social change. In order to study the role of digital media in social movements, we must aim to understand the sociotechnical ecology in which the combination of social dynamics and the affordances and limitations of digital media work together to reproduce culture and construct the identities of the movement, and therein shape the kind of social action possible.

NOTES

1. The HPA brands themselves "Dumbledore's Army for the Real World," adopting the name of the group of students who band together to fight against the tyrannical takeover of their school in the fifth Harry Potter novel.
2. Nerdfighters are a group of fans of John and Hank Green, professional YouTube video bloggers who celebrate intellectualism.
3. Charles Tilly, *From Mobilization to Revolution* (New York: McGraw-Hill, 1978).
4. Tom Boellstorff, *Coming of Age in Second Life: An Anthropologist Explores the Virtually Human* (Princeton University Press, 2010); Joel Penney and Caroline Dadas, "(Re) Tweeting in the Service of Protest: Digital Composition and Circulation in the Occupy Wall Street Movement," *New Media & Society* (2013).
5. Nancy Baym, *Personal Connections in the Digital Age* (Polity, 2010); Sherry Turkle, *Life on the Screen* (Simon and Schuster, 2011); Barry Wellman and Milena Gulia, "Net Surfers Don't Ride Alone: Virtual Communities as Communities," in *Networks in the Global Village: Communities and Cyberspace*, ed. Barry Wellman. (Boulder, CO: Westview, 1999), 331–366.
6. Andy Crabtree and Tom Rodden, "Hybrid Ecologies: Understanding Cooperative Interaction in Emerging Physical-digital Environments," *Personal and Ubiquitous Computing* 12, no. 7 (2008): 481–493; Mizuko Ito, "Technologies of the Childhood Imagination: Media Mixes, Hypersociality, and Recombinant Cultural Form," *Items and Issues* 4, no. 4 (2003): 2003–2004; Mirca Madianou and Daniel Miller, *Migration and New Media* (New York: Routledge, 2012).
7. Jennifer Terrell, "Transmediated Magic: Sociality in Wizard Rock," in *Information Technology: New Generations (ITNG), 2011 Eighth International Conference*, 2011, 879–883.
8. Henry Jenkins, "'Cultural Acupuncture': Fan Activism and the Harry Potter Alliance," *Transformative Works and Cultures* 10 (2011).
9. Ashley Hinck, "Theorizing a Public Engagement Keystone: Seeing Fandom's Integral Connection to Civic Engagement through the Case of the Harry Potter Alliance," *Transformative Works and Cultures* 10 (2011).

10. Neta Kligler-Vilenchik et al., "Experiencing Fan Activism: Understanding the Power of Fan Activist Organizations through Members' Narratives," *Transformative Works and Cultures* 10 (2011).
11. Melissa M. Brough and Sangita Shresthova, "Fandom Meets Activism: Rethinking Civic and Political Participation," *Transformative Works and Cultures* 10 (2011).
12. Jenkins, "'Cultural Acupuncture': Fan Activism and the Harry Potter Alliance."
13. "Muggles" are what magical people call those who are non-magical.
14. Henry Jenkins, *Convergence Culture: Where Old and New Media Collide* (NYU Press, 2006).
15. Shaowen Bardzell, "Feminist HCI: Taking Stock and Outlining an Agenda for Design," in *Proceedings of the SIGCHI Conference on Human Factors in Computing Systems*, (2010), 1301–1310, doi:10.1145/1753326.1753521.
16. Randal Edgar, "Bill to Legalize Same-Sex Civil Unions Slated for June 29 Vote by R.I. Senate Judiciary Committee," *Providence Journal*, last modified June 28, 2011, www.providencejournal.com/politics/content/20110628-bill-to-legalize-same-sex-civil-unions-slated-for-june-29-vote-by-r.i.-senate-judiciary-committee.ece.
17. Jenkins, "'Cultural Acupuncture': Fan Activism and the Harry Potter Alliance."
18. More information about Read Indeed can be found at www.readindeed.org/.
19. Jean E. Burgess and Joshua B Green, *YouTube: Online Video and Participatory Culture* (Polity Press, 2009); Madianou and Miller, *Migration and New Media*.
20. William W. Gaver, "Technology Affordances," in *Proceedings of the SIGCHI Conference on Human Factors in Computing Systems*, (1991), 79–84.
21. Henrik Serup Christensen, "Political Activities on the Internet: Slacktivism or Political Participation by Other Means?" *First Monday* 16, no. 2 (2011).
22. "Facebook Profile Pictures Go Red in Support of Gay Marriage Rights," *Huffington Post*, last modified March 27, 2013, www.huffingtonpost.com/2013/03/26/facebook-profile-pictures-red-gay-marriage_n_2957968.html.
23. Evgeny Morozov, "The Brave New World of Slacktivism," *Foreign Policy* 19 (2009).
24. Yu-Hao Lee and Gary Hsieh, "Does Slacktivism Hurt Activism?: The Effects of Moral Balancing and Consistency in Online Activism," in *Proceedings of the SIGCHI Conference on Human Factors in Computing Systems*, (2013), 811–820.
25. Evgeny Morozov, "Iran: Downside to the 'Twitter Revolution,'" *Dissent* 56, no. 4 (2009): 10–14.
26. Lori Kido Lopez, "Fan Activists and the Politics of Race in The Last Airbender," *International Journal of Cultural Studies* 15, no. 5 (2012): 431–445; Sun Jung, "Fan Activism, Cybervigilantism, and Othering Mechanisms in K-pop Fandom," *Transformative Works and Cultures* 10 (2011).
27. Jenkins, "'Cultural Acupuncture': Fan Activism and the Harry Potter Alliance."
28. W. Lance Bennett, Chris Wells, and Deen Freelon, "Communicating Civic Engagement: Contrasting Models of Citizenship in the Youth Web Sphere," *Journal of Communication* 61, no. 5 (2011): 835–856.
29. W. Lance Bennett, "The Personalization of Politics Political Identity, Social Media, and Changing Patterns of Participation," *The Annals of the American Academy of Political and Social Science* 644, no. 1 (2012): 20–39.
30. Francesca Polletta and James M Jasper, "Collective Identity and Social Movements," *Annual Review of Sociology* (2001): 283–305.

REFERENCES

Bardzell, Shaowen. "Feminist HCI: Taking Stock and Outlining an Agenda for Design." In *Proceedings of the SIGCHI Conference on Human Factors in Computing Systems*, 1301–1310, 2010. doi:10.1145/1753326.1753521.

Baym, Nancy. *Personal Connections in the Digital Age*. Polity, 2010.

Bennett, W. Lance. "The Personalization of Politics Political Identity, Social Media, and Changing Patterns of Participation." *The Annals of the American Academy of Political and Social Science* 644, no. 1 (2012): 20–39.

Bennett, W. Lance, Chris Wells, and Deen Freelon. "Communicating Civic Engagement: Contrasting Models of Citizenship in the Youth Web Sphere." *Journal of Communication* 61, no. 5 (2011): 835–856.

Boellstorff, Tom. *Coming of Age in Second Life: An Anthropologist Explores the Virtually Human*. Princeton University Press, 2010.

Brough, Melissa M, and Sangita Shresthova. "Fandom Meets Activism: Rethinking Civic and Political Participation." *Transformative Works and Cultures* 10 (2011).

Burgess, Jean E., and Joshua B. Green. *YouTube: Online Video and Participatory Culture*. Polity Press, 2009.

Christensen, Henrik Serup. "Political Activities on the Internet: Slacktivism or Political Participation by Other Means?" *First Monday* 16, no. 2 (2011).

Crabtree, Andy, and Tom Rodden. "Hybrid Ecologies: Understanding Cooperative Interaction in Emerging Physical-digital Environments." *Personal and Ubiquitous Computing* 12, no. 7 (2008): 481–493.

Edgar, Randal. "Bill to legalize same-sex civil unions slated for June 29 vote by R.I. Senate Judiciary Committee." *Providence Journal*. June 28, 2011. www.providencejournal.com/politics/content/20110628-bill-to-legalize-same-sex-civil-unions-slated-for-june-29-vote-by-r.i.-senate-judiciary-committee.ece (accessed February 1, 2012).

"Facebook Profile Pictures Go Red In Support Of Gay Marriage Rights." *Huffington Post*. March 27, 2013. www.huffingtonpost.com/2013/03/26/facebook-profile-pictures-red-gay-marriage_n_2957968.html (accessed February 1, 2012).

Gaver, William W. "Technology Affordances." In *Proceedings of the SIGCHI Conference on Human Factors in Computing Systems*, 79–84, 1991.

Hinck, Ashley. "Theorizing a Public Engagement Keystone: Seeing Fandom's Integral Connection to Civic Engagement through the Case of the Harry Potter Alliance." *Transformative Works and Cultures* 10 (2011).

Ito, Mizuko. "Technologies of the Childhood Imagination: Media Mixes, Hypersociality, and Recombinant Cultural Form." *Items and Issues* 4, no. 4 (2003): 2003–2004.

Jenkins, Henry. *Convergence Culture: Where Old and New Media Collide*. NYU Press, 2006.

———. "'Cultural Acupuncture': Fan Activism and the Harry Potter Alliance." *Transformative Works and Cultures* 10 (2011).

Jung, Sun. "Fan Activism, Cybervigilantism, and Othering Mechanisms in K-pop Fandom." *Transformative Works and Cultures* 10 (2011).

Kligler-Vilenchik, Neta, Joshua McVeigh-Schultz, Christine Weitbrecht, and Chris Tokuhama. "Experiencing Fan Activism: Understanding the Power of Fan Activist Organizations through Members' Narratives." *Transformative Works and Cultures* 10 (2011).

Lee, Yu-Hao, and Gary Hsieh. "Does Slacktivism Hurt Activism?: The Effects of Moral Balancing and Consistency in Online Activism." In *Proceedings of the SIGCHI Conference on Human Factors in Computing Systems*, 811–820, 2013.

Lopez, Lori Kido. "Fan Activists and the Politics of Race in the Last Airbender." *International Journal of Cultural Studies* 15, no. 5 (2012): 431–445.

Madianou, Mirca, and Daniel Miller. *Migration and New Media*. Routledge, 2012.

Morozov, Evgeny. "Iran: Downside to the 'Twitter Revolution.'" *Dissent* 56, no. 4 (2009): 10–14.

———. "The Brave New World of Slacktivism." http://neteffect.foreignpolicy.com/posts/2009/05/19/the_brave_new_world_of_slacktivism *Foreign Policy* 19 (2009).

Penney, Joel, and Caroline Dadas. "(Re) Tweeting in the Service of Protest: Digital Composition and Circulation in the Occupy Wall Street Movement." *New Media & Society*, pp. 140–154 (2013).

Polletta, Francesca, and James M Jasper. "Collective Identity and Social Movements." *Annual Review of Sociology* (2001): 283–305.

Terrell, Jennifer. "Transmediated Magic: Sociality in Wizard Rock." In *Information Technology: New Generations (ITNG), 2011 Eighth International Conference On*, 879–883, 2011.

Tilly, Charles. *From Mobilization to Revolution*. McGraw-Hill New York, 1978.

Turkle, Sherry. *Life on the Screen*. Simon and Schuster, 2011.

Wellman, Barry, and Milena Gulia. "Net Surfers Don't Ride Alone: Virtual Communities as Communities." *Networks in the Global Village* (1999): 331–366.

4 Dangerous Places

Social Media at the Convergence of Peoples, Labor, and Environmental Movements

Richard Widick

POSTCARDS FROM THE FUTURE OF CLIMATE CHAOS

From the advent of Indymedia at the 1999 battle of Seattle anti-World Trade Organization protests, to the worldwide diaspora of anti-globalization protests (2000–2003) and the great anti-war protests starting in 2003, all the way up through the United Nations climate protests in Copenhagen in 2009, WikiLeaks, Occupy Wall Street, and the Arab Spring, the digital communication revolution has been transforming how social movements are assembling themselves on a planetary scale. In the same way that these movements and ruptures express the transformative effects of new Internet technologies that came of age in the 1990s, so now does the emergent global climate justice movement of the 20-teens embody and express the transformative potential of emergent social media technologies that came of age in the 2000s.[1]

Looking backwards from these decades of technology-driven historical change, we now see clearly an equally profound continuity: Changing mass media have shaped every modern social movement, each in its own time and place. Each movement bears the mark of dawning communications and transportation technologies that were, in their time and place, transcending barriers to collective action and consequently reorganizing power-laden social relations. Where would the 19th-century abolition movement have gone without the Black Press that arguably began with the founding of *Freedom's Journal* in 1827?[2] How would the Civil Rights Movement have unfolded absent the publication of those horrific photos of Emmit Till's bludgeoned and river-bloated corpse in the September 15, 1955, issue of *Jet Magazine*?[3] The Montgomery bus boycott?[4] The news footage of viscous police dogs flashing teeth and chewing up peaceful kids at the Children's Crusade in Birmingham 1963? The March on Washington? What impact did constant TV news footage from Vietnam have on the free speech and anti-war movements of the 1960s? Or consider the modern environmental movement absent those Apollo 17 "blue marble" photos of December 7, 1972.[5] We should also mention the media storm unleashed when Commander Marcos and the EZLN revolted in Chiapas on DAY 1 of the North American Free Trade Agreement: January 1, 1994.[6]

What these examples show is how social movements really get moving when individuals are able to identify with each other through shared experience facilitated by images (especially visual but also narrative), reaching *through media* across every previous barrier of time and space to recognize the social and increasingly environmental conditions of their shared grievances. It might now seem cliché, but in 1999, when the Seattle anti-World Trade Organization protestors chanted down the police and National Guard with "The Whole World Is Watching! The Whole World Is Watching!" they were announcing the arrival of a new digital era in activism, protest, and resistance.

More than that, Seattle was a postcard from the future we are living out now, in the dawning era of global warming and rapid anthropogenic climate change. Every day brings new reports of new places suffering new environmental stresses and new species facing new hardship due to rising temperatures, rising seas, and rising ocean acidification, not to mention disappearing ice caps, retreating glaciers, shrinking water supplies, creeping deserts, and invading pests. Increasingly, local people naturally tuned into their local social and environmental conditions awaken to the fact that their unique place-based struggle shares a common logic with other places and ultimately with everyplace across the horizon of globalization: Some local natural or social resource—such as a community of labor—that had once been shared as a public good is now being legally privatized, designated as fungible (saleable, transferable property), and subjected to market forces. The results are predictable: Long-term public value streams emergent from rooted communities and stable ecosystems are converted into short-term private profits. Ascendant neoliberal economic globalization—defined as the universalization of private-property-rights-driven industrial production and exchange—brings with it the globalization of social and environmental problems and thus resistance and ultimately social movements.

As a crucial correlate of these monumental changes, emergent global activism serves as an indicator of just how far and fast they are happening. What do the new opportunities for digital and social media participation in ever-wider communities, publics, and movements mean for the future of social movements in general, and to the global climate justice movement in particular? This question of the role of information and communication technologies in social movements lay at the heart of my study of California's redwood timber wars, and now it guides my current research on climate justice.[7]

California's long-simmering redwood timber war exploded in 1985 when MAXXAM announced its clear-cut liquidation plan for the newly acquired Pacific Lumber Company and its principal old growth holdings in the Humboldt Bay region, including the famed Headwaters grove, and only simmered down again when victorious forest defenders succeeded in coercing the state and the federal government to buy Headwaters Grove for preservation in 1999. The decade following the movement to save Headwaters started with the fiery convergence of newly networked peoples, labor, and environmental movements at the anti-World Trade Organization protests in Seattle.

But whereas over the last quarter of the 20th century redwood forest defenders demanded transition to sustainable forestry and preservation of the last 1% of ancient redwoods (by 1985, 96% had already been cut, 3% had been preserved in parks, and the last 1%, which remained in private hands, had become the center of local land-use politics), and projected their concerns into the anti-globalization movement that burst on the scene in Seattle 1999, the climate justice movement now demands the same on a global scale—nothing less than the transformation of cultural/economic development away from its current tendency toward manifestly unjust and unsustainable dependence on pollution-heavy global privatization of nature by the fossil-fuel system, led by the big oil companies, and toward socially just and sustainable development dependent instead on democratically regulated renewable energies. These two struggles embody, each in their own time, both the social and environmental consequences of capitalist world system expansion.

IMAGINATION

The underlying, space-crunching communications and transportation technologies that make such global economic expansion possible also make possible the new, global protest movements. Today, for example, we observe how transnational peer-to-peer cultural production of shared knowledge drives the creation of collective political subjectivities that flash up wherever and whenever the big international institutions (WTO, IMF, WB, UNFCCC, etc.) convene to advance their objectives of global governance. Notwithstanding much debate concerning the relative strength or weakness of the *digital social ties* implied in that statement, what cannot be denied is how social media technologies are fueling the imaginations of legion erstwhile social movers, activists, youth, and untold other previously more sedentary social forces.[8] Not everyone can put their bodies into the street and, on a moment's notice, join an immigrants' rights march in Los Angeles, for example, but they can log on and channel some portion of their attention into the digital semiotic groundswell. What effect does that possibility have on their *imagination*, which I claim is *the crucial resource* for any and all social movements?

Why imagination? Before a person gets directly or physically involved in a movement, for example, by showing up at a meeting or joining a rally or donating money or starting to organize or changing her own daily life in ways that prefigure the world she hopes to achieve, she must first make the connection and imaginatively project herself into an absent collectivity, a group, about which she will learn precisely through *mass media*, the already ubiquitous reach of which is multiplied by symbiotic social media that channel its fodder ever further and faster.[9] How much of the blogosphere is in fact the reposting, with commentary, of content culled from mass media? This is one way in which the digital communications revolution produces deep change in the *practice* of both individual and collective subjectivity. The new possibilities it presents to all—for participation, for self education, and for adding our voices to the public debate over crucial ideas—changes the way we think about ourselves as belonging to this or that group, or being vested in this or that political process. It changes how we judge our own personal efficacy and hence our prefigurative fantasies of power and heroism.[10] Can I really participate in the United Nations international climate talks, for example, or the global climate justice movement? What would that look like? What's the climate buzz on social media? Climate movement groups and nongovernmental organizations (NGOs) are tweeting like crazy, and so is the Secretary General of the United Nations Framework Convention on Climate Change (UNFCCC), which convenes the UN climate talks (themselves fully online at unfccc.int). Social movements are nothing without these technological possibilities for seeing beyond oneself to identify with distant or wide-flung communities of grievance. Such projections rely on new fantasies that emergent semiotic channels of planetary social (mass) media make increasingly possible.[11]

DANGEROUS PLACES

A related and even more primary condition of such possibility is the fundamental role of *place* in every actual, concrete appearance of an individual's imaginative projection of self into community or identification with distant causes. Most people remain grounded in, and most attached, to their local relations, and when the open channel of social (mass) media reflects on their homegrown conditions, allowing them to see themselves in the face of such others, identification is possible and fantasies ignite. Daydreaming sets in. Look at that! Could I be part of that? Could I do that here?

Thus do today's changing technological conditions of possibility for collective subjectivity open up new and qualitatively distinct opportunities for social movements to channel up local, place-based attention to grievance and conflict into global publics that identify and self-organize under common knowledge of governance, economy, and other social forces that variously appear to exercise hegemony or otherwise tower over smaller-scale or individual interests. With such newly shared and so more confident knowledge supplanting or at least augmenting the symbolic figures (i.e., perceived authority figures, catastrophic events, unrealized desires, fatal losses, and unjust grievances) that had previously motivated people in their ongoing struggles, movements can be more effective, exercise more reach, and more successfully recruit.

Social media are helping make such places *dangerous* to the powers that be, and that have profited off those places for so long—dangerous because, as places hosting modern institutions of economic exchange based on private property rights, public spheres built on rights of free speech, and polities built on political rights of universal participation, their local histories of cultural and economic conflict are recorded in daily news, stored in local archives, and debated in media-driven political campaigns. When, in the course of events associated with colonization by the capitalist world economic system, unusual violence breaks out and starts producing corpses—as it inevitably does when proponents of modernity get busy installing their new systems over and in the place of previous ways and means of life—the ensuing reports and photographic evidence capture a snapshot of the social relations prevailing in that historical moment. Everyone chimes in to the open public sphere with opinions, analysis, and new facts. Reports are made and records are kept. Stories told and retold accumulate into archives of violence and become increasingly potent symbols and political weapons. Monuments and historical markers spring up. The event, the violence, and its archive get built into place. Such places remember, in other words—by which I mean they increasingly come to exist as such, as meaningful places, as archives of the objective violence of the social relations by means of which the place was originally colonized, developed, modernized, or otherwise internalized within the ascendant world order (culture) of global capitalism.

In the resulting *dangerous places* of the modernizing world, such constitutive violence lies just beneath the surface. It structures the historical archive within which contemporary social and environmental conflicts are conducted. Hence, *colonization by the culture system of modern capitalism*—with which necessarily prolix term I mean the dynamic institutional triad of constitutionally set up and legitimated private-property-rights-driven markets, free-speech-rights-driven public spheres, and political-rights-driven democratic polity—is the process by which the subjective, criminal violence of historical agents, acting as emissaries of the colonizing culture system, authorized by its laws and legitimated by its narratives, gets objectified in the deep cultural structures of place that come to preside over future political consciousness. Subjective violence by the victors of historical struggles pervades and eventually becomes the objective, structural violence of institutions.[12] Slavery made the United States a place where Jim Crow could make sense and work well for the powerful. Jim Crow, in turn, made a place where the prison industrial complex could make sense and big profits. This objective system of violence haunts the built environment with landmarks like Louisiana's Angola State Prison, which endures as a visual legacy of white power spanning each of these eras.[13] Indian genocide in the redwoods made a place where it now makes sense for white capitalists to fight with predominantly white labor over the spoils of industrial timber production on what had been the First Peoples' land. One hundred years of such struggle between big timber capital and labor over the spoils of industrial timber extraction, which cut 96% of the ancient redwood forests and built huge accumulations of timber capital as well as thriving working class mill towns, made Humboldt a place where it makes sense for forest defenders to revolt against the status quo and link their current struggles to the labor wars and Indian wars that set the social and environmental conditions of the present. What these two historical narratives share is their common modernity—they are both particular instances of the general story of how subjective, criminal violence set up the institutions of markets, public spheres, and polities everywhere in the new world that we now call developed, modern. Each is an allegory illuminating the creation of the social systems of objective violence that we take for granted today, and which form the cultural unconscious—the system of cultural assumptions—that inform everyday life in the United States.

Canadian political philosopher Charles Taylor calls this basic institutional set-up *the modern social imaginary*, using the term *imaginary* in a way that imbues the theoretical concept with psychological dynamism, and which suggests that the unconscious body might have a strong role to play in the process.[14] From this perspective, in what follows capitalism will come to be understood not merely as an isolated sphere of productive activity, separate from society, but rather as the objective system of violence embodied in legalized private property and the enterprises (firms, etc.) that can operate as such only because they are nested in a broader set of institutions (civil society, the state, etc.), the combination of which amounts to a new set of shared assumptions, a new moral order that is shared, above all, by those who have become, by force or by choice, or by some combination of such agencies, modern.[15]

MODERN SOCIAL IMAGINARIES

The term "social imaginary" refers to the shared self-understandings that are embodied in a group's characteristic set of institutionalized actions, and which define the group as such, as an object of experience. The shared understandings have objective ramifications because they are always already, by definition, *put into action*—they are ideas being performed without necessarily being conscious. For example, the shared idea that voting is good is embodied in the cultural practice of democracy, with obvious objective effects in the world. Any particular social imaginary, or culture, is distinguished as such, as unique, precisely by the constellation of such ideas and the practices within which they are embodied and expressed objectively. Today, modern societies share the assumptions discussed above, for example that private property is good and legitimate, that free speech is to be valued, and that polities should be ruled by their peoples. Free markets, open public spheres, and democratic governance are the hallmarks of modern legitimacy.

More useful than the widely used term "culture," the term social imaginary refers to values, expectations, norms, beliefs, morals, and ideas of what is good and sacred—but it frames these also, coterminously, as always already embodied and performed in collective, objective institutional practices. Emile Durkheim would have called them social facts.[16]

The term social imaginary moves us beyond the reductionism of either idealism or materialism, a path Marx himself took in writing that "Man makes history, but not under conditions of his own choosing." Explaining the remark, he continued: "The beginner who has learned a new language always translates it back to his mother tongue, but he assimilates the spirit of the new language and expresses himself freely in it only when he moves in it without recalling the old and when he forgets his native tongue."[17] These two dialectical statements embody the logic of structure and agency that drives sociological knowledge production, and which I place at the center of my own use of cultural, linguistic, psychoanalytic, economic, and environmental theory to further develop the term modern social imaginary.[18]

Looking closer at the term will be instructive: If the social is objective and collective, the term must be read *objective and collective imaginary*. And if the term *imaginary* refers to the imagination, and thus to the active, representational, meaning-making activity of a subject, the term must be read *objective collective active representation*. Finally, if we follow structuralism's use of Saussurian linguistics and construe the objective collective social order as a symbolic order—an a priori meaning-making system precisely comparable to a language system that subjects put to use—the term must ultimately be read as follows: Social imaginaries are *objective collective symbolic orders of and for active representation*. A social imaginary is thus a usable system of ideal elements already up and running in an institutional structure; a system of meaningful institutions into which people are born and which they therefore tend to embody and naturalize exactly like they do their first language. To every individual, the social imaginary within which it emerges as a thinking and acting subject exists as a structural condition of possibility of its experience as a member of the group, in the same way that its mastery of its mother tongue is a condition of possibility of its coherent speech in and among the same group. A social imaginary is thus something that people use, and must use, to make meaning. This concept applies a linguistic metaphor to all social life: Society is a conversation—actually more like an argument.

According to Taylor, what is *modern* about modern social imaginaries is the emergence in the period 1500 to the present of a specific set of practices that comes to dominate social life, not just social life in the places where they were created, but social life everywhere that they are exported, and each of which draws energy and legitimation from the idea of individual rights. In modern societies, those characterized by a *modern social imaginary*, the idea of individual rights promotes the strength and legitimacy, and hence the geographical extension, of one specific set of reciprocally constitutive institutions (practices): Again, these are private property markets, free speech public spheres, and polities ruled by the people. Modernization means precisely the extension of these institutional practices in time and space, a sweeping wave of social changes driven by the Euro-Anglo-American liberal cultural *discourse of rights*.[19]

Again, as this modern capitalist culture, this social imaginary, expands in space, colonizing new places that previously hosted some other social system, it invariably remakes them into what I call *dangerous places*—places that remember events of extraordinary violence in landscape, architecture, institutions, and mass media narratives and photojournalist images of dead bodies, weeping relatives, catastrophic poverty, starvation, oppression, denuded and poisoned landscapes, resistance, and war—but especially dead bodies, and doubly so when these are imbued with the absence of justice for the perpetrators.

To whom are such places of modern objective violence dangerous? How do they drive the formation of social movement publics? What pushes them upwards and outwards from local to global and universal significance? And how do the more recent social media technologies increasingly ensure the connection of these places to emergent global political subjectivities? By way of answering, I first revisit my ethnographic journey into California's redwood timber wars, and then I report back from my ongoing field research at the UN climate talks in Durban, South Africa (2011); Doha, Qatar (2012); and Warsaw, Poland (2013).

CALIFORNIA'S REDWOOD TIMBER WARS

California's narrow redwood ecozone reaches from the coast inland up to 30 miles, and stretches from Big Sur in the south to the Oregon border in the north. Between discovery in 1850 by white European ambassadors of the U.S. capitalist economic (culture) system, and the purchase of the last 1% of privately owned, unprotected acreage by Charles Hurwitz and his MAXXAM corporation, the big timber companies took 96% of the ancient redwoods, yielding some of the world's finest lumber for building and contributing greatly to the construction of California's great cities of San Francisco, Sacramento, and Los Angeles, as well as the rebuilding of San Francisco after the great fire of 1906.

What happened to the indigenous peoples who lived there, and to the workers whose labor made the whole affair profitable? The Wiyot people who inhabited Humboldt Bay were reduced from somewhere between 1,500 and 2,000 to perhaps 200 between first colonization in 1850 and the massacres of 1860. The Hupa, Karuk, and Yaruk tribes, which populated the redwood forested riverbanks of the Trinity, Arcata, and Klamath Rivers, and the Whilkut, Chilula, Nongatl, Chimariko, Mattole, Sinkyone, Lassic, and Wailaki tribes, which inhabited the wider Humboldt Bay redwood region, were reduced to a minimal threat by dint of murder, starvation, and ultimately forced relocation to camps and reservations.

With this genocide, the previously communally held native lands were opened to privatization by whites, who transformed them into legal property under compulsion by the U.S. state land system. Thus rendered for all-out industrial competition in redwood lumber production over the ensuing decades, the rising lumber barons subjected them to continually increasing scales of production and consolidation through acquisition and merger into massive corporate tree farms, sometimes reaching 200,000 to 300,000 acres (MAXXAM and Simpson timber, respectively, in 1985). Themselves subjected to unremitting price competition, they advanced their own interests through continual division and subdivision of the labor process; by speeding up their axes, saws, and mills in order to increase labor productivity; and by relentlessly substituting machinery for human labor.[20] And they fought labor organization with every tool they had, including blacklists and direct, murderous violence.[21]

Exploitation by the lumber barons provoked labor resistance, and what followed was common enough: the violent repression of redwood labor movements, and in the end a compromise that promoted smooth, rapid, and eventually massive escalation of production.

The result was nearly total deforestation. Ninety-six percent of the original giants were cut, and in the process the great lumber barons and their corporate followers laid many thousands of miles of logging roads without much thought to engineering their integrity. For generations they bled, and continue to bleed, large-scale erosion into the salmon-bearing streams, at once both destroying the salmon's magnificent productivity and raising the long-term cost of salmon and redwood production alike.

In this way, colonial genocide cleared the way for private-property-rights-driven capitalism, which came in and set the social and environmental conditions for the redwood timber wars that erupted in 1985. In that year, CEO Charles Hurwitz brought the MAXXAM Corporation into the redwoods on a wave of deregulated junk bond leverage. First he bought the local Pacific Lumber, owner of 200,000 plus acres, including most of the last 1% of uncut and unprotected, privately owned old growth (3% had been preserved in parks). Then he announced a plan to cut it all, roiling this once distant and obscure place that was already occupied by the remnant and marginalized tribes, who nevertheless had learned to share the deteriorating forests and rivers with generations of exploited labor and an unceasing tide of educated urban refugees who thought they were heading back to land and away from the harsh city life of politics and consumerism. The political awareness and organizational skills of this last group ended up transforming this erstwhile hinterland into a media hub and symbolic center of converging indigenous, labor, and environmental movements.

Woodland creatures played a crucial role at this juncture. Several endangered species use these forests, and so the forest defenders used two of them, the marbled murrelet and the spotted owl, and the Endangered Species Act (ESA) to fight back against Hurwitz. They sued repeatedly on behalf of the birds, fighting every timber harvest plan they could on a case-by-case basis, depending on which of California's Forest Practice Rules MAXXAM was violating at each particular site. They conducted a relentless campaign of civil disobedience as well, blocking roads and trespassing into active logging sites to shut or slow the cut down by putting their bodies in the way of the work being done. And finally in 1990 they staged the largest environmental protest to date—Redwood Summer, a whole season of direct-action civil disobedience modeled on Mississippi Summer, the 1964 civil rights campaign. The idea was the same—create an influx of outsiders capable of breaking through the monopoly on established reality exercised by the timber industry—just like the white monopoly exercised over power in the 1960s South. People came from all over the nation to shut down the logging and defend the ancient redwoods.

But right before the summer *season of protest* began, some still unknown individuals planted a bomb in the car of lead organizers Judi Bari and Darryl Cherney. They were not killed, but critical damage was done to their bodies, the Redwood Summer campaign, and the redwood forest defense. The FBI proceeded to arrest them for carrying the bomb and associated the movement with terrorism in the public sphere with several press releases and appearances. In the end the FBI never pressed any charges, because there was no evidence. But, by investigating the victims and not doing a wider inquiry, they tainted the movement in the media and contributed to the defeat of legislation then pending that would have radically transformed the timber industry in California—the California's *Forests Forever Initiative* state ballot initiative which was on ballot that fall and would have banned clear cutting as well as even residual harvesting of any trees over 150 years old. The measure was defeated by a narrow margin of 4%. That was a giant victory for industrial timber interests all over California, not just in Humboldt.

But in the following months, forest defenders launched more logging lawsuits against MAXXAM, and in his defense Hurwitz filed a 5th-Amendment-based so-called *takings* lawsuit against the federal government, claiming that the ESA murrelet regulations had taken *all of the value* of his property at Headwaters Grove.

Finally, in 1999 Hurwitz, the state of California, and the Federal government under Clinton settled the lawsuit out of court with the so-called *Headwaters Deal*, in which they exchanged combined funds and lands valued at around $500 million for the 2,700 acres of Headwaters Grove—even though Hurwitz had paid only double that amount for the whole company in 1985, which then held over 200,000 acres, the old growth mill town of Scotia with its 235 company houses, a giant welding company (later sold for $30 million), an office building in San Francisco (later sold for $50 million), and more.[22]

Going back to 1988, we see that MAXXAM had another problem brewing. In 1988 it acquired the Kaiser Aluminum Company in yet another leveraged buyout. Kaiser was global and unionized, and by 1998 the company was locked in heated contract negotiations with its United Steel Workers. When the negotiations broke down, the steel workers went on strike, MAXXAM locked them out, and, believe it or not, they shipped in laid-off timber workers from Humboldt to replace steel workers at their Spokane, Washington, factory. They even drove them onto the site in ominous looking buses with blacked-out windows. The steel workers promptly headed down to Humboldt and allied themselves with the forest defenders, setting the stage for United Steel Workers from Kaiser and Humboldt forest defenders to famously march together in Seattle against the WTO.

In the spring of 1999, I embarked on two years of field research on the scene of this struggle, living and working in Humboldt's ancient redwoods, participating in the timber wars, and dwelling as much as possible in the libraries and historical archives of the region. Using participant observation, interviews, and archival study, I traced the social and ecological conditions of the timber wars back across 150 years of colonization, industrialization, and deforestation, during which I ultimately recognized that these three consecutive historical phases can each be understood as distinct but related forms of conflict over property. First came the struggle for property in land—an epoch of colonial Indian wars; then a struggle for property in values produced by industrial labor directed at redwood ecology—an epoch of union struggles; and finally a struggle for property in ecology itself—an epoch of deforestation, environmental resistance, and converging labor and ecology movements. But these discoveries in the field and in the archives sent me back even further—all the way back to the modern *culture of rights* that characterizes the deep structure of American nationalism and market revolution.

Assembling these ideas in the interest of explaining the region's contemporary environmental politics, I was learning how the politics of timber war are performed on a cultural landscape built over successive decades of Indian wars, labor wars, and timber wars. In assembling the story and comparing public discourse in these three epochal struggles, I discovered how each had produced a particular moment of *extra*-ordinary violence around which social memory has crystallized over time: the genocidal massacre of Wiyot Indians during their world renewal ceremony in 1860, the killing of strikers at the gates of the Holmes-Eureka Mill during The Great Lumber Strike of 1935, and the car bombing of forest defenders in 1990. Representations of these events now saturate the living, symbolic, and built social world of Humboldt. Each spasm of *violence* provoked a media spectacle that captured an image of the social relations prevailing in that historical moment. The narratives and symbols they provoked, for example in newspaper reports, labor publications, court records, and historical accounts, now circulate continuously in Humboldt; they inhabit the museums, libraries, and mass media *archives*; they structure its built landscape and its architecture of social *memory*; and so they shape its practical cultures of timber production and environmental resistance. They haunt Humboldt's embattled landscape of company towns, museums, monuments, and parks as well as its raucous public debate over corporate forestry.

As an ethnographer of the timber wars, I discovered how these events became allegorical of the dominant tendencies and struggles in each epoch—how the stories are told and retold, how they accumulate meaning over time, how the texts accumulate, and how the retellings grow and enter peoples' lives and identities. For example, in Humboldt today, one still encounters these stories everywhere. When talking about the struggle against MAXXAM, conversations almost always lead back to the bombing of organizers Judy Bari and Darryl Cherney—the bombing punctuates the story. When people talk about it, and the bombing gets mentioned, mention of the violent event which seems to say, "see, that's what happens when environmental movements get really radical and then get close to victory by putting peoples' lives on the line, like in the civil rights movement, that's when somebody tries to pop them!" Such stories of extraordinary violence become a resource for the movements, which build on them and retell them, always relying on one or more communications media to propound their moral arguments and to broadcast their claims, educating people and building their own publics. Today, such stories are increasingly told and retold through new social media, in which the new possibilities of peer-to-peer coproduction multiplies their range and deepens their perspective considerably.

The case of Humboldt unfolded in an open public sphere in which opposing individuals representing competing interests openly debated the meaning of subjective acts of the most extraordinary violence, as they do in every new place that the modern social imaginary establishes itself, for, by the definition above, to be modern is to practice (property) rights-driven markets, (free speech) rights-driven publics, and (voting) rights-driven polities together. This performative institutional troika makes places into archives of social memory of constitutive violence that, over time, increasingly mediates future consciousness, and thus of course future projects and politics. It makes places dangerous namely to capital, by which term in this instance I mean those accumulations of objectified labor and ecological values and the nameable agents of their enjoyment. In Humboldt, that means the big timber corporations who must now tread more lightly on forest soils and communities that remember genocidal white colonial violence in the same long narrative/image as labor massacres and bombed out environmentalists. To see this idea telescoped in a single concrete particular image, visit the deforested, salmon-stripped mountain banks of the Eel River where it flows through MAXXAM's anti-union company town of Scotia, California—site of the 1860 massacre of the Wiyot peoples, reduced from around 2,000 pre-colonial population to 200 after just 10 years of white presence. The company has changed names, but the colonial, industrial, and environmental traces of its making are left for our perusal, and for our fantasies of power, participation, and potential prefiguration of converging indigenous peoples, labor, and environmental movements. That is the symbolic work that MAXXAM can do for progressive movements on the scene today.

This method can now be generalized and applied to new research. As I used the concept of modern social imaginaries to study local markets, publics, and polity in the redwoods, and discovered in the process how signature events of extraordinary violence allegorized the region's history of colonization, industrialization, and globalization, other researchers in conflict-torn regions at the erstwhile margins of the world economic system's expansion might similarly tune into local archives. Are they also accumulating dangerous, violent stories about primitive accumulation, labor struggle, and environmental struggle? Do they also embody the legacy of capitalism? Are they showing the common cause? Are they building into archival engines for converging peoples, labor, and environmental movements?

Global ethnographers of such *dangerous places* can now, using new social media, much more easily tune into the local, place-based modern social imaginaries and enter their archive of violent colonization, industrialization, and environmental degradation. They can encounter from afar the archival legacy of rights-driven markets, publics, and polity ruled by the people. They can dig up the images and narratives of extra-ordinary violence, raise them into public consciousness, and assemble them into dangerous stories about the common conditions and causes of emergent peoples, labor, and environmental movements. And they can channel these local stories into global public arenas, in support of local projects by identifying struggles across every social barrier.

With the ongoing rise of modernity, understood as the expansion to universal significance of the modern social imaginary, this world is being made into a single place, with reports coming in from its wide-flung, constituent *dangerous places* now assembling themselves into a planetary engine driving the global convergence of movements around the unfolding catastrophe of climate change. These places, as archives of violence, are precisely the substance—the mass media content—that new cyberactivists, as soon as they tune into the modern social imaginary and realize the possibilities it has objectified for them, can and are beginning to use in their newfangled construction of transnational collective subjects of social movement. Find a real place, enter the archive, do the history, discover the events that captured public attention for the violence they did, start your blog, open it to comments, post your evidence online, and open the channel up from your locale into the global semiotic flow of identificatory attentions that establish, with ever more certainty, the common logic of social movements in the 21st-century epoch of imperial globalization. One emergent global capitalist social imaginary. One planet, with only one atmosphere, as its industrial fodder. And one social movement (of movements) to the barricades!

CLIMATE JUSTICE NOW

As the summer of 2013 arrived, the United Nations was gearing up yet again for another international climate conference, hoping to make progress on two distinct work streams—first, a new treaty for adoption in 2015, and implementation in 2020, designed to govern global carbon policy in the post-2020 era, and second, a year-by-year effort to increase ambition in reducing CO2 emissions incrementally in the years leading up 2020. Like the Durban COP 17 in 2011 and the Doha COP 18 in 2012, the Warsaw conference of 2013 brought the familiar convergence of issue-driven, NGO-centered coalitions (like CAN, Greenpeace, etc.), as well an emergent, more radical distributed network movement—Climate Justice Now!

The convergence of people and movements at these climate COPs is reminiscent of those great spectacles of resistance that made the anti-globalization movement familiar to all—but there are important differences. A story from my fieldwork at COP 17 illustrates one driving force of the changing scene:

"Mic Check!" cried the middle-aged white woman, who turned out to be a Canadian representative of the Global Justice Ecology Project.[23]

"MIC CHECK!" came the sonorous reply from a crowd of around 200 folks, all of whom had UN badges granting them entry to the international climate talks.

"I've been coming to these COPs since 2004," she continued. "I'VE BEEN COMING TO THESE COPs SINCE 2004," repeating her words by shouting at the top of their lungs in the style that Occupiers all around the world have taken to calling *the human microphone.*

"They are dominated and controlled by the 1 percent."

"THEY ARE DOMINATED AND CONTROLLED BY THE ONE PERCENT."

"That will not change . . . "

"THAT WILL NOT CHANGE . . . "

"Unless we make it."

"UNLESS WE MAKE IT."

"And if we go . . . "

"AND IF WE GO . . . "

"We will not have . . . "

"WE WILL NOT HAVE . . . "

"The power to make that change."

"THE POWER TO MAKE THAT CHANGE"

"So I say . . . "

"SO I SAY . . . "

"Occupy the COP."

"OCCUPY THE COP!"

"Occupy the COP!"

"OCCUPY THE COP."[24]

Such was the scene inside Albert Luthuli International Convention Center on December 9, 2011, at COP 17 in Durban, South Africa. The UN climate talks were on the verge of collapse after 10 days that had failed to produce any significant agreement on the issues at hand—who and by how much and on what timetable should each nation commit to cutting greenhouse gasses, in the interest of heading off runaway global warming and climate change? Frustrated activists demanding "Climate Justice Now!" adopted the Occupy tactic and Mic Checked the 17th Conference of Parties (COP)—the annual global climate conference that the United Nations Framework Convention on Climate Change (UNFCCC) has convened in a different city every year since 1995.[25]

The national delegations had met. The environmental ministers had made their ritual three-minute statements. The NGOs had convened their official side events on every conceivable topic, from the Third World Network's panel "What must Durban deliver?" on opening day to "Multi-stakeholder Collaboration to Reinforce Adaptation Opportunities for African Pastoral Peoples," a panel convened by the Indigenous People of Africa Coordinating Committee (IPACC), featuring speakers from Conservation International, UNESCO, WMO, the Ministry of Water from Chad, and the director of the nomadic women's association of Chad.[26] And the global Day of Action had come and gone, bringing 15,000 protestors through the streets of Durban past city hall to the militarized perimeter of the Albert Luthuli International Convention Center.

My work was done, or so I thought, and late in the afternoon of the last scheduled day of negotiations, I headed to the central café at the Hilton and sat down for a late lunch. But then a sound caught my attention. It grew until I realized that the shouting and singing was clearly in protest. I jumped up from my table, switched on my video camera, and hustled inside the conference hall, wading into the agitated sea of bodies . . . The Occupation of COP17 was on, and I was there to witness it, quite by accident, not unlike my fortuitous arrival at the WTO protests in Seattle in 1999, the so-called Battle in Seattle that contributed so much to the anti-globalization movement.[27]

Yes, I had known the potential for protest—no, I didn't expect what happened next. Yes, I had been at the Occupy site in the designated protest zone outside the concrete barriers that made central Durban look like the U.S. green zone in Iraq. But even though I talked to everyone I could, and had been told to expect the unexpected, I had not heard the call to action. I had been asked several times, "are you on Facebook or Twitter?"—to which I had to respond that "sorry, no, my iPhone has no international SIM card, my local cell is just a phone, with no Internet, and the web connection at my local residence is not worth the trouble—so basically I'm off the network. But can you call me on my local phone if anything comes up?"

"Really?" replied one twenty-something international hipster from the rich world north, probably the U.K., "that's not how it works any more.

You've got to be online if you want to be in the movement and find out what's going on." That is how everyone except for me knew where to go. But thankfully I got lucky and happened on the scene, not as a protestor, but rather as a visual, participatory ethnographer shooting video, still photos, and conducting interviews in and among not just the converging social movements and activists who trail the COP around the world, year after year, but also the corporations that pursue their interests here and the political delegations that come to represent their countries.

Paradoxically, I proceeded to experience just how crucial new social media have become by having my own microcosm of service denial. As these reflections on COP 17 suggest, e-mail, blog, and web-based organizing have become essential *conditions of possibility* for converging social movement groups and activists, who flock to these big international conferences in order to participate in a truly global democratic experiment in self-governance. Now the social movements are going digital in ways we have to understand if we want to gauge their potential and compare them to previous movements. What would Seattle 1999 have looked like, we might ask, had there been an #OccupyWTO Twitter feed comparable to that of #OccupyCOP17? Perhaps there would have been a convergence of 500,000 indigenous, labor, and environmental activists and protestors, instead of the 50,000 that managed to shut down the WTO ministerial conference.

FROM ANTI-GLOBALIZATION TO THE CLIMATE JUSTICE MOVEMENT

One thing we learn from the sequence of events Seattle 1999-to-Warsaw COP 19 is that all of this digital globalism brings the local more dearly into play. Place-based movements become ever more relevant not just to the local scene, but to the global flow of signs constitutive of emergent global subjectivities, for example transnational social movements like the global climate justice movement. Everyone on the ground in Seattle had come from somewhere—far or near, and they came bearing the weight of their own witnessing, from their hometowns and villages across the globe, to confront power, as they see it, with a modicum of face-to-face criticism.

At this juncture, it is tempting to digress into a list of the hundreds of protest groups that, originating across the horizon of globalization, each from a concrete geographical place where the expanding world economic system, manifest in the activity of corporations that accumulate by externalizing costs on communities of labor and environment, provoke the grievances that set in motion the chains of identificatory events that allow, for example, a group of forest defenders from the redwood region of northern California to see their struggle against the MAXXAM Corporation as equivalent to those of native Mexicans and peasant farmers in Chiapas. They are defending their forests against the same or similar corporations that are destroying the redwoods and the salmon of Humboldt. We are Zapatistas—and Zapatistas are forest defenders. What makes these identifications possible are the communications and transportation technologies that are now trending toward unlimited access to global virtual co-presence. Communications channels, newly global and digital, are very simply the substance of collective identification, and the faster and wider they function, the faster and wider is it possible (not necessarily probable, but possible), for the identificatory chains of equivalence to grow.

Now it is 2014, the COP has come and gone from Warsaw 2013 and is heading for Lima, Peru, in December to work on the next climate treaty, which agreement will govern the international climate policy in the crucial post-2020 decades. That period will see either a 90% cutback in carbon emissions before 2030, or runaway climate change and an ensuing era of what Christian Parenti has called *climate chaos*—the disruption of human lifeways that is already developing on the front lines of climate change in the tropics of Africa, where warming is setting off human migrations and bloody sectarian battles on the postcolonial landscape of weaponized tribal groups and failed states.[28]

In full cognizance of the situation at hand, global activists are rising up like never before, constructing the widest and deepest social movement networks the world has ever seen. The emergent global climate justice movement is one such increasingly (socially) mediated network flow of attention, an infrastructure of and for the identification of struggles; it is a convergence of peoples, labor, and environmental movements that is already shaping the UN talks and thus the global policy response to global warming, and thus by extension the future of climate change, and by further extension the livability of our planet and all the present and future lives that depend on its natural systems.[29] Be sure to follow the negotiations on Twitter at @UN_ClimateTalks for the 140-character updates of the United Nations Framework Convention on Climate Change, and simply search the social media site for the handles of the big indigenous peoples, poor peoples, labor, and environmental groups. They are all there, hoping you will click their link and channel some modicum of your available attention into their particular public struggle. Maybe you will even follow them home, to the dangerous places and archives of violence that ground their participation in emergent global civil society.

CONCLUSIONS

The case of Humboldt shows how the capitalist world economic (culture) system, in its ongoing phase of globalization, drives the increasing integration and emergence of global civil society. Its market forces come, they colonize, industrialize and deforest or otherwise mine a place for its natural resources. And as the system rises and globalizes, so too do its public spheres rise and globalize.

But Humboldt is just a single case where this global process implodes in the local, producing the conditions of possibility for converging movements. Consider that the 2010 UN report titled *Universal Ownership* documented how the world's top 3,000 corporations produce so much external environmental cost that paying for them would eat up to 30% to 40% of their profits.[30] Those percentages constitute a conservative UN-style estimate. But from the standpoints of both economic history and business economics, which explain how firms plan their internal pricing, we know that the first rule of thumb is that avoided cost equals profit. Think of all the concrete, historical places of subjective-cum-objective violence where these corporations externalize their costs on communities of labor and nature.

In this way, the conditions of possibility of converging peoples, labor, and environmental movements have been and are being set up across the horizon of globalization, everywhere that colonization by the culture system of modern, western capitalism has come in and built societies modeled on its own constitutionally enumerated rights-driven private property markets, free speech public spheres, and polities ruled by the people. Each locally instantiated modern social imaginary is an archive on fire with violence, modern violence, remembering the living, symbolic, and built traces first of colonization, then of industrialization, and finally of the accumulating environmental disturbances wrought along the way.

These archives, as conditions of possibility that the hegemonic claims of the victors can and will be contested, now stand at the dawn of a new era, the era of social media. Cyberactivism is, and will increasingly become, the name of these conditions.

NOTES

1. On the global climate justice movement, visit IICAT, the International Institute of Climate Action & Theory (iicat.org); see also John Foran and Richard Widick "Breaking Barriers to Climate Justice," *Contexts: Understanding People in Their Social Worlds* 12, no. 2, 34–39; Patrick Bond, "Climate Justice," *Critical Environmental Politics*, ed. C. Death (Routledge 2014); and John Clammer, Culture, Development, and Social Theory (Zed Books, 2013), especially the chapter "Culture and Climate Justice," 144–161. Connect with the climate justice movement online by searching out the following groups: Climate Action Now (CAN), Friends of the Earth International (FOIE), Greenpeace, Climate-Justice-Now (C-J-N), SustainUs, 1Sky, and 350.org.
2. *The Black Press: Soldiers Without Swords*, a documentary film produced by Stanley Nelson (California Newsreel, 1998), tells the story of Black journalists from the abolition movement and the founding of the first Black newspaper, *Freedom's Journal* in 1827 by Frederick Douglas, to Ida B. Wells, the first female newspaper owner and civil rights crusader, Robert S. Abbot and his paper the *Chicago Defender*, the great migration, and the era of Martin Luther King.
3. "Nation Horrified by Murder of Kidnapped Chicago Youth," *Jet Magazine*, (September 25, 1955), 4–9.

4. For a useful compendium of now iconic news images that helped constitute the Civil Rights Movement, see the PBS series *Eyes on the Prize* (www.pbs. org/wgbh/amex/eyesontheprize/).

5. NASA photograph AS17–148–22727, http://spaceflight.nasa.gov/gallery/ images/apollo/apollo17/html/as17-148-22727.html.

6. See Big Noise Films' *Zapatista* (1998) for an indication of the power of media images at the dawn of the Internet age.

7. See Richard Widick, *Trouble in the Forest: California's Redwood Timber Wars* (Minneapolis: University of Minnesota Press, 2009); Foran and Widick, "Breaking Barriers to Climate Justice."

8. See, e.g., Malcom Gladwell, "Small Change," *The New Yorker*, (October 4, 2010); Lee Siegel, "Trouble by a Weak Connection," *New York Times*, (July 13, 2012); Evgeny Morozov, *To Save Everything, Click Here* (New York: Perseus Books, 2013) and *The Net Delusion: The Dark Side of Internet Freedom* New York: Perseus Books, 2013); Nicolas Carr, *The Shallows: What the Internet is Doing to our Brains* (New York: W.W. Norton, 2011).

9. Niklas Luhman, *The Reality of the Mass Media* (Stanford: Stanford University Press, 2000), 1: "Whatever we know about our society, or indeed about the world in which we live, we know through mass media."

10. The technological and cultural conditions of possibility of fantasies of power in the constitution of social movements is comparable to the role of fantasies of power in the reproduction of masculine domination in the occupational culture of financial trading floors; see Richard Widick, "Flesh and the Free Market," *Theory & Society* 32 (2003), 679–723. According to the sociologically inclined psychoanalyst Jacques Lacan, the human subject's (in our example, the social mover's) desire (to move) is always the desire of *the Other* (that is, the desire of the group, the culture—meaning that desire is always necessarily educated by the social world in which it is and must continue operating). The term "fantasy" indicates a scene, narrative, or imagistic series that presents to the imagination the staging of a desire that is always by definition in some measure unconscious; an unconscious source of desire is the group, the social, i.e., the necessary structure within which the subject is ensconced, and with which it must communicate and act, in the same way that the competent speaker is always necessarily unconscious to some extent of the language system being used to speak. Thus, in the foregoing, the subject's desire for omnipotence in the rebuttal of forces it experiences as towering over it and determining its fate is expressed in dreams, daydreams, and/or fantasies of successful opposition; that is the type of fantasy transformed by emergent technological conditions of possibility for collective identification through media—and that is what makes it so important to social movement studies. In a different register, and basing his arguments on cognitive psychology rather than psychoanalysis, in his classic book *Distinction: A Social Critique of the Judgment of Taste,* trans. Richard Nice, (Harvard University Press, 1984), 373–397, Pierre Bourdieu describes the same effect of culture on desire as "the choice of the necessary."

11. On the sociological uses of cultural sociology and psychoanalytic social theory in the study of place-based social movements, see Widick, *Trouble in the Forest*, 22–23; on using the same to study the United Nations climate talks and the global climate justice movement, see Richard Widick, "Invitation to Durban: Ethnography and the Politics of Climate Activism at COP17" (working paper, The International Institute of Climate Action and Theory, 2014), last modified January 19, 2014, www.iicat.org/invitation-to-durban-ethnography-and-the-politics-of-climate-change-at-cop17-durban-south-africa-nov-28-dec-9-2011/; Richard Widick, "What is Driving our Modern

Social Imaginaries? Turning to Cultural and Environmental Sociology for Answers," *Perspectives: Newsletter of the ASA Theory Section* 31, no. 2 (2009); and Richard Widick, ibid., "Flesh and the Free Market." For a relevant discussion of publics and public formation using comparable cultural and psychoanalytic ideas, see Mustafa Emirbayer and Mimi Sheller, "Publics in History," *Theory and Society* 28 (1999), 145–197.

12. On the distinction between subjective violence ("acts of crime and terror, civil unrest, international conflict") and objective violence ("'systemic' violence, or the often catastrophic consequences of the smooth operation of our economic and political systems"), see Slavoj Zizek, *Violence* (New York: Picador, 2008), 1–2; also Patchen Merkell and Candice Vogler "Violence and Redemption," *Public Culture* 15, no.1 (2003), 1–10, 1: "Violence haunts liberal political thought. The defining image of early modern European social contract theory—and an image that remains potent in contemporary contractarian moral and political theory—locates the possibility of civil society in a compact among men who are long accustomed to the use of force in the bloody business of self-assertion and self-preservation." The liberal state substitutes objective, normalized, legitimate, monopolized, and patient violence for the pathological, subjective violence of unorganized life.

13. See *The Farm: Angola USA* (Gabriel Films and Curtis Productions, 1998).

14. Charles Taylor, *Modern Social Imaginaries* (Durham: Duke University Press, 2004). For the best and usefully short treatments of the concept of social imaginaries, see Craig J. Calhoun, "Imagining Solidarity: Cosmopolitanism, Constitutional Patriotism, and the Public Sphere," *Public Culture* 14, no.1 (2002), 147–171; and Michael Warner, "Publics and Counterpublics," *Public Culture* 14, no.1 (2002), 49–90.

15. For an extended discussion of this cultural approach to the dynamism of modern capitalism and the basic set of institutions within which it is nested, see Widick, *Trouble in the Forest*, 20–41.

16. Emile Durkheim, *Rules of Sociological Method* (New York: Free Press, 1966), 2–3.

17. Karl Marx, "The Brumaire of Louis Bonaparte," in *The Marx-Engels Reader*, ed. Robert C. Tucker (New York: W.W. Norton, 1852/1978), 594–595.

18. Dialectical thought begins from the totality of the social system as a set of relationships between people, labor, its products, and the world. Concrete and particular events, processes, connections, and developments are viewed as inseparable from the whole without being reducible to it. For Theodor Adorno ("Sociology and Psychology," *New Left Review* 46 [1968], 67–80), concrete and particular cultural artifacts are intersectionional artifacts of social structure (institutions, symbolic order) and social action; their possible meanings are a function the social totality (see also *Negative Dialectics*, trans. E.B. Ashton [New York: Continuum, 1997]). In "A Portrait of Walter Benjamin" (*Prisms*, Cambridge, MA: MIT Press, 1967), 236, Adorno wrote: "[Walter Benjamin] never wavered in his fundamental conviction that the smallest cell of observed reality offsets the rest of the world." On dialectical thinking and ecological dialectics, respectively, see Bertell Ollman, "Why Dialectics? Why Now?" *Science & Society* 62, no. 3 (1998): 338–357 and David Harvey, *Justice, Nature and the Geography of Difference* (Cambridge: Blackwell Publishers, 1996).

19. On the constitutional tension between liberty and democracy, see Jenifer Nedelsky *Private Property and the Limits of American Constitutionalism: The Madisonian Framework and its Legacy* (Chicago: University of Chicago Press, 1994); Nedelsky shows how the U.S. Constitution's dual imperatives of democracy and liberty produce the schism between political rights and

civil rights that profoundly shapes U.S. political culture; also Knud Haakons-sen and Michael J. Lacey *Culture of Rights* (*Cambridge: Cambridge University Press*, 1991); Richard Flacks, *The American Left and the American Mind* (New York: Columbia University Press, 1988); and Jeffrey Alexander, *The Civil Sphere* (Oxford: Oxford University Press, 2006).

20. Environmental theorists debated the second contradictions in capitalism in the journals *Capital Nature Socialism* and *Monthly Review*. See especially John Bellamy Foster, "Capitalism and Ecology: The Nature of the Contradiction" (*Monthly Review* 54, no. 4, September 2002, 6–16) and James O'Connor, "Capitalism, Nature, Socialism: A Theoretical Introduction" *CNS* 1 (1988), 11–38; "On the Two Contradictions of Capitalism," *Capitalism Nature Socialism* 2, no. 3 (1991), 107–109; *Natural Causes* (New York: The Guilford Press, 1998); and "What is Environmental History? Why Environmental History," *Capital Nature Socialism* 8, no. 2 (1997), 1–27. Also John Bellamy Foster, *Capitalism Against Ecology* (New York: Monthly Review Press, 2002); "Marx's Ecological Value Analysis," *Monthly Review* 52, no. 4 (2000); "The Scale of Our Ecological Crisis," *Monthly Review* 49, no. 11 (1998), 5–17; and "The Absolute General Law of Environmental Degradation Under Capitalism" *Capitalism Nature Socialism* 3, no. 3 (1992). Further: Samir Amin, "A Note on the Depreciation of the Future," *Capitalism Nature Socialism* 3, no. 3 (1992): 21–22; Victor Toledo, "The Ecological Crisis: A Second Contradiction of Capitalism" *Capitalism Nature Socialism* 3, no. 3 (1992), 22–24; and Michael A. Lebowitz, "Capitalism: How Many Contradictions?" *Capitalism Nature Socialism* 3, no. 3 (1992), 22–24.

21. See especially Richard Widick, *Trouble in the Forest*, 175–223 on industrialization and labor history; 129–174 on colonization, the land system, and genocide; and 225–275 on the contemporary environmental movement and the conflict with the MAXXAM corporation over Headwaters Grove and the last 1% of the ancient redwoods. See also Owen C. Coy, *The Humboldt Bay Redwood Region, 1850–1875* (Los Angeles: California State Historical Society, 1929); Daniel Cornford, *Workers and Dissent in the Redwood Empire* (Philadelphia: Temple University Press, 1987); Brett H. Melendy, "One Hundred Years of the Redwood Lumber Industry, 1850–1950" (PhD dissertation, Stanford University, microfilm title B26, Stanford, 1952); and Frank Onstine, *The Great Lumber Strike of Humboldt County 1935* (Arcata: Mercurial Enterprises).

22. In fact, the deal was quite a bit more complex, involving land transfers between the Pacific Lumber Company and other local firms as well as the cash exchange, and the adoption of a habitat conservation plan restricting the company's activity on its remaining lands, etc.; see Widick, *Trouble in the Forest*, 13–20, 47–50, 261–269.

23. Visit the Global Ecology Justice Project online at http://globaljusticeecology.org/.

24. Richard Widick, field notes and audio recording produced during ethnographic research at the United Nations Framework Convention on Climate Change, COP 17, Durban, December 9, 2011.

25. The UNFCCC convened the Conference of Parties in Berlin 1995; Geneva 1996; Kyoto 1997; Buenos Aires 1998; Bonn 1999; The Hague 2000; Marrakech 2001; Milan 2003; Buenos Aires 2004; Montreal 2005; Nairobi 2006; Bali 2007; Poznan 2008; Copenhagen 2009; Cancun 2010; Durban 2011; Doha 2012; and Warsaw 2013.

26. For a crash course in the complexity of these climate COPs, and for the breadth of engagement by civil society groups, see the UNFCCC's official

schedule of side events: http://unfccc.int/files/meetings/durban_nov_2011/application/pdf/see_brochure_cop_17_cmp_7.pdf

27. See Alexander Cockburn, *Five Days that Shook the World: Seattle and Beyond* (New York: Verso, 2000); Eddie Yuen, *The Battle of Seattle* (New York: Soft Skull Press, 2001).

28. Christian Parenti, *Tropic of Chaos: Climate Change and the New Geography of Violence* (New York: Nation Books, 2011).

29. See especially Michael Hardt and Antonio Negri, *Empire* (Cambridge, MA: Harvard University Press, 2000), *Multitude: War and Democracy in the Age of Empire* (New York: Penguin Press, 2004), and *Commonwealth* (Cambridge, MA: Harvard University Press, 2009); also Manuel Castells, *The Rise of the Network Society* (Massachusetts: Blackwell, 1996).

30. United Nations Environment Program Finance Initiative, *Universal Ownership: Why Environmental Externalities Matter to Institutional Investors*, ed. Adam Garfunkel (2010), last modified October 2010, www.unepfi.org/fileadmin/documents/universal_ownership.pdf.

REFERENCES

Adorno, Theodor. "A Portrait of Walter Benjamin." In *Prisms*. Cambridge, MA: MIT Press, 1967.

———. "Sociology and Psychology." *New Left Review* 46 (1968).

———. *Negative Dialectics*. Translated by E. B. Ashton. New York: Continuum, 1997.

Alexander, Jeffrey. *The Civil Sphere*. Oxford: Oxford University Press, 2006.

The Black Press: Soldiers without Swords, directed by Stanley Nelson. 1998, California Newsreel. VHS.

Amin, Samir. "A Note on the Depreciation of the Future." *Capitalism Nature Socialism* 3, no. 3 (1992): 21–22.

Bond, Patrick. "Climate Justice." In *Critical Environmental Politics*, edited by C. Death. New York: Routledge, forthcoming.

Bourdieu Pierre *Distinction: A Social Critique of the Judgment of Taste*, translated by Richard Nice. Harvard University Press, 1984.

Calhoun, Craig J. "Imagining Solidarity: Cosmopolitanism, Constitutional Patriotism, and the Public Sphere." *Public Culture* 14, no. 1 (2002): 147–171.

Carr, Nicolas. *The Shallows: What the Internet Is Doing to Our Brains*. New York: W. W. Norton, 2011.

Castells, Manuel. *The Rise of the Network Society*. Massachusetts: Blackwell, 1996.

Clammer, John. *Culture, Development, and Social Theory*. Zed Books, 2013.

Cockburn, Alexander. *Five Days that Shook the World: Seattle and Beyond*. New York: Verso, 2000.

Cornford, Daniel. *Workers and Dissent in the Redwood Empire*. Philadelphia: Temple University Press, 1987.

Coy, Owen C. *The Humboldt Bay Redwood Region, 1850–1875*. Los Angeles: California State Historical Society, 1929.

Durkheim, Emile. *Rules of Sociological Method*. New York: Free Press, 1966.

Emirbayer, Mustafa, and Sheller, Mimi. "Publics in History." *Theory and Society* 28, no. 1, (1999): 145–197.

The Farm: Angola USA, Directed by Jonathan Stack, Liz Garbus, and Wilber Rideau. Gabriel Films and Curtis Productions, 1998.

Flacks, Richard. *The American Left and the American Mind*. New York: Columbia University Press, 1988.

Foran, John, and Widick, Richard. "Breaking Barriers to Climate Justice." *Contexts: Understanding People in Their Social Worlds* 12, no. 2, (2013): 34–39.

Foster, John Bellamy. "The Absolute General Law of Environmental Degradation under Capitalism." *CNS* 3, no. 3 (1992): 18–20.

———. "The Scale of Our Ecological Crisis." *Monthly Review* 49, no. 11 (1998).

———. "Marx's Ecological Value Analysis." *Monthly Review* 52, no 4. (2000).

———. *Capitalism against Ecology*. New York: Monthly Review Press, 2002.

———. "Capitalism and Ecology: The Nature of the Contradiction." *Monthly Review* 54, no. 4 (2002).

———. "A Planetary Defeat: The Failure of Global Environmental Reform." *Monthly Review* 54, no. 8, (2003): 8.

Gladwell, Malcom. "Small Change." *The New Yorker*. October 4, 2010.

Haakonssen, Knud, and Lacey Michael J. *Culture of Rights*. Cambridge: Cambridge University Press, 1991.

Hardt, Michael, and Negri, Antonio. *Empire*. Cambridge, MA: Harvard University Press, 2000.

———. *Multitude: War and Democracy in the Age of Empire*. New York: Penguin Press, 2004.

———. *Commonwealth*. Cambridge, MA: Harvard University Press, 2009.

Harvey, David. *Justice, Nature and the Geography of Difference*. Cambridge: Blackwell Publishers, 1996.

Lebowitz, Michael A. "Capitalism: How Many Contradictions?" *Capitalism Nature Socialism* 3, no. 3 (1992).

Luhman, Niklas. *The Reality of the Mass Media*. Stanford: Stanford University Press, 2000.

Marx, Karl, "The Brumaire of Louis Bonaparte." In *The Marx-Engels Reader*, edited by Robert C. Tucker (pp. 594–595). New York: W.W. Norton, 1978.

Melendy, Brett H. *One Hundred Years of the Redwood Lumber Industry, 1850–1950*. PhD dissertation, Stanford University, microfilm title B26, Stanford, 1952.

Merkell, Patchen, and Vogler, Candice. "Introduction: Violence, Redemption, and the Liberal Imagination." *Public Culture* 15, no. 1 (2003): 1–10.

Morozov, Evgeny. *The Net Delusion: The Dark Side of Internet Freedom*. New York: Perseus Books, 2013.

———. *To Save Everything, Click Here*. New York: Perseus Books, 2013.

NASA photograph AS17-148-22727, http://spaceflight.nasa.gov/gallery/images/apollo/apollo17/html/as17-148-22727.html.

"Nation horrified by Murder of Kidnapped Chicago Youth." *Jet Magazine*. September 25, 1955, 4–9.

Nedelsky, Jenifer. *Private Property and the Limits of American Constitutionalism: The Madisonian Framework and its Legacy*. Chicago: University of Chicago Press, 1994.

O'Connor, James. "Capitalism, Nature, Socialism: A Theoretical Introduction." *CNS* 1 (1988).

———. "On the Two Contradictions of Capitalism." *Capitalism Nature Socialism* 2, no. 3 (1991).

———. "What is Environmental History? Why Environmental History." *Capital Nature Socialism* 8, no. 2, (1997).

———. *Natural Causes*. New York: The Guilford Press, 1998.

Ollman, Bertell. "Why Dialectics? Why Now?" *Science & Society* 62, no. 3 (1998): 338–357.

Onstine, Frank. *The Great Lumber Strike of Humboldt County 1935*. Arcata: Mercurial Enterprises, 1980.

Parenti, Christian. *Tropic of Chaos: Climate Change and the New Geography of Violence*. New York: Nation Books, 2011.

Siegel, Lee. "Trouble by a Weak Connection." *New York Times*. July 13, 2012.

Taylor, Charles. *Modern Social Imaginaries*. Durham: Duke University Press, 2004.

Toledo Victor, "The Ecological Crisis: A Second Contradiction of Capitalism." *Capitalism Nature Socialism* 3, no. 3 (1992).

United Nations Environment Program Finance Initiative, *Universal Ownership: Why Environmental Externalities Matter to Institutional Investors*, edited by Adam Garfunkel. www.unepfi.org/fileadmin/documents/universal_ownership.pdf (2010).

Warner, Michael. "Publics and Counterpublics." *Public Culture* 14, no. 1 (2002): 49–90.

Widick, Richard. "Flesh and the Free Market." *Theory & Society* 32: (2003): 679–723.

———. *Trouble in the Forest: California's Redwood Timber Wars*. Minneapolis: University of Minnesota Press, 2009.

———. "What is Driving our Modern Social Imaginaries? Turning to Cultural and Environmental Sociology for Answers." *Perspectives: Newsletter of the ASA Theory Section* 31, no. 2, (November 2009).

———. "Invitation to Durban: Ethnography and the Politics of Climate Activism at COP17." Working Paper, The International Institute of Climate Action and Theory, 2014. www.iicat.org/invitation-to-durban-ethnography-and-the-politics-of-climate-change-at-cop17-durban-south-africa-nov-28-dec-9-2011/ (accessed January 19, 2014).

Yuen, Eddie. *The Battle of Seattle*. New York: Soft Skull Press, 2001.

Zapatista, directed by Rick Rowley. Big Noise Films, 1998. VHS.

Zizek, Slavoj. *Violence*. New York: Picador, 2008.

5 The Arab Spring and Its Social Media Audiences

English and Arabic Twitter Users and Their Networks

Axel Bruns, Tim Highfield, and Jean Burgess

The "Arab Spring" uprisings in 2011 saw widespread anti-government protests, and some régime changes, in many Middle Eastern and North African (MENA) countries, from Libya and Tunisia to Bahrain and Syria. Social media were among the tools used by protesters to organize themselves and to disseminate footage from rallies. These were not only used by local activists, but also attracted comments from a worldwide media audience, for example in Twitter hashtag conversations such as #egypt and #libya. These hashtags were used to mediate a wide range of practices of political participation among a diverse group of social media users—from distanced observation and information-sharing in a globalized "ambient journalism"[1] environment through to narration of direct experience and even coordination of on-the-ground activities. However, there is no reason to assume that these diverse activities were really "connected" via the hashtag, or that one geographically or culturally distinct group of users ever encountered another, hence highlighting the question of whether social media, in such contexts, facilitates the flow of information across social boundaries. This chapter addresses these questions via an analysis of language differences in social media communication focused on the Arab Spring and in doing so describes new methods for the analysis of large-scale Twitter data.

We focus on discussions on Twitter concerning the uprisings in Egypt and Libya, tracked between January and November of 2011. These two cases, showing citizen opposition to long-serving leaders, ultimately took different forms in their pursuit of revolution. The Egyptian uprising initially saw a short series of large protests in January and February of 2011, resulting in the ouster of President Hosni Mubarak. In Libya, anti-government protests quickly transformed into a civil war, resulting in months of bloodshed before the capture and death of Libyan leader Colonel Gaddafi. In both cases, developments were accompanied by widespread discussion on Twitter, in both Arabic and English. Our focus in this chapter is on the relative levels of activity in Arabic, English, and mixed-language tweets featuring the #egypt and #libya hashtags, and on the interactions between these different linguistic groups. This enables us to track the changing circumstances of these revolutionary conflicts, and to examine the relative contributions of different language groups to their discussion.

CONTEXT, BACKGROUND, AND APPROACH

The organization and coverage of public protests is one of many purposes for which Twitter has been used; many other social, political, and educational functions have also been identified.[2] However, the specific contribution made by the platform remains debatable. In June 2009, Twitter was viewed as the medium of choice for activists, both local and international, to dispute the Iranian election result using the #iranelection hashtag,[3] to the point that the Iranian protests were dubbed an (ultimately unsuccessful) "Twitter revolution." At the same time, opinions remain divided about the extent to which these and other protests were in a narrower sense *led* by activists using social media to express their views and orchestrate resistance.[4] From the evidence available, it appears that social media were *additional* communication tools for activists, rather than drivers of the demonstrations themselves.[5] The Arab Spring uprisings have attracted similar descriptions, as social media are used to share details about protests and generate support for movements, in a highly hybridized media environment[6] in which Twitter has achieved increased uptake both in the population at large and among news organizations and journalists themselves. Although the Egyptian and Libyan governments attempted to block domestic Internet access during the uprisings, protestors used workarounds to post to Twitter.[7] Once the Egyptian blackout was lifted, mobile phone videos were uploaded directly from the demonstrations to YouTube,[8] and shared through social media. The volume of tweets hashtagged #egypt or #libya highlights the attention that the uprisings received from Twitter users both domestic and further afield; however, there are questions about whether Twitter was a stable means of coordinating demonstrations on the ground, or primarily a channel for international observers to discuss the uprisings.[9]

Either way, coverage of the Arab Spring on Twitter provides important examples for the formation of issue publics through shared hashtags. By including "#egypt" or "#libya" in their tweets, Twitter users are connecting their comments to a wider discussion. Bruns and Burgess[10] argue that these conversations on common topics can create *ad hoc* issue publics, which can "respond with great speed to emerging issues and acute events." Such events include crises and emergencies, including civil unrest and natural disasters;[11] hashtags have been used to concentrate the flow of information from emergency authorities in such cases as the earthquakes in Christchurch, New Zealand (#eqnz), and the floods in Queensland, Australia (#qldfloods), both in 2011.[12] Indeed, the convention of using hashtags to mark topical tweets first spread (before becoming fully integrated into Twitter architecture) following their use in the coverage of wildfires in San Diego in 2007.[13]

Hashtagged discussions emerge without being controlled by any one organization or user. Politicians, journalists, and emergency authorities may all be contributing to the ongoing coverage, and may indeed be central figures to these discussions, but any account is able to use, or ignore, hashtags in their own tweets. Any Twitter user could include #egypt or #libya in their tweets, regardless of their proximity to the uprisings or involvement in the protests (the range of participants discussing #egypt is studied by Lotan et al.[14]). Discussion of events in Egypt, for example, also used the #Jan25 hashtag, signifying the "Day of Revolt" against President Hosni Mubarak. Whereas this hashtag was widely used, it was not studied here (tweets containing #Jan25 as well as #egypt are present within the dataset, however). In the present context, it should be especially noted that the use of these hashtags was not limited to English speakers, in spite of the use of the English names of these countries as hashtags. At the time of the uprisings, Arabic speakers were forced to use hashtags in Latin characters: although Twitter supports the use of non-Latin characters in tweets themselves, as of January 2012 it was still testing its official support for right-to-left languages, especially regarding hashtags.[15] A key reason that many Arab Spring tweets combined Arabic text with an English hashtag was that the platform could not yet support right-to-left hashtags; left-to-right hashtags, by contrast, are automatically converted on publication to links to Twitter searches for those tags, providing easy access to the wider discussion on the topic. Therefore, a substantial volume of tweets mainly in English (as the international *lingua franca*), using Latin characters, were united with an at times equally significant volume of tweets in Arabic (as the common language of the MENA region), using Arabic characters, under the #egypt and #libya hashtags.

An additional technological innovation, in response to local Internet restrictions, can also explain some of the crossover between Arabic tweets and the English hashtag #egypt; the *Speak2Tweet* tool provided by Google and Twitter enabled users to tweet by calling an international telephone number and leaving a voice message, which was subsequently turned into a tweet and automatically accompanied by the #egypt hashtag.[16] Here, too, comments in various languages were combined with an English hashtag, thus aggregating multilingual tweets about the Egyptian revolution, although this does not necessarily translate to greater links between linguistic groups.

The resulting heterogeneous, bi- or multilingual nature of these hashtags immediately raises questions about the structure of their participant communities. Were there two or more separate groups of commenters, writing in Arabic and English but using the same hashtag? To what extent were bilingual users acting as boundary riders, connecting different language communities and facilitating information flows between them? Previous studies of blogging within the MENA region have noted the presence of blogs written in English alongside sites in Arabic, leading Zuckerman to suggest that some of these sites may act as "bridgeblogs," intended to inform readers "from a different nation, religion, or culture."[17] Similarly, a study of Arabic language blogs found a group of sites from across the Levant acting as an "English bridge," writing in both English and Arabic (Etling et al., 2010).[18] Whereas Egyptian bloggers did not necessarily act in this way, they played "key roles in movement politics,"[19] using the Internet to circumvent the regulation of political organization offline.

Indeed, prior to the uprisings, Egyptian blogging was credited as having "intensified current trends in politics and media," following media outlets' increasingly critical coverage of the Mubarak régime.[20] Blogs became publishers of commentary or reports that could not be featured in the traditional media, even those opposed to Mubarak. As an active Egyptian blogosphere developed, the bloggers involved formed activist networks, in Egypt and abroad, and with international journalists and other foreign bloggers. These links enable the wider spread of information, sharing reports in Egypt and with a more distributed worldwide audience.[21]

But writing in different languages does not automatically mean that an individual is acting as a bridge between different groups of users. Herring et al.'s study of language networks on *LiveJournal* found that English, and other languages, would be featured within journal entries "in formulaic or emblematic uses," connecting users of different linguistic backgrounds even without a thorough understanding of the languages concerned.[22] The intent—or result—of using another language on *LiveJournal* is not to reach a new international audience, like Zuckerman's bridge bloggers, but to participate extensively within *LiveJournal*'s "cosmopolitan environment." Within the MENA region, bloggers will use both Arabic and English or Arabic and French in their posts, so these languages are strongly interconnected rather than used by distinct groups of bloggers.[23]

Use of English or Arabic may also be affected by the topics discussed in posts, and by the intended audience. Jansen's study of digital activism in the Middle East found that in Syria, Arabic was employed for discussion of "more general issues like government, unemployment, and poverty," whereas English was used for comments on specific activist issues, including individual cases of arrest or harassment.[24] Jansen argues that blogging in English may be aimed at drawing more global attention to particular issues. In their analysis of #sidibouzid tweets around the Tunisian revolution, Poell and Darmoni found that the most active users would post in multiple languages, tailoring their content for different audiences and acting to connect groups of users commenting on the uprising in Arabic, English, and French.[25] Although determining the subjects of tweets written in Arabic and English during the Arab Spring is beyond the scope of this chapter, the two languages (and others) may have been employed in different tweets by individual users for similar purposes (for a content analysis of #egypt tweets written in English, see Papacharissi and de Fatima Oliveira).[26]

Although the different languages represented in the datasets used here do not map onto distinct geographic regions, it is important to distinguish the patterns of social media use around the Arab Spring originating from local and international users. Howard et al., examining tweets containing geolocational data as well as the #egypt hashtag, found that the early discussions were led by users found outside Egypt and its neighbors. In the weeks leading up to Mubarak's resignation, a greater proportion of tweets came from local users (and from users who did not provide location information).[27] In addition, Freelon's analysis of several Arab Spring hashtag datasets found that spikes in Twitter activity in most discussions were led by international users, rather than those within the MENA region.[28] Whereas language is not in itself an accurate means of determining location, comparing the use of English and Arabic tweets over the same period allows us to examine whether spikes in activity are led by particular linguistic groups.

In this study, we investigated the following questions through our comparison of Latin and non-Latin tweets:

1. Do tweets containing Latin and non-Latin characters follow similar patterns in responding to the events of the Arab Spring?

Based on previous research into online communication in the region, it would be expected that the use of English (and other Latin languages) would be prominent within the #egypt and #libya hashtags, however:

2. Is this use consistent throughout the uprisings, or does the volume of tweets from different language groups follow more varied patterns of troughs and spikes in response to specific events?

And finally:

3. Are the different language groups (Latin and non-Latin) interconnected? And is there evidence of bridging between these groups of Twitter users?

The presence of bridges in other online contexts suggests that an examination of user interactions in the #egypt and #libya hashtags would find some users acting as bridges between Arabic and English speakers. These hashtags also provide an automatic tie between the groups, through Twitter's conversion of hashtags into hyperlinks. However, this does not necessarily mean that bridging is taking place; we examine the networks of @replies and retweets within the datasets to identify connections between users tweeting in Latin and non-Latin languages. As part of this examination, this study also establishes methods for identifying, and comparing, the languages used within large datasets of tweets, which have applications for further research into multilingual social media discussions.

METHODS

Our datasets were collected through the Twitter API. Using a modified version of the open source tool *yourTwapperkeeper* (see Bruns),[29] we tracked #egypt and #libya from early 2011 (Jan. 23, 2011, for #egypt and Feb. 16, 2011, for #libya); for the purposes of our analysis, our data collection period terminates on November 30, 2011. Due to the vagaries of collecting data from the Twitter API, we cannot expect to have gathered a fully comprehensive dataset for either hashtag: Given the long timeframe of data collection, unavoidable outages both on Twitter's and on our side will have combined to create several brief gaps in the archives. Further, as the API is the only sanctioned access point to Twitter data at scale, it is impossible to independently verify exactly how much data may have been excluded from collection: Short of comparing datasets with other researchers tracking these hashtags over the same period, there is no reliable method for finding gaps in the data (see also Freelon on similar limits to his study).[30] This is a fundamental problem of all research drawing on third-party APIs; it is an unavoidable aspect of doing "big data" research.[31]

At the same time, the overall volume of tweets that we did capture is immense, and sufficient as a basis for the examination of broad patterns in Twitter activity. A chronological overview of the data points to obvious gaps: for #egypt, we received no tweets at all on Jan. 31, Feb. 5–7, Mar. 31, Apr. 1–2, Aug. 2–4, Sept. 15, Oct. 16, and Nov. 23, 26, 27, and 29, 2011; for #libya, we are missing data for Mar. 31, Apr. 1, Apr. 15, Aug. 2–4, Sept. 15, Oct. 16 and 21, and Nov. 26 and 29, 2011.[32] This means that for #egypt, we missed 16 days in over 10 months of data collection; for #libya, we missed 11 days in nine and a half months.

yourTwapperkeeper datasets are available in simple comma- or tab-separated value formats, containing the tweets themselves and a range of additional metadata; most importantly, these metadata include the numerical Twitter ID and username of the sender, as well as the exact timestamp of the tweet. Further metadata can be extracted from the tweets: chiefly, this includes the usernames of any Twitter users mentioned (through @replies or retweets), and the—usually shortened—URLs of any links included with the tweet. Further processing also reveals the specific type of tweet: By parsing its syntax, it is possible to distinguish between simple @replies and retweets (in the form "RT @user . . . ", "MT @user . . . ", "via @user . . . " or " "@user . . . " "—that is, enclosing the original tweet in quotation marks), or to identify tweets as *original* tweets that neither @reply to nor retweet another user.

In the present context, it is especially important to distinguish between tweets in different languages. The Twitter API itself does not provide sufficient information to make immediate distinctions: Whereas amongst the metadata returned by the API is a language code for each tweet, that code is simply inherited from the language setting made globally by the tweet sender, and does not reflect the specific language of the tweet itself. Tweets by an Egyptian user, tweeting in Arabic, who left their global Twitter profile setting at the English default would be marked as "English"; tweets by a French user who set their profile to French but converses in English and Arabic would be marked as French. The specific language of tweets can only be ascertained by individually analyzing each tweet itself, then.

For the purposes of the present analysis, working with datasets that largely contain tweets in English and other European languages on the one

hand, and in Arabic on the other, this analysis can be considerably simplified: A useful approach to distinguishing these two groups is to examine
whether tweets are written in Latin or non-Latin characters. Whereas the
non-Latin group will also contain tweets in various other scripts (Chinese,
Japanese, Korean, etc.), the presence of such languages in our present datasets is negligible in comparison to Arabic script; additionally, in an analysis of conversational networks between Twitter users, such third language
groups should form distinct conversational networks at a distance from the
dominant Arabic and English groups. Similarly, any major distinctions in
the Latin group should indicate the presence of various European languages.

Because all standard Latin characters and punctuation marks have been
assigned ASCII character codes below 128, a simple method for coding
tweets as "Latin" or "non-Latin" is to count the number of characters with
a code above 127 in a tweet. Should that number pass a certain threshold,
the tweet is coded as "non-Latin." Through a trial and tuning process,[33]
we determined that a threshold of 10 non-Latin characters results in a reliable distinction between Latin and non-Latin tweets. This threshold value
is preferable to a strict zero as it allows for the presence of several accented
characters as they are common in various European languages (äöüß, áéíóú,
etc.) as well as for "fancy" punctuation marks (" instead of ", etc.), all of
which have also been assigned character codes above 127.

Such automated coding of tweets was implemented using *Gawk*, a pro-
grammable command-line tool for processing CSV/TSV data files.[34] In addition to coding the tweets themselves, we can also calculate a cumulative
language score for each Twitter user participating in these datasets, indicating what percentage of their tweets was in non-Latin scripts. This can
be used to distinguish different Twitter user groups: those posting mainly
in Latin characters (in the present context, mainly in English); those posting mainly in non-Latin characters (mainly in Arabic), and those using a
mixture of scripts (and thus perhaps acting as information brokers between
different language communities). Similarly, we can calculate the ratio of
Latin and non-Latin tweets across all users per timeframe (e.g., per day or
hour), to show when different language communities were especially active.

Beyond this coding of language, we also extracted a range of other metrics from the Twitter datasets (see Bruns for an extended discussion of these
metrics and the methods used to obtain them):[35] We track the number of
tweets made (also broken down into tweet categories including original
tweets, @replies, retweets, and tweets containing URLs) as well as the number of active users per timeframe; further, for each user we determine the
number of hashtagged tweets sent and received (again also broken down
into the different tweet categories).

Finally, following the 1/9/90 rule that has become the unofficial standard
for analyses of user communities where activity broadly follows a "long
tail" distribution,[36] we divide the userbase of active contributors into three
groups: one group of lead users, which contains the most active 1% of

participants; a second group of highly engaged users, which contains the next 9% of active participants; and a third group comprising the remaining 90% of least active users. These divisions are determined by ranking users on the basis of the number of tweets they have contributed to the hashtag: The top 1% of users on this ranked list are included in the first group, the next 9% in the second group, and the remaining userbase in the third group. Finally, a fourth group contains all those whose usernames are mentioned in @replies and retweets, but who did not themselves post to the hashtag. For each of the first three groups, we again track their contribution to the hashtag over time, and determine overall patterns of activity such as their relative use of original tweets, @replies, retweets, or tweets containing URLs.

OVERALL PATTERNS

Based on this methodology, we are able to determine overall patterns for both #egypt and #libya, over the total period covered by each dataset—Jan. 23 to Nov. 30, 2011, for #egypt and Feb. 16 to Nov. 30, 2011, for #libya.

#egypt

In total, we captured some 7.48 million #egypt tweets from over 445,000 unique users between Jan. 23 and Nov. 30, 2011. Twitter activity for #egypt peaks at a significantly higher level during the early stages of the revolution than at any other subsequent point (Figure 5.1). Whereas, unfortunately, data for several days in this early period (Jan. 31, Feb. 5–7) are missing from our overall dataset (visible as gaps in the graphs that follow), the resignation of President Mubarak on Feb. 11 has the greatest resonance in the available data: We recorded more than 205,000 #egypt tweets from over 82,000 unique users on this day. During this early stage, the composition of the Twitter community was also markedly different from that recorded during the majority of the overall period: Throughout almost all of February, tweets using Latin characters retained the majority; it was only on Feb. 26 that the balance first swung towards non-Latin tweets. From then on, the situation was markedly different: from Mar. 1 to Nov. 30, an average of more than 75% of the #egypt tweets sent each day were composed in non-Latin characters.

This demonstrates a substantial shift in attention: whereas during the first month, and especially around the key days of régime change, a significant number of non-Arabic-speaking users participated, their interest dissipated as the situation moved from outright revolution to a more long-term reshaping of the political system; the remaining #egypt userbase (an average of over 7,000 unique users per day, posting nearly 24,000 tweets per day during the Mar. 1 to Nov. 30 period) was likely to be composed largely of

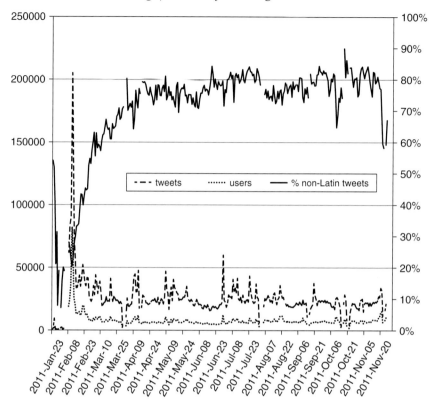

Figure 5.1   #egypt tweets and unique users per day, compared with daily percentage of non-Latin tweets

Egyptian locals and expatriates with a more direct interest in the continuing process of change.

One additional possible explanation for these changes is also the existence of the alternative hashtag #Jan25, referring to the so-called "Day of Revolt" that ignited the protest movement against the Mubarak régime. Notably, our data record only a relatively minor spike of less than 9,500 #egypt tweets on Jan. 25, substantially less than the over 205,000 tweets on Feb. 11; it is conceivable that the majority of early Twitter activity around the Egyptian protests took place under the #Jan25 hashtag, shifting to #egypt only once the initial aim of the protests (Mubarak's resignation) was achieved, and as the further passage of time made the #Jan25 tag seem anachronistic. The #Jan25 tag may also have had substantially greater resonance with directly involved local users, participating in or closely following the Jan. 25 protests, than with onlookers further afield; it is possible, therefore, that #Jan25 hashtag activities attracted a proportionally larger number of Egyptian (and generally Arabic-speaking) Twitter users, in turn leaving

#egypt to be dominated by English speakers, and that this imbalance only changed once a greater number of Arabic speakers transitioned to #egypt.

Such shifts in the userbase can also be traced by examining the relative contributions made by each of the three user groups outlined above. Figure 5.2 indicates the percentage of all daily tweets contributed by the three groups, and shows significant activity by the normally less active groups, especially during the first stage: Until the end of February, the lead users contributed only an average of 36% of all tweets per day; from March onwards, the same group accounts for an average of 60% of all tweets each day. In other words, this early stage saw a substantially larger presence of—in the long term—less engaged users; when these users exit the hashtag conversation as the "hot" phase of the revolution comes to an end, the two user groups who have a more long-term commitment to discussing

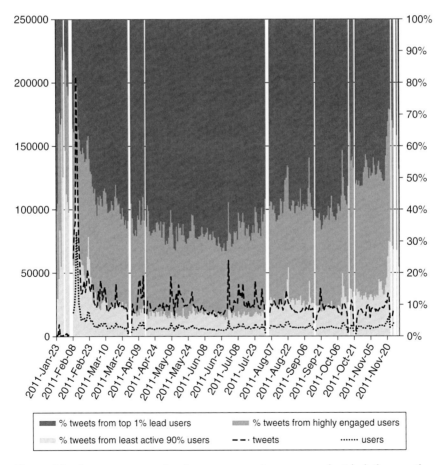

Figure 5.2 #egypt tweets and unique users per day, compared with daily contributions by different user groups

political change in Egypt increasingly come to dominate the conversation. But it should also be noted that from July onwards, lead users are again pushed back in favor of a greater contribution, especially from the second group of users: This may point both to the growing frustration with the slow pace of changeover from the Supreme Council of the Armed Forces to a civilian administration, which began to be voiced at this time, and to the building anticipation of popular elections, which began on Nov. 28, 2011. It is interesting to note that whereas the balance of contributions by the three groups gradually shifts from mid-year, the total volume of #egypt tweets remains relatively stable.

For further illustration, Figure 5.3 specifically compares the daily contributions made by the least active group with the daily percentage of tweets in a Latin character set, and points to a strong correlation between these metrics. Especially during the early stage of the revolution, the presence

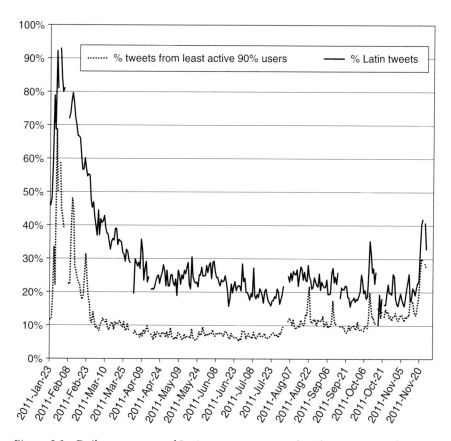

Figure 5.3 Daily percentage of Latin tweets, compared with percentage of tweets from least active

of a large number of normally relatively inactive users also coincides with a large number of Latin (i.e., mainly English) tweets; this implies that Arabic-language users are especially well represented in the leading groups of the most active contributors to #egypt, whereas less active contributors are more likely to be from non-Arabic backgrounds, and may have been attracted to the #egypt discussion largely because of the widespread media coverage of the revolution, but have limited interest in the longer-term process of political change.

These differences also become apparent from a further examination of the activity patterns for each of the three groups (Figure 5.4). As is to be expected, the lead users are responsible for a disproportionate percentage of all #egypt tweets; this 1% of most active users contributed nearly 56% of all tweets. Their tweets are also substantially more likely to be original tweets (that is, neither @replies nor retweets—64% of their tweets fall into this category); by contrast, the majority of the tweets contributed by the least active user group—65%—are retweets. The leading user group is also most likely to share URLs: some 56% of their tweets contain hyperlinks to external resources, compared with under 40% for each of the other two groups.

A further striking difference between these three groups is evident from their language preferences. For the lead group, an average of nearly 75% of their tweets use non-Latin characters; this reduces to 63% for the highly engaged users, and drops to 43% for the large group of least engaged users.

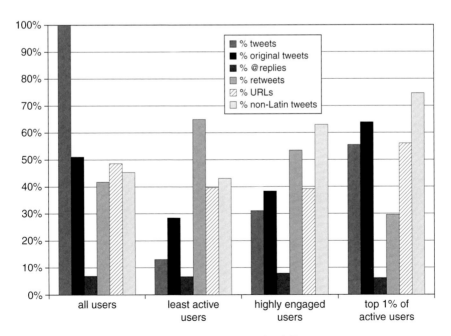

Figure 5.4   #egypt contribution patterns across the different user groups

This means that Arabic speakers are relatively overrepresented amongst the most engaged groups, whereas the least engaged group of users contains a substantially larger number of non-Arabic speakers.

#libya

Patterns in the #libya dataset are somewhat different from those for #egypt, as Figure 5.5 indicates. Over the course of the data collection period, we captured over 5.27 million tweets originating from more than 476,000 users. Total usage of the hashtag spikes early on at over 320,000 tweets per day on Feb. 21, 2011, as first reports of unrest are covered by world media, but after this relatively brief moment of heightened activity, the #libya hashtag continues to operate at a much lower volume: From the start of April, the daily average remains at a comparatively low 10,500 tweets. As in #egypt, the number of unique users contributing to the hashtag each day generally

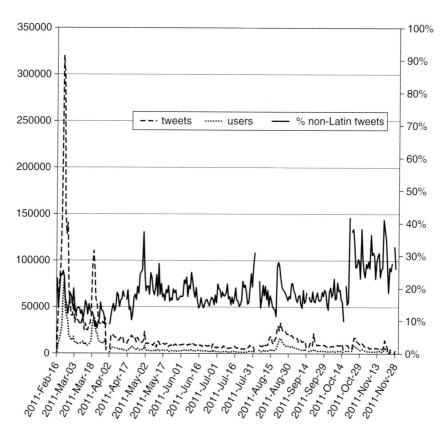

Figure 5.5   #libya tweets and unique users per day, compared with daily percentage of non-Latin tweets

correlates with the number of tweets; it peaks at over 80,000 on Feb. 22, but reaches only an average of 3,600 for the period after April 1.

A notable difference from #egypt emerges with the percentage of Arabic (i.e., non-Latin) tweets per day: Here, #libya shows a surprisingly limited number of tweets using non-Latin characters. From Feb. 16 to Oct. 15, the average percentage of non-Latin tweets remains at a lowly 18%; it rises to 29% only during the last one and a half months. Contrary to #egypt, fluctuations in language use cannot be traced back to the relative contributions made by the different user groups: at 23%, the percentage of non-Latin tweets posted by the top 1% group of lead users over the entire period differs little from that of the least active group, at 27%.

Rather, an explanation for the generally comparatively low number of Arabic tweets in the #libya dataset must be sought in the user demographics, and in the nature of the conflict. In Egypt, where protests were centered on demonstrations in the urban setting of Cairo, significant use of Twitter in covering the crisis may well have been considerably more likely than in Libya, where régime change was achieved only after a long military campaign unfolding across the country; additionally, differing Internet and social media take-up, and subsequent blocking of access to such communication tools, is likely to have influenced the respective level of domestic Twitter use in these countries. Media reports during the Libyan civil war, suggesting that the Gaddafi régime attempted to block Libya's access to the global Internet, would explain the low number of Arabic tweets in the #libya dataset; further, the substantial rise in Arabic tweets from Oct. 20, 2011, may indicate that such restrictions were lifted as the régime fell (Gaddafi himself was killed on that day).

Figure 5.6 again compares overall daily activity with the respective contributions made by the three user groups. As before, the top 1% of most active users is generally responsible for the vast majority of all tweets; over the entire period, they contribute some 57% of all tweets, whereas the least active group only contributes 16% of all tweets. Again, however, the contribution of the less active user groups also rises considerably when the overall number of tweets peaks; on Aug. 23, for example, the lead user group accounts for less than 27% of all tweets, with the other two groups driving overall hashtag activity on that day (the day rebels overran Gaddafi's Bab al-Azizia compound in central Tripoli).

Compared to #egypt, the activity patterns for these different user groups in #libya (Figure 5.7) show few notable trends. There is, as expected, a marked difference in the overall level of contributions made by the three groups; the lead users are also somewhat less likely to send retweets (56% of their tweets were retweets, compared to 66% of the tweets made by the least active group), and more likely to post original tweets (36% compared to 27%). There also is no clear pattern in the relative use of Latin or non-Latin scripts; differences between the groups are relatively minor.

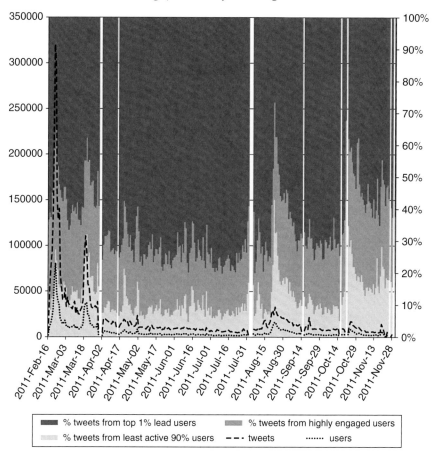

Figure 5.6   #libya tweets and unique users per day, compared with daily contributions by different user groups

This is remarkably different from #egypt, where lead users were substantially more likely to post original tweets (65% of their messages were neither @replies nor retweets), and to do so in Arabic (nearly 75% of their tweets used non-Latin script). What these observations strongly suggest is the relative absence—because of Internet blockages or a more limited take-up of Twitter—of a domestic *élite* of Libyan Twitter users reporting on the latest developments, as well as of an active ex-pat community to take up and disseminate their messages further. Twitter as a communications tool *was* used to document and discuss the unfolding events of the Libyan civil war—but more so by interested onlookers outside of the country, mainly using English to communicate, than by Libyan locals and their compatriots abroad.

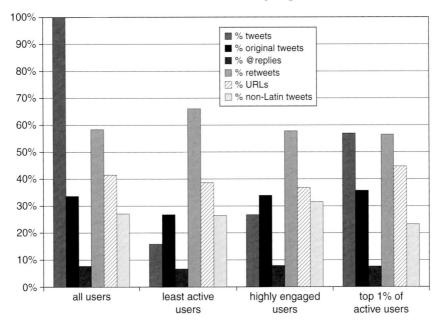

Figure 5.7   #libya contribution patterns across the different user groups

INTERACTIONS BETWEEN LANGUAGE GROUPS

There are clear differences in the *Twitter* audiences for the #egypt and #libya streams, and the make-up of these groups changes substantially over the course of 2011. Of particular interest is the presence of different language groups, and the potential for interactions between them: Our interest is in determining to what extent information originating from predominantly Arabic-speaking Twitter participants is able to reach English-speaking users, and vice versa. Such interactions can be traced by examining the flow of @replies and retweets (collectively, @mentions) between participating accounts; for both #egypt and #libya they consist largely of retweets, because (as Figures 5.4 and 5.7 have demonstrated) less than 10% of all tweets are genuine @replies. For our analysis, this is useful: Retweets are generally used by Twitter contributors to pass along incoming information to their own networks of followers; where we find evidence of significant connection between Arabic- and English-language users, we may assume that information is transmitted across language boundaries.

To examine these questions, we focus on four distinct periods selected from the overall Twitter feeds for #egypt and #libya. For #egypt, we examine the period of Feb. 1–28, which sees the major spike in Twitter activity, and is characterized by a relatively high number of users (many from the less engaged groups) tweeting in Latin characters, and the period of June 15 to Sept. 15, marked by a steady but less spectacular daily volume of tweets and a predominance of non-Latin tweets. For #libya, we examine Feb. 16 to Mar. 15, a comparable one-month period during the early stages of the uprising, reaching daily volumes surpassing even those seen in #egypt but notable for the comparative absence of non-Latin tweets, and Aug. 1 to Sept. 30, with steady levels of activity and a slightly higher incidence of non-Latin tweets. For each of these periods, we again divide participating users into the three groups of lead users, highly engaged users, and least active users, as well as a final group of passive Twitter accounts whose usernames are mentioned in hashtagged tweets, but who do not themselves post hashtagged tweets during the period.

We also calculate for each user the percentage of their tweets that use more than our threshold value of 10 non-Latin characters. On this basis, we divide the overall userbase along new lines: into groups using predominantly Latin characters (less than 33% of their tweets pass the non-Latin threshold); predominantly non-Latin characters (more than 66% of their tweets are non-Latin); and mixing both Latin and non-Latin tweets (between 33% and 66% of their tweets use non-Latin characters). Such distinctions can only be made for active contributors to the hashtags, of course; for the group of passive accounts that are merely mentioned, we are unable to determine their position across the language divide. In the network graphs that follow, accounts with predominantly Latin (i.e., mostly English-language) tweets will be shown in blue; those with mainly non-Latin (i.e., Arabic) tweets in green; users posting a mixture of Latin and non-Latin tweets are marked in an intermediate color that reflects that mix; passive accounts, finally, are shown in grey. Connections between users are shown in the color of the originating user.

#egypt

The two periods in the overall #egypt dataset that we examine here are marked by a substantial shift in the language mix, from a substantial majority of Latin tweets to an even more significant predominance of non-Latin tweets. Figure 5.8 shows the relative presence of the three different language groups within the total community of users, as well as within the groups of more and less active users.

During the Feb. 1–28 period, users tweeting predominantly in Latin characters clearly dominate: more than 78% of all users fall into that category, whereas only 4% and 18%, respectively, belong to the "mixed" and "non-Latin" groups. The distribution within the least active user group largely matches this distribution. Towards the more active end, however, the distribution changes considerably: Only 67% of the highly active group, and only 55% of the lead users, tweet predominantly in Latin characters, whereas the presence of "non-Latin" users grows to 22% and 33%. The

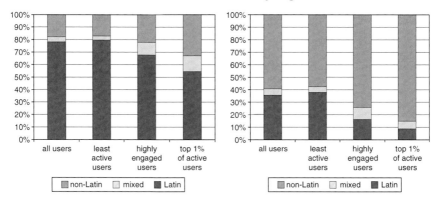

Figure 5.8   #egypt language groups as percentage of total userbase, February 1–28 and June 15 to September 15

most remarkable difference is for the mixed-language group, however: Constituting only 3% of the least active group, they account for 10% of the highly active group, and make up nearly 13% of the lead user group. This indicates a considerable difference in commitment to the #egypt discussion: Whereas larger numbers of English speakers may be interested enough to tweet or retweet the occasional message relating to the situation in Egypt, even at this early stage Arabic-speaking Twitter users are prepared to participate in significantly more depth.

Several months later, similar patterns persist, but the balance has shifted much further towards the "non-Latin" group. They now constitute nearly 60% of the total userbase, and are again considerably overrepresented amongst the more engaged groups; over 85% of all lead users tweet predominantly in non-Latin characters. Similar to the earlier period, too, mixed-language contributors are disproportionately represented amongst the more active groups; here, however, they constitute a larger proportion of the second, highly engaged group (at nearly 10%), but only 6% of the lead user group. One explanation for this shift may be that the "mixed" group is more likely to include native Arabic speakers who use English as a second language than native English speakers with some knowledge of Arabic; as the overall stream of the #egypt discussion shifts more towards the use of Arabic in these later months, users who were in the "mixed" group during the earlier phase of the uprising may now be posting Arabic-language tweets so frequently that they have moved into the "non-Latin" group as we have defined it.

Figure 5.9 compares the total network of Twitter exchanges between users through @replies and retweets during these periods. Connections are depicted in the color of the originating user: @replies and retweets by "Latin" users are shown in blue; those by "non-Latin" users in green, and those by users tweeting in a mixture of character sets in the corresponding

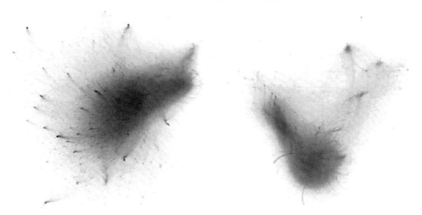

Figure 5.9   #egypt @reply/retweet networks, February 1–28 and June 15 to September 15. This figure is reproduced in the color plate section.

mixed color. The balance between predominantly blue (Latin) and green (non-Latin) regions in the network shifts substantially from the Feb. 1–28 period to the June 15 to Sept. 15 period. During the former period, in fact, some 68% of all connections through @replies and retweets originate from the "Latin" user group, 10% from the "mixed" group, and 22% from the "non-Latin" group.[37] During the latter, the situation is reversed, and even more one-sided: Only 18% of all @mentions originates from "Latin" users, 9% from "mixed" users, and 73% from "non-Latin" participants. If the least active group of contributors is excluded from this calculation, the situation changes slightly: For the earlier period, the "Latin" group now accounts for a slightly lower 64% of all @mentions; for the later period, however, the contribution of "non-Latin" users rises yet further, to over 78% of all @mentions. Several outliers may be detected in these network graphs (especially amongst "non-Latin" users in the June–September period); it is likely that ideological, geographic, or other sociodemographic factors are responsible for their separation from the core of the network.

The overall flows of information across the network, for which @replies and retweets provide a proxy measure, can be examined further by visualizing aggregate flows (Figure 5.10). These graphs show that interaction by "Latin" and "non-Latin" groups during both periods is largely amongst themselves: The indicators of self-linking are considerably more prominent in Figure 5.10 than any connections across language boundaries. During February, some 80% of all @replies and retweets by "Latin" users reference others in the same group; 65% of the @mentions by "non-Latin" users mention other "non-Latin" participants. For "Latin" users, in fact, the second most prominent source of information are "passive" accounts: 10% of their tweets reference those accounts (amongst which news organizations and other sources will play an important role), often likely retweeting information while adding the "#egypt" hashtag to the original messages. Where

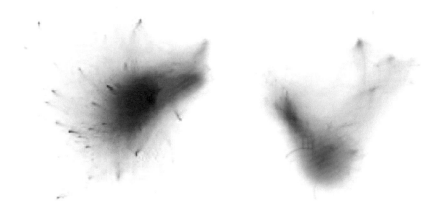

Figure 5.9   #egypt @reply/retweet networks, February 1–28 and June 15 to September 15

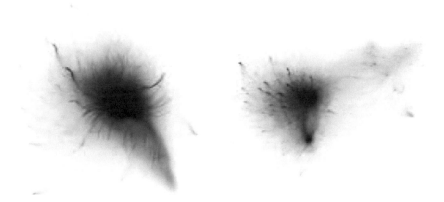

Figure 5.12   #libya @reply/retweet networks, February 16 to March 15 and August 1 to September 30

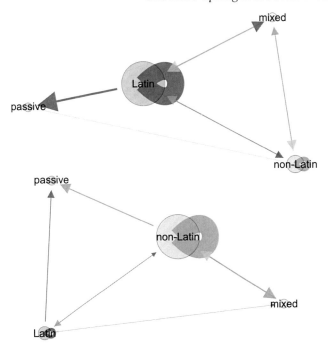

Figure 5.10   Aggregate #egypt @reply/retweet networks, February 1–28 and June 15 to September 15

they look beyond their own group, by contrast, "non-Latin" users divide their attention almost equally between "mixed" (14%) and "Latin" (16%) sources; they draw on passive accounts only for 5% of their @mentions. The "mixed" group, finally, acts considerably differently: Only 15% of their @replies and retweets are directed at other mixed-language users, but 42% reference "Latin" accounts and 37% connect to "non-Latin" accounts. Therefore, whereas the overall contribution of the "mixed" group to #egypt is relatively minor, their main role appears to be an attempt to bridge the major language groups.

During the period of June 15 to Sept. 15, the situation is reversed, and more: As originators of only 18% of all @mentions, "Latin" users now play an even lesser role than "non-Latin" users did during February. Due in part to their overall dominance, the "non-Latin" group is similarly self-focused: Over 82% of their tweets mention other "non-Latin" users, with between 4% and 7% mentioning each of the other three groups. Conversely, as #egypt is now predominantly a non-Latin Twitter stream, the remaining "Latin" users are also forced to look beyond their own group for more information: Whereas 56% of their tweets continue to reference other "Latin" participants, 11% draw on the "mixed" group, and 14% contain @mentions of "non-Latin" users. Indeed, if the 90% least active users are excluded from the analysis, the cross-language links from "Latin" to "non-Latin" users increase from 14% to over 19% (and from 11% to 12% for links to the "mixed" group): Those "Latin" users who are amongst the most active overall contributors to #egypt are also significantly more likely to seek information beyond their own group. The "Latin" group also remains especially focused on "passive" accounts; however, some 19% of their tweets continue to inject information from such non-participating accounts into the #egypt discussion through retweeting. Finally, more so than during the earlier period, the "mixed" accounts have also accepted the dominance of "non-Latin" accounts: 53% of their @mentions reference those accounts, compared to only 21% referring to "Latin" users. Intra-group @mentions remain characteristically low for this group: Only 14% of their @mentions refer to fellow mixed-language accounts.

#libya

Dominated throughout by "Latin" users, the situation in the #libya hashtag differs considerably from that in #egypt. During the early phase of the revolution, the overall #libya userbase presents what is nearly a mirror image of the situation in #egypt: Some 82% of all participating users during this time fall into the "Latin" category (Figure 5.11). However, when broken down into the groups of more or less engaged users, the distribution of language groups becomes more complicated: Whereas the second most active group again includes a larger number of "non-Latin" and mixed-language users, that trend is reversed again for the leading user group. "Non-Latin" users constitute 14% of the least active group, 20% of the second group of highly engaged users, but again only 14% of the lead group; by contrast, the mixed-language group accounts for only 3% of the least active group, 8% of the highly engaged group, and nearly 9% of the leading group. It appears that similar to #egypt, during this early phase the #libya hashtag attracted

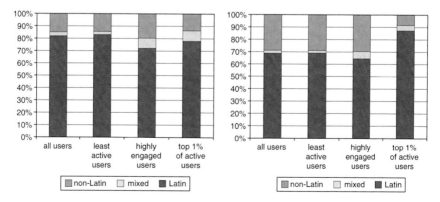

Figure 5.11 #libya language groups as percentage of total userbase, February 16 to March 15 and August 1 to September 30

a substantial number of relatively random English-language commenters, a comparatively large number of fairly active Arabic-speaking users, but also a substantial number of very highly active English-language participants.

This pattern is even more pronounced for the August–September period. By this time, users tweeting mainly in non-Latin characters have become substantially more active in the #libya community; they now account for 29% of the total userbase, and constitute 30% of the highly engaged user group. Surprisingly, however, they have not only failed to make any inroads into the lead user group, but have indeed been pushed out of this group by an even more active English-language élite, to the point where they now constitute only 8% of that lead group. Further, the mixed-language group also appears to have been squeezed out of the overall hashtag community by this increasing language polarization: Now accounting for only 2% of the total #libya userbase, they also constitute only 6% of the highly engaged group, and 4% of the lead user group.

Figure 5.12 again compares the overall network of @replies and retweets across the two periods we have chosen (Feb. 16 to Mar. 15 and Aug. 1 to Sept. 30, respectively), and shows a gradual thinning of and cluster formation in the network: Not only do connections between the predominantly "Latin" and "non-Latin" sections of the network weaken from the earlier to the latter period, but even within these sections themselves distinct, loosely connected clusters emerge (available space in this chapter does not permit us to examine the unifying traits of these distinct clusters). During the earlier period, nearly 80% of all connections through @mentions originated from the "Latin" group of users, whereas the "non-Latin" group accounted for just over 13%; the "mixed" group contributed only 7% to the total number of @mentions. This distribution remains steady once the least active 90% of users are removed from the network, too. In August and September, during

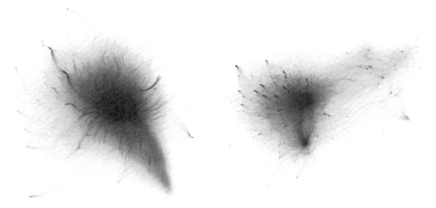

Figure 5.12   #libya @reply/retweet networks, February 16 to March 15 and August 1 to September 30. This figure is reproduced in the color plate section.

the final battle for control of Tripoli, the situation becomes more polarized: Whereas at 79%, the "Latin" dominance remains steady, the contribution of the "mixed" group drops to only 4%, and that of "non-Latin" users increases to nearly 17%; if only the top 10% of most active users are considered, however, the "Latin" group now accounts for over 85% of all @ mentions, and the "non-Latin" group drops back to just over 10%.

An analysis of the aggregate flow of information further supports these observations. Figure 5.13 is clearly dominated by the presence of "Latin" users, who largely make intragroup @mentions (more than 85% of their @ mentions are directed to other "Latin" participants, in both periods); where they connect outside their own group at all, they do so mainly to "passive" Twitter accounts (8% and 11% of their @mentions, respectively, are pointing to that group during the two periods, whereas @mentions of any of the other groups fail to account even for as little as 4% of the total @replies and retweets sent by "Latin" users).

Nonetheless, a small but internally active group of "non-Latin" users does remain: Respectively, during the two periods, 66% and 76% of the @ mentions originating from "non-Latin" users are directed at other members of that group. During February–March, "Latin" users are the next most important information source for "non-Latin" users at 16%, followed by mixed-language users at 11% and "passive" accounts at 6%; in August and September, however, external, "passive" sources become more important (at 9%), whereas @mentions of the "Latin" and "mixed" groups drop to 8% and 6%, respectively. Finally, whereas in #libya the efforts of the "mixed" group of users do not amount to a substantial level of activity, it is nonetheless notable that their information-sourcing processes do not reflect the balance of power that prevails within the #libya community: Whereas during both periods, over 50% of their @mentions refer to "Latin" users, a similarly considerable over 30% of their mentions are directed to the significantly smaller group of "non-Latin" users. This intermediary group of mixed-language users does continue to play a role in enabling an information flow across language boundaries, therefore, even if their more limited presence in the #libya hashtag means that direct connections between "Latin" and "non-Latin" users must play a greater role here, compared to #egypt.

CONCLUSION

Space available in this chapter has allowed us to examine only the broad patterns of Twitter usage by Arabic and English speakers in the Egyptian and Libyan uprisings, and to point to the relative presence of highly active élite users in each case; even this already highlights significant differences between the two cases. These differences are clearly aligned with sociodemographic and technological distinctions between the countries, as well as with the different course of events followed by each revolution.

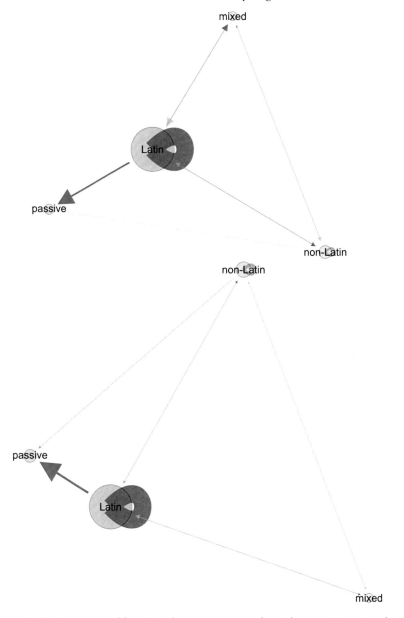

Figure 5.13 Aggregate #libya @reply/retweet networks, February 16 to March 15 and August 1 to September 30

We found that there is a substantially larger group of Arabic-speaking users participating in the #egypt discussion than in #libya; this observation supports research that found—albeit on the basis of geolocated tweets, which account for only a minute percentage of all messages on Twitter—that the Egyptian Twitter population is larger by an order of magnitudes than the Libyan population.[38] As a consequence, discussion under the #libya hashtag is likely to consist largely of outsiders looking in, rather than—as in #egypt—of locals and expatriates discussing the unfolding political crisis in their country.

Even in #egypt, however, we found a substantial shift over time, from a comparative dominance of users tweeting in Latin characters to an overwhelmingly Arabic-speaking userbase. This shift may be driven in part by the early prominence of alternative hashtags—chiefly, the #Jan25 hashtag, which referenced to the date of the first major demonstrations, and which subsided thereafter. But our analysis has also shown the already considerable presence of an Arabic-speaking élite amongst the top 1% of most active contributors to #egypt even at this early stage; as other users shifted from #Jan25 to #egypt proper, and as long-term interest by international participants waned, this established élite became the nucleus around which a largely Arabic-language discussion unfolded.

Our analysis of activity patterns in #egypt and #libya provides a complement especially to Lotan et al.'s analysis of the activities of a small group of highly active Twitter users who commented on the uprisings in Tunisia and Egypt.[39] Where that study traced patterns of dissemination for a limited number of high-profile examples, our research points to the degree to which information exchanges are able to bridge existing language divides. Although outside the scope of the present chapter, further work will be able to examine the relative prominence of specific news sources (as URLs cited in tweets, and/or as major Twitter contributors themselves) in the English- and Arabic-language networks, and the extent to which such resources are shared across the language divide, or specific to one or the other of these language communities; this will shed further light onto the relative uses of Twitter for disseminating both mainstream and eyewitness accounts of the uprisings to local and international followers of these hashtags.

Such analyses also enable us to move beyond simplistic arguments about whether or not the events of the Arab Spring constituted "Twitter revolutions" (see, e.g., Sullivan[40] and Morozov[41] for examples of the opposing perspectives in this argument). The differences we have found between the Egyptian and Libyan uprisings already point to the fact that the real situation is far more complex, and not only highly dependent on national and regional specificities, but also considerably changeable over time. The substantial level of Arabic tweets in the case of #egypt certainly points to the fact that Twitter—and, by extension, other online media—did play a role in informing, organizing, and reporting protest activities in the country (and most likely continue to do so now, as post-election unrest persists), but this does not necessarily translate into support for the popular narrative of Egypt as a social media revolution. In Libya, the situation is notably different—here, the consistent lack of local Twitter activity makes it difficult to escape the conclusion that other, more conventional forms of communication were significantly more important to the successful pursuit of régime change, and that Twitter interest in the uprising was driven largely by onlookers from further afield. Future research will show whether—in the wake of these political transformations—Twitter and other online and social media will become established in the long term as tools for political communication in both countries.

NOTES

Axel Bruns, Jean Burgess, and Tim Highfield, "The Arab Spring and Social Media Audiences: English and Arabic *Twitter* Users and Their Networks," *American Behavioral Scientist* 57, no. 7 (2013), 871–898. Copyright © 2013 by Sage Publications. Reprinted by Permission of SAGE Publications.

1. Alfred Hermida, "From TV to Twitter: How Ambient News Became Ambient Journalism," *M/C Journal* 13, no. 2 (2010), last modified July 25, 2013, http://journal.media-culture.org.au/index.php/mcjournal/article/view/220.
2. Kate Crawford, "Following You: Disciplines of Listening in Social Media," *Continuum* 23, no. 4 (2009), doi:10.1080/10304310903003270; Alex Burns and Ben Eltham, "Twitter Free Iran: An Evaluation of Twitter's Role in Public Diplomacy and Information Operations in Iran's 2009 Election Crisis," *Record of the Communications Policy & Research Forum 2009*, Sydney (November 19–20, 2009), last modified July 25, 2013, www.networkinsight. org/publications/record_of_the_2009_cprf.html/group/16.
3. Devin Gaffney, "#IranElection: Quantifying Online Activism" (paper presented at WebSci10, Raleigh, NC, Apr. 26, 2010), last modified July 25, 2013, http://journal.webscience.org/295.
4. Barrie Axford, "Talk about a Revolution: Social Media and the MENA Uprisings," *Globalizations* 8, no. 5 (2011), doi:10.1080/14747731.2011.621281; Walid El Hamamsy, "BB = BlackBerry or Big Brother: Digital Media and the Egyptian Revolution," *Journal of Postcolonial Writing* 47, no. 4 (2011), doi :10.1080/17449855.2011.590325; Malcolm Gladwell, "Does Egypt Need Twitter?" *The New Yorker: News Desk*, (February 2, 2011), last modified July 25, 2013, www.newyorker.com/online/blogs/newsdesk/2011/02/does-egypt-need-twitter.html; Evgeny Morozov, "Facebook and Twitter Are Just Places Revolutionaries Go," *The Guardian: Comment Is Free*, (March 7, 2011), last modified July 25, 2013, www.guardian.co.uk/commentisfree/2011/mar/07/facebook-twitter-revolutionaries-cyber-utopians.
5. Malcolm Gladwell, "Twitter, Facebook, and Social Activism: Small Change—Why the Revolution Will Not Be Tweeted," *The New Yorker*, (October 4, 2010), last modified July 25, 2013, www.newyorker.com/reporting/2010/10/04/101004fa_fact_gladwell.
6. Andrew Chadwick, "The Hybrid Media System" (paper presented at the 6th European Consortium for Political Research General Conference, Reykjavík, Iceland, August 25–26, 2011).
7. Jillian C. York, "Egypt: A Voice in the Blackout, Thanks to Google and Twitter," *Global Voices*, (February 1, 2011), last modified July 25, 2013, http://globalvoicesonline.org/2011/02/01/egypt-a-voice-in-the-blackout-thanks-to-google-and-twitter/.
8. El Hamamsy, "BB = Blackberry."
9. Genevieve Barrons, "'Suleiman: Mubarak Decided to Step Down #egypt #jan25 OH MY GOD': Examining the Use of Social Media in the 2011

Egyptian Revolution," *Contemporary Arab Affairs* 5, no. 1 (2012), doi:10.1 080/17550912.2012.645669.

10. Axel Bruns and Jean Burgess, "The Use of Twitter Hashtags in the Forma-tion of *Ad Hoc* Publics" (paper presented at the 6th European Consortium for Political Research General Conference, University of Iceland, Reykjavík, August 25–27, 2011), last modified July 25, 2013, http://eprints.qut.edu. au/46515/.

11. Kate Starbird and Jeannie Stamberger, "Tweak the Tweet: Leveraging Microblogging Proliferation with a Prescriptive Syntax to Support Citizen Reporting," *Proceedings of the 7th International ISCRAM Conference, Seattle, WA, May 2010*, last modified July 25, 2013, http://repository.cmu. edu/silicon_valley/41/.

12. Axel Bruns and Jean Burgess, "Local and Global Responses to Disaster: #eqnz and the Christchurch Earthquake," *Proceedings of Earth: Fire and Rain—Australian & New Zealand Disaster and Emergency Management Conference, Brisbane, Australia, 16–18 April 2012*, last modified July 25, 2013, http://eprints.qut.edu.au/50739/; Axel Bruns, Jean Burgess, Kate Crawford, and Frances Shaw, *#qldfloods and @QPSMedia: Crisis Commu-nication on Twitter in the 2011 South East Queensland Floods* (Brisbane: ARC Centre of Excellence for Creative Industries and Innovation, 2012), last modified July 25, 2013, http://cci.edu.au/floodsreport.pdf.

13. Chris Messina, "Twitter Hashtags for Emergency Coordination and Disaster Relief," *Factory City*, (Oct. 22, 2007), last modified July 25, 2013, http:// factoryjoe.com/blog/2007/10/22/twitter-hashtags-for-emergency-coordina tion-and-disaster-relief/; Kate Starbird and Jeannie Stamberger, "Tweak the Tweet."

14. Gilad Lotan, Erhardt Graeff, Mike Ananny, Devin Gaffney, Ian Pearce, and danah boyd, "The Revolutions Were Tweeted: Information Flows during the 2011 Tunisian and Egyptian Revolutions," *International Journal of Com-munication* 5 (2011), last modified July 25, 2013, http://ijoc.org/ojs/index. php/ijoc/article/view/1246.

15. Twitter, "Twitter Translation Center Adds Right-to-Left Languages," *Twit-ter Blog*, (January 25, 2012), last modified July 25, 2013, http://blog.twitter. com/2012/01/twitter-translation-center-adds-right.html.

16. Ujjwal Singh, "Some Weekend Work That Will (Hopefully) Enable More Egyptians to Be Heard," *Google Blog*, (February 1, 2011), last modified July 25, 2013, http://googleblog.blogspot.com.au/2011/01/some-weekend-work-that-will-hopefully.html.

17. Ethan Zuckerman, "Meet the Bridgebloggers," *Public Choice* 134, nos. 1–2 (2008): 48, doi:10.1007/s11127–007–9200-y.

18. Bruce Etling, John Kelly, Robert Faris, and John Palfrey, "Mapping the Ara-bic Blogosphere: Politics and Dissent Online," *New Media & Society* 12, no. 8 (2010), doi:10.1177/1461444810385096.

19. Etling et al., "Mapping the Arabic Blogosphere," 1240.

20. Tom Isherwood, "A New Direction or More of the Same? Political Blogging in Egypt," *Arab Media & Society* 6 (2008), 13, last modified July 25, 2013, www.arabmediasociety.com/?article=693.

21. Tom Isherwood, "A New Direction," 9.

22. Susan C. Herring, John C. Paolillo, Irene Ramos-Vielba, Inna Kouper, Elijah Wright, Sharon Stoerger, Lois Ann Scheidt, and Benjamin Clark, "Language Networks on LiveJournal," *Proceedings of the 40th Hawaii International Conference on System Sciences, Los Alamitos, CA: IEEE Press, 2007*, 9, doi:10.1109/HICSS.2007.320.

23. Bruce Etling et al., "Mapping the Arabic Blogosphere," 1229.

24. Fieke Jansen, "Digital Activism in the Middle East: Mapping Issue Networks in Egypt, Iran, Syria and Tunisia," *Knowledge Management for Development Journal* 6, no. 1 (2010), 48, doi:10.1080/19474199.2010.493854.
25. Thomas Poell and Kaouthat Darmoni, "Twitter as a Multilingual Space: The Articulation of the Tunisian Revolution through #sidibouzid," *NECSUS: European Journal of Media Studies* 1, no. 1 (2012), last modified July 25, 2013, www.necsus-ejms.org/twitter-as-a-multilingual-space-the-articulation-of-the-tunisian-revolution-through-sidibouzid-by-thomas-poell-and-kaouthar-darmoni/.
26. Zizi Papacharissi and Maria de Fatima Oliveira, "Affective News and Networked Publics: The Rhythms of News Storytelling on #Egypt," *Journal of Communication* 62 (2012), doi:10.1111/j.1460–2466.2012.01630.x.
27. Philip N. Howard, Aiden Duffy, Deen Freelon, Muzammil Hussain, Will Mari, and Marwa Mazaid, *Opening Closed Régimes: What Was the Role of Social Media During the Arab Spring?* (Seattle: Project on Information Technology and Political Islam, 2011), 16–17, last modified July 25, 2013, http://pitpi.org/?p=1051.
28. Deen Freelon, "The MENA Protests on Twitter: Some Empirical Data," DFreelon.org, (May 19, 2011), last modified July 25, 2013, http://dfreelon.org/2011/05/19/the-mena-protests-on-twitter-some-empirical-data/.
29. Axel Bruns, "Switching from *Twapperkeeper* to your *Twapperkeeper*," *Mapping Online Publics*, (June 21, 2011), last modified July 25, 2013, www.mappingonlinepublics.net/2011/06/21/switching-from-twapperkeeper-to-yourtwapperkeeper/.
30. Deen Freelon, "The MENA Protests."
31. danah boyd and Kate Crawford "Critical Questions for Big Data," *Information, Communication & Society* 15, no. 5 (2012), doi:10.1080/1369118X.2012.678878.
32. All dates and times here are in Cairo time.
33. See http://mappingonlinepublics.net/2012/01/28/creating-basic-twitter-language-metrics/ for details.
34. Axel Bruns, "Creating Basic Twitter Language Metrics," *Mapping Online Publics*, (January 28, 2012), last modified July 25, 2013, www.mappingonlinepublics.net/2012/01/28/creating-basic-twitter-language-metrics/.
35. Axel Bruns, "Taking Twitter Metrics to a New Level," *Mapping Online Publics*, (January 2, 2012), last modified July 25, 2013, www.mappingonlinepublics.net/2012/01/02/taking-twitter-metrics-to-a-new-level-part-1/, www.mappingonlinepublics.net/2012/01/02/taking-twitter-metrics-to-a-new-level-part-2/, www.mappingonlinepublics.net/2012/01/02/taking-twitter-metrics-to-a-new-level-part-3/, www.mappingonlinepublics.net/2012/01/02/taking-twitter-metrics-to-a-new-level-part-4/.
36. Chris Anderson, "The Long Tail," *Wired* 12, no. 10 (2004), last modified July 25, 2013, www.wired.com/wired/archive/12.10/tail.html; Chris Anderson, *The Long Tail: Why the Future of Business Is Selling Less of More* (New York: Hyperion, 2006); Steven J. J. Tedjamulia, Douglas L. Dean, David R. Olsen, and Conan C. Albrecht, "Motivating Content Contributions to Online Communities: Toward a More Comprehensive Theory," *Proceedings of the 38th Annual Hawaii International Conference on System Sciences (HICSS), Los Alamitos, CA: IEEE Press, 2005,* doi:10.1109/HICSS.2005.444.
37. Here and throughout, these percentages refer to the relative number of connections (network edges) between users from these different language groups; we do not take into account the frequency with which such connections between any pair of participants may have been repeated during each timeframe (i.e. the specific weight of each network edge).

38. Beatrice Karanja, "New Research Reveals How Africa Tweets," *African Arguments*, (January 26, 2012), last modified July 25, 2013, http://africanarguments.org/2012/01/26/new-research-reveals-how-africa-tweets-by-beatrice-karanja-portland-communications.
39. Gilad Lotan et al., "The Revolutions Were Tweeted."
40. Andrew Sullivan, "Could Tunisia Be the Next Twitter Revolution?" *The Atlantic: The Daily Dish*, (January 13, 2011), last modified July 25, 2013, www.theatlantic.com/daily-dish/archive/2011/01/could-tunisia-be-the-next-twitter-revolution/177302/.
41. Evgeny Morozov, "Facebook and Twitter."

REFERENCES

Anderson, Chris. "The Long Tail." *Wired* 12, no. 10 (2004). www.wired.com/wired/archive/12.10/tail.html (accessed July 25, 2013).
———. *The Long Tail: Why the Future of Business Is Selling Less of More*. New York: Hyperion, 2006.
Axford, Barrie. "Talk about a Revolution: Social Media and the MENA Uprisings." *Globalizations* 8, no. 5 (2011): 681–686. doi:10.1080/14747731.2011.621281.
Barrons, Genevieve. "'Suleiman: Mubarak Decided to Step Down #egypt #jan25 OH MY GOD': Examining the Use of Social Media in the 2011 Egyptian Revolution." *Contemporary Arab Affairs* 5, no. 1 (2012): 54–67. doi:10.1080/17550912.2012.645669.
boyd, danah, and Kate Crawford. "Critical Questions for Big Data." *Information, Communication & Society* 15, no. 5 (2012): 662–679. doi:10.1080:1369118X.2012.678878.
Bruns, Axel. "Switching from *Twapperkeeper* to *yourTwapperkeeper*." *Mapping Online Publics*, June 21, 2011. www.mappingonlinepublics.net/2011/06/21/switching-from-twapperkeeper-to-yourtwapperkeeper/ (Accessed July 25, 2013).
———. "Taking Twitter Metrics to a New Level." *Mapping Online Publics*. January 2, 2012. www.mappingonlinepublics.net/2012/01/02/taking-twitter-metrics-to-a-new-level-part-1/, www.mappingonlinepublics.net/2012/01/02/taking-twitter-metrics-to-a-new-level-part-2/,www.mappingonlinepublics.net/2012/01/02/taking-twitter-metrics-to-a-new-level-part-3/,www.mappingonlinepublics.net/2012/01/02/taking-twitter-metrics-to-a-new-level-part-4/ (accessed July 25, 2013).
———. "Creating Basic Twitter Language Metrics." *Mapping Online Publics*. Jan. 28, 2012. www.mappingonlinepublics.net/2012/01/28/creating-basic-twitter-language-metrics/ (accessed July 25, 2013).
Bruns, Axel, and Jean Burgess. "The Use of Twitter Hashtags in the Formation of *Ad Hoc* Publics." Paper presented at the 6th European Consortium for Political Research General Conference, University of Iceland, Reykjavík, August 25–27, 2011. http://eprints.qut.edu.au/46515/ (accessed July 25, 2013).
———. "Local and Global Responses to Disaster: #eqnz and the Christchurch Earthquake." *Proceedings of Earth: Fire and Rain—Australian & New Zealand Disaster and Emergency Management Conference, Brisbane, Australia, 16–18 April 2012*. http://eprints.qut.edu.au/50739/ (accessed July 25, 2013).
Bruns, Axel, Jean Burgess, Kate Crawford, and Frances Shaw. *#qldfloods and @QPSMedia: Crisis Communication on Twitter in the 2011 South East Queensland Floods*. Brisbane: ARC Centre of Excellence for Creative Industries and Innovation, 2012. http://cci.edu.au/floodsreport.pdf (accessed July 25, 2013).
Bruns, Axel, Jean Burgess, and Tim Highfield. "The Arab Spring and Social Media Audiences: English and Arabic *Twitter* Users and Their Networks." *American Behavioral Scientist* 57, no. 7 (2013): 871–898.

Burns, Alex, and Ben Eltham. "Twitter Free Iran: An Evaluation of Twitter's Role in Public Diplomacy and Information Operations in Iran's 2009 Election Crisis." *Record of the Communications Policy & Research Forum 2009.* Sydney, November 19–20, 2009. www.networkinsight.org/publications/record_of_the_2009_cprf.html/group/16 (accessed July 25, 2013).

Chadwick, Andrew. "The Hybrid Media System." Paper presented at the 6th European Consortium for Political Research General Conference, Reykjavík, Iceland, August 25–26, 2011.

Crawford, Kate. "Following You: Disciplines of Listening in Social Media." *Continuum* 23, no. 4 (2009): 525–535. doi:10.1080/10304310903003270.

El Hamamsy, Walid. "BB = BlackBerry or Big Brother: Digital Media and the Egyptian Revolution." *Journal of Postcolonial Writing* 47, no. 4 (2011): 454–466. doi:10.1080/17449855.2011.590325.

Etling, Bruce, John Kelly, Robert Faris, and John Palfrey. "Mapping the Arabic Blogosphere: Politics and Dissent Online." *New Media & Society* 12, no. 8 (2010): 1225–1243. doi:10.1177/1461444810385096.

Freelon, Deen. "The MENA Protests on Twitter: Some Empirical Data." *DFreelon. org*, May 19, 2011. http://dfreelon.org/2011/05/19/the-mena-protests-on-twitter-some-empirical-data/ (accessed July 25, 2013).

Gaffney, Devin. "#IranElection: Quantifying Online Activism." Paper presented at WebSci10, Raleigh, NC, Apr. 26, 2010. http://journal.webscience.org/295 (accessed July 25, 2013).

Gladwell, Malcolm. "Twitter, Facebook, and Social Activism: Small Change—Why the Revolution Will Not Be Tweeted." *The New Yorker*. Oct. 4, 2010. www.newyorker.com/reporting/2010/10/04/101004fa_fact_gladwell (accessed July 25, 2013).

———. "Does Egypt Need Twitter?" *The New Yorker: News Desk*. Feb. 2, 2011. www.newyorker.com/online/blogs/newsdesk/2011/02/does-egypt-need-twitter.html (Accessed July 25, 2013).

Hermida, Alfred. "From TV to Twitter: How Ambient News Became Ambient Journalism." *M/C Journal* 13, no. 2 (2010). http://journal.media-culture.org.au/index.php/mcjournal/article/view/220 (accessed July 25, 2013).

Herring, Susan C., John C. Paolillo, Irene Ramos-Vielba, Inna Kouper, Elijah Wright, Sharon Stoerger, Lois Ann Scheidt, and Benjamin Clark. "Language Networks on LiveJournal." *Proceedings of the 40th Hawaii International Conference on System Sciences.* Los Alamitos, CA: IEEE Press, 2007. doi:10.1109/HICSS.2007.320.

Howard, Philip N., Aiden Duffy, Deen Freelon, Muzammil Hussain, Will Mari, and Marwa Mazaid. *Opening Closed Régimes: What Was the Role of Social Media During the Arab Spring?* 16–17. http://pitpi.org/?p=1051 (accessed July 25, 2013).

Isherwood, Tom. "A New Direction or More of the Same? Political Blogging in Egypt." *Arab Media & Society* 6 (2008): 1–17. www.arabmediasociety.com/?article=693 (accessed July 25, 2013).

Jansen, Fieke. "Digital Activism in the Middle East: Mapping Issue Networks in Egypt, Iran, Syria and Tunisia." *Knowledge Management for Development Journal* 6, no. 1 (2010): 37–52. doi:10.1080/19474199.2010.493854.

Karanja, Beatrice. "New Research Reveals How Africa Tweets." *African Arguments.* Jan. 26, 2012. http://africanarguments.org/2012/01/26/new-research-reveals-how-africa-tweets-by-beatrice-karanja-portland-communications (accessed July 25, 2013).

Lotan, Gilad, Erhardt Graeff, Mike Ananny, Devin Gaffney, Ian Pearce, and danah boyd. "The Revolutions Were Tweeted: Information Flows during the 2011 Tunisian and Egyptian Revolutions." *International Journal of Communication* 5 (2011): 1375–1405. http://ijoc.org/ojs/index.php/ijoc/article/view/1246 (accessed July 25, 2013).

Messina, Chris. "Twitter Hashtags for Emergency Coordination and Disaster Relief." *Factory City.* Oct. 22, 2007. http://factoryjoe.com/blog/2007/10/22/twitter-hashtags-for-emergency-coordination-and-disaster-relief/ (accessed July 25, 2013).

Morozov, Evgeny. "Facebook and Twitter Are Just Places Revolutionaries Go." *The Guardian: Comment Is Free.* March 7, 2011. www.guardian.co.uk/commentis free/2011/mar/07/facebook-twitter-revolutionaries-cyber-utopians (accessed July 25, 2013).

Papacharissi, Zizi, and Maria de Fatima Oliveira. "Affective News and Networked Publics: The Rhythms of News Storytelling on #Egypt." *Journal of Communication* 62 (2012): 266–282. doi:10.1111/j.1460–2466.2012.01630.x.

Poell, Thomas, and Kaouthat Darmoni. "Twitter as a Multilingual Space: The Articulation of the Tunisian Revolution through #sidibouzid." *NECSUS: European Journal of Media Studies* 1, no. 1 (2012). www.necsus-ejms.org/twitter-as-a-mul tilingual-space-the-articulation-of-the-tunisian-revolution-through-sidibouz id-by-thomas-poell-and-kaouthar-darmoni/ (accessed July 25, 2013).

Singh, Ujjwal. "Some Weekend Work That Will (Hopefully) Enable More Egyptians to Be Heard." *Google Blog.* February 1, 2011. http://googleblog.blogspot.com.au/2011/01/some-weekend-work-that-will-hopefully.html (accessed July 25, 2013).

Starbird, Kate, and Jeannie Stamberger. "Tweak the Tweet: Leveraging Microblogging Proliferation with a Prescriptive Syntax to Support Citizen Reporting." *Proceedings of the 7th International ISCRAM Conference, Seattle, WA, May 2010.* http://repository.cmu.edu/silicon_valley/41/ (accessed July 25, 2013).

Sullivan, Andrew. "Could Tunisia Be the Next Twitter Revolution?" *The Atlantic: The Daily Dish*, January 13, 2011. www.theatlantic.com/daily-dish/archive/2011/01/could-tunisia-be-the-next-twitter-revolution/177302/ (accessed July 25, 2013).

Tedjamulia, Steven J.J., Douglas L. Dean, David R. Olsen, and Conan C. Albrecht. "Motivating Content Contributions to Online Communities: Toward a More Comprehensive Theory." *Proceedings of the 38th Annual Hawaii International Conference on System Sciences (HICSS).* Los Alamitos, CA: IEEE Press, 2005. doi:10.1109/HICSS.2005.444.

Twitter. "Twitter Translation Center Adds Right-to-Left Languages." *Twitter Blog.* January 25, 2012. http://blog.twitter.com/2012/01/twitter-translation-center-adds-right.html (accessed July 25, 2013).

York, Jillian C. "Egypt: A Voice in the Blackout, Thanks to Google and Twitter." *Global Voices.* February 1, 2011. http://globalvoicesonline.org/2011/02/01/egypt-a-voice-in-the-blackout-thanks-to-google-and-twitter/ (accessed July 25, 2013).

Zuckerman, Ethan. "Meet the Bridgebloggers." *Public Choice* 134, nos. 1–2 (2008): 47–65. doi:10.1007/s11127-007-9200-y.

6 Twitter as the People's Microphone
Emergence of Authorities during Protest Tweeting

Alexander Halavais and Maria Garrido

The elections in Iran in 2009, and the protests that followed, have been called the "Twitter Revolution." The phrase is ambiguous: Was the revolution in Iran, or in the way the technology of protest affects public perceptions? In public protests that have followed, microblogging—publicly disseminating short messages on the Internet—has continued to be employed by protesters and by the public observing protests. The use of Twitter during the London G20 protests, the Iranian elections, and other protests made 2009 a turning point for Twitter as a political tool.[1] Whereas there are a wide range of ways in which individuals tweet,[2] a set of protest-oriented tweeting styles emerged out of these events: tweets that called protesters to action, kept them coordinated and informed during protests, and established what was important about the events: what they meant.

To understand the character of microblogging during protests, and the ways in which public discourse is shaped, we recorded and analyzed tweets during the Group of Twenty (G20) protests in Pittsburgh in late September of 2009. This represents a fairly inchoate phase in the use of Twitter during protests, and was small in scale relative to many of the protests that would follow. In this chapter, we describe the ways in which tweeting related to the events of the protest, which twitterers emerged as influential during the protests, and what this might mean for the use of mobile microblogging during future political actions.

SOCIAL MOVEMENTS AND SOCIAL MEDIA

Golnaz Esfandiari, in an article in *Foreign Policy*, argues that the attention paid to Twitter during the Iranian Elections is misplaced, and that many of the twitterers were not, in fact, engaged in the protests.[3] In many cases, those tweeting about the events in Iran were not in Tehran at all, but scattered across the globe. In practice, new networked technologies function in a number of ways within grassroots social movements and the protests they foster.[4] One of those functions is to organize the protest itself, drawing together disparate groups into collective action. In addition, the technologies may be used extemporaneously to coordinate actions on the ground, quickly shifting to meet new challenges. The final way in which net-worked technologies have been used is to shape the public narratives around events. Assuming that the purpose of such protests is to change the public discourse, in some ways, this last locus of action is especially important. It is difficult to deny that Twitter affected the public perception of what occurred in the streets of Tehran or during the Occupy Wall Street movement.

Of course, media in various forms have affected the ways in which social movements not only communicate their message, but organize themselves and effect change.[5] The protests at the Seattle meeting of the WTO in 1999 are often seen as a turning point for use of the Internet and other networked technologies to organize protest, to manage it, and to communicate it to a wider public.[6] In particular, political action has been aimed at creating media-friendly narratives in the hope of multiplying the intended message. Approaches to shaping mass media coverage have certainly not diminished; social media simply add another tool to the repertoire of the activist. How-ever, the nature of the tool—a simple communication protocol that requires no special training or infrastructure—represents a particularly "lightweight" way of putting a message out and having it reach a wider audience or create a pool of shared media experiences.[7]

One of the most common observations about new social movements is that there appears to be a change in the ways in which they are organized and led. Olson, in 1965, argued for the importance of structured organi-zations to help put into action the shared interests of a "latent group" of citizens with shared interests and vision. But new technologies allow for less structured and more liquid forms of organization that can unite the inter-ests of these groups "from below."[8] Unlike traditional organizations that might recruit members through a strategic organizational effort, authority in networked social movements is "polycentric," drawing on a multitude of hubs and authorities.[9] Some have gone so far as to suggest that the new net-worked politics is entirely rhizomatic[10] and represents a perfectly distributed crowd, free from authoritative leaders.[11] In practice, of course, networked politics is a messy mix of emergent leaders and a cobweb of connections. Garrido and Halavais found this to be the case in the web structures of global social movements, where the Zapatista movement provided a cat-alyst for global, grassroots collaboration.[12] This uneven mix of hierarchy and anarchy, or "heterarchy"[13] not only distributes authority throughout a network, but assigns that authority dynamically from among its members.

TWITTER AND PROTEST

Twitter is used in a range of ways during a protest, but to have a significant influence, tweets need to be read by a large number of people. Those who have large numbers of followers have the equivalent of a megaphone on the network, but real audience reach can also be achieved through retweeting. Retweeting is the act of taking the tweet of another user and reproducing verbatim (sometimes with comment) to that user's own followers. This retweet may be reproduced by yet another user, in a chain of retweets. In some cases, this may become a cascade of retweets as a particular tweet sweeps across a community.[14] This differs from many social networking sites, most notably Facebook, in which relationships are more often reciprocal. Rather than social groupings, clusters, or communities, the relationships on Twitter lend themselves to an analysis of influence and authority.[15] As Braun and Gillespie suggest, this places Twitter in a position that is somewhat different from many other forms of social media, and was marked by a change in both the way Twitter represented itself to users (by asking what they were doing), and how it might relate to the diffusion of news.[16] Lotan et al. show that Twitter hosts an interesting space of flows between those who are tweeting from an institutional role (journalists, researchers, activists) and those relaying their personal interactions.[17]

The Occupy Wall Street (OWS) movement reclaimed a longstanding form of human technology, what is referred to variously as the "People's Microphone" or "Human Megaphone." When megaphones were banned in Zuccatti Park, protesters used call and response to broadcast a speech through the crowd. Although it was slow and cumbersome for a speech to be broken up and passed along this way, it was effective, and allowed individuals to participate as a conduit for the message. Some saw this in stark contrast with the new social media, but it is easy to see how such a human structure could be extended or replaced by social media.[18] A tweet is a slight thing—on average it is not only short, but unlikely to be read by many people. But once taken up and rebroadcasted to wider and wider audiences (and sometimes on to the traditional mass media), it provides the potential for an individual to have an extraordinary reach. Whereas there are a number of ways of measuring influence on Twitter,[19] retweets have often been used as a significant indicator of explicit influence.[20] The OWS movement deployed multiple media to reach their ends,[21] but Twitter represents a structural analog to the human microphone. Understanding who gets to be the source of messages in this network is important to understanding new forms of leadership for today's activism.

The G20 meeting in the American city of Pittsburgh, which occurred on the 24th and 25th of September 2009, followed a larger London meeting, in which police found themselves unprepared for the size of the crowds and were criticized for managing the protests badly. The U.S. meeting was originally planned for New York City, but eventually scheduled for Pittsburgh mainly for reasons of logistics. As with earlier meetings on the topic of global economic cooperation, a range of groups planned to come to Pittsburgh to voice their concerns, supported by activist organizations based in the city, including the Pittsburgh Organizing Group (POG) and the G-20 Resistance Project. Permits for meetings and demonstrations were initially denied by the city, and once granted, protestors were not allowed near the time or place of the official G20 meetings. As a result, many of the marches and meetings were conducted without permits, providing a pretext for police action. From the first day, the Pittsburgh meetings were marked by what many saw as an overwhelming police presence, sometimes ridiculously disproportionate to the number of protestors.[22]

Although the media framing of the event is open to interpretation,[23] the conflict between police and protesters dominated the popular discussion, particularly in the immediate aftermath of the meetings. The role of Twitter was perhaps not as closely watched in Pittsburgh as it was in London, but it remained an important part of the coverage and became particularly noted after the arrests in the weeks following of two activists who had been actively tweeting during the event. As with earlier protests, both participants in the protests and observers actively tweeted during the days surrounding the meetings.

This presents us with a set of basic exploratory questions regarding the G20 protests in Pittsburgh. First, when did people tweet? How did the volume of tweets relate to events on the ground? This provides us with some idea of how (if at all) Twitter use might co-occur with events of importance.

Second, who were the most influential twitterers? Whereas this could be answered in a number of ways, we operationalize influence as retweeting, for the reasons noted above. Who became the most retweeted users? Did this relate to particular kinds of events? What was the relationship of these users to the protests?

Finally, what is it that the most influential twitterers tweeted about? That is, how (if at all) did the tweets of the most influential, retweeted participants differ from the tweets of all of the other twitterers who affixed the #g20 hashtag?

MEASURING THE TWITTERVERSE

The U.S. Library of Congress announced some years ago that it had acquired a relatively complete archive of tweets from Twitter,[24] although at the time of writing this archive is not widely accessible to researchers.[25] Researchers have relied on third-party resellers of Twitter data, like Gnip, or have collected their own data. For this work, we used an application called The Archivist, collecting from three client computers in different locations to provide redundancy in case of network outages or heavy tweeting that might test the cap on Twitter requests. Neither of these were issues during the collection period.

Twitter has no explicit community functions, but hashtags (a keyword prepended with the # character) are used to mark emergent publics.[26] Hashtags represent an important and effective way of constraining discussions to a particular topic over a particular period of time.[27] We recorded tweets resulting from a search for the #g20 hashtag, from midnight of September 20 to midnight of September 29, and a total of 30,296 tweets were recorded. The dataset included #g20 tweet activity three days prior to the meeting, the two days when the meeting took place, and four days after it concluded. These data have been made available to interested researchers and have already been used by Earl et al. to describe the role of police-related tweeting during the protests.[28]

Once these tweets were collected, it was possible to code for both formal characteristics and semantic content. The formal characteristics of the whole tweet dataset provide some indication of when tweeting was most popular, how many different users were tweeting at a given time, who was retweeting whom, what hashtags were used, and other basic characteristics of the tweets.

Finally, those twitterers who were most frequently retweeted were ranked by number of raw retweets. To do this, tweets were searched for the stand-alone "RT," "MT" (for "modified tweet") or "via" followed by a user name. Soon after the period in question, Twitter changed the way in which it handled retweets, providing a process of indicating the source in metadata rather than in the text of the tweet itself, but this change had not yet taken effect.[29] In terms of the focus of retweets, there seemed to be an inflection point after the top 20 retweeted twitterers, and so we decided to see what differentiated these top 20 twitterers from the 6,204 others who contributed a #g20 tagged tweet during the nine-day period.

This indicator of retweet success was used primarily for its simplicity. In addition we examined authority within the retweet network based not just on local retweets of individuals, but the larger network of retweets. In other words, just as Google charts not just how many incoming hyperlinks a given page has, but how widely linked it is by the network at large, we were able to find an indication of which sources of tweets had the largest influence on the network as a whole.[30] Some twitterers may only be retweeted by a few, very influential, twitterers, but this would otherwise be hidden in direct retweet counts. The centrality of the retweet network was measured using PageRank (implemented in the networkx package for Python) for the nine days, and each day separately in order to determine how authority might have changed over the period of study. PageRank provides not just the most retweeted users, but those that are most likely to see their retweets travel well beyond themselves consistently;[31] it is an attempt to measure the central sources of information flow.

Once the formal structure of the G20 twittersphere had been examined, a subset of roughly 10% randomly selected tweets from the collection was evaluated by human coders to determine what the prevailing topics were over the course of the protest. Rather than starting with a hypothesis, we carefully read through the tweets, establishing an emergent set of codes, and engaging in constant comparison.[32] Through this iterative process, we developed a set of codes that represented, as cohesively as possible, a taxonomy of tweeting categories and topics during the protest. Recent studies take a similar grounded iterative approach for analyzing content of tweets during political protests.[33] A final coding scheme was agreed upon among the three coders and tested once more on a subset of tweets to ensure comprehensiveness. The coding scheme included 11 categories of codes covering a variety of topics, as well as one category for tweets that did not fit cohesively into any of the other categories and a category for those tweets with content in non-English languages or otherwise illegible to the coders. (See Table 6.1 for a summary of the tags and examples of tweets included in each category.) Many of these find alignment with the categories of tweeting behavior Penney and Dadas discovered in surveying OWS protesters.[34]

There were instances where a tweet was coded across multiple categories. These multiply coded tweets were more prevalent among those that addressed police actions, protest actions, and opinions of the events on the ground. A smaller percentage of tweets that included commercial and non-commercial news coverage of the events also showed co-occurrence with opinions of media coverage, from the perceived accuracy of the coverage to the frequency in which media outlets reported on the events.

A total of 5,976 tweets were hand coded following the coding framework outlined above. This subset included all the tweets that were most central in the network during this nine-day period (a total of 2,988 tweets from the top 20 twitterers) and a randomly selected sample of the same size of tweets from the whole data set to determine if there were differences in the manifest content of the tweet that could help explain why some tweets were more retweeted than others.

Table 6.1   Coding categories for sample of G20 tweets

About Twitter
Instruction
Local Response
Mass Media Opinion
Media Coverage
Non-commercial / Alternative Media
Not Legible
Opinions
Other
Police Actions
Political Issues
Position / Geolocation
Protestors' Actions

Zarella provides some insight into what gets retweeted most often on Twitter as a whole, including tweets with hashtags, links, and explicit calls for retweeting.[35] Suh et al. examine a large corpus of tweets and look at how other formal elements of the tweets, including characteristics of those being retweeted, might affect the retweetability of a particular tweet.[36] Given that we were looking at a particularly constrained Twitter public, we were interested in the ways in which topic or style might be related to retweeting. Although this may not represent a causal relationship (in fact, it seems that oft-retweeted users may share a background in professional media communications), it provides a useful perspective on what constitutes a message worth sharing in the protest context.

ETHICAL ISSUES

Before discussing what we found in investigating the G20 tweets, it is important to take a moment to address the ethical questions surrounding the study of public tweets on Twitter. By "public tweets" we refer to those tweets that are published to the web in real time and can be read by any user—the default for Twitter—unlike Twitter streams that are made explicitly private by the user. Most researchers consider these public tweets to be equivalent to observing interactions in public spaces, which is generally seen by human subjects committees as outside their purview because it has a very low risk of harm. This is true both because users should have no expectation that their tweets are private and because we as researchers had no interactions with the individuals we are studying that might put them in harm's way.

Not all human subjects boards agree on the status of Twitter as a public space, and there are elements of this particular case that bear further consideration, particularly around the ephemerality of the medium and the potential harm of recontextualizing these tweets. Users of Twitter might have some expectation that their tweets, while public and recordable, will most likely go unnoticed.[37] After all, millions of tweets go unnoticed every day: unread, unsaved, and destined to be unsearchable on the site after some time has passed. And if a user closes her account, the tweets become immediately unsearchable via Twitter, although they may exist in various personal and public archives, as well as having been copied via retweets into other streams. Whereas tweets are archived for both commercial and research purposes, these archived tweets are not easily accessed, and when reported on at all are likely to be referred to only in the aggregate. As a result, there may be some expectation that tweets are public, but only for a while.

It may also be that these tweets can be used against the interests of those who send them. Often there are elements of criminality during protests, and what constitutes criminal action may be murky. This proved to be especially true in the case of Pittsburgh. In the weeks after the protest, two participants were arrested for broadcasting police movements on Twitter. It would have been difficult to predict that use of the platform in this way would be judged as a violation of law, and clearly a public archive of protest-related tweets would be helpful to police investigating such uses. Moreover, the kind of analysis of content and structure presented here could help to identify influential individuals and groups, a task taken on by police forces both in authoritative regimes and in more democratic ones as part of the "negotiated management" of public protest.[38]

For these reasons, what initially appeared to be a relatively simple ethical decision became more fraught. We had initially identified particular Twitter users who were part of the core retweeted 20, but in what follows we do not refer to them directly if they appear to represent an individual, rather than an organizational, Twitter handle. We also continue to make our archived materials available to interested researchers in order to further social scientific inquiry, although we now provide these data only on request. These are small changes to our original approach, but we think they represent a measured effort to respond to privacy concerns.

TWEET PEAKS

One easy way of discovering what the totality of tweets tells us is by examining the frequency of tweets over time, rather than the content of those tweets directly. Discovering information through traffic patterns has long been an element of signals intelligence[39] and in other contexts, tracking online "chatter" in social media provides a map to social events and attitudes.[40] Google has used traffic related to mentions of influenza as means of surveillance of the virus,[41] and Twitter itself has used such frequency peaks to map conversations surrounding the World Cup.[42] Traffic analysis has more recently been used in other work to show the relationship between traffic around a particular hashtag on Twitter and protest activities.[43]

As shown in Figure 6.1, the distribution of tweets over the nine-day period was far from consistent. The frequency of tweets hit their nadir each morning at six o'clock, and there are a clear set of peaks. These peaks are easily associated with events during the protests, both due to their temporal correlation and the content of the tweets during the spike. The highest spike was at around 4 p.m. local time on September 24 (marked B in Figure 6.1), when police countered protesters with tear gas and stun grenades and for the first time deployed a crowd control weapon called a "sound cannon."[44] Other spikes also generally corresponded to clashes between police and protesters, including the arrests of Greenpeace activists rappelling from a bridge to hang a sign (A), marked increase in helicopter patrols (C), standoffs during speeches and the march (D), and video of police snatching someone off the street, seemingly at random (E). These spikes were marked by increases both in the number of twitterers and the frequency with which they tweeted. They also included efforts—mainly from those who disagreed with the protesters—to flood the #g20 hashtag with repeated identical tweets.

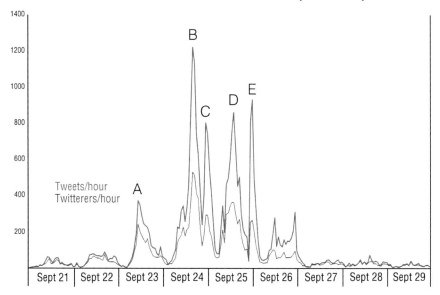

Figure 6.1   Frequency of tweets and number of twitterers using the #g20 hashtag each hour

TWITTER AUTHORITIES

As with many such linked systems, the distribution of retweets in the Pittsburgh G20 twitter data includes a relatively small number of highly retweeted users, and very large number of users at the periphery who might retweet (see Figure 6.2). Indeed, of the 6,224 total users that tagged a tweet with #g20, 2,255 never retweeted another #g20 tagged tweet, they simply added their own voice. As would be expected, the distribution of retweets follows a power law, with the most retweeted user receiving 2,177 retweets, and this number dropping dramatically with rank. The tenth ranked user received only 28 retweets.

Whereas PageRank can tell us which twitterers have their voices carry best within the network during the protests, they provide less indications of how those users came to that position. One possibility is that they emerged from the crowd to become very popular. To test for this possibility, we once again turned to the network over time, determining the PageRank not just of the network as a whole, but in daily increments (Figure 6.3). Notable here is that the peaks in twitter volume do not necessarily occur with peaks in centrality among our most central twitterers overall. In other words, those peaks, which were largely driven by events occurring each day, were in large part popular in nature: They consisted of a relatively large number of users tweeting relatively frequently, and not necessarily retweeting the same message repeatedly. Many of those who became central to our network reached

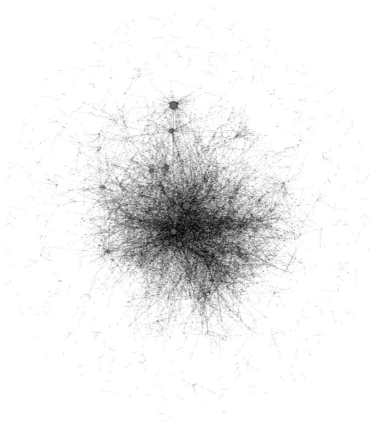

Figure 6.2   Network of retweets for all nine days. Node size based on PageRank (Gephi/OpenOrd).

that position late in the protests, and seemingly around retweeted summaries of earlier events, not breaking news.

What is clear is that among these top retweeted twitterers, it was not a matter of continual growth in popularity, or a learning process. Instead, it seems that the tweets that they made that were most heavily retweeted were largely situational, and they moved up and down in terms of centrality from day to day, ranging from near the top to well into the triple-digit ranks. In all cases, they remained part of the core of retweeted users, but the top 20 on any given day was likely to have only partial overlap with the other days of the protest.

We also see that there are clearly different kinds of information and news that are tweeted as original tweets and "rebroadcast" through a retweet network. As a whole, the tweets from the G20 protest were remarkable in that a seemingly large number were made by those present in Pittsburgh at the time. During the heaviest peaks of tweeting, this meant that individuals

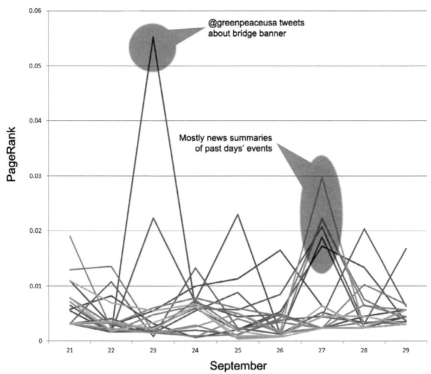

Figure 6.3   PageRank of top 20 twitterers for each of the nine days recorded

were sharing their own perspective, providing timely updates with their own information or views. During less eventful periods, it meant that they were more likely to share items from other, authoritative sources of news and opinion.

Who are these users? There is no simple answer to this question, but by examining the profile pages for each of the twitter accounts, we can obtain some understanding of who these users are and potentially their interest and involvement in the protest. Several of them, including two accounts for Greenpeace, represented established nongovernmental organizations with an interest in issues surrounding global economic policy. Although during the protests it may have been a single person tweeting for these organizations, the profile identified it as an official Twitter handle only, making it a more-or-less official organ of communication for the organization. In addition to organizing demonstrations, they provided information about protestors' rights and safety. Several of the accounts represented those who were either tweeting officially for local news organizations, journalists who were tweeting on their own from personal accounts (e.g., a producer for CNN), or accounts for what might be considered alternative news organizations. Along with an organization set up especially to coordinate the G20 protests, these twitterers represented fairly traditional sources of authority. All had significant experience getting messages out and heard. In many cases, the tweets they produced that were then echoed among other protest tweeters included links to their websites with more complete stories.

That these were among the more popular twitterers is perhaps not surprising. Not only did many of them have extensive experience as professional communicators, they benefitted from the familiarity of their institutional affiliations. Whereas in most cases it was unclear who the individual behind the tweet was, the organization was well known. As evident in Figure 6.3, above, most of them became central in the later part of the protests, when more was known and the dominant narrative of the protest was being established. Many of these retweets included links to stories in the mainstream national and local media.

What is perhaps surprising is that seven of the twitterers were individuals, with a variety of different approaches to the protest. Several had long tweeted about issues relating to globalism and activist causes, but some seemed to have simply fallen into the protests by happenstance. One of them, a student in Pittsburgh, tweeted throughout the protest, and after the period under study noted that her tweeting on topics of fashion would now resume. She had turned her view to the protest because it was part of her life, and in the process, became a widely retweeted contributor. These unusual twitterers were perhaps the most interesting of the collection, because they represent the democratic ideal—anyone can tweet—more closely than some of the other kinds of accounts that were highly retweeted. As noted below, many of these people happened to be in the right place at the right time, and were able to provide a credible first-person account of events as they happened.

In the end, then, we have a mixed bag. On one hand, those with institutional influence within the community continue to exercise this influence in the twittersphere. On the other, there are clear cases of those who otherwise would not have had a voice being elevated by the community into positions in which their voice is heard more widely. Some of this is, no doubt, shaped by the content of these tweets.

TWEET CONTENT

In order to understand the division between heavily retweeted and less retweeted twitterers, we categorized the semantic content of their tweets. Overall, the three most prominent topics of discussion across the #g20 tweets had to do with what was happening on a minute-by-minute basis. These were categorized as *Police Actions*, *Protestors' Actions*, or *Opinions of On-the-ground Events*, with fully 30% of the tweets relating to police activities. In other words, when compared to broader ideas, theories, calls to actions, and a myriad of other topics of tweeting, a substantial number were related to concrete current events; or to use Lasswell's taxonomy of the functions of communication media, they were heavily focused on immediate surveillance of the ongoing protest.[45]

The difficulty in sorting out tweets that related to clashes between police and protestors led us to allow multiple tagging of tweets, rather than exclusionary categories. By far, the most common tweets addressed issues of police interacting with protestors. As in London, many of these helped protestors to understand the location and movement of police forces:

> Police scanner: looking for best point to set up LRAD near Liberty & Grant area; major police presence at 5th & Ross #g20 #reportg20
>
> Munhal & Homestead police purchased riot gear. Now protecting ex-Steel PUMP HOUSE, edge of river, spot o Pinkerton's Guards past riot. #g20

In particular the events on September 24 on the University of Pittsburgh campus, which included the tear gassing of students trapped in campus buildings, produced a spike in Twitter activity:

> HAPPENING NOW: Students chanting "Show me what a police state looks like!" at line of cops on campus. #g20
>
> I wrote up a long account of what happened last night at #g20 on Pitt's campus. On page of Reddit.com

And as noted above, some of the heaviest tweeting came when police deployed less-lethal weapons against the protestors:

> PLEASE SPREAD THIS: Non-Violent #G20 Protesters Blasted by LRAD [as seen on #futureof] http://is.gd/3Ftzd
>
> Pic of LRAD Sonic Weapon @[user] Some kind of piercing siren to disperse crowds is coming from truck #g20 http://twitpic.com/iz16n

The discussion around protestor actions in some ways mirrored that of discussions of police action, with about 20% of the total being tagged as relating to protestors' activities. Many of these were either prescriptive or descriptive accounts of protestor activities and progress:

> Claiborne says there are about 40 tents now and more coming. "It's getting kind of crowded up there. We had 2 move some tents around." #g20
>
> RT @G20IMC Students March For Education For All http://bit.ly/7xA6w #g20 #reportg20 #university #college #knowledge #economy #jobs #tcot #p2

A number of posts provided updates of clashes between protestors and police:

> protestors clash with police http://tinyurl.com/ydbj4hv #g20 #Pittsburgh
> I have lost the main marches. Police from several cities are here blocking streets #myg20 #g20 Thursday 3:57pm

Whereas most of these posts were simply relating factual information, just over a fifth of the posts also editorialized, making clear what the twitterer thought of the events and its players. This included the use of hyperbole and sarcasm, or suggested that what was being reported or claimed by the news or officials was wrong.

Less than 10% of the sample (281 tweets in total), provided what might be considered instruction to those on the ground. This included pointing people toward particular sources of information (news outlets or twitterers in positions where they could gain information), as well as calls for protestors to report incidents, and how to protect themselves from the effects—both immediate and lingering—of tear gas.

Part of the reason we were interested in the content of these tweets was to see if particular topics during a protest resulted in a larger number of retweets. It is important to note that there was some diversity in posting patterns. Some of the top 20 most retweeted twitterers actually tweeted relatively infrequently compared to the number of retweets they received. Some created tweets that were not originally tagged #g20, and that hashtag was added by those who passed on the tweet. That said, there is some commonality in the nature of the tweets more frequently passed on.

As demonstrated in Figure 6.4, those who focused on the most popular topics—police, protestors, and clashes between the two—were also most likely to be retweeted. This was true both of those who tweeted "on the front lines" and from those who provided mainstream coverage of the events after the fact. There were other significant differences, including a tendency not to reference activist or nontraditional sources of media (no doubt this is due to the relationship of several of the top 20 with traditional news media and national nongovernmental organizations), but by far the most marked difference was that the top twitterers focused on what was going on around them at that moment.

This was particularly true of those twitterers who were not institutionally based. With some exceptions (Greenpeace tweeted its unfurling of a banner on a major bridge as it happened, for example), the institutional twitterers tended to reflect and retweet the observations of those participating in events in real time. Although there may be structural components that predict the successful twitterer, it is also true that being in the right place at the right time and conveying events around you clearly can quickly connect an otherwise obscure twitterer to a large audience.

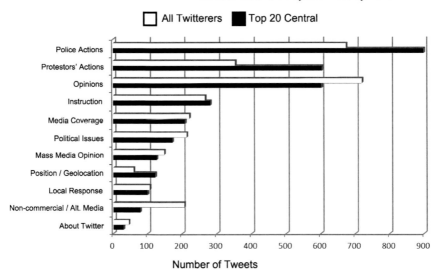

Figure 6.4 Comparison of tweet topics between sample of all tweets and tweets by the top 20 retweeted users

IN CONTEXT

It is difficult to know what can be generalized from a single protest event. As noted, the Pittsburgh G20 happened at a point of inflection for Twitter and social movements, and was followed by social media use during the Arab Spring and well after. There are elements that are particular to Pittsburgh—it was less geographically central than some of the other G20 meetings for example. And every event and protest is different.[46] Nonetheless, there are intriguing insights we can draw from the use of Twitter during this protest.

It seems clear that whereas institutions with significant credibility within the community retain that credibility and authority in the twittersphere, and have a natural advantage in attracting retweets, there is also significant potential for new voices and ideas. From London on, journalists not only used Twitter as a way of understanding protests, but as a way of getting out their own reports.[47] Indeed, the G20 twittersphere seemed to represent a shared space between more traditional institutions and individuals, perhaps in contrast to representations of Twitter and related social media as a space of explicit resistance to traditional media authorities.[48] This does not mean that Twitter cannot be used to resistant ends, and there are a number of clear examples of where this has been the case,[49] just as there are cases where it has been used more effectively against resistance.[50] But it is also clear that it is not a space in which external bases of influence suddenly disappear. The halo effect of reputation "outside" of Twitter is not limited to more established institutions: The most central account in the retweet network was the

Resist G-20 account, which established itself from the outset as a source of news and opinion around the protest in organizing in more traditional ways, and apparently carried this reputation over to Twitter. The combination of externally verified expertise and retweets, both of which build credibility,[51] led to a reinscription of some expected sources of influence.

Twitter is not a separate space, and social capital gained in other mediated and non-mediated venues matters. But it is also the case that Twitter provides for amazing influence mobility. Clearly, the initial structural position or external credibility of the twitterer is not the only source of retweetability; some tweets are better than others.[52] Some of the most influential twitterers during the protest had no apparent claim to that position other than interest in what they had to say in their tweets. Frequently, this was not something that set the narrative for the event, but rather something that was of immediate interest and provided surveillance of the event, sometimes mixed with in-group framing (humor, etc.). This provides interesting possibilities moving forward, particularly for movements that are organized around more cooperative, radically democratic, or anarchistic lines.

We can see how one's reputation outside of Twitter can be reflected and represented within the system itself. This can be seen in efforts to create parody and fake accounts on Twitter, and the response by Twitter of offering "verified accounts." Other researchers have suggested that retweeted tweets are more credible as well, creating a spiral of credibility as a message is propagated through the network.[53] But even more valuable is understanding how those who may not otherwise have a voice can either individually or collectively gain that voice.

The social media landscape changes quickly. It is hard to predict whether Twitter will remain the platform of choice for those during protests five or 10 years from now. Even the ways in which Twitter is used—the integration of pictures and video, for example—has changed rapidly over the last several years. Understanding how bottom-up, easily accessed microblogging can change the ways in which crowds of people communicate among themselves and with wider publics will remain a significant challenge for the foreseeable future.

The work described here represents an initial investigation into how such technologies may be employed, and hints at a tension between established reputation and emergent twitterers during protests. More such work is needed. At a macro level, we need to work toward tools and theory for making sense of large-scale interaction and understanding the content and structure of online communication both during events like protests and over the lifetime of a social movement. But these attempts at understanding the macro level structure must be mated with ethnographic work that examines micro-interactions and helps us to understand how these structures are reflected in individual decisions of when and how to engage with others.

NOTES

1. Alexandra Segerberg and W. Lance Bennett, "Social Media and the Organization of Collective Action: Using Twitter to Explore the Ecologies of Two Climate Change Protests," The Communication Review 14, no. 3 (2011): 197.
2. Alice E. Marwick and danah boyd, "I Tweet Honestly, I Tweet Passionately: Twitter Users, Context Collapse, and the Imagined Audience," New Media & Society 13, no. 1 (2010): 114.
3. Golnaz Esfandiari, "Misreading Tehran: The Twitter Devolution," Foreign Policy (2010), Last modified July 1, 2013, www.foreignpolicy.com/articles/2010/06/07/the_twitter_revolution_that_wasnt.
4. R. Kelly Garrett, "Protest in an Information Society: A Review of Literature on Social Movements and New ICTs," Information Communication Society 9, no. 2 (2006): 202.
5. Todd Gitlin, The Whole World Is Watching: Mass Media in the Making and Unmaking of the New Left (Berkeley, CA: University of California Press, 1980).
6. Levi Margaret and David Olson, "The Battles in Seattle," Politics & Society 28, no. 3 (2000): 309.
7. Bruce Bimber, A.J. Flanagin, and Cynthia Stohl, "Reconceptualizing Collective Action in the Contemporary Media Environment," Communication Theory 15, no. 4 (2005): 365.
8. Sandra González-Bailón, "Online Networks and Bottom up Politics," in Society and the Internet: How Information and Social Networks Are Changing Our Lives, eds. William H. Dutton and Mark Graham (Oxford, UK: Oxford University Press, forthcoming).
9. W. Lance Bennett, "Communicating Global Activism: Strengths and Vulnerabilities of Networked Politics," Information Communication Society 6, no. 2 (2003): 143.
10. Harry Cleaver, "Computer-Linked Social Movements and the Global Threat to Capitalism," last modified July 1, 2013, https://webspace.utexas.edu/hcleaver/www/polnet.html.
11. Richard Kahn and Douglas Kellner, "New Media and Internet Activism: From the 'Battle of Seattle' to Blogging," New Media & Society 6, no. 1 (2004): 87.
12. Maria Garrido and Alexander Halavais, "Mapping Networks of Support for the Zapatista Movement: Applying Social Network Analysis to Study Contemporary Social Movements," in Cyberactivism: Online Activism in Theory and Practice, eds. Martha McCaughey and Michael D. Ayers (New York: Routledge, 2003), 165–184.
13. Warren McCulloch, "A Heterarchy of Values Determined by the Topology of Nervous Nets," Bulletin of Mathematical Biology 7, no. 2 (1945): 89.
14. Eytan Bakshy, Jake M Hofman, Winter A Mason, and Duncan J Watts, "Everyone's an Influencer: Quantifying Influence on Twitter Categories and Subject Descriptors," in Proceedings of the Fourth ACM Conference on Web Search and Data Mining, 65–74, 2011.
15. Eytan Bakshy, Jake M. Hofman, Winter A. Mason, and Duncan J. Watts, "Everyone's an Influencer: Quantifying Influence on Twitter Categories and Subject Descriptors," in Proceedings of the Fourth ACM Conference on Web Search and Data Mining, 65–74, 2011; 2011; Haewoon Kwak, Changhyun Lee, Hosung Park, and Sue Moon, "What Is Twitter, a Social Network or a News Media? Categories and Subject Descriptors," in Proceedings of WWW 2010, 112: 591–600, ACM Press, 2010.

16. Joshua Braun and Tarleton Gillespie, "Hosting the Public Discourse, Hosting the Public," Journalism Practice 5, no. 4 (2011): 383.

17. Gilad Lotan, Mike Ananny, Devin Gaffney, and danah boyd, "The Revolutions Were Tweeted: Information Flows During the 2011 Tunisian and Egyptian Revolutions," International Journal of Communication, 5 (2011): 1375.

18. Homay King, "Antiphon: Notes on the People's Microphone," Journal of Popular Music Studies 24, no. 2 (2012): 238.

19. Meeyoung Cha, Hamed Haddadi, Fabrício Benevenuto, and Krishna P. Gummadi, "Measuring User Influence in Twitter: The Million Follower Fallacy," 4th International AAAI Conference on Weblogs and Social Media (ICWSM), 2010.

20. Carolina Bigonha, Thiago N. C. Cardoso, Mirella M. Moro, Virgílio A. F. Almeida, and Marcos A. Gonçalves, "Detecting Evangelists and Detractors on Twitter," in 18th Brazilian Symposium on Multimedia and the Web, 107, 2010.

21. Sasha Costanza-Chock, "Mic Check! Media Cultures and the Occupy Movement," Social Movement Studies 11, nos. 3–4 (2012): 375.

22. Candi Carter Olson and Brittany Duncan, "Pittsburgh's Flair for Protest II: An Oral History Interview with G20 Research and Activist and University of Pittsburgh Sociology Student Brittany Duncan. [Audio]," last modified July 1, 2013, http://d-scholarship.pitt.edu/2782/.

23. Rachel V. Kutz-Flamenbaum, Suzanne Staggenborg, and Brittany J. Duncan, "Media Framing of the Pittsburgh G-20 Protests," in *Research in Social Movements, Conflicts and Change*, eds. Jennifer Earl and Deana A. Rohlinger (Bingley, UK: Emerald Group Publishing, Ltd., 2012), 109–138.

24. Matt Raymond, "How Tweet It Is! Library Acquires Entire Twitter Archive." Library of Congress Blog, last modified July 1, 2013, http://blogs.loc.gov/loc/2010/04/how-tweet-it-is-library-acquires-entire-twitter-archive/.

25. Victor Luckerson, "What the Library of Congress Plans to Do with All Your Tweets," Time, February 25, 2013, last modified July 1, 2013, http://business.time.com/2013/02/25/what-the-library-of-congress-plans-to-do-with-all-your-tweets/.

26. Axel Bruns and Jean Burgess, "The Use of Twitter Hashtags in the Formation of Ad Hoc Publics," 6th European Consortium for Political Research General Conference 64 (August 2011): 1.

27. Wolfgang Reinhardt, Martin Ebner, Günter Beham, and Cristina Costa. "How People Are Using Twitter During Conferences," in 5th EduMedia Conference, eds. V. Hornung-Prahauser and M. Luckmann, 145–156, 14: 2009.

28. Alexander Halavais, "#g20 Tweets." A Thaumaturgical Compendium, 2009, last modified July 1, 2013, http://alex.halavais.net/g20-tweets.

29. Evan Williams, "Why Retweet Works the Way That It Does," EVHEAD, 2009, last modified July 1, 2013, http://evhead.com/2009/11/why-retweet-works-way-it-does.html.

30. Jon M. Kleinberg, "Hubs, Authorities, and Communities," ACM Computing Surveys 31, no. 4es (1999): art. 5.

31. Daniel M. Romero, Wojciech Galuba, Sitaram Asur, and Bernardo A. Huberman, "Influence and Passivity in Social Media," in Machine Learning and Knowledge Discovery in Databases, eds. Peter A. Flach, Tijl De Bie, and Nello Cristianini (Berlin: Springer Berlin Heidelberg, 2011), 18–33.

32. Kimberly A. Neuendorf, *The Content Analysis Guidebook* (Thousand Oaks, CA: Sage Publications, 2002); Barney Glaser and Anselm Strauss, *The*

Discovery of Grounded Theory: Strategies for Qualitative Research (Chicago: Aldine de Gruyter, 1967).

33. Kartikeya Bajpai and Anuj Jaiswal, "A Framework for Analyzing Collective Action Events on Twitter," in Proceedings of the 8th International ISCRAM Conference, Lisbon, Portugal, 2011.

34. Joel Penney and Caroline Dads, "(Re)tweeting in the Service of Protest: Digital Composition and Circulation in the Occupy Wall Street Movement," New Media & Society (2013).

35. Dan Zarella, "Science of ReTweets," 2009, last modified July 1, 2013, http://danzarrella.com/the-science-of-retweets-report.html.

36. Bongwon Suh, Lichan Hong, Peter Pirolli, and Ed H. Chi, "Want to Be Retweeted? Large Scale Analytics on Factors Impacting Retweet in Twitter Network," in SocialCom 2010 IEEE Second International Conference on Social Computing, eds. Ahmed K Elmagarmid and Divyakant Agrawal, (IEEE, 2010), 177.

37. Sarah Vieweg, "The Ethics of Twitter Research," in Revisiting Research Ethics in the Facebook Era Challenges in Emerging CSCW Research, Association for Computing Machinery (ACM), 2010.

38. Patrick F. Gillham, "Securitizing America: Strategic Incapacitation and the Policing of Protest Since the 11 September 2001 Terrorist Attacks," Sociology Compass 5, no. 7 (2011): 636.

39. George Danezis and Richard Clayton, "Introducing Traffic Analysis," in Digital Privacy: Theory, Technologies, and Practices, eds. Alessandro Acquisti, Stefanos Gritzalis, Costas Lambrinoudakis, and Sabrina De Capitani di Vimercati (Boca Raton, Florida: Auerbach Publications, 2008), 95–113.

40. D. Gruhl, R. Guha, David Liben-Nowell, and A. Tomkins, "Information Diffusion Through Blogspace," eds. Stuart I Feldman, Mike Uretsky, Marc Najork, and Craig E Wills, ACM SIGKDD Explorations Newsletter 6, no. 2 (2004): 491–501.

41. Herman Anthony Carneiro and Eleftherios Mylonakis, "Google Trends: A Web-based Tool for Real-time Surveillance of Disease Outbreaks," Clinical Infectious Diseases an Official Publication of the Infectious Diseases Society of America 49, no. 10 (2009): 1557.

42. Matt Graves, "The 2010 World Cup: A Global Conversation," Twitter Blog, 2010, last modified July 1, 2013, http://blog.twitter.com/2010/07/2010-world-cup-global-conversation.html.

43. Kartikeya Bajpai and Anuj Jaiswal, "A Framework for Analyzing Collective Action Events on Twitter," in *Proceedings of the 8th International ISCRAM Conference*, Lisbon, Portugal, 2011; Jennifer Earl, Heather McKee Hurwitz, Analicia Mejia Mesinas, Margaret Tolan, and Ashley Arlotti, "This Protest Will Be Tweeted: Twitter and Protest Policing During the Pittsburgh G20," *Information, Communication & Society* 16, no. 4 (May 16, 2013): 459.

44. Urbina, Ian. "Protesters Are Met by Tear Gas at G-20 Conference." New York Times, 2009, last modified July 1, 2013, www.nytimes.com/2009/09/25/us/25pittsburgh.html.

45. Harold D. Lasswell, "The Structure and Function of Communication in Society," in The Communication of Ideas, ed. Lyman Bryson (New York: Harper & Bros., 1948), 37–51.

46. Cf. Lotan et al., 2011.

47. Bibi Van der Zee, "Twitter Triumphs," Index on Censorship 38, no. 4 (November 1, 2009): 97.

48. Leah A. Lievrouw, "Oppositional and Activist New Media: Remediation, Reconfiguration, Participation," in PDC 06 Proceedings of the Ninth

Conference on Participatory Design Expanding Boundaries in Design Volume 1, 115–124, 2006.

49. E.g., Alicia Qi, Alicia Tan Min, "Shut up and Sit down: Singapore's Social Movements through Twitter," Flow.tv 9, no. 14 (2009), last modified July 1, 2013, http://flowtv.org/2009/05/shut-up-and-sit-down-singapore's-social-movements-through-twitter-alicia-tan-min-qi-national-university-of-singapore.

50. Evgeny Morozov, "Technology's Dubious Role in Thailand's Protests," Foreign Policy Net.Effect (2009), last modified July 1, 2013, http://neteffect.foreignpolicy.com/posts/2009/04/17/technologys_dubious_role_in_thailands_protests.

51. Meredith Ringel Morris, Scott Counts, Asta Roseway, Aaron Hoff, and Julia Schwarz, "Tweeting Is Believing? Understanding Microblog Credibility Perceptions," in Proceedings of the ACM 2012 Conference on Computer-Supported Collective Work, 441–450. ACM, 2012.

52. Daniele Quercia, Jonathan Ellis, Licia Capra, and Jon Crowcroft, "In the Mood for Being Influential on Twitter," 2011 IEEE Third Intl Conference on Privacy Security Risk and Trust and 2011 IEEE Third Intl Conference on Social Computing, Section VI (2011): 307.

53. Carlos Castillo, Marcelo Mendoza, and Barbara Poblete, "Information Credibility on Twitter," in Proceedings of the 20th International Conference on the World Wide Web, 675–684, Hyderabad, India, 2011.

REFERENCES

Bajpai, Kartikeya, and Anuj Jaiswal. "A Framework for Analyzing Collective Action Events on Twitter." In *Proceedings of the 8th International ISCRAM Conference*. Lisbon, Portugal, 2011.

Bakshy, Eytan, Jake M. Hofman, Winter A. Mason, and Duncan J. Watts. "Everyone's an Influencer: Quantifying Influence on Twitter Categories and Subject Descriptors." In *Proceedings of the Fourth ACM Conference on Web Search and Data Mining*, 65–74, 2011.

Bennett, W. Lance. "Communicating Global Activism: Strengths and Vulnerabilities of Networked Politics." *Information Communication Society* 6, no. 2 (2003): 143–168.

Bigonha, Carolina, Thiago N. C. Cardoso, Mirella M. Moro, Virgílio A. F. Almeida, and Marcos A. Gonçalves. "Detecting Evangelists and Detractors on Twitter." In *18th Brazilian Symposium on Multimedia and the Web*, 107–114, 2010.

Bimber, Bruce, A. J. Flanagin, and Cynthia Stohl. "Reconceptualizing Collective Action in the Contemporary Media Environment." *Communication Theory* 15, no. 4 (2005): 365–388.

Braun, Joshua, and Tarleton Gillespie. "Hosting the Public Discourse, Hosting the Public." *Journalism Practice* 5, no. 4 (2011): 383–398.

Bruns, Axel, and Jean Burgess. "The Use of Twitter Hashtags in the Formation of Ad Hoc Publics." *6th European Consortium for Political Research General Conference* 64, August (2011): 1–9.

Carneiro, Herman Anthony, and Eleftherios Mylonakis. "Google Trends: A Web-based Tool for Real-time Surveillance of Disease Outbreaks." *Clinical Infectious Diseases an Official Publication of the Infectious Diseases Society of America* 49, no. 10 (2009): 1557–1564.

Carter Olson, Candi, and Brittany Duncan. "Pittsburgh's Flair for Protest II: An Oral History Interview with G20 Research and Activist and University of Pittsburgh Sociology Student Brittany Duncan. [Audio]," 2009. http://d-scholarship.pitt.edu/2782/ (accessed July 1, 2013.

Castillo, Carlos, Marcelo Mendoza, and Barbara Poblete. "Information Credibility on Twitter." In *Proceedings of the 20th International Conference on the World Wide Web*, 675–684. Hyderabad, India, 2011.

Cha, Meeyoung, Hamed Haddadi, Fabrício Benevenuto, and Krishna P. Gummadi. "Measuring User Influence in Twitter: The Million Follower Fallacy." *4th International AAAI Conference on Weblogs and Social Media (ICWSM)*, 2010.

Cleaver, Harry. "Computer-linked Social Movements and the Global Threat to Capitalism." 1999. https://webspace.utexas.edu/hcleaver/www/polnet.html (accessed July 1, 2013).

Costanza-Chock, Sasha. "Mic Check! Media Cultures and the Occupy Movement." *Social Movement Studies* 11, nos. 3–4 (2012): 375–385.

Crumley, Carole L. "Heterarchy and the Analysis of Complex Societies," edited by Robert M. Ehrenreich, Carole L Crumley, and Janet E Levy. *Archeological Papers of the American Anthropological Association* 6, no. 1 (1995): 1–5.

Danezis, George, and Richard Clayton. "Introducing Traffic Analysis." In *Digital Privacy: Theory, Technologies, and Practices*, edited by Alessandro Acquisti, Stefanos Gritzalis, Costas Lambrinoudakis, and Sabrina De Capitani di Vimercati (pp. 95–113). Boca Raton, Florida: Auerbach Publications, 2008.

Earl, Jennifer, Heather McKee Hurwitz, Analicia Mejia Mesinas, Margaret Tolan, and Ashley Arlotti. "This Protest Will Be Tweeted: Twitter and Protest Policing During the Pittsburgh G20." *Information, Communication & Society* 16, no. 4 (May 16, 2013): 459–478.

Esfandiari, Golnaz. "Misreading Tehran: The Twitter Devolution." *Foreign Policy*. 2010. www.foreignpolicy.com/articles/2010/06/07/the_twitter_revolution_that_wasnt (accessed July 1, 2013).

Galuba, Wojciech, Dipanjan Chakraborty, Karl Aberer, Zoran Despotovic, and Wolfgang Kellerer. "Outtweeting the Twitterers—Predicting Information Cascades in Microblogs." In *3rd Workshop on Online Social Networks WOSN 2010*, 2010.

Garrett, R Kelly. "Protest in an Information Society: A Review of Literature on Social Movements and New ICTs." *Information Communication Society* 9, no. 2 (2006): 202–224.

Garrido, Maria, and Alexander Halavais. "Mapping Networks of Support for the Zapatista Movement: Applying Social Network Analysis to Study Contemporary Social Movements." In *Cyberactivism: Online Activism in Theory and Practice*, edited by Martha McCaughey and Michael D. Ayers (pp. 165–184). Routledge, 2003.

Gillham, Patrick F. "Securitizing America: Strategic Incapacitation and the Policing of Protest Since the 11 September 2001 Terrorist Attacks." *Sociology Compass* 5, no. 7 (2011): 636–648.

Gitlin, Todd. *The Whole World Is Watching: Mass Media in the Making and Unmaking of the New Left*. Berkeley, California: University of California Press, 1980.

Glaser, Barney, and Anselm Strauss. *The Discovery of Grounded Theory: Strategies for Qualitative Research*. Chicago: Aldine de Gruyter, 1967.

González-Bailón, Sandra. "Online Networks and Bottom up Politics." In *Society and the Internet: How Information and Social Networks Are Changing Our Lives*, edited by William H. Dutton and Mark Graham. Oxford, UK: Oxford University Press, forthcoming.

Graves, Matt. "The 2010 World Cup: A Global Conversation." *Twitter Blog*, 2010. http://blog.twitter.com/2010/07/2010-world-cup-global-conversation.html (accessed July 1, 2013.

Gruhl, D, R Guha, David Liben-Nowell, and A Tomkins. "Information Diffusion Through Blogspace," edited by Stuart I Feldman, Mike Uretsky, Marc Najork, and Craig E Wills. *ACM SIGKDD Explorations Newsletter* 6, no. 2 (2004): 491–501.

Halavais, Alexander. "#g20 Tweets." *A Thaumaturgical Compendium*, 2009. http://alex.halavais.net/g20-tweets (accessed July 1, 2013).

———. "Structure of Twitter: Social and Technical." In *Twitter and Society*, edited by Axel Bruns, Katrin Weller, Jean Burgess, Merja Mahrt, and Cornelius Puschmann. New York: Peter Lang, forthcoming.

Juris, Jeffrey S. "The New Digital Media and Activist Networking Within Anti-Corporate Globalization Movements." *The ANNALS of the American Academy of Political and Social Science* 597, no. 1 (2005): 189–208.

Kahn, Richard, and Douglas Kellner. "New Media and Internet Activism: From the 'Battle of Seattle' to Blogging." *New Media & Society* 6, no. 1 (2004): 87–95.

King, Homay. "Antiphon: Notes on the People's Microphone." *Journal of Popular Music Studies* 24, no. 2 (2012): 238–246.

Kleinberg, Jon M. "Hubs, Authorities, and Communities." *ACM Computing Surveys* 31, no. 4es (1999): art. 5.

Kutz-Flamenbaum, Rachel V., Suzanne Staggenborg, and Brittany J. Duncan. "Media Framing of the Pittsburgh G-20 Protests." In *Research in Social Movements, Conflicts and Change*, edited by Jennifer Earl and Deana A. Rohlinger (pp. 109–138). Bingley, UK: Emerald Group Publishing, Ltd., 2012.

Kwak, Haewoon, Changhyun Lee, Hosung Park, and Sue Moon. "What Is Twitter, a Social Network or a News Media? Categories and Subject Descriptors." In *Proceedings of WWW 2010*, 112:591–600. ACM Press, 2010.

Lasswell, Harold D. "The Structure and Function of Communication in Society." In *The Communication of Ideas*, edited by Lyman Bryson (pp. 37–51). New York: Harper & Bros., 1948.

Levi, Margaret, and David Olson. "The Battles in Seattle." *Politics & Society* 28, no. 3 (2000): 309–329.

Lievrouw, Leah A. "Oppositional and Activist New Media: Remediation, Reconfiguration, Participation." In *PDC 06 Proceedings of the Ninth Conference on Participatory Design Expanding Boundaries in Design Volume 1*, 115–124, 2006.

Lotan, Gilad, Mike Ananny, Devin Gaffney, and danah boyd. "The Revolutions Were Tweeted: Information Flows During the 2011 Tunisian and Egyptian Revolutions." *International Journal of Communication* 5 (2011): 1375–1406.

Luckerson, Victor. "What the Library of Congress Plans to Do with All Your Tweets." *Time*. February 25, 2013. http://business.time.com/2013/02/25/what-the-library-of-congress-plans-to-do-with-all-your-tweets/ (accessed July 1, 2013).

Marwick, Alice E, and danah boyd. "I Tweet Honestly, I Tweet Passionately: Twitter Users, Context Collapse, and the Imagined Audience." *New Media & Society* 13, no. 1 (2010): 114–133.

McCulloch, Warren. "A Heterarchy of Values Determined by the Topology of Nervous Nets." *Bulletin of Mathematical Biology* 7, no. 2 (1945): 89–93.

Morozov, Evgeny. "Technology's Dubious Role in Thailan's Protests." *Foreign Policy Net.Effect* (2009). http://neteffect.foreignpolicy.com/posts/2009/04/17/technologys_dubious_role_in_thailands_protests (accessed July 1, 2013).Morris, Meredith Ringel, Scott Counts, Asta Roseway, Aaron Hoff, and Julia Schwarz. "Tweeting Is Believing? Understanding Microblog Credibility Perceptions." In *Proceedings of the ACM 2012 Conference on Computer-Supported Collective Work*, 441–450. ACM, 2012.

Neuendorf, Kimberly A. *The Content Analysis Guidebook*. Thousand Oaks, California: Sage Publications, 2002.

Penney, Joel, and Caroline Dads. "(Re)tweeting in the Service of Protest: Digital Composition and Circulation in the Occupy Wall Street Movement." *New Media & Society* (2013).

Poell, Thomas, and Erik Borra. "Twitter, YouTube, and Flickr as Platforms of Alternative Journalism: The Social Media Account of the 2010 Toronto G20 Protests." *Journalism* 13, no. 6 (2011): 695–713.

Qi, Alicia Tan Min. "Shut up and Sit down: Singapore's Social Movements Through Twitter." *Flow.tv* 9, no. 14 (2009). http://flowtv.org/2009/05/shut-up-and-sit-down-singapore's-social-movements-through-twitter-alicia-tan-min-qi-national-university-of-singapore (accessed July 1, 2013.Quercia, Daniele, Jonathan Ellis, Licia Capra, and Jon Crowcroft. "In the Mood for Being Influential on Twitter." *2011 IEEE Third Intl Conference on Privacy Security Risk and Trust and 2011 IEEE Third Intl Conference on Social Computing*, Section VI (2011): 307–314.

Raymond, Matt. "How Tweet It Is! Library Acquires Entire Twitter Archive." *Library of Congress Blog*, 2010. http://blogs.loc.gov/loc/2010/04/how-tweet-it-is-library-acquires-entire-twitter-archive/ (accessed July 1, 2013).

Reinhardt, Wolfgang, Martin Ebner, Günter Beham, and Cristina Costa. "How People Are Using Twitter During Conferences." In *5th EduMedia Conference*, edited by V. Hornung-Prahauser and M. Luckmann (pp. 145–156). 14: 2009.

Romero, Daniel M., Wojciech Galuba, Sitaram Asur, and Bernardo A. Huberman. "Influence and Passivity in Social Media." In *Machine Learning and Knowledge Discovery in Databases*, edited by Peter A. Flach, Tijl De Bie, and Nello Cristianini (pp. 18–33). Berlin: Springer Berlin Heidelberg, 2011.

Rucht, Dieter. "The Quadruple 'A': Media Strategies of Protest Movements Since the 1960s." In *Cyberprotest: New Media, Citizens and Social Movements*, edited by Wim Van De Donk, Brian D. Loader, Paul G. Nixon, and Dieter Rucht (pp. 25–48). New York: Routledge, 2004.

Segerberg, Alexandra, and W. Lance Bennett. "Social Media and the Organization of Collective Action: Using Twitter to Explore the Ecologies of Two Climate Change Protests." *The Communication Review* 14, no. 3 (July 2011): 197–215.

Suh, Bongwon, Lichan Hong, Peter Pirolli, and Ed H. Chi. "Want to Be Retweeted? Large Scale Analytics on Factors Impacting Retweet in Twitter Network." In *SocialCom 2010 IEEE Second International Conference on Social Computing*, edited by Ahmed K Elmagarmid and Divyakant Agrawal, 2010:177–184. IEEE, 2010.

Urbina, Ian. "Protesters Are Met by Tear Gas at G-20 Conference." *New York Times*. 2009. www.nytimes.com/2009/09/25/us/25pittsburgh.html (accessed July 1, 2013).

Van der Zee, Bibi. "Twitter Triumphs." *Index on Censorship* 38, no. 4 (November 1, 2009): 97–102.

Van Laer, Jeroen, and Peter Van Aelst. "Internet and Social Movement Action Repertoires." *Information Communication Society* 13, no. 8 (2010): 1146–1171.

Vieweg, Sarah. "The Ethics of Twitter Research." In *Revisiting Research Ethics in the Facebook Era Challenges in Emerging CSCW Research*. Association for Computing Machinery (ACM), 2010.

Williams, Evan. "Why Retweet Works the Way That It Does." *EVHEAD*, 2009. http://evhead.com/2009/11/why-retweet-works-way-it-does.html (accessed July 1, 2013).

Wu, Shaomei, Jake M. Hofman, Duncan J. Watts, and Winter A. Mason. "Who Says What to Whom on Twitter." In *Proceedings of the 20th International Conference on the World Wide Web*, 705–714. ACM Press, 2011.

Ye, Shaozhi, and S. Felix Wu. "Measuring Message Propagation and Social Influence on Twitter.com." In *Social Informatics: Second International Conference*, 6430:216–231. Laxenburg, Austria, 2010.

Zarella, Dan. "Science of ReTweets." 2009. http://danzarrella.com/the-science-of-retweets-report.html (accessed 1 July 2013).

7 From Crisis Pregnancy Centers to Teenbreaks.com

Anti-abortion Activism's Use of Cloaked Websites

Jessie Daniels

The campaign to dissuade women from having abortions dates back many decades in the United States. Since the 1960s, some anti-abortion activists have used deceptive tactics to discourage and divert women who are seeking abortions, deny them service, and persuade them to carry their pregnancy to term. Primarily, these sorts of tactics have been deployed through facilities known as "Crisis Pregnancy Centers" (CPCs). More recently these brick-and-mortar facilities and the deceptive practices traditionally associated with them have been joined by online strategies that do not replace, but rather augment, the established methods. In this chapter, I examine the mutually reinforcing practices of online and offline deception used by anti-abortion activists as a way to explore central issues for cyberactivism. I argue that a key struggle for all activists in the digital era is one over "facts." Ultimately, such battles are about *epistemology*, or *how* we know what we say we know. In this political struggle over how we come to know and agree upon facts, those who create cloaked sites rely on the limitations of current, narrow formulations of Internet literacy that contribute the ability to persuade through deception. I conclude the chapter by pointing the way forward to a critically engaged praxis that combines Internet literacy with a critical consciousness of power.

Activism around the issue of abortion has been a flashpoint of the culture wars in post-civil rights era United States (Ginsberg 1998; Luker 1985). Whereas the popular discussion of abortion in the 19th century appeared uncontroversial as the emerging medical profession claimed specialized knowledge about gestation and termination, the late 20th- and early 21st-century struggle over abortion has been rancorous, violent, and sometimes deadly. It is commonplace for anti-abortion protesters to confront women with pictures of bloody fetuses as they try to access abortion services, and some radical anti-abortion activists have assassinated abortion providers, such as Dr. Tiller (Hopkins 2009). As Luker argues, this shift in the place that abortion occupies in the political landscape reflects the way it has become a proxy for the place and meaning of motherhood with women on either side clearly drawn from "two different views of motherhood [that] represent in turn two very different kinds of social worlds" (1985, 193).

The reality of the current popular Internet is that search engines, web addresses (URLs), and graphic user interfaces (GUIs) represent a new kind of battleground over ideas and politics. For example, a candidate running for office today may be the target of a "Google Bomb"—a clever way of using a search engine to undermine a carefully crafted public persona, as I discuss further below. Or, when a woman who is supposedly an average mom appears in a video spot (run simultaneously on cable television and YouTube) voicing her concern about "big government interfering with her grocery shopping," she may actually be a spokesperson for the beverage industry and part of a multimillion dollar "astroturf" campaign. Or, a site that appears to be a tribute to an African American civil rights leader may actually be a "cloaked site" hosted by a white supremacist organization, such as www.martinlutherking.org. Deception is certainly not a new practice, but it plays out in new ways within the context of Internet technologies like URLs, GUIs, and Google search algorithms.

Deception is not a new strategy, certainly, in the CPC movement. Before the rise of the popular Internet, many in the CPC movement used a range of deceptive tactics in print media, in face-to-face interactions, and over the telephone. I will take up these tactics in more detail below, but for now, it is to cloaked sites which I turn, as they are effective tools anti-abortion activists are using in their cyberactivist struggle.

CLOAKED SITES

Cloaked sites are easily encountered using popular search engines, such as Google (Daniels 2009a; 2009b). Cloaked websites are published by individuals or groups who conceal authorship in order to deliberately disguise a political agenda. The use of the term "cloaked" to refer to a website appeared the first time in Ray and Marsh's 2001 article in which the authors refer to www.martinlutherking.org as a "cloaked site" (Ray and Marsh 2001). Others have used the terms "counterfeit," "hoax," and "urban legend" to refer to some of these sites (e.g., Deutsch 2004). However, such terms lack a conceptual clarity because they miss the key element of a *hidden political agenda*.

Cloaked websites are similar to previous versions of print and electronic media propaganda in which the authorship, source, or intention of a publication or broadcast is obscured (Cull, Culbert, and Welch 2003; Jowett and O'Donnell 2006). In a study of revolutionary and counterrevolutionary electronic communication using radio, the authors (Soley and Nichols 1986) distinguish between these three types of propaganda: 1) "white" propaganda in which stations openly identify themselves (e.g., *Radio Free Europe*), 2) "grey" propaganda in which stations are purportedly operated by dissident groups within a country although actually they might be located in another nation (e.g., the supposedly anti-Castro *La Voz del CID* [Frederick 1986]), and 3) "black" propaganda stations that transmit broadcasts by one side disguised as broadcasts by another (e.g., the "*Lord Haw-Haw*" broadcasts of the "English voice of Nazi Germany," [Doherty 1994]).[1] Websites like radio broadcasts or printed media can be used to advance the goals of propagandists;[2] and, as with "black" and "grey" propaganda, cloaked websites are rendered more effective precisely because they conceal their intention (Stauber, Rampton, and St. John 1996). There has been a good deal of attention to the use of the Internet to advance clearly declared political agendas by easily identifiable authors from marginalized subcultures (Kahn and Kellner 2003, 2004). Generally, scholars have seen this as a good thing because of the participatory aspect in the face of large, corporate monopolies controlling media (Kahn and Kellner 2003, 2004; Langman 2005; Jenkins et al. 2006); yet, relatively little has been written about websites that intentionally conceal, disguise, or obfuscate their authorship in order to advance a political agenda (Daniels 2009a; 2009b). Cloaked websites are not the exclusive purview of white supremacists; such sites disguise any number of political agendas. In order to expand on this point about the range of agendas that can be hidden through cloaked sites, in the section that follows, I explore a number of examples of cloaked websites representing a range of political perspectives.

Perhaps the most widely known example of a cloaked site is that of www.GWBush.com,[3] which was set up in the early days of Bush's first presidential campaign. The activist group behind this project, known collectively as ®™ark, in collaboration with two other activists known as The Yes Men, have views that would be considered far left-wing on the American political landscape. ®™ark is primarily interested in drawing attention to the system of corporate power and challenging the legal convention in the United States of corporate personhood; The Yes Men are anti-globalization activists (Meikle 2002, 114–115).[4] This cloaked www.GWBush.com site was very effective in getting attention and fooling web users, in part because of the clever use of a domain name similar to the official campaign's URL, which was www.GeorgeWBush.com, and in part because it used the same graphics as the official site. In the days after its initial launch, a number of reporters were taken in by the site and phoned the Bush campaign to ask for clarification on policy issues (Meikle 2002, 116). Bush and his campaign advisors strenuously objected to the site, going so far as to issue a cease-and-desist letter to its creators and file a complaint with the Federal Election Committee (Meikle 2002, 116–118). It was in response to this cloaked site that George W. Bush twice remarked "there ought to be limits to freedom" (Meikle 2002, 118). Whereas www.GWBush.com was referred to in mainstream press accounts as a "spoof" or "hoax" (and even by the creators as "parody"), I argue that these terms elide the pointed political message that motivated the creation of the site. For example, the www.GWBush.com site intentionally concealed the authorship at first, and it was very difficult for many, even quite skilled web users, to discern that ®™ark was behind the site. The political agenda of the site was also not clear at first. The apparent disconnect between George Bush's well-known conservatism and the language on the cloaked site about "corporate responsibility" had reporters calling the official Bush campaign site for comment about their new policy positions (Meikle 2002, 118). In this instance, once the authorship of ®™*ark* was revealed, the political agenda of the cloaked site became clearer. This was a strategy by a left-leaning group, but there is a range of political agendas disguised by cloaked sites.

Far-right racist groups and individuals also design cloaked sites. Perhaps the most pernicious cloaked site is one that is intended to disguise a far-right, racist political agenda is the aforementioned www.martinlutherking. org site, hosted by the white supremacist portal Stormfront, which is run by Don Black (Daniels 2009a). This site was one of the earliest ones on the web, and has been maintained continuously since it first appeared in the late 1990s. And, in 2007, an anonymous and clever Internet user known as "Bleachboy" registered the domain name "cnnheadlienews.com." Even with the misspelled "lie" (rather than "line"), many people were taken in by the cloaked site, when it posted a deceptive looking article claiming, "*Radical Hispanic separatist organization MEChA (Movimiento Estudiantil Chicano de Aztlan) is taking responsibility for setting the wildfires in California, confirmed Governor Arnold Schwarzenegger.*" Although quickly discredited by journalists, the piece was repeated as true throughout the conservative, anti-immigration blogosphere.

The fact that people believe the misstatements, half-truths, and lies on cloaked sites highlights the unique epistemological challenge of activist websites in the digital era. Before the Internet, we relied on a system of gatekeepers such as editors, publishers, broadcasters, and librarians, all of whom mediated information for knowledge seekers. The rise of the popular Internet has not eliminated these gatekeepers, but it has opened a new venue for a kind of publishing that is not mediated by any sort of vetting process. Mostly, this opens new opportunities for a wider range of ideas to be shared by a broader array of groups and individuals; and, at the same time, it raises some disturbing questions about how we acquire and verify knowledge. In particular, the deceptive strategies of cloaked sites are even more disturbing when considered in light of cognitive research on how people remember (or misremember) facts. Researchers found that false claims, if repeated, are remembered as true (Skurnik, Yoon, Park, and Schwarz 2005). This is especially vexing in the case of cloaked sites that purport to offer scientific information about reproductive health.

DECEPTION AS ANTI-ABORTION CYBERACTIVIST STRATEGY

Cloaked websites can also conceal hidden political agendas connected to reproductive health and the volatile area of abortion politics, as does "Teen Breaks" (www.teenbreaks.com), which first appeared online in 2005.

The two main elements of cloaked sites, concealing authorship and a hidden political agenda, are both evident at this site.

Concealing Authorship

It is difficult to tell who is behind Teen Breaks, and that is intentional. Unlike most sites on the web, there is no "who we are" or "about us" page on Teen Breaks. At the very bottom of the main page, in small print, the publisher is noted as the "Rosetta Foundation," but there is no link to that Foundation, nor any text describing the supposed Foundation's goals. In fact, a separate Internet search reveals that Sandra Choate Faucher is the president of the Rosetta Foundation. According to several online sources, Faucher is a long-time pro-life activist (www.wrtl.org/events/bios/SandyFaucher.aspx). Not revealing Faucher's involvement with the site is another way to conceal authorship. In terms of the Rosetta Foundation, there is little evidence that it exists as an organization beyond obfuscating the authorship of the website.

Hidden Political Agenda

To all but the most astute political observer and experienced Internet veteran, the site appears to be a legitimate source of reproductive health information. In fact, it disguises an anti-abortion political agenda. On a page called "Complications for Girls," the site quotes literature from the conservative activist group *Focus on the Family* to support the notion that there are many (and exclusively) negative physical and emotional consequences of abortion that form an alleged "post-abortion syndrome" (www.teen breaks.com/abortion/complicationsgirls.cfm). This supposed "syndrome" is not a clinically recognized medical condition with a biological etiology (Robinson et al. 2009). However, some literature has begun to point to the social and cultural stigma around abortion as harmful to those who have the procedure (Kumar, Hessini, and Mitchell 2009). Neither the *American Psychiatric Association* nor the *American Psychological Association* recognizes "post-abortion syndrome" as a diagnosable disorder. In fact, the term "post-abortion syndrome" is an especially effective rhetorical strategy of the anti-abortion movement to advance its agenda by instilling fear in women about what will happen to them if they have the procedure (Hopkins and Reicher 1997; Kelly 2012).

The powerful combination of the concealed authorship and hidden political agenda is amplified by other digital elements of Teen Breaks. The site deploys a very sophisticated use of domain name. The web address, or URL (universal resource locator), teenbreaks.com does not signal the political intentions of the site, but rather the target audience. The professional-looking design of the site, with an animated graphic of young people playing video games and sharing glimpses of each other's mobile devices across the top, also helps convey a sense of legitimacy and distract from questions of authorship. Further, the site does not employ extreme or overt movement rhetoric, either in words (e.g., "murder") or in images (e.g., bloody, aborted fetuses). This is striking given how prominent these are at so many anti-abortion actions. Instead, the tone of the language at the site is moderate and reasoned. The user interface, layout, and moderate sounding rhetoric along with the concealed authorship and hidden political agenda combine to make Teen Breaks a pernicious presence on the web.

The danger in a cloaked site of this type is that young girls or women might stumble upon the site through an Internet search for reliable reproductive health information. At the very least, the site may confuse people, or, it may persuade some that "post-abortion syndrome" is a reality. This was true of the young people (ages 15–19) that I interviewed as they searched for information about civil rights and inadvertently came upon cloaked sites; most were confused by the deceptive sites (Daniels 2009a; 2009b). And, the way that I originally learned of Teen Breaks was through an undergraduate student classroom presentation. At the end of a 15-week semester on finding and assessing health information online, I assigned students to make a presentation "about any health issue" and the way it was being addressed online. One student made her presentation on "post-abortion syndrome" and used Teen Breaks as her example. This student was not an ideologue or ardent anti-abortion advocate; she was simply completing the assigned task as she understood it. When she completed her presentation, I took her and the rest of the class through a learning exercise to see if we could find who was behind the Teen Breaks site. Part of what we discovered together is that the authorship on the site itself was concealed; there was nothing on the site that discussed who had created it beyond the small print mentioning "The Rosetta Foundation." From there, we worked together as a class to find the information (described elsewhere) about Sandra Choate Faucher, a pro-life activist who runs the site. There are consequences from this sort of misinformation beyond the confusion this student experienced.

In a worst-case scenario, cloaked sites such as Teen Breaks may actually succeed at their movement goals. That is, they may convince some girls or women that they must endure an unwanted pregnancy and childbirth rather than end a pregnancy for fear of the fictitious syndrome and misdirection away from abortion services. The cloaked site Teen Breaks is in many ways a digital version of the brick-and-mortar Crisis Pregnancy Centers designed to prevent women from accessing abortion services.

CRISIS PREGNANCY CENTERS BEFORE THE INTERNET

The Crisis Pregnancy Center movement is a subculture of the larger anti-abortion movement (Kelly 2013). It began in the late 1960s and, initially at least, was largely driven by one man. Robert Pearson opened the first Crisis Pregnancy Center (CPC) in Hawaii in 1967 and continued to work on expanding the movement throughout the next decades. Whereas crisis pregnancy centers (CPCs) are typically associated with Evangelical Christian charities, such as Care Net, Heartbeat International, and the National Institute of Family and Life Advocates (Kelly 2012, 2013), the early movement began with Pearson's connection to and networks among those affiliated with the Catholic Church. In 1984, Pearson authored a 93-page printed manual, *How to Start and Operate Your Own Pro-Life Outreach Crisis Pregnancy Center*, published by his own "Pearson Foundation," which circulated widely via regular mail among anti-abortion activists and served as a catalyst for the expansion of the centers. In the manual, Pearson outlines some of the deceptive tactics that would come to characterize the tactics of many CPCs, including:

> Do not indicate you are pro-life. If she is seeking an abortion and indicates she won't come in because she knows we are pro-life, assure her we can still help her by giving her all the information on abortion.

And, these notes about interior décor:

> Make sure your decor does not expose your purpose.
>   Keep a few baby items hidden away in your Center, so that you are not advertising your pro-life views. But sometimes the gift of a little baby outfit before she leaves, is the very thing that will clinch the mother's decision for life.

All the instructions in the manual are geared toward one goal "to find and assist those women who might be seeking an abortion to change their mind." Throughout the 1980s and 1990s, CPCs continued to grow and gain power through the support of organizations such as Focus on the Family, the Christian Action Council (now known as Care Net), and the National Institute of Family Life Advocates.

The manual urges local operators to use "neutral advertising," to seek listings in the printed Yellow Pages telephone directory alongside abortion clinics and to adopt "dual names," one to "draw abortion-bound women" and one to attract donations from people against abortion (Gross 1987). CPCs would also use the alphabetical taxonomy of the Yellow Pages to their advantage. In the 1986 issue of the Nynex Yellow Pages, the category "Abortion Alternatives" appears before "Abortion Providers," thus positioning CPCs before abortion providers. So, for example, if a woman were to look for an abortion provider in the Manhattan yellow pages, she would first see an ad for "Pregnancy Help, Inc." Such an ad might read, "Pregnant? Need Help? Free Pregnancy Test." Although it appears that this group might perform abortions, it does not. Apart from the central misunderstanding about whether the centers perform abortions or make referrals, there are other inaccuracies. For instance, The Manhattan Pregnancy

Services (a CPC) advertisement says that it offers "accurate abortion information," yet materials presented at all the centers are filled with statistics about the dangers of abortion that have been disputed by the Centers for Disease Control (Gross 1987).

The Christian organizations that were originally behind CPCs, such as Pearson's Catholic network and the Evangelical Care Net, also funded roadside billboards. Accurate numbers about how many billboards and at what cost are difficult to come by, but these were a key strategy for the CPCs. The billboards would typically include a question in large letters, "Crisis Pregnancy?" and then a 1–800 telephone number, with a reassuring and vague, "We Can Help." The telephone number would connect callers to a 24-hour toll-free "hotline" staffed by volunteers who would direct women to a CPC in their geographic region.

As CPCs proliferated, some municipalities have tried to stop these deceptive practices by creating regulations that "Crisis Pregnancy Centers" had to clearly post their positions on abortion and contraception. The New York City Council, following in the footsteps of Baltimore and Austin, is the latest city government to take up legislation to at least force these clinics to fess up. However, such attempts at regulating these deceptive practices have been struck down by higher courts. In June 2012, the U.S. Court of Appeals for the Fourth Circuit ruled that the deceptive "Crisis Pregnancy Centers" are allowed to deceive women and that this is not against the law.

Ironically enough, as various governmental entities tried to take action against CPCs, they began to change tactics. For example, Care Net issued a statement formalizing their new commitment to the evangelical community, including "Our Commitment to Care" condemning deception (Kelly 2013). Meanwhile, the CPCs have grown well beyond their grassroots beginnings and are now thoroughly institutionalized within the political landscape in the United States. Between 2001 and 2005, CPCs received $30 million in federal funds through a variety of mechanisms (Murphy 2011). A thorough exploration of the success of the CPC movement is beyond the scope of this chapter, but the strategies and tactics of the movement before the Internet are what is most relevant here.

Before the rise of the popular Internet, the CPC movement used a variety of media strategies to deceive and misdirect "abortion seeking" women. These mostly print-based strategies included: Pearson's printed manual, the listings in the Yellow Pages and the manipulation of alphabetical taxonomy, that is, using "AA" before the names of CPCs so that they appear first in the alphabetical listings of the Yellow Pages, and billboards along busy highways, with images of a distressed woman and the words "Pregnant? In trouble? Call us, we can help." They combined these mechanisms with a 24-hour "hotline," or telephone number staffed by volunteers who would direct women to the nearest brick-and-mortar CPC, where they would be given more printed materials with "facts" that are disputed by reputable authorizes like the Centers for Disease Control. All of these are forms of media that the CPC used in variously deceptive ways to misdirect women away from abortion services in the era of the popular Internet.

Of course, not all anti-abortion activists use deceptive practices, and the deceptive practices discussed here are some of the more radical examples. It might be useful to think of CPC deception as a continuum. At the most extreme end is Pearson, but there are more moderate subcultures of the movement, such as Care Net and HBI, that engage in less egregiously deceptive practices. For example, Peggy Hartshorn, founder and president of Heartbeat International (HBI), an anti-abortion organization, objects to the association with Pearson (Hartshorn 2006). Similarly, the group Care Net's counselor training manual disavows the kind of deception that Pearson advocates (Care Net 1995).[5] Still, the strategies in both online and brick-and-mortar CPCs do work in reciprocally strengthening ways across different levels of deception.

In the Internet era, the CPC buildings that house "clinics" exist simultaneously with cloaked sites such as Teen Breaks. These two instances of the anti-abortion movement subculture—one material (the CPC buildings) the other digital (the cloaked site)—offer mutually reinforcing practices of online and offline deception as forms of activism and cyberactivism. What both these sets of practices highlight are the ways that the struggle over "facts" is integral to political struggle in the digital era.

WAYS OF KNOWING: A SITE OF CYBERACTIVIST STRUGGLE

A key struggle for cyberactivists across a range of issues is the struggle over "facts" and what are agreed-upon truths. In the digital era, activists strategize about how to change people's minds about an issue as much as how to deploy state power in their favor. In his three-volume work, *The Network Society*, first published in 1996–1998, Manuel Castells offers an analysis of social movements in the digital era, or, in his terms the Information Age. Castells takes as his case studies the feminist, environmentalist, and white supremacist movements. He writes:

> Social movements in the Information Age are essentially mobilized around cultural values. The struggle to change the codes of meaning in the institutions and practice of the society is *the essential struggle in the process of social change in the new historical context, movements to seize the power of the minds, not state power.* (Castells 1997, emphasis added)

This insight about seizing the power of minds, rather than state power, is a crucial one for understanding cyberactivism. As I have written elsewhere about the contemporary focus of the white supremacist movement online, the focus of struggle now is around changing people's minds about the history of slavery, about the civil rights movement, and about the place of racial equality in a democracy, rather than about approaching the State for a change in the legitimation of rights or a redistribution of resources.

Whereas the use of lies in political propaganda to achieve nefarious ends is neither new nor unique to digital media (Corn 2003; Conason 2003; George 1959), the emergence of cloaked websites does illustrate a central feature of the broader use of propaganda in the current political context; that is, the use of sometimes difficult-to-detect lies and baseless "facts" to further a political agenda. Indeed, a key feature of the mainstream right-wing movement's political success in the United States has been the challenge to "fact-based reality" by building a knowledge production network of counter intellectuals who produce a steady flow of manufactured "facts" that suit a conservative, faith-based agenda that includes pseudo-science like "intelligent design," "reparative therapy to cure homosexuality," and "abstinence-only" sex education. Ultimately, these are disputes about epistemology, or how we know what we say we know, and these battles are fought along the lines of political ideology rather than any notion of scientific validity.

Traditional epistemologies tied to enlightenment notions of reason and objectivity divorced from lived experience suggest that universal *Truth* is knowable. Scientists committed to such an epistemology follow strict methodological rules intended to distance themselves from the values, vested interests, and emotions generated by their race, class, gender, sexuality, or unique lived experience. Some feminists and postmodern theorists have argued that knowledge is always partial, situated, and embodied. Such an epistemology makes universal *Truth* as an impossibility because only a relational truth between *knower* and *known* is possible. Postmodern epistemologies also make claims for social justice problematic (if not impossible) because there can be no standard upon which to base such claims. There are many ways in which knowledge, distributed via the Internet, is the realization of postmodern epistemologies because of the way it opens publishing ideas without the gatekeepers of traditional publishing avenues and the ways it allows for the possibility of identity formation of "minds" without regard for identities rooted in geographically rooted selves. All ideas, and notions of expertise, are up for renegotiation in this new digital era. For social movement activists, this opens a whole new field of political struggle around meaning.

The tautological strategy of using conservative sources to substantiate conservative "facts" is a commonplace tactic of the right-wing propaganda machine in the United States. Indeed, a cottage industry of conservative think tanks, pundits, and writers churning out scientific distortions has emerged to conduct a "war on the Enlightenment" ideal of rationality (Goldberg 2006, 80–105). In an ironic twist, the mainstream right-wing has, under the guise of cultural tolerance for diverse views, engaged in a full assault on "fact-based reality" in which conservatives have created their own version of postmodern, radical deconstructionism where "truth" is no longer possible (Goldberg 2006, 102).

Critical theorists associated with the Frankfurt School such as Adorno stressed the importance of critical thinking by arguing that it is a constitutive feature of the struggle for self-emancipation and social change (Giroux 2006, 8). Whereas there is certainly room for a critique of the ways that rationality contributes to systems of domination, the hidden political agendas of cloaked websites suggest the need for a renewal in the cultivation of rationality and critical thinking.

MULTIPLE CRITICAL/MEDIA LITERACIES

Cloaked sites, and other intentionally deceptive online practices, require a new set of skills. Rather than simply offer a critique of these deceptive practices, I want to signal a way forward to a critically engaged praxis that combines Internet literacy with a critical consciousness of power relations. The presence of difficult-to-detect propaganda on the Internet makes necessary a new set of skills for deciphering such deception, what one cultural critic refers to as "crap detection" skills for the digital era (Rheingold 2012). Fortunately, there is also a whole range of new tools specifically designed to help with deciphering "crap" on the Internet.

Digital tools change frequently, so it is important to learn *how to learn* new tools. Some of these new tools include: Alexa Web (www.alexa.com/), Snopes (www.snopes.com/), and SourceWatch (www.sourcewatch.org/).

Alexa Web (www.alexa.com/) is a strong resource for finding out more about a particular website, who visits it often, and what kinds of search queries lead people to the site. So, for example, if you were to go to the site and enter teenbreaks.com into the search field and then click on the tab "Contact Information," you would learn that Sandra Choate Faucher is the main contact person, along with her mailing address and her email (scfaucher@aol.com).

Snopes proclaims itself to be "the definitive Internet reference source for urban legends, folklore, myths, rumors, and misinformation" and can sometimes be useful for debunking persistent myths about reproductive health. For example, the page on "Impregnable Defenses" counters the notion that a woman (or, a "gal") cannot get pregnant the first time she has sex (www.snopes.com/pregnant/conceive.asp).

Source Watch (www.sourcewatch.org) is an excellent resource for deciphering cloaked sites that may be used as part of a front group. For instance, whereas you might think that something called *The Independent Women's Forum* is a pro-feminist lobby, it is actually an anti-feminist organization predominately funded by conservative U.S. foundations, including the Koch brothers' Claude R. Lambe Foundation—and Source Watch would be an excellent place to discover this (www.sourcewatch.org/index.php?title=Independent_Women%27s_Forum).

These tools are a necessary but not sufficient array of tools that may enable one to decipher cloaked sites and other forms of propaganda online.

Along with these, one needs a broader set of skills, or "literacies" in order to not be duped by cloaked sites. Kellner has written extensively about the need for new, and multiple, literacies for the digital era (Kellner 1998; 2000, 2004; Kahn and Kellner 2005; Kellner and Share 2005, 2007). He offers first a critique of the way that we have come to think of "computer literacy," tied as it is to the *A Nation at Risk* report of 1983 and up to the present call for integration of technology across the curriculum and the standards-based approach of the No Child Left Behind Act of 2001 and 2004's U.S. National Educational Technology Plan. Instead, Kellner wants to re-vision education related to technology in a way that foregrounds democracy in and through multiple literacies. It is this project that I want to build on here. Multiple critical media literacies, such as learning to check suspicious websites with the tools described above, must be joined with a critical understanding of power relations. It is both of these, a fluid understanding of technologies and a grasp of power relations, that are necessary to meet the challenge of parsing propaganda and facts in the digital era.

CONCLUSION

Anti-abortion activists have augmented the legacy of deceptive practices employed through Crisis Pregnancy Centers with cloaked sites. Teen Breaks brings together key elements of cloaked sites, concealing authorship and disguising a political agenda, and deftly combines this with a slick graphic design and layout, moderate rhetoric, and a URL that reveals little about the intent of the site. These deceptive online strategies echo those of the pre-Internet Crisis Pregnancy Centers that used the printed Yellow Pages, road-side billboards, and 24-hour "hotline" to dissuade women from obtaining abortions. In the current era, these two sets of strategies—one material and analog, the other digital—are mutually reinforcing and work together to shore up misinformation, such as the notion that there is a "post-abortion syndrome" that supposedly plagues women who have the procedure.

One of the many promises of digital media is that it opens up the possibility for multiple perspectives. Understanding multiple perspectives is an important corrective to the racism, sexism, and homophobia generated by corporate-owned media outlets; and, this is a vital contribution of participatory media (Jenkins et al. 2006). However, the downside of an open web is that individuals are left to decipher vast amounts of information from an unmediated and unvetted universe of people publishing their own words. If the wonder of the open Internet is that anyone can create and publish content online, it is also simultaneously the distress, as those who intend to deceive create and publish cloaked websites. The chief danger of sites like Teen Breaks is the same as the brick-and-mortar Crisis Pregnancy Centers: that women will be denied an important health service to which they have a constitutionally protected right. Beyond that significant threat is another.

Deceptive cloaked sites like Teen Breaks also challenge what we know to be "fact" and, in so doing, undermine the epistemological foundation of social movements that would seek to guarantee a woman's right to access an abortion. And this is a very grave threat, indeed.

NOTES

1. While the crudely color-coded designations of "white" "grey" and "black" are problematic linguistic constructions for the way they reinscribe racial connotations, the distinctions drawn by these conceptualizations are useful for understanding cloaked websites.
2. "Propaganda is the deliberate, systematic attempt to shape perceptions, manipulate cognitions, and direct behavior to achieve a response that furthers the desired intent of the propagandist," Garth S. Jowett and Victoria O'Donnell, *Propaganda and Persuasion*, 4th edition (London: Sage Publications, 2006).
3. The site is no longer on the web, but the creators have a web page that chronicles the saga and offers screenshots of some earlier versions of the site, along with audio of Bush's "freedom ought to have limits" reaction. Available online at: www.rtmark.com/bush.html, last modified June 22, 2013.
4. "The Yes Men" chronicle their unique version of activism in the documentary film *The Yes Men*, (2003). Their involvement in the GWBush.com action is available online here: http://theyesmen.org/hijinks/gwbush.
5. I am indebted to Kimberly Kelly for her insights on the various subcultures of the CPC movement.

REFERENCES

Care Net. *Serving with Care and Integrity*. Lansdowne, VA: Care Net, 1995.

Castells, Manuel. *The Power of Identity, Vol. II, The Information Age: Economy, Society and Culture*. Oxford: Blackwell, 1997.

Conason, Joe. *Big lies: The Right-Wing Propaganda Machine and How It Distorts the Truth*. New York: St. Martin's Griffin, 2004.

Corn, David. "The Lies of George W." In *Bush: Mastering the Politics of Deception*. New York: Crown Publishers, 2003.

Cull, Nicholas John, David Holbrook Culbert, and David Welch. *Propaganda and Mass Persuasion: A Historical Encyclopedia, 1500 to the Present*. Santa Barbara, CA: ABC-CLIO, 2003.

Daniels, Jessie. "Cloaked Websites: Propaganda, Cyber Racism & Epistemology in the Digital Era." *New Media & Society* 11, no. 5 (August 2009a): 659–683.

Daniels, Jessie. *Cyber Racism: White Supremacy Online and the New Attack on Civil Rights*. Lanham, MD: Rowman & Littlefield, 2009b.

Deutsch, C.H. "Compressed Data; Bhopal Critics in Web Hoax Against Dow Chemical." *The New York Times*. December 9, 2002.

Doherty, Martin. "Black Propaganda by Radio: The German Concordia Broadcasts to Britain 1940–1941." *Historical Journal of Film, Radio and Television* 14, no. 2 (1994): 167–197.

Frederick, Howard H. *Cuban-American Radio Wars: Ideology in International Telecommunications*. New York: Ablex Publishing Corporation, 1986.

George, Alexander L. *Propaganda Analysis: A Study of Inferences Made from Nazi Propaganda in World War II*. Row, Peterson, 1959.

Ginsburg, Faye D. *Contested lives: The Abortion Debate in an American Community.* Berkeley, CA: University of California Press, 1998.

Giroux, Henry A. 2006. *Theory and Resistance in Education: Towards a Pedagogy for the Opposition.* Englewood Cliffs, NJ: Praeger/Greenwood.

Goldberg, Michelle. *Kingdom coming: The Rise of Christian Nationalism.* New York: W. W. Norton & Company, 2006.

Gross, Jane. "Pregnancy Centers: Anti-Abortion Role Challenged." *The New York Times.* January 23, 1987. www.nytimes.com/1987/01/23/nyregion/pregnancy-ccnters-anti-abortion-role-challenged.html (accessed July 10, 2013).

Hartshorn, Peggy. Pregnancy Help Centers: Prevention, Crisis Intervention, Healing: Putting It All Together. (2006). Heartbeat International, Inc. www.heartbeatservices.org/pdf/Putting_It_All_Together.pdf (accessed July 10, 2013).

Hopkins, Nick, and Steve Reicher. "Social Movement Rhetoric and the Social Psychology of Collective Action: A Case Study of Anti-Abortion Mobilization." *Human Relations* 50, no. 3 (1997): 261–286.

Hopkins Tanne, Janice. "US Abortion Doctor Murdered in Kansas." *BMJ* 338 (2009).[1]

Jenkins, Henry, Katie Clinton, Ravi Purushotma, Alice J. Robinson, and Margaret Weigel. "Confronting the Challenges of Participatory Culture: Media Education for the 21st Century. Chicago, IL: The John D. and Catherine T. MacArthur Foundation." Digital Media and Learning Initiative, 2006. : www.newmedialiteracies.org (accessed July 10, 2013).

Jowett, Garth S., and Victoria O'Donnell. *Propaganda & Persuasion.* Thousand Oaks, CA: Sage, 2011.

Kahn, Richard, and Douglas Kellner. "Internet Subcultures and Oppositional Politics." *The Post-Subcultures Reader* (2003): 299–314.

———. "New Media and Internet Activism: From the 'Battle of Seattle' to Blogging." *New Media & Society* 6, no. 1 (2004): 87–95.

———. "Reconstructing Technoliteracy: A Multiple Literacies Approach." *E-Learning and Digital Media* 2, no. 3 (2005): 238–251.

Kaufman, Marc. "Pregnancy Centers Found to Give False Information on Abortion." *Washington Post.* July 18, 2006: A8.

Kelly, Kimberly. "In the Name of the Mother: Renegotiating Conservative Women's Authority in the Crisis Pregnancy Center Movement." *Signs* 38, no. 1 (2012): 203–230.

———. "Evangelical Underdogs: Intrinsic Success, Organizational Solidarity and Marginalized Identities as Religious Movement Resources." Unpublished paper (2013).

Kellner, Douglas. "Multiple Literacies and Critical Pedagogy in a Multicultural Society." *Educational Theory* 48, no. 1 (1998): 103–122.

———. "New Technologies/New Literacies: Reconstructing Education for the New Millennium." *Teaching Education* 11, no. 3 (2000): 245–265.

———. "Technological Transformation, Multiple Literacies, and the Re-visioning of Education." *E-Learning and Digital Media* 1, no. 1 (2004): 9–37.

Kellner, Douglas, and Jeff Share. "Toward Critical Media Literacy: Core Concepts, Debates, Organizations, and Policy." *Discourse: Studies in the Cultural Politics of Education* 26, no. 3 (2005): 369–386.

———. "Critical Media Literacy, Democracy, and the Reconstruction of Education." *Media Literacy: A Reader* (2007): 3–23.

Kumar, Anuradha, Leila Hessini, and Ellen MH Mitchell. "Conceptualising Abortion Stigma." *Culture, Health & Sexuality* 11, no. 6 (2009): 625–639.

Langman, Lauren. "From Virtual Public Spheres to Global Justice: A Critical Theory of Internetworked Social Movements." *Sociological Theory* 23, no. 1 (2005): 42–74.

Luker, Kristin. *Abortion and the Politics of Motherhood.* Berkeley, CA: University of California Press, 1985.

Meikle, Graham. *Future Active: Media Activism and the Internet.* New York: Routledge, 2002.

Murphy, Kate. "Regulating CPCs: Consumer Protection or Affront to Free Speech?" *The Nation.* October 31, 2011.

Ray, Beverly, and George E. Marsh. 2001. "Recruitment by Extremist Groups on the Internet." *First Monday* (2). www.firstmonday.org/issues/issue6_2/ray/index. html (accessed July 10, 2013).

Rheingold, Howard. *Net Smart: How to Thrive Online.* Cambridge, MA: MIT Press, 2012.

Robinson, Gail Erlick, Nada L. Stotland, Nancy Felipe Russo, Joan A. Lang, and Mallay Occhiogrosso. "Is There an 'Abortion Trauma Syndrome'? Critiquing the Evidence." *Harvard Review of Psychiatry* 17, no. 4 (2009): 268–290.

Skurnik, Ian, Carolyn Yoon, Denise C. Park, and Norbert Schwarz. "How Warnings about False Claims Become Recommendations." *Journal of Consumer Research* 31, no. 4 (2005): 713–724.

Soley, L. C., and J. C. Nichols. 1986. *Clandestine Radio Broadcasting: A Study of Revolutionary and Counterrevolutionary Electronic Communication.* Englewood Cliffs, NJ: Praeger.

Stauber, John C., Sheldon Rampton, and Burton St. John III. "Toxic Sludge Is Good for You." *Public Relations Review* 22, no. 2 (1996): 192–193.

Yes Men Fix the World (2009). Documentary film.

8 Art Interrupting Business, Business Interrupting Art

Re(de)fining the Interface between Business and Society

Constance Kampf

Tensions between global corporations and digital artists who use business as an artistic and activist medium reveal rough edges in the interface between business and society. This interaction can be seen as a space where the interface between business and society is being challenged, with artists performing online art that raises awareness about hidden aspects of business practices. As digital artists place the spotlight on activities and business strategies that are not part of corporate plans for communicating their "transparency," they also work to reconfigure and re(de)fine this interface.

To set the scene for understanding digital activism, this chapter examines a partial history of digital artist activism focused on ®™ark and etoy, two artist collectives that were networked and cooperated on some projects in the late 1990s. The focus is on two projects and their impacts: Toywar and Vote-Auction. The chapter moves on to look at later projects from the two artist duos emerging from them—the activist group The Yes Men, emerging from ®™ark, and the actionist[1] group UBERMORGEN, which includes one of the founders of etoy.

Projects by these artist groups are examined through a lens based on dimensions of transparency.[2] These dimensions allow for a critical examination of transparency and demonstrate some inherent tensions between what is revealed and concealed in communication between business and society. This, in turn, addresses the notion of knowledge that leads to new possibilities for understanding and action.

To address power, this paper introduces a *savoir/pouvoir* connection (a "verbing" of the nouns for knowledge and power) as a concept for examining processes underlying a transformative relationship between knowledge and power in the interface between business and society. The *savoir/pouvoir* connection comes from the verb forms of the words for knowledge and power used by Foucault. As Foucault discusses the Archeology of Knowledge (1969) in an interview with Georges Chabonnier, he uses s*avoir* and *pouvoir* in discussing knowledge and power. He describes an end goal of his method of archeology as understanding transformation, thus a change is assumed.[3]

The *savoir/pouvoir* connection is based in Foucault's use of the notion of *dispositif*[4]—an understanding of context that allows for a focus on configurations of power or domination that are made up of different positions, thoughts, actions, hooks, ideas, and physical things. In the process of creation and identification of *dispositifs* of power or domination, which act as underlying forces affecting configurations of power and knowledge (Foucault 1976/1997, 13–14, 39), the available means of knowing and ability to act are (re)established. This *savoir/pouvoir* connection relates to online activism/actionism due to the enhanced affordances offered by Internet technologies, such as Gurak's characteristics of speed and reach observed in early Internet-based protests against business (1997), and the phenomenon of interaction between conventional media sources and Internet users as both consumers and content providers.[5] These factors expand the means and opportunity for building and transforming *dispositifs* which, in turn, affect opportunities to know and resulting understandings of possibilities for action.

A BRIEF (AND PARTIAL) HISTORY OF DIGITAL ARTIST ACTIVISM TOWARDS BUSINESS

Digital artist activism towards business can be seen as a reflection and extension of artists creating art that reflects, refines, and works to re(de)fine our understanding of the world around us. From the Dada artists focused on destroying the language that created war propaganda after World War I to the surrealists putting together pieces intended to provoke us into questioning our underlying assumptions about the world around us to Andy Warhol's 1962 exhibition of soup cans that presented a commercial product as art, key artists have been creating works that cause us to question interfaces between language and society, as well as business and society during the latter half of the 20th century. Lievrouw[6] describes Dada and the Situationist art led by Guy Debord in the 1950s and 1960s as being part of the roots of Internet activism. According to Hans Bernhard of UBERMORGEN,[7] the art movement most influencing his work is the Austrian Actionism movement led by Otto Mühl. In an interview from 2000, Mühl describes art as making the invisible visible.[8] This type of art offers an example of art parallel to Kenneth Burke's[9] description of "art . . . as equipments for living, that size up situations in various ways and keep with correspondingly various attitudes" because it first provokes and then focuses on revealing and questioning underlying assumptions about how the world around us works.

In the 1990s, artist collectives such as etoy and ®™ark continued the tradition of activist/actionist art intended to raise awareness and provoke, by revealing and questioning underlying assumptions at the interface of business and society. The act of revealing these assumptions can be understood as revealing a contested form of transparency—intended to cause people to question their assumptions about corporations and how they affect society. One example of this is the way ark derives their name from "registered trademark," and uses the genre of mutual funds to encourage people to invest in projects with cultural, rather than capital, yields. Thus, through the ensuing reflection, common understandings of the interface between business and society can be refined and even re(de)fined. This interface can be understood as points of interaction between business and society.

®™ark began in the 1990s and has a website dated from 2000, explaining it as a limited liability corporation focused on cultural, rather than economic, capital.[10] It collected projects submitted by others, and set up 20 different mutual funds as an early form of crowdfunding to solicit donations or work for projects with different areas of focus, such as corporate law, media, communication, etc.[11] Through this system, ®™ark supported many projects, some by other artists. The focus of ®™ark's web presence is on mobilizing widespread support for projects through soliciting donations of money and/or labor.

The founders of ®™ark are Jaques Servin and Igor Vamos, who use aliases in their work. One of the aliases, Andy Bilchbaum, is an Americanization of an alias invented by European artists UBERMORGEN as Andreas Bilchbauer, demonstrating the interconnection between the American activists and European actionists. Servin and Vamos went on to form The Yes Men duo, currently active through creating events by impersonating political and business officials and putting videos about it on the Internet. In the FAQs on their website, they describe themselves as having ". . . impersonated World Trade Organization, Dow Chemical Corporation, and Bush administration spokesmen on TV and at business conferences around the world . . . (a) in order to demonstrate some of the mechanisms that keep bad people and ideas in power, and (b) because it's absurdly fun."[12] The WTO project was funded, co-organized, and made possible by UBERMORGEN.[13] They describe their main goal as focusing attention "on the dangers of economic policies that place the rights of capital before the needs of people and the environment."[14] This can be seen as a form of culture jamming.[15] However, rather than choosing Lasn's meme and meta-meme focus, they engage in "tactical embarrassment"[16]—designed to raise the awareness by exposing powerful entities to public scrutiny. This can be seen through the way they introduce themselves on their website:[17]

> We're The Yes Men, Andy Bichlbaum and Mike Bonanno. Two guys who couldn't hold down a job until they became representatives of Exxon, Halliburton, Dow Chemical, and the US federal government.

They continue the description of The Yes Men in their FAQ section with "As The Yes Men, they use humor, truth and lunacy to bring media attention to the crimes of their unwilling employers."[18]

Recent Yes Men projects include the 2009 Balls across America project[19] in which they designed a ridiculous looking survival suit to shut out the environment. They used these balls in protests from 2006 onwards, describing them as a "gated community for one" for corporate managers to protect themselves. The suit was introduced when they impersonated Halliburton employees at a conference for catastrophic climate change in 2006. For more recent projects through the Yes Lab,[20] they teamed up in 2012 with Greenpeace to create a prank oil well drink dispenser that went out of control at an event celebrating Shell Oil's arctic drilling program.[21] They put out a video on YouTube, which later went viral with more than 843,000 hits.[22] In 2013, they teamed up with another activist group to create online exposure of the European Investment Bank for its "dodgy climate portfolio," which supported not only environmentally clean businesses, but also businesses using coal and other dirty energy sources.[23] The Yes Men and Yes Lab activism projects coordinate with other groups and address a wide range of issues. Their goal is to generate media coverage, and communicate new perspectives on organizations that are trying to stage communication and control public knowledge about their actions. These new perspectives are linked to reframing current media issues such as calling attention to arctic oil controversies, or the relationship between finance and social responsibility.

The artist collective *etoy* was founded in 1994 by a group of seven artists. They use the domain name etoy.com, and describe themselves as working not to have individual identities as artists, but rather a collective, corporate identity. Currently, their website states that they are a collective of 25 artists. This group has won prizes for their work, including the Ars Electronica prize in 1996. Their early projects included: the etoy.TANK-SYSTEM, which became a core business model for the group, and Toywar, which was the site of action for the war between etoy and eToys.com.

The etoy.TANK-SYSTEM has been expanded to include a system of bright orange shipping containers that they set up on a temporary basis at different locations around the world and document online. An example of a project using these orange shipping containers is etoy.DAY-CARE[24] in which they used orange shipping containers to set up a project to introduce children to their art, parodying the socialization of corporate advertising directed at children. In one of the film clips demonstrating the daycare program, the children are dressed in white jumpsuits with 3D barcodes on the back, representing corporate efforts to affect the identity of young children as consumers and future workers.[25] Here, the children are presented as being future workers for etoy, and future consumers of electronic art. The group is currently active, and their corporate history can be found online.[26] On this page, they use an image of fluctuations in their share value, which are addressed on the timeline as well. After a disagreement, one of the founders, Hans Bernhardt, left etoy and went on to found UBERMORGEN with his partner, lizvlx, in 1998.

UBERMORGEN is an actionist artist duo who describes themselves as sculpting in business as their medium and creating pieces designed to affect our knowledge of global business, and the interrelations between business and society. They abstain from calling themselves activists because of the political connotations of the term,[27] and see the Viennese Actionism movement led by Otto Mühl as an important influence on their work.

Two key pieces that they worked on were the "Vote-Auction" in 2000, which was supported by ®™ark, and "Google Will Eat Itself" (GWEI) from 2005–2007, supported by other independent digital artists. GWEI focused on revealing hidden information about Google's Adsense and calling their business model into question. They also created a fun, noncritical piece called "The Sounds of E-bay," which they showed in art galleries around the world, including South Africa.[28] The latter piece creates songs based on e-bay user names and allows you to download them. When I asked Hans Bernhard why they were not consistently critical in their work, his response was that they were artists first, and found it to be too much to not have lighter elements in their work as well. They create artworks online and include pieces that could fit with Lasn's culture jamming, but art and actionism, rather than activism, is more central to their purpose. They document both their work and reactions to it, particularly in the media or legal actions and communication from the corporate world, and arrange art exhibits with the documentation in galleries around the globe—including New York, Tokyo, and Paris.[29] GWEI was nominated for a Transmediale award in 2006, and has received awards from other digital artist venues as well.

The significance of these artists lies in the affordances of the Internet, which allowed a reach and capacity to literally interrupt business in the case of Toywar, arguably the most expensive art work in history[30] because it cost the company eToys.com billions of dollars and sent them into bankruptcy proceedings. This interruption can be understood as an impact of the combination of engagement and mobilization emerging from networking between digital artist activists both about and through Internet technologies.

CHALLENGING *DISPOSITIFS* OF KNOWLEDGE AND POWER

To challenge *dispositifs* of knowledge and power, an examination of power and how it relates to transparency as a form of knowledge is in order. This section begins with a discussion of power, and examines MacKenzie's (2005) notions of performative power with their limitations, then discusses how power can be approached from a transformative perspective rooted in Foucault. To examine the interface between business and society, the concept of defining an interface between business and society will be explored, followed by a description of dimensions of transparency (Kampf 2012; Kampf and Cox 2012), which offers a means of operationalizing this transformation. These concepts will be used as a basis for explaining the operationalization of a *savoir/pouvoir* connection also based in Foucault. This connection is intended to highlight processes of knowledge and practice that lay the groundwork for change in society.

POWER

In terms of power, the interface between business and society can be seen as a space where power is a dynamic force—and divergent interests are continually vying for power in the form of control for frames of reference, which, in turn, control understanding and interpretation of the options available for action. MacKenzie (2005) defines performative power as having three distinct challenges that come into conflict with each other—efficacy, efficiency, and effectiveness. These elements make up what he calls the machinic performance, situated in the field of performance theory. He describes different arrangements of these elements functioning to support interactions between organizations and their context. This could be applied either directly within organizations or to activist/actionist groups interacting in a larger sphere with corporations, as in the etoy case. He goes on to use DeLeuze and Guitttari's notion of *desiring machines* to set up distinctions between official and informal, and reproducing and resistant desiring machines. These concepts allow him to conclude that digital artist activists have a challenge in forming alliances within sociotechnical machines in order to contest them.

This *machinic* analysis is situated in a performative frame of reference, and offers a view of the etoy case addressing a set of separate levels for understanding performances interacting among each other—at the cultural, organizational and technical levels. However, machinic analysis does not foreground key elements in the process approach needed to understand the dynamic interface and possibilities for transformation in the relationships connecting business and society used in the frame of this chapter. Thus, the impacts of digital artist activist works are used as context for machinic analysis, and foregrounded as part of change processes in this analysis based on understanding the *savoir/pouvoir* connection, dimensions of transparency, and the processes (re)shaping the interface between business and society.

To move to a process approach, a different notion of power is used here, rooted in the French language used by Foucault to describe the relationship between knowledge and power.[31] This word choice used not the French nouns for these concepts (*connaissance & puissance*), but rather the French verb forms—*savoir* and *pouvoir*. These verbs can be translated into English as "to know" and "to be able." Thus, the notion of power here is rooted in people's ability to know, and their consequent ability to act. Foucault explains his work with these concepts not as his focus, but rather as part of the process of people becoming subjects in a dual sense of the word—both as having the agency and reflection to act as subjects and to be subjected to power through limits to both their ability to act and know. He sees these limits as created by institutions. And through this lens, we can understand the approaches of ®™ark, The Yes Men, UBERMORGEN, and etoy as introducing new perspectives and practices to challenge power structures by creating and practicing alternative forms of knowledge. By doing so, they enable people to act more reflexively in the interface between business and society, thus laying the groundwork for consequent shifts in the balance of power.

TRANSPARENCY AND THE *SAVIOR/POUVOIR* CONNECTION

To begin to understand notions of transparency and the *savoir/pouvoir* connection, the interface between business and society will be examined, followed by a description of dimensions of transparency (Kampf 2012; Kampf and Cox 2012). These concepts will be used as a basis for explaining the operationalization of a *savoir/pouvoir* connection based in Foucault. This connection is intended to highlight processes of knowledge and practice that lay the groundwork for change in society.

TOWARDS A DEFINITION FOR THE INTERFACE BETWEEN BUSINESS AND SOCIETY

The notion of an interface between business and society relies on connecting concepts across three key fields of scholarship—sociotechnical design, culture, and Corporate Social Responsibility (CSR). Here, we will look at selected concepts from each of the fields to build a rich notion of the interface between business and society, focusing on their synthesis as a space for artistic criticism by digital artist activists.

First, we will look at mapping the concept of sociotechnical design and user interfaces for software to a macro level. Suchman et al.'s concept of sociotechnical design in terms of the cultural production of new forms of practice offers a place to begin understanding cultural production for organizations. In turn, as wider sections of society share technologies and interfaces offered by search engines, websites, and social media, these interfaces can be seen as part of the cultural production of the macro-level interface between business and society.

From a perspective based in culture, this macro level can be described through Pold's conception of a cultural process with a "cybernetic interface." He describes the interface as follows:[32]

> The interface works in two ways, translating the machine to us and us to the machine. It renders the computer sensible, and it is the sense-organs of the computer, whereby it becomes a part of human culture. This double sensory process entails a contemporary relationship between interface and perception: Perception becomes mediated and cybernetic. However, as the interface-cultural loop in the above pointed out, this relationship is not purely techno-biological, but draws on

complex cultural processes, where culture, human-beings, organizations, societies, increasingly incorporate cybernetic behavior.

Pold's interface is cultural in nature, and affects perception. It reflects a process-based focus, in which Pold finds a natural space for artists to critically engage with society.

When we add business to the equation, we not only have this notion of cybernetic behavior affecting organizations, society, and ultimately culture from a sociotechnical perspective, but we need to add the notion of Corporate Social Responsibility (CSR), describing the interface between business and society from a corporate perspective. This perspective is based in corporate models for stakeholders, which place the corporation at the center—such as Freeman's (1984) model for managing stakeholders. Another key model underlying CSR scholarship is Carroll's CSR pyramid (1991). This model is significant because it equates the basic needs of the corporation to economic needs in the context of describing morality in business. He posits the corporation as the basic economic unit in society, and, in doing so, sets up a strategy model for CSR with economics as an assumed base. The model has been contested in Asia (Hendeberg and Lindgren 2009; Muzawir, 2011), but is generally accepted in North America and Europe. Together these two models for understanding the interface between business and society—the stakeholder management model and the CSR pyramid model—focus on business having basic needs that are economic in nature, and higher-level, less fundamental needs for ethics and philanthropy. The implications of the corporate perspective on the interface between business and society include corporations striving to manage their stakeholders. Consequently, corporations engage in the conversation about CSR to influence the frame of reference for defining and measuring it. This process can be described as (re)producing economic logics of social responsibility.

In sum, at the interface between business and society, three key processes can be understood as (1) cultural production of practice, (2) a cultural process of interface (re)design that produces new possibilities for action, and (3) a corporate process of (re)producing economic logics of social responsibility. These processes can be understood as incongruent and working at odds with one another.

DIMENSIONS OF TRANSPARENCY

Processes at the interface between business and society rely on knowledge in terms of what is commonly called transparency. However, the notion of transparency is by nature selective. This selection is rhetorical in the sense that it works to define not only the available means of persuasion in Aristotle's terms, but also of participation in the key processes at the interface of business and society. ®™ark, etoy, UBERMORGEN, and The Yes Men, as digital artist activists, work to shift transparency by challenging corporate notions of transparency rooted in economic logics of social responsibility through introducing new cultural productions of practice and (re)designing interfaces between business and society.

Ways in which these digital artist activists accomplish their (re)design of the interfaces can be seen through dimensions of transparency (Kampf 2012; Kampf and Cox 2012). The first dimension of transparency is the audience dimension. This dimension focuses on tensions between what is known and not known in order for the interface between business and society to continue functioning as a system. These tensions can be seen through the development of a reflexive audience independent of the system. Digital artist activists act as this reflexive independent audience.

The second dimension of transparency is the accountability dimension. This dimension looks at corporate staging of transparency, focusing on tensions between staging and alignment to the context, and examines ways in which corporations act to reduce diversity in perspectives as part of communicating transparently. Here digital artists act to (re)introduce diversity in perspectives.

These two dimensions of transparency—audience and accountability—offer a means of describing how and why digital artist activists work to interrupt business at the interface between business and society. They demonstrate ways in which digital artist activists operationalize transparency by acting as a reflexive, independent audience and communicating multiple perspectives at the interface of business and society. This operationalizing transparency affects subjectivity—in the dual sense laid out by Foucault (1982)—the agency gained as people becomes reflexive subjects, and the effects of being subjected to power acting on the self. This approach to subjectivity assumes a relationship between knowledge and power that will be examined as the *savoir/pouvoir* connection.

THE *SAVIOR/POUVOIR* CONNECTION

The *savoir/pouvoir* connection refers to the introduction of additional perspectives that affect possibilities for people and corporations to act in the interface between business and society, and lay the groundwork for change. Through this lens, ®™ark, The Yes Men, etoy, and UBERMORGEN can be seen as digital artist activists who introduce new perspectives to contest corporate streamlining of perspectives and (re)configure this *savoir/pouvoir* connection, laying the seeds for transformation. An example of this can be seen in project Vote-Auction by UBERMORGEN, discussed in detail later. Vote-Auction questioned whether votes in the U.S. elections were really for sale to corporate interests, created a parody site pretending to buy and sell votes, and brought the issue to the media around the world. Resulting discussions in European and worldwide media included analysis of the role of the U.S. in a post cold war society, and "awareness regarding campaign

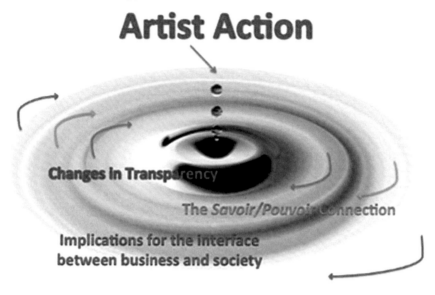

Figure 8.1   Metaphoric view of artist action as a rock thrown in the pond

financing and the impact of the middle man (advertisment agencies, consultants, brokers) on democracy in the U.S."[33] Resulting actions included legal
action to shut down websites, which led to legal discussions and changes in
Internet law about disputes related to the legal and illegal shut down of the
domains used for the project.

These three layers of analysis—from dimensions of transparency at an
operational level to the *savoir/pouvoir* connection and the resulting implications of the interface between business and society are demonstrated in
Figure 8.1. Here the artist action is pictured as making an impact like a rock
thrown in a pond. As soon as the rock makes contact with the water, the
effects of that contact ripple out over the water. Each of these constructs can
be seen as a layer of the ripples.

DIGITAL ARTIST ACTIVIST PROJECTS WITH IMPACT

To take a closer look at the interface between business and society through
the perspectives of digital artist activists, we will examine three of the projects mentioned earlier in the chapter in depth—Toywar, Vote-Auction, and
Google Will Eat Itself (GWEI). The lens used to examine these projects has
multiple perspectives built into it, beginning with (1) how each project illuminates a part of the intersection between business and society, (2) ways
in which new perspectives are operationalized and introduced through the

audience and accountability dimensions of transparency, and (3) implications for impact related to the *savoir/pouvoir* connection present in the context of each case.

TOYWAR (1999–2000)

Background

What happens when a U.S.-based online toy company worth billions of dollars (eToys.com) takes on a small collective of European digital artists (etoy.com) in cyberspace? The obvious answer would be, the billionaires win. However, in this case the artists fought back, and the company ended up filing for bankruptcy. How did this happen and what was at stake?

The case started with eToys.com customer complaints about obscenities on the etoy.com website, which they reached by mistake. The etoy.com domain was registered in 1995[34] and the artists were working to establish their own art brand since 1994, long before eToys.com existed. Thus, etoy.com was forced into interacting with eToys.com. The toy company, eToys.com, offered to purchase the etoy.com domain, but the artist collective refused because they had used the domain before eToys.com became a company, and had developed their own brand in Europe, winning a digital art prize among other points of recognition. So the toy company eToys.com resorted to legal action, and obtained a court injunction from a California court against the artist collective etoy.com, ordering them to cease and desist using their website or pay fines. This tipping of the scales towards the commercialization of the Internet created an issue for activism. So, as the digital artist collective etoy.com re-opened their website at a new domain, they called it Toywar.com. And they engaged as artist activists in an effort to attack eToys.com, as a symbol of a corporate-focused Internet. This project was described on the etoy.com site[35] as:

> the TOYWAR.com NET.ART.PRODUCT was designed in November 1999 to prevent the destruction of the etoy.ART-BRAND and to research the potential of an elaborate, effective but playful resistance system against the old fashioned corporate bulldozing power used by eToys Inc. (one of the biggest e-commerce companies in the world / incorporated 1996) who attempted unsuccessfully to take over the etoy.com art brand.

This project attracted help from digital artist activists around the world, including ®™ark. According to Hans Bernhard, ®™ark did a lot to support this fight with their network of operatives and institutions and connections.[36] These connections played a game together in which players earned points by actions that resulted in lowering eToys.com stock. According to MacKenzie (2005), one of the supporting sites, the Electronic Disturbance

Theater, a group of artist activists led by Ricardo Dominguez using technology and art to engage in civil disobedience,[37] staged a virtual sit-in from December 15–25, 1999, through which people could log into their website and participate in a denial of service attack on eToys.com. Other tactics included email campaigns to eToys.com investors, as well as the press.

In the end, eToys.com filed for bankruptcy March 7, 2001. eToys.com was eventually sold for 3.5 million dollars—significantly lower than the 8.65 billion that eToys.com was valued at the height of its stock price (Wishart and Bochsler 2003).

Illuminating a Technology Supported Power Shift at the Intersection of Business and Society

etoy.com described the outcome of Toywar[38] as:

> TOYWAR.com did not follow common political strategies: TOYWAR. com successfully mobilized the net-community (among them hundreds of journalists), involved the enemy in an insane TOYWAR situation (preventing overview by fighting on too many layers with the help of 1799 soldiers) and turned eToys' aggressions against themselves (martial arts for the net) until art finally neutralized the naive power of money. By playing a game on the web, in the court room and on the NASDAQ the etoy.CORPORATION and supporters forced eToys to step back from their aggressive intention.

Their notion of "martial arts for the net"[39] that allows art to neutralize the *naïve power* of money highlights tensions at the intersection of business and society—and calls into question the value of money versus the resources that they were able to coordinate with the purpose that eToys.com provided them by their attack on the etoy.com domain.

This project demonstrates a power shift in which power comes not from money, but knowledge and networking among artists across the world. The effects of this application of "martial arts for the net" were catastrophic for eToys.com. And, at least in this case, knowledge about technology and networking proved more powerful than money. eToys.com conceded the domain name to etoy.com with no conditions in order to end the project. One question about this type of power shift is whether this type of power shift was possible due to the surprise element—in which eToys.com did not even realize until it was too late that they were being engaged on so many different levels via technology. The other outcome is that this case can serve as an example to both business and artists that power structures are not set, but rather negotiable through creative applications of knowledge about technology and resources provided by large networks of mobilized people.

The Audience and Accountability Dimensions of Transparency in Toywar

In understanding the Toywar project, the audience and accountability dimensions of transparency can be applied to understand both eToys.com and etoy.com, showing how they engaged with transparency in different manners.

The audience dimension of transparency "can be seen as being a range of possibilities with two different endpoints—selection of audiences for optimum functionality of the system, or broadening of the audience for optimum communication" (Kampf 2012). The first side—selection of audiences, focuses on who knows, and who does not know in order to maintain the system. The second side is transformative in nature, focusing on broadening the audiences in order to enable change in the system. eToys.com was selective in their choice of audiences and focused on maintaining an offline system of power in which the money and resources of corporations dominate. When they tried to bring that system into a larger space by engaging with online domain names, they communicated with etoy.com and with the courts, but not with broader public audiences. This use of the audience dimension focuses on what the public does not know in order to maintain power. It is an example of omission rather than what Christensen called staging (2002).

In contrast, the etoy.com approach to the audience dimension of transparency was on the transformative end of the spectrum, broadening the audience to people who knew about technology and would be angry at the idea of a pre-existing domain name being taken away (or attacked) by a corporation. In their approach to the project, the Toywar game was open and available online, and the project was supported and described on other sites, such as the ®™ark site and the Electronic Disturbance Theater (MacKenzie 2005). This extended audience engaged in actions designed to transform the system of power, and shift power from the resources provided by money, formal institutions, and limited audiences to a larger set of audiences including supporters on the sites in their networks, some of whom engaged as part of the 1,799 etoy soldiers working together.

For the accountability dimension of transparency, there are also two ends to a continuum, which differ from the audience dimension of transparency. Instead of conserving the status quo and transformation, the accountability continuum has one endpoint in alignment with the context (dynamic) and the other transforming the context through strategy. The salient feature of this dimension is diversity of perspectives. In the alignment end of the scale, diversity of existing perspectives is recognized. In the transformative end of the scale, diversity of perspectives is actively reduced, and specific and often simplified perspectives are supported by corporate communication to stage transparency. eToys.com and etoy.com both act to stage transparency through their corporate communication practices. Thus, both eToys.com and etoy.com engaged in the transformative end of the scale by staging their communication and focusing on their own perspectives.

Of the two dimensions of transparency—audience and accountability—etoy.com was consistently at the transformative end of the continuum. This combination of transforming the context through enlarging the audience and narrowing the diversity of perspectives enabled etoy.com and its supporters to shift the balance of power.

The *Savoir/Pouvoir* Connection and Implications through Toywar

The *savoir/pouvoir* connection was defined earlier as the introduction of additional perspectives to counter corporate streamlining of ideas and to affect possibilities for action in the interface between business and society. In the case of Toywar, etoy.com, ®™ark, and the Electronic Disturbance Theater introduced the knowledge of ways to practice online versions of civil disobedience directed at a corporation as a means of responding to unfair legal action. Due to the success of this performance, seeds about the possibilities for networked people in contesting and questioning corporate actions with counter-actions in public forums have been laid. This encourages corporations to account for the risk of inciting online counter-actions to their choices for acting in the interface between business and society, thus affecting corporate strategy.

Implications for the Interface between Business and Society

The implications for the interface between business and society can be seen through three key processes: (1) Cultural production of practice; (2) cultural processes of interface (re)design that produces new possibilities for action, and (3) corporate processes of (re)producing economic logics of social responsibility. In the Toywar case, the cultural production of practice can be seen focused on a subculture of online activists who used their technical skills as a form of resistance to corporate power. This cultural production of practicing directed online action against a specific business can be understood as creating a temporary shift from power based in economic resources to power based in networked practices. As a result of this cultural production of practice, the resulting process of interface (re)design can be seen as raising both corporate awareness and public awareness about corporations by demonstrating economic consequences to their social actions related to cyberspace. Finally, the third process was simply not part of this case, as eToys.com did not engage in (re)producing corporate logics of social responsibility related to this case. The change in cultural practices of resistance with direct economic consequences at the interface between business and society demonstrates the dynamic notion of power in this interface and the emergent power of technology-enabled activists to contest business strategies.

VOTE-AUCTION (2000–2006)

Background

In contrast to Toywar, which was a response to a direct corporate power play towards a group of people for their domain name rights, Vote-Auction was initiated by a student, James Baumgartner, and was subsequently bought out by the artist activist duo, UBERMORGEN and a subsidiary company they set up in Bulgaria. The project ran from 2000–2006 and was UBER-MORGEN's "feature media hacking performance in the year 2000."[40] The purpose of the project was to highlight the role of business in U.S. governmental elections through satire by setting up a forum for voters to sell their votes in the U.S. election to the highest bidder. On the Vote-Auction site archive home page,[41] the title reads "Bringing Capitalism and Democracy closer together." The site was noticed by CNN, and featured in the show "Burden of Proof" on October 24, 2000. The hosts appeared to completely miss the satire in the site, and the transcript[42] of the opening dialogue reads:

> *GRETA VAN SUSTEREN, CO-HOST*: But the race for the White House between Bush and his opponent, Vice President Al Gore, could be vulnerable because of the Internet. A Web site run by an Austrian holding company has been offering to buy American votes in this November's election.
>
> *COSSACK*: www.vote-auction.com was shut down over the weekend under the order of a Cook County, Illinois judge. But Saturday night, the site resurfaced under a slightly different name, suggesting voters ask for a donation this time instead of selling their votes.

Here, they treat the satire seriously, as if they believe that votes are actually being sold on it. One feature of the site that CNN may have overlooked was the description under the category "statistics," which is described as:

> Pollsters use them, politicians use them, liars use them, and now [v]ote-auction.com is using them too. Check out some interesting statistics on the type of person who registers with voteauction.com. We at [V]ote-auction are proud to announce our web-stats: We currently receive around **150.000 unique visits per day.**

Under this link they show statistics about average sellers and buyers of votes that look official. The crowning touch was Burden of Proof's phone call to

Hans Bernhard during the show. The transcript of this part of the show highlights UBERMORGEN's key point with the piece:[43]

> *VAN SUSTEREN*: Hans, why in the world do you think it is any of your business to get involved in this American election?
>
> *BERNHARD*: Yes, we are interested in providing a forum in order to create a perfect market. That's also our slogan, bringing capitalism and democracy closer together. This is actually our task and we see this as a worldwide operation. The US election is just a test pilot for us in order to do research, in order to bring out this perfect market.
>
> *VAN SUSTEREN*: Does your Web site buy, sell, solicit, ask for donations, or use anything else in terms of getting American votes?
>
> *BERNHARD*: No, we don't do that. We are just a plain forum for campaign contributors and voters to come together for free market exchange. That's all what we do.
>
> *COSSACK*: Tell me exactly, sir, how that you attempt to accomplish this. As I understand it, prior to having your Web site taken down before, you would—if I wanted to, I could sell you my vote, and then you would take that vote and then, I suppose, turn it around and sell it to the candidate who would pay you the highest amount of money. *WHY ISN'T THAT JUST FLAT VOTER FRAUD?*
>
> *BERNHARD*: No, we don't buy or sell votes. We don't do that. We just facilitate a platform where we want to have this market done. And we see that there is a big future for this. We bring this business to business. You know, we have consultants. They cut like 10–15 percent for themselves, and they sell a vote to the campaigns.
>
> *WILLIAM WOOD, CHIEF COUNSEL, SEC. OF STATE OF CALIFORNIA*: Very briefly, what this individual has described is illegal in California. . . .
>
> *VAN SUSTEREN*: Is it a quid pro quo, though? Or how different is it from this, sort of, like, you know, you give your $1,000 campaign contribution on November sixth and November eighth you show up at your Congressman's office and say: Remember me? I'm a big contributor. I would like to talk to you about some project? How is that different?
>
> *WOOD*: Well, it's absolutely different because it's fundamentally different. The actual buying of the vote is just that. It is that simple. It is the buying of some individual's vote. One of the things in the United States that we have prized above all is the vote.

The subsequent discussion on the show then turns to explaining whether or not campaign donations are similar to the buying and selling of votes, which is one of the key points of the satire—from UBERMORGEN's perspective, it is already being done, why not open it up to the free market?

The other point that Hans is bringing out is the definition of the free market and legal structures for assigning responsibility. He abdicates responsibility by stating "We are just a plain forum for campaign contributors and voters to come together for free market exchange. That's all what we do." This clear abdication of responsibility is linked to the notion of supporting a free market, and bringing democracy and business "closer together." He uses a corporatesque public relations language to parody the concerns of the CNN hosts, who simply are unable to understand the satire. The video of this show and the legal documentation generated by Vote-Auction were used by UBERMORGEN in nine installations around the globe, in major cities including Madrid, Johannesburg, Helsinki, Barcelona, Malmo, and Graz. Hans also credits support from other artist-activists such as Kenneth Aronson of Hell.com "who forwarded their whole website to our IP for 2–3 days."[44] They also received an award of distinction from Prix Ars Electronica 2005 for the Vote-Auction piece.

Illuminating the Role of Business in Politics at the Intersection of Business and Society

The outcomes of this project included over 2,500 media pieces around the globe featuring the site, and bringing out discussion around how the voting system works with respect to business contributions and vote selling in the United States. Hans also explained that it brought out discussions about the new role of the United States in a post cold war world in the media in Austria, Germany, and Bulgaria. He explained significant impacts as including the raising of awareness regarding campaign financing and the impact of "the middle man"—advertisement agencies, consultants, brokers—on democracy in the United States. Hans also saw the sheer volume of media produced by the satire site as an example of how current media works carelessly—even at some of the most important outlets—so that information about this case was forwarded without being checked and random information was added to the story as it was released. He also estimated that the reach of Vote-Auction was approximately 500 million people.[45]

One of the most significant impacts from the artists perspective was that it showed the "weakness of the democratic system and the electoral process by seeing how much energy, money and sheer force was put into fighting the purely artistic (some might say political) platform Vote-Auction—millions of dollars were spent in legal fees, injunctions, court orders, judges salaries, clerks, Fedex/UPS (delivery fees), etc."[46]

A second significant outcome from the artists' perspective was the impact on Internet Law. During the Vote-Auction projects, two domains were taken away from UBERMORGEN—one legally and one illegally. This led to ICANN using Vote-Auction as "an example for how to create useful legislation and how to resolve domain disputes and illegal shut-downs of domains."[47]

The Audience and Accountability Dimensions of Transparency in Vote-Auction

The Vote-Auction case is clearly a case where both the audience and accountability dimensions of transparency are transformative in nature. In the audience dimension, UBERMORGEN worked to bring out discussion around vote selling and campaign contributions to a larger audience—the U.S. public. This specific target of the average voter on the Vote-Auction website was meant to get people thinking about how much their vote was worth, and the extent to which they had a voice in U.S. democracy compared to the voice of corporations.

In terms of the accountability dimension of transparency, their actions were also on the transformative end, focusing on delivering a message with a specific frame of reference supporting the exchange of votes for donations as part of a free market experiment. However, their effect was the opposite, delivering alternative voices questioning accepted paradigms for campaign financing and the corporate responsibility in supporting free markets. Thus, in terms of the accountability dimension of transparency, they used alignment both with the context and the transformational act of limiting the message to a "free market" framework, which worked to UBERMORGEN's and Vote-Auction's advantage.

The *Savoir/Pouvoir* Connection and Implications through Vote-Auction

The *savoir/pouvoir* connection in Vote-Auction focused around the introduction of additional perspectives on campaign donations and the roles of the media and free markets in U.S. elections. This notion of the voice and worth for the vote of a single consumer is set up as a counterpoint to the corporate streamlining of ideas that make recognition and donations by corporations to political campaigns seem to be necessary and the way that campaigns ought to function. This connection raised awareness of corporate practices with respect to voting donations in the United States and around the world, and affected the topics of discussion related to the U.S. elections in 2000 through media outlets. On a more concrete level of action, through the project UBERMORGEN affected the possibilities for action in the interface between business and society with respect to how domain name disputes are handled. Because UBERMORGEN used a corporate entity to own their project, the consequences to the project also become, in turn, consequences for all corporations.

Implications for the Interface between Business and Society

The implications of UBERMORGEN's project Vote-Auction for the interface between society and business is seen through all three of the key processes: (1) cultural production of practice, (2) a cultural process of interface (re)design that produces new possibilities for action, and (3) a corporate process of (re)producing economic logics of social responsibility.

The cultural production of practice, auctioning votes, that UBERMOR-GEN used was a mock process, actually (re)producing what UBERMOR-GEN explains is a history of buying and selling votes—which they support with a few examples from history beginning with George Washington buying drinks for "each of the 391 voters in his district" when he ran for a seat in the Virginia House of Burgesses, and ending with Paul Allen's purchase of the Seattle Seahawks and subsequent payment for elections costs and a four million dollar advertising campaign to build a new stadium in lieu of gathering the required signatures.[48] They engage in this process in two ways—first they create the mock process, then they use it to highlight current practices in campaign donations which they find akin to selling votes. Second, they describe their strategy as a radical corporate marketing strategy, calling into question Public Relations and marketing practices currently used by corporations. Thus, UBERMORGEN's cultural production of practice can be seen as producing the practice of satire, which exposes the mechanisms underlying the oppositions to their mock corporate stances.

The cultural process of interface re(de)sign was accomplished through the changes they inspired in policy and law for handling issues related to Internet domains. This process was also set in motion with respect to getting the media to discuss and bring to the surface corporate practices for campaign donation. Although the campaign donation process itself has not been redesigned with respect to Vote-Auction, it can be argued that the project initiated a process of interface (re)design in the sense that questions about business donations to political campaigns became a common topic for discussion in reaction to the extreme form of "vote-selling" parodied by Vote-Auction.

Finally, in terms of reproducing economic logics of corporate social responsibility, UBERMORGEN satirically reproduces the logic of facilitating an open market and lack of responsibility for ways in which people use the Vote-Auction platform on CNN. The use of satire in reproducing economic logics is intended to provoke a protesting response, which the CNN hosts of Burden of Proof do at Hans' insistence that the site does not sell or buy votes, but rather sets up the opportunity for a free market.

GOOGLE WILL EAT ITSELF (GWEI) (2005–2007)

Background

Google Will Eat Itself (GWEI) is described by UBERMORGEN as "GWEI—Google Will Eat Itself is to show-case and unveil a total monopoly of information, a weakness of the new global advertisement system and the renaissance of the 'new economic bubble'—reality is, Google is currently valued more than all Swiss Banks together (sic)."[49] The project consists of a combination of hacking Google Adsense, setting up an NGO called "Google to the People," which anyone could sign up to join during the project and using the capital generated by the performance to buy shares of Google stock, which were then donated to the NGO. UBERMORGEN earned over 405,000 U.S. dollars worth of revenue, and used it to purchase 819 shares of Google stock. On their website, they announce how long it will take at their rate of earnings from hacking Adsense to buy out Google—in this case, 202,345,117 years.[50] This project used "bots" and fake accounts to hack Google Adsense, creating clicks that were valued financially, but yet had no connection to people who might actually purchase a product. The key points emerging from the project focus both on the fragility of the Adsense model as a business model, and the point that Google is selling us, therefore the people should own Google. In addition to the online archive of the piece, complete with legal documents from Google asking them to cease and desist, as well as photos of checks from Google, UBERMORGEN also presented the piece in galleries in Paris, Toyko, Seoul, Sao Paulo, Johannesburg, Milan, and more. Their exhibitions included both the online parts of the piece, and diagrams of the hacking system, which were deliberately vague to keep Google from finding all of their fake Adsense accounts.

UBERMORGEN describes the project on their website archive[51] as follows:

> We generate money by serving Google text advertisments on a network of hidden Websites. With this money we automatically buy Google shares. We buy Google via their own advertisment! Google eats itself— but in the end "we" own it!
>
> By establishing this autocannibalistic model we deconstruct the new global advertisement mechanisms by rendering them into a surreal click-based economic model.
>
> After this process we hand over the common ownership of "our" Google Shares to the GTTP Ltd. [Google To The People Public Company] which distributes them back to the users (clickers) / public.

Here, UBERMORGEN stresses their deconstruction of global advertisement mechanisms as demonstrating the surreal ability to literally generate money out of nothing. They cause viewers to question the value of the Adsense model, as well as the assumptions about Google's worth through their sidebar on this same page, which shows the current value per share of Google and the amount of years (over 202 million years) that it would take for their system to cause Google to literally "eat itself" and become owned by the NGO "Google to the People."

Illuminating the "Google Bubble" at the Intersection of Business and Society

UBERMORGEN's outcomes with GWEI include nominations for art awards, and the attention of Google, which has seen that their Adsense system can be hacked. Although they sent a cease-and-desist letter to UBER-MORGEN, and disabled one of the fake Adsense accounts, they did not locate the others. As the project finished in 2007, it currently offers a historical perspective on Google Adsense and the surreal timeframe in which the project was able to generate a fairly large sum of money. This is in contrast to the more tangible outcomes of the Toywar and Vote-Auction projects. Although the outcomes are less tangible, the subject matter questioning the role of Google in society, as well as their business model in Adsense and their current stock value succeeds in illuminating the Google bubble as an economically fragile system.

The Audience Dimension of Transparency in GWEI

UBERMORGEN uses the audience dimension of transparency most strongly in GWEI. One of the effects of the project is to give viewers hidden information about how Google's Adsense model works. This information appears to be unknown to even Google itself. This effect can be understood in terms of UBERMORGEN's establishment of a "surreal" environment where real money is generated out without human eyes on the advertisements, leading to questions concerning the real value of the Adsense "click" model. Thus, the audience gains knowledge about Adsense and Google's inability to distinguish between sophisticated hacking and real eyes on the ads which, in turn, enables them to begin to question the system, and lays seeds for transformation.

The *Savoir/Pouvoir* Connection and Implications through GWEI

The *savoir/pouvoir* connection in GWEI is about changing our assumptions and awareness with respect to Google and other global e-corporations who are selling us as their product. With the introduction of the NGO Google to the People, GWEI calls into question issues of ownership—should a cultural resource as important as Google be privately owned or publicly held? They also call into question the value of Google stock, using the surreal number of 202,345,117 years before the GWEI project would own Google at the rate they were earning. As people begin to question the viability of current global e-business, a space for new actions opens up.

Implications of GWEI for the Interface between Business and Society

The implications of GWEI for the interface between business and society include the cultural production of practice, and suggestions for a (re) design in the interface between business and society. However, it does not connect with the process of corporate communication of social responsibility. Instead, GWEI engages in the cultural production of deconstructing global e-business. Their suggestion for a resulting (re)design at the interface between business and society focuses on ownership—asserting that since Google is really selling us, it should be the property of the people.

CONCLUSIONS

These three cases—Toywar, Vote-Auction, and GWEI—all affect the inter-section between business and society in different ways, because their activism is targeted towards business, and the artists creating these pieces use legal business structures as part of their approach to art—literally "sculpting" in the medium of business. Toywar demonstrates the shifts in power that can occur when financially wealthy entities show aggression towards networked artists focused on building wealth in terms of cultural capital. Vote-Auction demonstrates satire as a mechanism for exposing the mechanisms underlying current practices and using the media to draw attention to them. Finally, GWEI creates a surreal system of money-making that draws attention to potential weaknesses in Google's Adsense business model, as well as ques-tions of ownership related to the knowledge-based technologies that Google creates, yet which rely on work and knowledge created by everyone else.

Their effects on the interface between business and society can be seen from a perspective rooted in two dimensions of transparency—the audience and accountability dimensions. These dimensions of transparency can be used to see ways in which each project operationalizes a *savoir/pouvoir* connection that highlights opportunities for transformation and introduces new possibili-ties for action at the interface of business and society. Toywar introduced issues of power and Internet domain ownership—demonstrating that legal action can be contested by a collection of small actions spread out over a world-wide network as a form of protest. Through parody, Vote-Auction introduced issues of free speech and domain regulation, which affected Internet law, as well as discussions about the role of corporations in elections and impacts of U.S. elections on other nations in international media forums. Through the use of an NGO called "Google to the People" and hacking Adsense, GWEI introduced the notion of a "Google bubble" and questioned the Adsense busi-ness model they use. This final project raised questions about what Google is really selling, and asked why we are buying ourselves—knowledge that we produce—through Google. These questions highlight the intersection between business and society, showing how business draws on society, and could be seen as repackaging society in order to sell it back to the producers.

The combination of these three layers of analysis (dimensions of trans-parency, the *savoir/pouvoir* connection, and the interface between business and society) offers a multilayered framework for both creating and analyz-ing the processes for transformation at the interface between business and society. Due to online activism/actionism relying on the speed and reach of the Internet for effect, this multilayered framework allows for a look at online actions, networks, and modes of distribution in terms of their configurations and effects in opening up spaces for new actions that can affect the configurations of *dispositifs* of power and dominance underlying current structures of power and knowledge.

The idea for a multilayered framework for understanding and creating transformation also opens up a space for asking new questions. For example, which concepts other than transparency can operationalize a *savoir/pouvoir* connection? And, on a higher level, what do other conceptualizations of power reveal about processes of transforming the interface between business and society? Can the process of transformation of the interface between business and society be better understood through more or fewer layers of interaction? And is this transformation a necessary part of the interaction between artist activists and business, in which art interrupts business as business interrupts art?

NOTES

This project was funded in part by a grant from the Aarhus University Ideas Fund for a project together with Media Studies faculty Christian Ulrik Andersen, Soren Pold, and Geoff Cox.

1. Hans Bernhard, email message to author, July 9, 2013.
2. Constance Kampf and Geoff Cox, "Using Digital Art to Make the Tensions between Capital and Commons Transparent: Innovation in Shaping Knowledge of Internet Business Practices as a Form of Cultural Knowledge," in *Proceedings of the Cultural Attitudes Towards Technology and Communication Conference, Aarhus, Denmark* (Perth, Australia: Murdoch University Press, 2012); Constance Kampf, "Revealing the Socio-Technical Design of Global E-Businesses: A Case of Digital Artists Engaging in Radical Transparency," *International Journal of Sociotechnology and Knowledge Development* 4, no. 4 (2012), 18–31.
3. Savoir and Pouvoir can be used as both nouns and verbs in French. In the verb form, they are "to know" and "to be able." In their noun forms, they are differentiated from Connaissance and Puissance, also translated to English as knowledge and power. Connaisance can be understood as a recognized form of knowledge, whereas savoir indicates an individual's wisdom collected from a combination of connaissances across fields and their experience. Puissance can be understood as having impact on an individual level, and pouvoir as having power from the respect of others. These concepts are rich and the distinctions are not directly translatable to English. Therefore I am simplifying it to the verb forms for the purposes of focusing on the dynamics of transformation here.
4. For a discussion on the role of *dispositif* in Foucault's work, see Matti Peltonen, "From Discourse to Dispositif: Michel Foucault's Two Histories," *Historical Reflections Reflexions Historiques* 30, no. 2 (Summer 2004), 205–219.
5. For an example of how people experiencing the Tsunami in 2004 used media websites to communicate and provide content for understanding the situation, see Liza Potts, "Designing for Disaster: Social Software Use in Times of Crisis," *International Journal of Socio-Technology and Knowledge Development* 1, no. 2 (2009), 33–46. doi:104018/jskd.2009040104.
6. Leah Lievrouw, *Alternative and Activist New Media* (Cambridge UK: Polity Press, 2011) Kindle edition.

7. Hans Bernhard, email communication to the author, July 9, 2013.

8. Andrew Grossman.,"An Actionist Begins to Sing: An interview with Otto Muhl," September 4, 2002. translated by Robert Grossman, last modified November 17, 2005, www.archivesmuehl.org/filmen.html.

9. Kenneth Burke, *The Philosophy of Literary Form: Studies in Symbolic Action*, 3rd edition (Berkeley: University of California Press, 1974), 304.

10. ®™ark, "Frequently Asked Questions," last modified July 26, 2003, www.rtmark.com/faq.html.

11. ®™ark, "The Mutual Funds | New Projects," last modified May 7, 2003, www.rtmark.com/funds.html.

12. Yes Men, "Frequently Asked Questions," last modified May 15, 2013, http://theyesmen.org/faq.

13. Hans Bernhard, email communication to the author, July 9, 2013.

14. ®™ark, "The Mutual Funds | New Projects," last modified May 7, 2003, www.rtmark.com/funds.html.

15. Kalle Lasn, *Culture Jam: How to Reverse America's Suicidal Consumer Binge—And Why We Must* (New York: HarperCollins, 2000).

16. Yes Men, "The Working Tactics Poster Series," last modified May 7, 2003, www.rtmark.com/tactics.html.

17. Yes Men, "Frequently Asked Questions," last modified May 15, 2013, theyesmen.org/faq.

18. Yes Men, "Frequently Asked Questions," last modified May 31, 2013, theyesmen.org/faq.

19. Yes Men, "Balls across America," last modified May 12, 2013, theyesmen.org/hijinks/ballsacrossamerica.

20. Yes Men, "Yes Lab," last modified June 1, 2013, yeslab.org.

21. Yes Men, "Shell's Epic Party Fail, reveal date June 7, 2012," last modified June 1, 2013, yeslab.org/shellfail.

22. Logan Price, "#ShellFAIL: Private Arctic Launch Party Goes Wrong," YouTube video, last modified June 20, 2012, www.youtube.com/watch?v=NMUFci_V4mU.

23. Yes Men, "Bank's Dodgy Climate Portfolio Revealed," last modified February 28, 2013, yeslab.org/eib.

24. etoy, "etoy.DAYCARE," last modified June 1, 2013, www.etoy.com/projects/daycare/.

25. etoy, "etoy DAY-CARE trailer," last modified June 1, 2013, etoy.com/files/movies/daycare/index.html.

26. etoy, "etoy.HISTORY," last modified June 1, 2013, history.etoy.com/.

27. Hans Bernhard, communication with the author via email, July 10, 2013.

28. UBERMORGEN, "THE SOUND OF EBAY—UBERMORGEN.COM—GENERATIVE MUSIC—DOWNLOAD SONGS—SEE VISUALS," last modified May 15, 2013, www.sound-of-ebay.com/100.php.

29. UBERMORGEN, "GWEI—Google Will Eat Itself," last modified May 15, 2013, www.gwei.org/index.php

30. Søren Bro Pold, "Interface Perception the Cybernetic Mentality and Its Critics: UBERMORGEN.com," in *Interface Criticism: Aesthetics Beyond Buttons*, eds. Christian Ulrik Andersen and Søren Bro Pold (Aarhus, Denmark: Aarhus University Press, 2011).

31. Foucault, *Le sujet et le pouvoir*, volume 4 (Paris: Gallimard, D&E, 1982), last modified June 1, 2013, foucault.info/documents/foucault.power.en.html. Note that I did not translate, but worked with the source in French. I have 10 years experience with the French language and have lived in both France and Tunisia, speaking mainly French in University contexts.

32. Søren Bro Pold (2011), 109.

33. Hans Bernhard, email communication to the author, May 7, 2013.
34. etoy.CORPORATION, "etoy.HISTORY file 13-10-95," last modified July 20, 2013, history.etoy.com:9673/history/stories/entries/58/.
35. etoy.CORPORATION, "Projects Toywar 1999/2000," last modified May 12, 2013, www.etoy.com/projects/toywar/.
36. Hans Bernhard, email communication to the author, July 9, 2013.
37. Zach Blas, "On Electronic Civil Disobedience: Interview With Ricardo Dominguez," Reclamations Blog, UC Berkeley, (January 7, 2012), last modified January 12, 2012, www.reclamationsjournal.org/blog/?ha_exhibit=interview-with-ricardo-dominguez.
38. etoy.CORPORATION, "Projects Toywar 1999/2000," last modified May 12, 2013, www.etoy.com/projects/toywar/.
39. etoy.CORPORATION, "Projects Toywar 1999/2000," last modified May 12, 2013, www.etoy.com/projects/toywar/.
40. UBERMORGEN.com, "Vote-Auction," last modified 2006, www.vote-auction.net/.
41. UBERMORGEN.com, "[V]ote-Auction.com," vote-auction.net/index00.htm.
42. CNN, "CNN Transcript—Burden of Proof: Bidding for Ballots: Democracy on the Block—October 24, 2000," last modified 2001, edition.cnn.com/TRANSCRIPTS/0010/24/bp.00.html.
43. Ibid.
44. Hans Bernhard, email communication to the author, May 7, 2013.
45. Ibid.
46. Ibid.
47. Ibid.
48. UBERMORGEN, "History," vote-auction.net/history.htm.
49. UBERMORGEN, "GWEI-Google will eat itself," last modified December 11, 2005, gwei.org/pages/texts/detail.html. accessed May 12, 2013.
50. UBERMORGEN, "Google Share and how much of Google do we own?" last modified May 31, 2013, www.gwei.org/pages/google/googleshare.php.
51. UBERMORGEN, "GWEI-Google will eat itself," last modified May 31, 2013, www.gwei.org/index.php.

REFERENCES

Aristotle 'On Rhetoric': A Theory of Civic Discourse. translated by George A. Kennedy. New York/Oxford: Oxford University Press, 1991.
®™ark. Frequently Asked Questions. 2000. www.ark.com/faq.html (accessed May 15, 2013).
———. "The Mutual Funds | New Projects." www.rtmark.com/funds.html (accessed May 15, 2013).
Bernhard, Hans. Communications via email with the author, May–July, 2013.
Burke, Kenneth. Philosophy of Literary Form. Berkeley: Berkeley University Press, 1974, 293–304.
Blas, Zach. "On Electronic Civil Disobedience: Interview With Ricardo Dominguez." *Reclamations Blog.* January 7, 2012. UC Berkeley. www.reclamations journal.org/blog/?ha_exhibit (accessed July 15, 2013).
Carroll, Archie B. "The Pyramid of Corporate Social Responsibility: Toward the Moral Management of Organizational Stakeholders," *Business Horizons,* July–August 1991.
Christensen, Lars T. "Corporate communication: the challenge of transparency." *Corporate Communications: An International Journal,* 7 no. 3 (2002): 162–168.
CNN. Burden of Proof Transcript October 24, 2000. http://edition.cnn.com/TRANSCRIPTS/0010/24/bp.00.html (accessed May 17, 2013).

etoy.CORPORATION. "etoy DAY-CARE Trailer." http://etoy.com/files/movies/daycare/index.html (accessed June 1, 2013).

———. "etoy.HISTORY file 13–10–95." http://history.etoy.com:9673/history/stories/entries/58/ (accessed July 20, 2013).

———. "Projects Toywar 1999/2000." www.etoy.com/projects/toywar/ (accessed May 12, 2013).

Foucault, Michel. Michel Foucault parle de l'Archéologie du savoir, 2 mai 1969, interview de Georges Chabonnier au mic. Posted by Anthony Le Cazals, May 14, 2013 (accessed June 2, 2013).

———. Il faut défendre la société, Cours au Collège de France, 1976, edited by Mauro Bertani and Alessandro Fontana. Paris: Hautes Études des Editions du Gallimard et des Editions du Seuil, France, 1997.

———. Le sujet et le pouvoir. Paris: Gallimard, D&E Vol. 4, 1982. http://foucault.info/documents/foucault.power.en.html (accessed June 1, 2013).

———. *Beyond Structuralism and Hermeneutics*, 2nd edition, edited by Hubert L. Drefus and Paul Rabinow (pp. 208–226). Chicago, IL: The University of Chicago Press, 1983.

Freeman, R. Edward. *Strategic Management: A Stakeholder Approach*. Boston: Pitman, 1984.

Grossman, Andrew. "An Actionist Begins to Sing: An Interview with Otto Muhl." September 4, 2002. Translated by Robert Grossman. www.archivesmuehl.org/filmen.html (accessed June 15, 2013).

Gurak, Laura. *Persuasion and Privacy in Cyberspace: The Online Protests over Lotus MarketPlace and the Clipper Chip*. New Haven, CT: Yale University Press, 1997.

Hendeberg, Simon, and Fredrik Lindgren. "CSR in Indonesia: A Qualitative Study from a Managerial Perspective Regarding Views and Other Important Aspects of CSR in Indonesia." BA thesis, Högskolan Gotland, Sweden, 2009. p. 36. http://hgo.diva-portal.org/smash/get/diva2:240404/FULLTEXT01 (accessed January 15, 2013).

Kampf, Constance. "Revealing the Socio-Technical Design of Global E-Businesses: A Case of Digital Artists Engaging in Radical Transparency." *International Journal of Sociotechnology and Knowledge Development* 4, no. 4 (2012): 18–31. doi:10.4018/jskd.2012100102 (accessed July 1, 2013).

Kampf, Constance, and Geoff Cox, "Using Digital Art to make the Tensions between Capital and Commons Transparent: Innovation in Shaping Knowledge of Internet Business Practices as a Form of Cultural Knowledge." In *Proceedings of the 2012 Conference on Cultural Attitudes towards Technology and Communication, Aarhus, Denmark*. Perth, Australia: Murdoch University Press, 2012, 16–24. http://issuu.com/catac/docs/catac12_proceedings_part_1?e=?e p://issuu.com (accessed May 1, 2013).

Lasn, Kalle. *Culture Jam: How to Reverse America's Suicidal Consumer Binge—And Why We Must*. New York: HarperCollins, 2000.

Lievrouw, Leah. *Alternative and Activist New Media*. Cambridge UK: Polity Press, 2011. Kindle edition.

MacKenzie, Jon. "Hacktivism and Machinic Performance," *Performance Paradigm: A Journal of Performance and Contemporary Culture* 1 (2005). www.performanceparadigm.net/journal/issue-1/articles/hacktivism-and-machinic-performance/ (accessed May 15, 2013).

Muzawir, Mohd Rizal. Corporate Social Responsibility in the Context of Financial Services Sector in Malaysia. PhD thesis, Cardiff University, UK, 2011. http://orca.cf.ac.uk/21878/1/2011MuwazirMRPhD.pdf (accessed November 12, 2012).

Peltonen, Matti. "From Discourse to Dispositif : Michel Foucault's Two Histories." *Historical Reflections* [Reflexions Historiques] 30, no. 2 (Summer 2004): 205–219. http://hdl.handle.net/10224/4098 (accessed July 3, 2013).

Pold, Søren Bro. "Interface Perception the Cybernetic Mentality and Its Critics: UBERMORGEN.com." In *Interface Criticism: Aesthetics Beyond Buttons,* edited by Christian Ulrik Andersen and Søren Bro Pold. Aarhus, Denmark: Aarhus University Press, 2011.

Potts, Liza. "Designing for Disaster: Social Software Use in Times of Crisis." *International Journal of Socio-Technology and Knowledge Development*, 1, no. 2: 33–46. 2009, doi:10.4018/jskd.2009040104.

Price, Logan. "#ShellFAIL: Private Arctic Launch Party Goes Wrong." YouTube video. www.youtube.com/watch?v (accessed July 7, 201).

Suchman, L., J. Bloomberg, J.E. Orr, and R. Trigg. "Reconstructing Technologies as Social Practice." *American Behavioral Scientist*, 43 (1999): 392.

UBERMORGEN. "Google Share and How Much of Google Do We Own?" www.gwei.org/pages/google/googleshare.php (accessed May 31, 2013).

———. "GWEI-Google Will Eat Itself." http://gwei.org/pages/texts/detail.html (accessed May 12, 2013).

———. "History." http://vote-auction.net/history.htm (accessed May 12, 2013).

———. "Vote-Auction." www.vote-auction.net/ (accessed May 14, 2013).

———. "[V]ote-Auction.com." http://vote-auction.net/index00.htm (accessed May 14, 2013).

Wishart, Adam, and Regula Bochsler. *Leaving Reality Behind: etoy vs eToys.com & Other Battles to Control Cyberspace.* New York: HarperCollins Publishers, 2003.

The Yes Men. "Balls across America." http://theyesmen.org/hijinks/ballsacrossamerica (accessed May 12, 2013).

———. "Bank's Dodgy Climate Portfolio Revealed." (Reveal date Feb. 28, 2013.) http://yeslab.org/eib (accessed June 5, 2013).

———. "Frequently Asked Questions." http://theyesmen.org/faq (accessed May 15, 2013).

———. "Shell's Epic Party Fail." (Reveal date June 7, 2012.) http://yeslab.org/shellfail (accessed June 1, 2013).

———. "The Working Tactics Poster Series." www.rtmark.com/tactics.html (accessed July 15, 2013).

———. "Yes Lab." http://yeslab.org (accessed June 1, 2013).

9 Cyberactivism of the Radical Right in Europe and the USA
What, Who, and Why?

Manuela Caiani and Rossella Borri

In November 2012, four activists of the neo-Nazi website Stormfront.org were arrested in Italy and accused of racial discrimination and incitement to racial hatred. The *Stormfront*, considered to be "the biggest hate website" by the American media, was born in the 90s, and from its operational base in Florida, now manages 15 forums all over the world, from Portugal to New Zealand. It posts lists of Jewish families along with insults against pro-immigrant actors. In 2008 it had 80,000 visitors, which increased by 2,000 per day after the election of Barack Obama.[1] In Austria, *the Austrian Freedom Party* (FPÖ) presently claims to have around 80,000 Facebook fans, as does the *British National Party*.[2] These online supporters "are not just armchair activists: many are party members and voters and they are more likely to demonstrate than the national average."[3]

These events are not isolated, instead they are emblematic of the shift by collective actors of many of their political and social activities to the online arena. In fact, as argued by social movement scholars, the Internet offers several advantages for the mobilization of political actors including low costs, fast and efficient communication connecting isolated individuals and groups from around the world, and a good tool for the coordination and socialization that overcomes problems of leadership and helps transnationalization. The main focus is the way the Internet and the new ICTs (Information Communication Technologies) are used by civil society groups to promote, organize, and diffuse protests online, as well as the organizational and structural changes of the movements fostered by web interactivity.[4]

This is even truer for "radical" actors, who are able to use the Internet as an alternative arena in which to express their views. Indeed, as observed by Back et al.,[5] more than a decade ago in their study on neo-fascist web subcultures, the Internet "possesses the potential to offer this small, geographically dispersed movement a means to communicate, develop a sense of common purpose, and create a virtual home symbolically." This is the new face of politics and political expression, also for "the distinct" and "until now ignored" "category of online supporters of [right-wing] groups"[6] and the Internet will, therefore, increasingly become an object of interest and research for social scientists who want to understand these (new) political movements.[7]

In what ways and how frequently do right-wing organizations use the Internet for their online political activism? And *for what* specific functions? Furthermore, *who* are the right-wing groups most active in the cybersphere? And what are the *opportunities* and the *challenges* provided by new technology for these organizations?

Taking recent trends into account, we will shed light on these issues by focusing on different types of right-wing groups (political parties, political movements, subcultural youth groups)[8] in seven western democracies (Italy, Spain, France, Germany, Austria, the United Kingdom, and the United States) and using a combination of quantitative and qualitative data. We will use the information gathered from *45 interviews* with representatives of extreme right organizations from the seven countries. Employing this information, integrated with a formalized content analysis of 336 right-wing websites, we will attempt to establish the specific functions of right-wing websites for several different political purposes. We will reflect on the most significant differences and similarities in the use of the web between different types of right-wing groups characterized by different organizational resources (e.g., nature, size, budget). Although our aim is mainly exploratory, the results will be interpreted from a theoretical point of view, drawing on insights from social movement studies and the research on politics and the Internet (ICTs and CMC literature).

In what follows, after presenting our methods (second section), we shall explore the main aspects of the extreme right's cyberactivism in Europe and the U.S. in recent years (comprising the "for what," third section), as well as the opinions and viewpoints of right-wing groups on this subject. Furthermore, we will analyze the differences (degree and forms) in the use of the web relating these to the organizational features of the different types of right-wing organizations (the "who," fourth section), and reflect on the advantages and disadvantages of the Internet for them (the "why" in fifth section).

METHODS AND SOURCES

Our analysis is based on *45 semi-structured interviews* with representatives of the most relevant right-wing organizations active in the seven selected countries. In order to offer a detailed description of the cyberactivism of the entire right-wing sector on the basis of sources of different kinds (academic literature, electoral data, reports from watch dog organizations), our sampling strategy involved identifying 3–4 potential interviewees in each of the three main categories of extreme right groups (i.e., political parties, political movements, and subcultural youth groups), for a total of between 9 and 12 organizations per country. In practice, we were able to conduct a total 45 interviews.[9]

The semi-structured questionnaire, containing both closed and open questions, focused on changes in the communication and mobilization strategies of extreme right groups (actions, targets, national, and crossnational contacts, etc.) due to the advent of the Internet era, as well as ascertaining their judgment and opinions concerning the impact of the Internet on them. In the second part, questions about their group's organizational characteristics (budget, size) were asked, plus open-ended questions investigating their motives for online participation, etc., which allowed us to better interpret the answers to the closed questions.

The interview data were integrated, by means of a common research design, with a systematic web content analysis of the websites of these and other extreme right organizations in the seven countries (a total of 336 websites were analyzed). Content analysis is a research method that uses a set of procedures "to make valid inferences from text. These inferences are about the sender(s) of the message, the message itself, or the audience of the message."[10] In our analysis, we visited each website and used a formalized codebook to record data (with quantitative and qualitative variables) on specific features of the use of websites by these groups related to their political communication and mobilization (e.g., propaganda, identity formation).[11]

RIGHT-WING ACTIVISM IN CYBERSPACE: FOR WHAT (FUNCTIONS)?

Our data from the interviews indicate that today the Internet has become an essential tool for right-wing activities, both in terms of enabling mobilization and facilitating communication. Indeed, as emerges from our analysis (Fig.1), in all seven countries, the large majority of the extreme right organizations (81%, without no significant differences between the three types of groups) considers the web particularly useful ("a lot") with regard to all kinds of organizational activities, from communication, propaganda, and advertising to arranging meetings, recruitment of new members, and the diffusion of the organization's ideals, describing it as "an open window on communication with the world (. . .), we could not get along without today" (Interview [Int.] 33). In particular, 78% of interviewed groups claim that the Internet is "very" helpful in the diffusion of their ideals, values, and ideology; 94% find it helpful for the communication and the promotion of the group propaganda; and another 93% for the recruitment of new members.[12] Moreover, a large majority of the interviewees (71%) also agreed that the Internet is a very useful means for strengthening the group's identity. A smaller, but still significant portion of organizations (40%) stress that the Internet is also very important for them as a tool for mobilization (with the cyberspace functioning, as we will see later on, both as place where their activists can meet and interact, and as a useful platform for staging events such as, for instance, web conferences, e-petitions, mail-bombings, or online electoral campaigns) and for fundraising (37%).

In sum, the Internet emerges as especially relevant for far right groups, as the representative of the *Insurgent* organization explains, stressing that

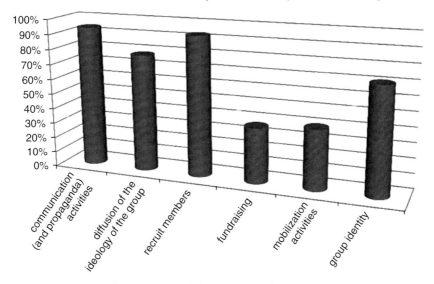

Figure 9.1 Uses of the Internet by right-wing organizations
Source: Our data from interviews with right-wing organizations (all countries: AT, DE, ES, FR, IT, UK and the U.S.), N= 45.

his network does not "operate as an organization, but as lone wolf in small cells" with the aim of "reaching like-minded people (. . .).Working on the web we do not need to have meetings like an organization, where government agencies, among others, can infiltrate" (Int. 19). As it has been observed, the Internet provides the benefit of a place, "safe" from state control and direct physical confrontations with opponents (Back et al. 1998, Ibid. p. 73).

These findings are in line with those resulting from our content analysis of right-wing websites.[13] Looking at the main functions of the use of the web by right-wing groups, we see that in fact the Internet is strongly used by them for communicating with the public (0.45 on the index), as well as for diffusing propaganda (0.34) and promoting their ideology (0.67). The use of the websites for stimulating debates and fostering the creation of a virtual community online is still present, but to a lesser extent for extreme right websites (0.16). Even less developed, according to our data, is the usage of the Internet for mobilization (either online or offline) (0.13), although there are significant signals of right-wing usage of the Internet for building a network of transnational contacts (0.22), which, as social movement literature argues, can be the base for transnational mobilization and identities.[14]

Communication, Propaganda, and Cyber Cascades

When looking at the specific web-based activities of right-wing groups, we see that—as far as communication and propaganda are concerned—more than half of the organizations publish information on their websites about the offline "reachability" (56%) of the group, such as a street address or a phone and fax number, and almost all of them (83.3%) provide an e-mail address. In addition, more than half of the organizations' websites offer a section in which they post "articles, papers and dossiers" (57.7%)[15] and a "news section" (50.6%), which contains a type of news coverage, taking information from other newspapers or TV programs. This can be considered an efficient way to set and illustrate the agenda of the group to the public of potential activists, as clarified by the representative of a German regional political movement "with the Internet, one can first of all engage in a 'larger' kind of propaganda," "reaching almost everyone you want" (e.g., Int. 12). In addition, we have to note that the possibilities opened up by the Internet go beyond written texts to also give relevance to images and audiovisual contents that exceed rationality and touch the emotional aspects of politics[16]—a possibility our analyzed extreme right organizations are totally aware of. One third of them (33%) contain on the website "symbols" referring to the fascist past (such as swastikas, eagles, or *fasci littori*, as well as eagles, wolves, lions, Celtic images, runes, Celtic crosses, etc.) or banners (26.5%) targeting particular social and/or political "enemies."[17] In this respect, many organizations often emphasize the Internet's utility as an "advertising tool" for diffusing the group's "opinions and standpoints" (Int. 04);[18] and others stress, what in communication studies is called "cyber cascades," explained by the representative of a German regional political movement as the "multiplying effect" of the Internet, in which information spreads like wildfire,[19] "since the message is not only spread via our own homepage, but also via other homepages and websites of groups linked with us (. . .). In this way, we can reproduce our ideas extremely fast and reach up to 100,000 people" (Int. 12).

On this point, it is worth noting that 14.3% of the analyzed organizations also publish an archive of the group's press releases on their websites and more than one-third (36.6%) offer bibliographical references to, broadly speaking, far right literature of any kind.[20] In fact, according to many organizations, "the Internet stands out in comparison with other advertising tools with regard to its low cost," which is a crucial aspect for these minor groups, as pointed out by the speaker of the *English Democrats*, because they are "a relatively small party, just started out, for which cheapness is important. In the U.K. the established parties spend millions of pounds in the elections, but we cannot do that" (Int. 16). Similarly, the representative of the *British Freedom Party* states that the Internet "has allowed [them] to decrease the costs to effectively communicating to thousands of members and supporters instantly via website, email, and social media" (Int. 15). Indeed the "democratic potential" of the Internet is clearly identified by some of these groups. For example, the spokesperson of the German right-wing online media, *Mupinfo*, asserts that "in principle today everybody can send their own news—if it's read or not, only depends on the request and the readers' interests" (Int. 13). Similarly another German right-wing activist emphasizes that "if you wanted to reach an unlimited number of people in the past, you would either need to be in a TV or radio station or you would have to edit a newspaper—weekly, magazine, or whatever. This means that the possibility to reach people was limited to a number of privileged people. Now, to the contrary, everybody has, at least potentially, this possibility" (Int. 14). It appears that, for the extreme right, this new form of media represents an important source of interest and discussions for politics, circulation of information and opinions, knowledge on topics of general interest and, above all, of soliciting the engagement of people.[21]

TRANSMIT GROUP IDEOLOGY

In addition to communicating with actual and potential members, the capacity of the Internet to generate new collective identities is highlighted by social movement scholars[22] who say that the web is used as an arena for the sharing of norms and values among different individuals and groups, building in this way a broader sense of community. In fact, according to our web content analysis, 74.1% of the right-wing websites have a section where they illustrate the doctrine and belief of the group (e.g., "about us," "who we are") and 60.1% of cases have a section that contains information about the goals of the group (e.g. our "mission statement," "statute," "constitution," "manifesto," "what we want").[23] On the website of the German *NPD Die Volksunion*,[24] one can read a manifesto calling for "Work, family, patria (. . .). Jobs for Germans, local oriented national economy against globalization, national democracy, healthy homeland and environment." Furthermore, many extreme right organizations stress the importance of the Internet for diffusing their ideology, for example the representative of the Italian subcultural right-wing movement *Casapound* recalls what it meant to do politics, "and especially right-wing politics," before the advent of the web:

> First of all, the Internet helps to convey our ideas and principles. Before it we had for the same purpose to organize a series of rallies throughout the country or print a book, which however allowed us to reach only a limited number of people, and often only those already interested in the matter (. . .) and who are not afraid of stigmatization (because approaching a right-wing rally can create problems). The added value of the Internet is that even those people who are simply curious, even without being sympathizers, can access a series of documents on our website (for example, our program) and get closer to our ideas. (Int. 31)

Other organizations also emphasize this empowerment role of the Internet in terms of the opportunity it gives them to find like-minded people. As some representatives of these groups explain, on the web, "people do not feel alone, because you can find whatever material, political or other, you are interested in (. . .) and, furthermore, you can find others interested in same things" (Int. 17). In this sense, the Internet is seen especially important for groups (as they often identified themselves) that do not hold mainstream ideas, "because it allows people to gain moral support from others they see as holding their views. It also allows for remote peer-pressure to help people comply with our strong ethical code of conduct" (Int. 23). Another finding of our web content analysis is the extensive use of websites by these organizations to construct their public 'image' and to publish rules or "norms of conduct" characterizing the group and the "good activist." For example, explicitly inciting violence is rare on the extreme right websites analyzed (only in 3.6% of cases), whereas more common are assertions stressing that the group is nonviolent and does not incite violence or racism, as in the case of the forum of the Austrian group *Südtiroler Freiheit*,[25] where it is stated: "The movement distances itself from every racist or extremist comment as well as from comments that offend someone's honor or endanger the youth."[26]

The transmission of ideology and propaganda (through the web) is an important aspect of collective action, and as social movement research has argued, "framing work may help to mobilize individuals and ultimately lower resource costs by retaining their emotional commitment to action" (Bennett and Sergeberg 2012, 13).

FORMING (OUR) NICHE IDENTITY

In respect to the Internet being seen as a new arena of debates, our web content analysis showed that only 10.4% of the organizations organize "online surveys" and "questionnaires" promoting a discussion among their visitors on their websites,[27] and rarer still are spaces of direct debate and chat-lines where all users can participate at the same time directly on the groups' websites (only 8%). Anyway, among the various interactive tools directly available on the organizations websites, asynchronous spaces of debate prevail over "real time" tools such as chat-lines. Forums of discussion (where any kind of issues are debated)[28] and mailing lists are indeed more prevalent (in 24.4% of cases) and they are indeed considered by most of the right-wing groups interviewed as very important. For example the representative of the organization *White Revolution* explains that "having had a discussion forum, chat, Internet newsletter, and other participatory activism online (. . .) was crucial for its organization in establishing the 'brand' and forming our niche identity within the movement at large" (Int. 18; see also Int. 20).

Most youth and local organizations are especially convinced about the positive role of web discussions for building their in-group identity, as for instance in the case of the organization *Jungen Nationaldemokraten*, where it was stressed that "due to the increased information transfer (. . .), the Internet has a crucial role to play in this context" (Int. 02, 06). In fact, in their opinion, through virtual fora "it is probably easier for members to inform their fellow men about our organization than just having a party newspaper lying around" (Int. 10) and furthermore, the "members start to feel they belong to our organization via the homepage and the topics that are discussed there" (Int. 12).

Thus, considering all this, how to explain the more limited use of the organizations websites/Internet for creating cyber-communities of debate? We could relate this result to the fact that the websites are no longer considered by right-wing organizations, along with many other collective actors (e.g., from the Left) as the best arena to promote cyber debates, and that other, more direct online platforms, such as the new social media associated with the web 2.0, are today becoming more prominent for this purpose. Indeed, according to our interview data, 76% of the organizations declare that they make use of "social networks" such as Facebook, Myspace, Twitter, Orkut, Kibop. For example, the representative of the Italian movement *Patria Nostra* stresses that "it is on Facebook that most of the online activity of the group takes place," (Int. 27) and he appears particularly enthusiastic about the effectiveness of these tools (e.g., Ints. 27, 36, 18, 15). As noted previously, the online social media for many of these groups "often dwarfs their formal membership, consisting of tens of thousands of sympathizers and supporters (. . .). This nascent, messy, and more ephemeral form of politics is becoming the norm for a younger, digital generation."[29]

Mobilization

Finally, turning to mobilization via the web, our web content analysis shows that for many of these groups, this Internet-related function often goes beyond the virtual arena and enters the sphere of real-life activism. Although only a small percentage of extreme right organizations attempt to organize protest actions (such as "e-petitions," "mail-bombings," etc.) directly on the web (5.7%), more than one quarter of them (25.6%) offer an "event calendar/agenda" of the group on their websites, which provides information on meetings, demonstrations, and concerts among activists. Moreover, another 21.1% of far right organizations publicize online their own ongoing political campaigns, as in the case of the Austrian *FPO* (www.fpoe.at/), which promotes its electoral campaign using key words such as "the social party of the homeland. Instead of Euro-billions for EU-broke-countries, our money for our people. Us for Austria, SPÖ/ÖVP for speculators & counterfeiters of financial statements"; or the case of the *British People's Party* Women's Division (www.bpp.org.uk/) protesting online against Muslim organizations and practices (against animals). Also our interviews confirm the existence of a strict relationship between the online and offline activism of right-wing groups, even though many of them declare to "favor(s) the sphere of 'real' activities and not only virtual activisms" (Int. 36). Moreover, highlighting the "amplifying effect of the Internet" for offline actions, the spokesperson of the Italian group *Movimento Nazional Popolare* explains that the Internet—and in particular YouTube—allows the public dissemination of videos of their meetings, conferences, press conferences, and also street demonstrations, for example, "the demonstration in Foggia to commemorate the fallen of the Second World War" (Int. 26). The representative of the Spanish party *Falange Autentica* describes a conference event organized by his party, which is reaching more people due to the Internet because "it is filmed and then spread through online social networks" (Int. 36). Similarly, the President of the French *Bloc Identitaire* told us that when they occupied a Quick Halal "some activists entered the restaurant wearing masks, and, because everything was filmed, the video was later released on the web" (Int. 37).

In addition, more than one quarter (26.8%) of the organizations possess a "newsletter" on their websites providing information about the possibilities for participation in upcoming offline events, as for example in the case of an Austrian political movement that explains that its organization uses the Internet for "announcing seminars, trainings, also rallies and events" (Int. 07). Similarly, a German activist stresses they use the Internet for advertising their activities, which "are mostly public appearances like demonstrations, vigils, rallies and (. . .) trainings" (Int. 14); and the spokesperson of a U.S.-based organization explains that they "send out alerts to members via automated email to keep them apprised of important action items" (Int. 23). Therefore, confirming what has been suggested by previous research, our analysis demonstrates that the Internet appears to play a significant role for right-wing groups during elections.[30] As the spokesperson of the *Jungen Nationaldemokraten*, the youth organization of the NPD party, highlights, "we create homepages for the candidates" or "use social networks—that are a much quicker way of communicating" and everyone "can always comment on the day-to-day politics" of our party (Int. 10).

These results not only suggest the potential of the Internet for (right-wing) mobilization, but also stress that with the diffusion and development of the new technologies and their social uses, the distinction between the online and offline dimensions is disappearing and "crossbreeding processes between the Net and the social and political reality are establishing".[31]

WHO PARTICIPATES IN THE WEB-SPHERE?

Social movement research has stressed that strategic choices of collective actors are influenced by their specific characteristics, including the availability of material and symbolic resources.[32] For example, it is noted that a high level of resources (financial, organizational, formal) endorsed by an organization might facilitate a more intensive use of the web[33] because running a well-organized, technically sophisticated and updated website requires money and professional skills. However, beyond material resources, symbolic and cultural ones might also play a role in facilitating or limiting the development of (online) strategies. For instance, it is said that youth organizations may be more active in their use of the web because "there is a generational migration to online political spaces,"[34] whereas political parties and in general more institutionalized and formalized organizations tend to rely more on face-to-face communication and on traditional channels of communication of the group.[35]

Considering this, we expected to find important differences in the (degree and forms of) the strategic use of the Internet among different types of extreme right organizations. Consequently, our web content analysis confirmed that the level of activism on the web varies according to the type of extreme right group (Figure 9.2).

In particular, neo-Nazi, nostalgic revisionist and cultural groups, as well as right-wing political parties, emerge as the most active on the web,[36] whereas political movements, subcultural youth groups, and right-wing nationalist organizations use online repertoires less frequently. The most limited groups in the use of the Internet are commercial and single issue organizations. This is also in line with our interviews, which show that subcultural youth groups are significantly more affected by problems accessing the web (75% of them) than political parties (17%) and movements (29%).

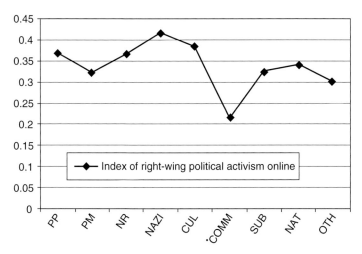

Figure 9.2 Right-wing cyber activism by different types of groups in the United States and Europe (index)
Source: Our data from web content analysis; all countries (AT, DE, ES, FR, IT, UK, and the United States), N=336; mean values are showed. Legend: PP (Political Parties), PM (Political Movements), NR (Nostalgic and Revisionist Orgs.), NAZI (neo-Nazi Orgs.), CUL (Cultural Groups), COMM (Commercial Orgs. and Publishers), SUB (Youth Subcultural Orgs.), NAT (Nationalistic and Patriotic Orgs.), OTHER (Single Issues and Not Classifiable Orgs.).

More than the intensity, it is the forms of Internet use that vary a lot according to the types of extreme right organizations interviewed. In this respect, according to our data, right-wing political parties and nostalgic and cultural movements are those most likely to use the websites to fulfill functions such as "communicating" and "informing" the public, a more traditional usage of the Internet as an additional channel to the usual political means of consensus-seeking.[37] On the other hand, subcultural youth organizations and neo-Nazi groups are those most likely to use the Internet in a more innovative way, being particularly active both in "mobilizing" through the web (but on this aspect so also are prominent political parties) and in "internationalizing" themselves.[38] As exemplified by the words of the representative of the youth organization *Gioventù Italiana*, "our values are those of a governmental Right, therefore a moderate Right characterized by social and also pro-Europe values (. . .), a right projected towards the future" (Int. 07). Furthermore, traditional right-wing organizations such as the nostalgic, revisionist, and negationist groups, as well as the cultural groups, are characterized by high levels of political activism within the new arena of the Internet, particularly concerning the promotion of virtual debate, propaganda, and ideology (together with neo-Nazi groups as regards this latter function).[39]

Here, it seems that the offline identity of the group (i.e., belonging to the same sector of the extreme right milieu) influences the preferences for specific forms cyberactivism; however, other types of offline organizational characteristics also seem to have an impact on their online behavior, as the chairman of the German political party *BGD* stresses, "the Internet does not work for itself (. . .)," instead "it is necessary to have enough resources for "the intensive working and editing on the homepage" (Int. 08).

Membership Size and Online Recruitment Practices

According to our interview data, the size of the right-wing organizations analyzed varies widely, ranging from small groups with only a few members (under 10) to up to groups of 20,000 members. In particular, it is worth mentioning that neo-Nazi and subcultural youth groups, which have also emerged from our web content analysis as the most active organizations for several of the functions, are also those, on average, with the highest number of members (with a median value of 2,400 adherents). They are followed by right-wing political parties and movements (with a median value of 900 and 700, respectively). In parallel, we also see from our web content data that many right-wing groups use their websites for recruitment activities (49.7% of cases, which increases to 78% and 59.3% in the case of youth subcultural and neo-Nazi organizations), and in particular the promotion of "multimedia materials" meant especially to attract young people. With respect to this matter, the spokesperson of an Austrian political party explains that "the young generation is very strongly focused on the Internet" and that "the reachability of this target group is therefore higher through the web" (Int. 02). Similarly the U.S. *White Revolution* group stresses that, in the case of his organization, "the website was precisely created with music and graphics and a delivery to appeal to the youth, who are more Internet-savvy and have ready access online" (Int. 18). These multimedia materials usually consist of video and music downloads characterized by political contents (such as fascist and Nazi songs,[40] as well as songs from far right bands,[41] or audio files of sermons and speeches of leaders from the Fascist past).[42] In fact, the importance of these tools to attract (young) members is clearly evident to right-wing groups, as stated by the spokesperson of the Austrian political party HPÖ, who stresses that many young people are represented in social networks and if there is an advertisement, the whole thing gets more interesting for them (Int. 04); and ". . . younger people visit our homepages because of stickers or propaganda material, which we distribute"—explained the representative of a German regional political movement (Int.12).

If the Internet is considered a useful recruitment tool for modern organizations, this holds especially true when it comes to radical groups, which often work between visible and invisible activities and, as emphasized, often are "politically isolated and socially stigmatized." The spokesperson of the Spanish party *Falange Autentica* explains that "thanks to the web, those citizens that would not approach the group through public acts, approach it instead through the Internet, in its intimacy, to read and get informed" (Int. 36). However, as with any other "digitalized" collective actors,[43] the relationship between the online–offline environments is also an issue for right-wing organizations, and in particular, how to measure, beyond its potentiality the actual Internet's efficacy in reaching out to supporters. In the words of the spokesperson of the English Democrats: "(. . .) One can send out e-mails to its members, but the fact that you sent it, doesn't mean it's read (. . .).You cannot be sure that your message gets across as if talking to a person" (Int. 16).

Financial Resources and Internet Activism

When looking at the level of financial resources of right-wing organizations in relation to their cyberactivism, our interview data show firstly, and with very few exceptions, that these groups have relatively small budgets (accounting for below 10,000 euros per year for 63% of groups) and secondly, that the subcultural youth groups who are very active on the web according to our analysis, are also the poorest ones in terms of finances. This, in part, contradicts our hypothesis that organizations that are better equipped with financial resources have a greater online presence. However it may also suggest that the groups which are scarcely endorsed with material resources in the offline sphere have to rely more on the web, in an attempt to increase the possibilities of success of their political action, creating a sort of "boomerang effect." In fact, our data from the web content analysis showed that more than one-third of right-wing groups (37.5%) use the Internet to sell some kind of merchandise. These include clothes, militaria, and souvenirs from World War II (caps, helmets, medals, weapons, uniforms, flags, T-shirts with Mussolini images, SS uniforms); books; magazines; CDs and videos; stickers, posters, and calendars;[44] and other memorabilia, which, as they stress, help in "funding organizational activities and programs" (Int. 18). The representative of the French *Front National de la Jeunesse,* for example, told us that "the e-shop of his organization, developed in occasion of the Presidential campaign, brought a significant innovation in the organization's fund raising activities" (Int. 42); and another leader of a political movement explains that his organization "receives more than 50% of the budget online" through the selling of products and donations via the homepage (Int. 05). In this respect, we found that the Internet offers many possibilities to right-wing organizations for financially supporting their group, not only through the use of websites but also via other types of social medias (e.g., see the *British freedom party*, Int. 15). Nevertheless, there are also some organizations that still prefer offline methods of fundraising (e.g., via ordinary mail), either because they think "it is a much more effective way to acquire donations," (e.g., see Ints. 08, 06) or because, as explained by the *Vanguard News Network,* they are "banned by paypal due to censorship" (Int. 17).

In sum, all this suggests a link between collective actors' values and identities offline and their approach to Internet technologies.[45]

WHY (CYBERACTIVISM)? ADVANTAGES AND DISADVANTAGES OF ONLINE POLITICS FOR RIGHT-WING ORGANIZATIONS

Some commentators are skeptical whether the online environments, due to the absence of "real people,"[46] can become substitutes for face-to-face interactions and social processes. Others are more optimistic, underlining the transformative potential of the new information and interactive technologies for civil society organizations. Some scholars have even argued that to consider new technologies only as tools of information and help in the organization of political mobilization is reductive.[47] Instead, beyond influencing the traditional logic of collective action, it should be argued that digital media could lead to a new logic of "connective action" (or "connective action networks") where communication becomes a prominent part of the organizational structure, giving birth to new types of mobilized actors based on personalized content sharing across media networks.[48]

As highlighted in the previous section, even in the case of right-wing extremists, the digital arena has undeniably facilitated communications between individuals and organizations. However, the actual extent to which the web interactivity has produced a substantial change in the political activism of these groups is still controversial. Why then do right-wing organizations use the Internet for their activities? What are the advantages and challenges of this new medium for them?

Right-wing organizations were asked about their general perceptions and evaluation of the Internet, and how they judged the impact of the new ICTs on them.[49] The analysis confirmed a broad consensus on the usefulness of the Internet, but within very different conceptions of the virtual arena, which meant very different things to various collective actors. First, our data show a duality in terms of the Internet's impact on the political activism of right-wing groups: according to 56% of the organizations, the internet has profoundly affected the way they communicate and behave; whereas for 44%, it is simply an additional tool used to present themselves to the world. More interestingly, there are no differences between countries and the various organizational types on this point.[50]

In particular, exploring the advantages of online politics for right-wing organizations, many groups focus on what the enthusiasts among social scientists indicated as the *participation* and *pluralism* impact of the web.[51] The Internet is thus perceived by these groups as having allowed an expansion of, not only the "users," but also of the producers of (political) information. This includes, in their view, an improvement in their external communication, with "ideas spread wider and faster" (Int. 19) and the opportunity for "reaching every corner of the world" (Ints. 22, 34); in other words "a wider audience than through offline actions" (Ints. 34, 35, 36). Many organizations also add that this is especially true for minor groups (like those of the radical right), and stress that today "online activities are more important than the offline ones" (Int. 34). Another point emphasized by right-wing groups regarding the advantages brought about by the ICTs is the possibility of overcoming the *"censorship"* of traditional media ("the predominately left press," Int.13), particularly in cases explained by many (especially American) organizations, where "the access to the mainstream media [is] controlled and limited by Jewish censorship." Therefore, the Internet has become an "alternative media outlet, as well as social media network and educational outreach" (e.g., Int. 20) for many right-wing groups. The *horizontal and bidirectional aspect* of the Internet is also emphasized by these groups ("to bring in more opinions from supporters," Int. 15), and in this sense the Internet is judged as being "very positive for the organizations," because "you most likely get feedbacks, as one can write comments on the articles and also written replies" (Int. 12).

Despite this positive overview, according to our findings, 60% of organizations still consider online activities to be less important than real-life activities (Figure 9.3).

Indeed, among the side effects of the Internet, many right-wing organizations emphasize the crucial step of *personal contacts* for many of their political processes, because "with pure online activities you won't reach anything in most of the cases, there always needs to be a main pillar in the reality" (e.g., Int. 14). This is especially true for right-wing political parties

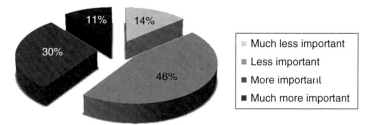

Figure 9.3   Importance of online vs. offline activities according to right wing organizations (%)
Source: Data from our interviews (N=45); all countries (AT, DE, ES, FR, IT, UK and the USA).

who emerge still strongly attached to offline politics, because according to them, "the outcome of online activities is too limited," and "you can't win an election by just being on the Internet" (e.g., Int. 16). For example, in the case of a political communication function, the chair of the German political party *BGD* explains that they hoped "to reach many people with this medium and to get a lot of reactions, but this has never happened" (Int. 08). Similarly, other organizations highlight the weakness of politics on the web, for the *selection biases* (e.g., gender, age) it introduces among the people you address. As revealed by the representative of an American organization "[we] primarily reach men" (Int. 21); "women only become members via personal contacts, because they are ideological-wise not so interested" (Int. 12). Similarly, the spokesperson of the German political party *NPD* clarifies that they "need to use other ways, because many people don't even have access to the Internet, especially people from lower classes" (Int. 09). Some organizations even declare they have had better success with "the good old letter post" (Int. 09) when trying to attract new supporters.

In addition, some organizations also emphasize the negative side to the Internet's broadening of their organization's visibility, which can "expose you to much *censorship*" as "being on the Internet also means that one is more open to the public and therefore to the attacks coming from the people" (Int. 06).[52] For example, the spokesperson of a German right-wing group complains that "despite no violation of law from his group, there are constant attempts of censorship (. . .): deletion of Facebook accounts without comments or closure of web partners by state authorities" (Int. 13) and the chairman of the Austrian political party *Die Bunten* claims that his "e-mail transfer is permanently monitored, so we are very much controlled by the state" (Int. 1). In sum, for many such groups "the Internet's safety is limited and therefore you can only use it conditionally" (Int. 09).

Similarly, the supposed benefit of achieving one-to-many communication is questioned by some right-wing organizations who point out the disadvantages for the so-called *disintermediation.*[53] In such cases, organizations might be exposed to the consequences deriving from messages by single activists, whose views are not always in line with those of the group itself, as the representative of *Nuova Destra Sociale* stresses, "the problem is that the Internet brings everything to the organizations, even crazy people that are then refused" (Int. 24).

More generally, right-wing groups are critical of the fact that online politics can *diminish political participation* instead of increase it,[54] warning that "we do not have to rely too much on the Internet, as other organizations do, by neglecting real practices" (Int. 24). Indeed in their view, although "online activities help to spur and increase real world activism (. . .), it is a two-edged sword, as sometimes Internet activism discourages and makes unnecessary real-world activism and contacts in the minds of participants" (e.g., Int. 20).

Whereas most of the interviewees believe that the Internet is an advantageous medium for carrying out their activities, some however, doubt its *actual effectiveness*. Here, the issue of the relationship between online and offline reality comes in to play. For instance, the spokesperson of a U.S. political movement emphasizes that their "goals are not easy ones as they go against entrenched and established interests. Therefore, it is hard to measure progress with so few milestones" (Int. 23). Problems arising from the actual return to using the web for their political action are perceived as crucial, especially when dealing with the (diffusion of) organization ideology. As explained by the spokesperson of the Austrian *HPÖ* party most of their ideals, which are related to the party-internal side, can only be diffused if the concerned people know each other in person (Int. 04). Similarly, there are also those organizations that question the power of the Internet in strengthening the *identity* of their group, and appear scarcely convinced of the Internet's ability in this regard. For instance, the speaker of the *NPD* party stresses that "the identity of an organization can never be strengthened or weakened by the Internet (. . .), since the "personal communication from person to person directly in a room is much more important than the web" (Int. 09). Also, the chairman of the political party *BGD* explains that the Internet is "only there to post information and say what we think and that we are here (. . .); however, it has not had any results in strengthening our identity" (Int. 08). Indeed, according to many interviewees "as for the identity, for the internal solidarity, one needs to know each other in person—the Internet is simply too superficial for that" (Int. 04).

Other right-wing groups confirm this perception of the Internet as a useful tool for doing politics but that it "cannot be compared to *personal level* contacts" for the activation of people (e.g., Ints. 12, 11). In this way some of them are, as they stress "more active on the street than on the web" (e.g., Int. 12). For instance, the spokesperson of an Austrian youth movement states that they are, above all, "an organization which lives from personal exchange and meetings" (Int. 07) and others say that "if you want to get really in contact with interested persons, potential members or like-minded people, this will only work on a personal level" (Int. 04); indeed, "it is more at that level that one can convince the people about the values one stands for" (Int. 12). Research on social movements and the Internet is still controversial regarding the 'real' political effects of the virtual arena (on the organizations as well as on members; e.g., more mobilization? more transnationalization?), and right-wing groups are aware that focusing on the 'cyber dimension' of the Internet does not imply that it is the only place where they act, construct their identities, and express their views. In any case, our results prove that right-wing social actors do not relate to the Internet as a 'monolitic unity,'[55] but rather they shape the technology in a way largely dependent on additional factors, such as the structure of social and political opportunities.

CONCLUSION

In the light of several purposes that the literature suggests the Internet can fulfill for civil society organizations, we have examined those that are actually exploited by right-wing groups and to what extent. First, our data from the interviews and web content indicate that the Internet seems deeply integrated with the strategy and identity of these radical right-wing groups. They use it to promote and disseminate their ideology, recruit new members and organize events.[56] Websites can indeed be considered in this sense as "different emerging structures of online civic participation"[57] also for the radical right. Some political uses of the Internet, however, emerged as being more difficult for these groups, as demonstrated by the continued moderated presence of interactive virtual debates on group websites, (even though this is probably counterbalanced by their wide use of social networks, like Facebook) as well as the organizations of online mobilization.

Second, our study has also highlighted that right-wing forms of cyberactivism do not emerge in a vacuum, but are instead related to specific contextual (advantages and disadvantages) and organizational factors. Although we did not find many differences among different types of organizations in the intensity of the use of the Internet, suggesting that online action has become part of the repertoire of action of the milieu of the radical right, we did, however, find that organizational resources matter with respect to the forms of online activism adopted.[58]

In addition, we also noted that the organizational context in which the mobilization takes place (i.e., collective actors' values and identities offline) seems to influence their approach to Internet technologies where more institutionalized and hierarchical organizations make for a more traditional and instrumental usage of the web than less formalized and more fluid networks such as the youth and neo-Nazi subcultural groups. This raises the issue of the supposed "equalizing" effects of the Internet, also concerning right-wing groups (is this new medium favoring organizations already rich in resources?). However, there are also indications that "the use of the web did not simply reify existing political structures," implying some transformations in the actors themselves.[59] Beyond the transformation in the organizational strategies (action, communication, recruitment, etc.) the Internet has indeed produced a change in the constituency of these organizations: first of all, by altering the relationship among activists (and between activists and their organizations) in the direction of virtual rather than face-to-face interactions; second, by generating a rejuvenation of the membership due to the generational (youth) migration to the web; and third, by attracting members who would otherwise never come in contact with the group. Moreover, it emerged that through the Internet and, in particular, through the new tools for communication offered by the web, right-wing radical groups are progressively becoming 'producers' of political information. In these cases, communication ceases to be simply an instrumental activity aimed at achieving specific purposes of the organization. Conversely, for organizations that opt to include online activism among their activities (or even more, they choose to give up offline activities and to operate exclusively online), communication becomes a real and characterizing feature of the organizational structure, as observed by Bennett and Segerberg.[60]

Finally, our study has also pointed out that the evaluation of the limits and potentialities of the Internet, by right-wing groups, can help in understanding their use (degree and forms) of the web. Although the importance of the Internet to function as a bridge between online and offline reality is widely recognized by extreme right movements which feel themselves to be the object of political, social, and media stigmatization, such organizations are also well aware of its weaknesses in this regard. Such weaknesses include target selection biases (or the problem of the 'digital divide'—as we could say in the language of CMC—that in countries like Italy is still quite relevant), the risk to undermine 'real' political participation of their members, and difficulties (for some groups more than for others) in Internet access and activities, to mention only a few. In sum, our study has shown that, whereas for some right-wing organizations the Internet may imply a more positive balance of opportunities, adding new channels to the traditional tools of politics, other groups in the same country may stand to lose influence, as a result of their difficulties in exploiting all the potentialities of this new instrument and arena of communication.

Some questions, however, concerning right-wing cyberactivism remain unanswered. First of all, what is the real added value of online activism for these groups if many of them still tend to be wary of web activities compared to the 'real' ones? Is it just a matter of resistance to innovation or do they have some concrete motivations for such mistrust? Such as, for example, the diffused claim that cyberactivism, with its virtual interactions, cannot be considered as reliable and solid as real-life face-to-face activism, even in the case of radical right organizations (for which the cost of participation is high)? As we have seen, for these groups the Internet performs an effective function of communication and promotion of (their) offline events. However, is it really able to retain group activists (i.e., would virtual activists, who often hide behind pseudonyms, be willing to support their organization in the real world if necessary)?

Further studies on more cases and countries, as well as at the micro levels of activists, would be necessary to improve our understanding of radical right-wing cyberactivism. In particular, in order to explore the underlying mechanisms behind the relationship between virtual and real-world political activism in more detail, wider comparative works, both on more countries and on different types of online political radicalism, are desirable for the future.

NOTES

This chapter is part of a larger comparative project "The Dark Side of the Web: Right-Wing Political Mobilization Using the Internet," coordinated by Manuela Caiani at the IHS (Vienna) and sponsored by the Austrian National Bank (Jubiläumsfondsprojekt ONB, Nr. 14035). We thank Patricia Kröll for conducting the interviews for the Austrian, English, German, and American cases and for her useful suggestions concerning this part. The authors contributed to the writing of the chapter 50% each.

1. Marco Pasqua, "Stormfront: Condannati e Gestori del Sito: 'Associazione a Delinquere di Stampo Neonazista'," Il Messaggero, last modified April 8, 2013, www.ilmessaggero.it/primopiano/cronaca/stormfront_condannati_i_gestori_del_sito_laquoassociazione_a_delinquere_di_stampo_neo-Nazis taraquo/notizie/263857.shtml.
2. Jamie Bartlett, Jonathan Birdwell, and Mark Littler, *The New Face of Digital Populism* (London: Demos, 2011), last modified January 13, 2014, www.marklittler.co.uk/After_Osama.pdf.
3. Ibid., 18
4. See, among others, W. Lance Bennett, "Communicating Global Activism: Strengths and Vulnerabilities of Networked Politics," *Information, Communication & Society*, 6, no. 2 (2003):143–168; W. Lance Bennett, "Communicating Global Activism: Some Strengths and Vulnerabilities of Networked Politics," in *Cyberprotest: New Media, Citizens and Social Movements*, ed. Wim Van de Donk, Brian D. Loader, Paul G. Nixon, and Dieter Rucht (London: Routledge, 2004), 109–128; W. Lance Bennet and Alexandra Segerberg,"Digital Media and the Personalization of Collective Action." *Information, Communication & Society* 14, no. 6 (2011):770–799; W. Lance Bennett, Terry Givens, and Christian Breunig, "Communication and Political Mobilization: Digital Media Use and Protest Organization among Anti-Iraq War Demonstrators in the U.S.," *Political Communication*, 25 (2008): 269–289; Davide Calenda and Lorenzo Mosca, "Youth Online: Researching the Political Use of the Internet in the Italian Context," in *Young Citizens in the Digital Age: Political Engagement, Young People and New Media*, ed. B. Loader (New York and London: Routledge, 2007), 52–68; Matteo Cernison, "Social Movement Organizations and the Web: An Online Trace of the Global Justice Movement," (PhD dissertation, European University Institute, Florence, 2008); Donatella della Porta and Lorenzo Mosca, "Democrazia in rete: stili di comunicazione e movimenti sociali in Europa," *Rassegna Italiana*

di Sociologia, 4 (2006): 529–556; Alice Mattoni, *Media Practices and Protest Politics. How Precarious Workers Mobilise* (United Kingdom: Ashgate, 2012); Dieter Rucht, "The Internet as a New Opportunity for Transnational Protest Groups," in *Economic and Political Contention in Comparative Perspective*, ed. Maria Kousis and Charles Tilly (Boulder: Paradigm Publishers, 2012), 70–85; Laura Stein, "Social Movement Web Use in Theory and Practice: A Content Analysis of US Movement Websites," *New Media & Society*, 11 (2009): 749–771; Jeroen Van Laer and Peter Van Aelst, "Internet and Social Movement Action Repertoires," *Information, Communication & Society*, 13, no. 8 (2010): 1146–1171. For a complete overview, see Wim Van de Donk et al., *Cyberprotest. New Media, Citizens and Social Movements* (London: Routledge, 2010).

5. Les Back, Michael Keith, and John Solomos, "Racism on the Internet: Mapping Neo-Fascist Subcultures in Cyberspace," in *Nation and Race*, eds. J. Kaplan and T., Bjorgo (New York: New York University Press, 1998), 98.

6. There are still a limited number of empirical studies on right-wing movements and their use of the web, the exception being the use of the Internet by right-wing political parties for electoral campaigns (e.g., see Carlos Cunha et al., "Southern European Parties and Party Systems, and the New ICTs," in *Political Parties and the Internet. Net Gain?* eds. Rachel Gibson, Paul Nixon and Stephen Ward (New York and London: Routledge, 2003), 70–98. For other recent studies, see Michael Chau and Jennifer Xu, *A Framework for Locating and Analyzing Hate Groups in Blogs*, paper to the Pacific Asia Conference on Information Systems, Kuala Lumpur, Malaysia, July 6–9, 2006, and Zuev (2010).

7. Bartlett, Birdwell, and Littler, *Digital Populism*, 30.

8. In terms of analytical classification, in this study we define a group as belonging to the extreme/far/radical right family (we will use these terms interchangeably) when it exhibits in its ideological cores nationalism, xenophobia, antiestablishment critiques and sociocultural authoritarianism (law and order, family values). See Cas Mudde, *Populist Radical Right Parties in Europe*, (Cambridge: Cambridge University Press, 2007).
   Despite being referred to as "far-right," empirically many of these groups are not easily placed according to traditional political categories, often combining elements of leftwing and rightwing philosophy, mixed with populist language and rhetoric.

9. The interviews, conducted mainly by phone, were held between 2010 and 2011. The length of the interviews varied between 30 minutes to one hour. We had initial difficulties in establishing the first preliminary contacts with extreme right organizations, and, in general, in achieving our ideal interview-sample (made of 3–4 orgs. x 3 organizational types x 7 countries = a total of an ideal sample of 63/84 organizations). The response rate was about 30%.
   The people interviewed within the selected organizations were those in charge of designing the organization's mobilization and communication strategies. In particular, they were either leaders (presidents or general secretaries), members of the leading bodies (e.g., members of the executive boards, spokesmen, or regional party leaders) or held a position of high prominence within the selected organization (general delegates or secretaries or website chief editors).

10. Robert P Weber, *Basic Content Analysis* (Newbury Park, CA: Sage, 1990), 9.

11. The web content analysis, conducted for the seven countries between August 2009 and January 2011, has been done by coders (country language speakers) trained in the sampling selection and coding procedure. For details on

the codebook and its measurements, see also Caiani Manuela and Linda Parenti, *European and American Extreme Right Groups and the Internet* (Abingdon, UK: Ashgate, 2013).

12. In the questionnaire we asked our interviewees to evaluate, on a four point scale (from "not at all" to "a lot"), the extent to which the Internet helps their organization in (a) the diffusion of its ideals and values; (b) better performing and communicating its activities; (c) reaching their supporters; (d) fundraising; (e) having crossnational and national contacts (with other organizations and with political actors and institutions). Finally, our partners were asked (through an open question, then recoded according to the same scale) if they also consider the Internet a means for strengthening the identity of the group.

13. We have classified the uses of the websites by right-wing groups that have emerged from the analysis in six broad categories: *communication* (including those activities through the website aiming at keeping a communication channel with the members, e.g., providing information about the reachability of the organization, such as address, email, telephone number, etc.; feedback forms, etc.; *propaganda* (including uses of the website aimed at providing materials for the "political education" of actual and potential members, such as the presence of hate symbols and slogans, multimedia materials, news section, documentation and material, e.g., articles, papers, dossier, references to bibliographical sources, etc.; *identity* (including the uses of the website as an arena for fostering debates and discussions, e.g., with the presence of forum of discussion, chats, surveys etc.; *ideology* (when the website is used to diffuse basic information on the mission of the group, e.g., "about us", "our goals"); *mobilization* (concerning the use of Internet as a tool of activation of members and sympathizers for offline as well as online actions, e.g., publicizing political campaigns, promoting online petitions, providing instructions for off line actions etc.; and *internationalization* (related to the use of the web to build transnational contacts with other extremist groups and to appeal to an international audience, e.g., content of the website translated in other languages, etc.). Each (lower-level) feature was recorded as a dummy variable, attributing a value of 1 if a given feature is present and zero if it is not found on the website. The six additional indexes of the forms of Internet usage derive from the sum of the lower-level indicators (normalized and standardized in order to be comparable among them and vary from 0 to 1). See also Caiani and Parenti 2013.

14. Bennett, "Global Activism," 143–168.

15. See for example the website of the Austrian subcultural group *Der Funke* (www.der-funke.info).

16. Lorenzo Mosca and Cristian Vaccari, eds., *Nuovi media e nuova politica? Partecipazione e mobilitazione online da MoveOn al Movimento 5 stelle* (Milano: Franco Angeli, 2012), 24.

17. See for example the right-wing websites: www.rvfonline.com/ or http://sioeengland.wordpress.com/.

18. As for example the case of the French right-wing magazine Reflechir & Agir, for which, "the Internet allows potential readers from abroad to know about the magazine, to establish contacts with the editors and subscribe" (Int. 38).

19. Cass R. Sunstein, *Republic.com 2.0* (Princeton: Princeton University Press, 2007).

20. As the case of the Austrian group *Wiener Nachrichten Online*, which offers on its website (www.wno.org/) a very long and detailed bibliographic list (e.g., on far right intellectuals such as Thilo Sarazin, Andreas Thierry, David Irving), and for every book a small description.

21. Peter Dahlgren, *Media and Political Engagement: Citizens, Communication and Democracy* (Cambridge and New York: Cambridge University Press, 2009).

22. E.g., della Porta and Mosca, "Democrazia in rete."
23. For example, "to be a nation, is the religion of our time" is stated as a goal of the group on the website of the Austrian Alpen-Donau (www.an-wien. nw.am/); and on the BNP website, a section is devoted to explaining that "the group exists to secure a future for the indigenous peoples of these islands in the North Atlantic which have been our homeland for millennia."
24. www.npd.de.
25. www.suedtiroler-freiheit.com/.
26. On the website of the organization *Imperial Klans of America*, it is stated that the organization will "suspend or banish any member immediately if they speak of or promote illegal actions. If anyone is found to be committing crimes they are immediately put up for suspension or banishment". For other examples, see: www.aime-et-sers.com/, www.present.fr; http://logr.org/ leerostfriesland/, and www.ab-rhein-neckar.de/index2.html
27. For example, on the website of the Austrian nationalistic group *Südtiroler Schützenbund* (www.schuetzen.com/) we find the following survey: "Did the 'firenight' (Feuernacht, namely attacks against of a group of southern Tyroleans in the year 1961) harm the peaceful coexistence between the different ethnic groups?"—with different options of answers: 1. Yes, because of this, the Italians started to feel uncomfortable; 2. No, because the peaceful coexistence was neither in the interest of the Italians nor of the Germans. 3. The peaceful living together was prevented by the Italian politics, not by the attacks.
28. This includes discussions on current social and political issues (e.g., see the forum of the group www.militaria.com; www.aime-et-sers.com), as well as more violent verbal attacks against social and political enemies (e.g., see www. ilmessaggero.it/primopiano/cronaca/stormfront_condannati_i_gestori_ del_sito_laquoassociazione_a_delinquere_di_stampo_neo-Nazistaraquo/ notizie/263857.shtml).
29. Bartlett, Birdwell, and Littler, *Digital Populism*, 15.
30. See for example, Randolph Kluver et al., *The Internet and National Elections: A Comparative Study of Web Campaigning* (London: Routledge, 2007).
31. Mosca and Vaccari, *Nuovi Media*, 17.
32. Donatella della Porta, *Social Movements, Political Violence and the State* (Cambridge: Cambridge University Press, 1995); John McCarthy and Mayer N. Zald, *Comparative Perspectives on Social Movements: Political Opportunities, Mobilizing Structures, and Cultural Framings* (Cambridge: MA: Cambridge University Press, 1996).
33. Donatella della Porta and Lorenzo Mosca, "Searching the Net: Websites' Qualities in the Global Justice Movement," *Information, Communication and Society*, 12 (2009): 783.
34. Stephen Coleman and Jay G. Blumler, *The Internet and Democratic Citizenship* (Cambridge: Cambridge University Press, 2009), 86.
35. Sidney Tarrow, *Global Movements, Complex Internationalism, and North-South Inequality*, paper presented at the workshop on Contentious Politics, Columbia University, October 27, 2003 (quoted in della Porta and Mosca, "Democrazia in rete," 546).
36. Accounting, respectively, for a score of 0.42, 0.37, 0.38, and 0.37 on the index of cyberactivism.
37. The scores of political parties and political movements on these indexes are 0.53 and 0.46, respectively, for communication and 0.50 and 0.44 for information. In the cases of cultural and nostalgic movements, the scores are 0.46 and 0.36, respectively, for communication and 0.46 and 0.47 for information.

38. The scores of subcultural and neo-Nazi groups on the index of internationalization are 0.42 and 0.24, respectively, and 0.19 and 0.17, respectively, on the index of mobilization. In the latter case, the score of political parties is 0.19.
39. As for propaganda via the web, the scores on the indexes are 0.53 for nostalgic revisionist and negationist groups and 0.38 for cultural movements. As for the use of the web for diffusing ideology, the values are 0.73 for nostalgic revisionist and negationist groups, 0.86 for cultural movements, and 0.83 for neo-Nazi groups.
40. As for example on the website *Benito Mussolini. Un omaggio al Duce* (http:// spazioinwind.libero.it/mussolini/index2.htm).
41. See for example the German site www.freies-netz-sued.net/.
42. For example, on the German website of the *Nationaler Widerstand Berlin Brandenburg*, it is possible to download the last words of Rudolf Hess at the Nuremberg trial.
43. Bennett and Segerberg, "Digital Media."
44. German right-wing organizations also often sell online subscriptions to newspapers and far right magazines. See the websites of the group Junge Nationaldemokraten (www.jn-buvo.de/index.php/ueber-uns).
45. E.g., Andrew Chadwich, "Internet Politics," (Oxford: Oxford University Press, 2006).
46. E.g., Kevin Gillan, Jenny Pickerill, and Frank Webster, *Anti-War Activism* (Basingstoke: Palgrave Macmillan, 2008), 35–36.
47. Bennett, "Global Activism," 143–168.
48. Bennett and Segerberg, "Digital Media," 1–2.
49. The questions on the questionnaire were: "How do you perceive the potential role of the Internet more generally in your organization?" "Is the Internet for your organization just another way of presenting itself publicly, or has it affected the way in which you communicate with policy-makers, the media or your supporters more substantially?"
50. Also confirmed by the Cramers' V coefficient.
51. E.g., Jeffrey M. Ayres, "From the Streets to the Internet: The Cyber-Diffusion of Contention," *The Annals of The American Academy of Political and Social Science*, 566 (1999): 132–143; Daniel J. Meyers, "Social Activism through Computer Networks," in *Computing in the Social Science Humanities*, ed. O.V. Burton (Urbana: University of Illinois Press, 2001), 124–139; Pippa Norris, *Digital Divide: Civic Engagement, Information Poverty and the Internet World-Wide* (Cambridge, MA: Cambridge University Press, 2001).
52. As the representative of a group tells, the "Jew-controlled governments attempt to deny access to our websites by deeming our content as 'hate' and sponsoring browsers that don't allow users to access White sites" (Int. 17).
53. Sunstein, *Republic.com*, 32.
54. Stephen Coleman, "The Lonely Citizen: Indirect Representation in an Age of Networks," *Political Communication*, 22 (2005): 197–214.
55. Laszlo Bruszt, Balazs Vedres, and David Stark, "Shaping the Web of Civic Participation: Civil Society Websites in Eastern Europe," *Journal of Public Policy*, 25, I (2005): 149–163.
56. Bartlett, Birdwell, and Littler, *Digital Populism*, 30.
57. Bruszt, Vedres, and Stark, "Civic Society Websites," 151.
58. della Porta and Mosca, *Democrazia in Rete*.
59. Kluver et al., *The Internet and National Elections*, 262.
60. Bennett and Segerberg, "Digital Media," 1–2.

REFERENCES

Ayres, Jeffrey M. "From the Streets to the Internet: The Cyber-Diffusion of Contention." *The Annals of the American Academy of Political and Social Science* 566 (1999): 132–143.

Back, Les, Michael Keith, and John Solomos. "Racism on the Internet: Mapping Neo-Fascist Subcultures in Cyberspace." In *Nation and Race*, edited by J. Kaplan and T. Bjorgo. New York: New York University Press, 1998.

Bartlett, Jamie, Jonathan Birdwell, and Mark Littler. *The New Face of Digital Populism*. London: Demos, 2011. [Online]. www.marklittler.co.uk/After_Osama.pdf (accessed January 14,2014).

Bennett, W. Lance. "Communicating Global Activism: Strengths and Vulnerabilities of Networked Politics." *Information, Communication & Society* 6, no. 2 (2003): 143–168.

Bennett, W. Lance. "Communicating Global Activism: Some Strengths and Vulnerabilities of Networked Politics." In *Cyberprotest: New Media, Citizens and Social Movements*, edited by Wim Van de Donk, Brian D. Loader, Paul G. Nixon and Dieter Rucht (pp. 109–128). London: Routledge, 2004.

Bennett, W. Lance, Terry Givens, and Christian Breunig. "Communication and Political Mobilization: Digital Media Use and Protest Organization among Anti-Iraq War Demonstrators in the U.S." *Political Communication* 25 (2008): 269–289.

Bennett, W. Lance, and Alexandra Segerberg. "Digital Media and the Personalization of Collective Action." *Information, Communication & Society*, 14, no. 6 (2011): 770–799.

Bruszt, Laszlo, Balazs Vedres, and David Stark. "Shaping the Web of Civic Participation: Civil Society Websites in Eastern Europe." *Journal of Public Policy* 25, I (2005): 149–163.

Caiani Manuela, and Linda Parenti. *European and American Extreme Right Groups and the Internet*. Abingdon, UK: Ashgate, 2013.

Calenda, Davide, and Lorenzo Mosca. "Youth Online: Researching the Political Use of the Internet in the Italian Context." In *Young Citizens in the Digital Age: Political Engagement, Young People and New Media*, edited by B. Loader (pp. 52–68). New York and London: Routledge, 2007.

Cernison, Matteo. *Social Movement Organizations and the Web: An Online Trace of the Global Justice Movement*. Ph.D. thesis, European University Institute, Florence, 2008.

Chadwich, Andrew. *Internet Politics*. Oxford: Oxford University Press, 2006.

Chau, Michael, and Jennifer Xu. *A Framework for Locating and Analyzing Hate Groups in Blogs*. Paper to the Pacific Asia Conference on Information Systems, Kuala Lumpur, Malaysia, July 6–9, 2006.

Coleman, Stephen. "The Lonely Citizen: Indirect Representation in an Age of Networks." *Political Communication* 22 (2005): 197–214

Coleman, Stephen, and Jay G. Blumler. *The Internet and Democratic Citizenship*. Cambridge: Cambridge University Press, 2009.

Cunha, Carlos, Irene Martin, James Newell, and Luis Ramiro. "Southern European Parties and Party Systems, and the New ICTs." In *Political Parties and the Internet. Net Gain?*, edited by Rachel Gibson, Paul Nixon, and Stephen Ward (pp. 70–98). New York and London: Routledge, 2003.

Dahlgren, Peter. *Media and Political Engagement: Citizens, Communication and Democracy*. Cambridge and New York: Cambridge University Press, 2009.

della Porta, Donatella. *Social Movements, Political Violence and the State*. Cambridge: Cambridge University Press, 1995.

della Porta, Donatella, and Lorenzo Mosca. "Democrazia in rete: stili di comunicazione e movimenti sociali in Europa." *Rassegna Italiana di Sociologia*, 4 (2006): 529–556.

della Porta, Donatella, and Lorenzo Mosca. "Searching the Net: Websites' Qualities in the Global Justice Movement." *Information, Communication and Society*, 12 (2009): 771–792.

Gillan, Kevin, Jenny Pickerill, and Frank Webster. *Anti-War Activism*. Basingstoke: Palgrave Macmillan, 2008.

Kluver, Randolph, Nicholas Jankowski, Kristen Foot, and Steven M. Schneider. *The Internet and National Elections: A Comparative Study of Web Campaigning*. London: Routledge, 2007.

Mattoni, Alice. *Media Practices and Protest Politics. How Precarious Workers Mobilise*. United Kingdom: Ashgate, 2012.

McCarthy, John D., and Mayer N. Zald. *Comparative Perspectives on Social Movements: Political Opportunities, Mobilizing Structures, and Cultural Framings*. Cambridge, MA: Cambridge University Press, 1996.

Meyers, Daniel J. "Social Activism through Computer Networks." In *Computing in the Social Science Humanities*, edited by O. V. Burton (pp. 124–139). Urbana: University of Illinois Press, 2001.

Mosca Lorenzo, and Cristian Vaccari, eds. *Nuovi media e nuova politica? Partecipazione e mobilitazione online da MoveOn al Movimento 5 stelle*. Milan: Franco Angeli, 2012.

Mudde, Cas. *Populist Radical Right Parties in Europe*. Belgium: University of Antwerp, 2007.

Norris, Pippa. *Digital Divide: Civic Engagement, Information Poverty and the Internet World-Wide*. Cambridge, MA: Cambridge University Press, 2001.

Pasqua, Marco. "Stormfront: Condannati e Gestori del Sito 'Associazione a Delinquere di Stampo Neonazista'" Il Messaggero, www.ilmessaggero.it/primopiano/cronaca/stormfront_condannati_i_gestori_del_sito_laquoassociazione_a_delinquere_di_stampo_neo-Nazistaraquo/notizie/263857.shtml (accessed January 14, 2014).

Rucht, Dieter. "The Internet as a New Opportunity for Transnational Protest Groups." In *Economic and Political Contention in Comparative Perspective*, edited by Maria Kousis and Charles Tilly (pp. 70–85). Boulder: Paradigm Publishers, 2005.

Stein, Laura. "Social Movement Web Use in Theory and Practice: A Content Analysis of US Movement Websites." *New Media & Society*, 11 (2009): 749–771.

Sunstein, Cass R. *Republic.com 2.0*. Princeton: Princeton University Press, 2007.

Tarrow, Sidney. *Global Movements, Complex Internationalism, and North-South Inequality*. Paper presented at the workshop on Contentious Politics, Columbia University, October 27, 2003.

Van de Donk, Wim, Brian D. Loader, Paul G. Nixon, and Dieter Rucht. *Cyberprotest. New Media, Citizens and Social Movements*. London: Routledge, 2004.

Van Laer, Jeroen, and Peter Van Aelst. "Internet and Social Movement Action Repertoires." *Information, Communication & Society*, 13, no. 8 (2010): 1146–1171.

Weber, Robert P. *Basic Content Analysis*. Newbury Park, CA: Sage, 1990.

APPENDIX

Quoted interviews with right-wing organizations:

ID. 01 Political party "Die Bunten." October 7, 2011. Austria.
ID. 02 Anonymous political party. November 9, 2011. Austria.
ID. 04 Political party "HPÖ." November 25, 2011. Austria.
ID. 05 Media organization. November 28, 2011. Austria.
ID. 06 Organization "ÖLM." December 2, 2012. Austria.
ID. 07 Anonymous political movement. December 2, 2012. Austria.
ID. 08 Political party "BGD." October 28, 2011. Germany.
ID. 09 Political party "NPD." November 4, 2011. Germany.
ID. 10 Organization "JN." January 9, 2012. Germany.
ID. 11 Anonymous political movement. January 22, 2012. Germany.
ID. 12 Anonymous regional political movement. February 5, 2012. Germany.
ID. 13 Organization "MUPINFO." March 3, 2012. Germany.
ID. 14 Single activist. March 16, 2012. Germany.
ID. 15 Political party "British Freedom Party." February 19, 2012. United Kingdom.
ID. 16 Political party "The English Democrats." March 29, 2012. United Kingdom.
ID. 17 The network "VNN." January 10, 2012. United States
ID. 18 Organization "White Revolution." January 10, 2012. United States
ID. 19 The network "The Insurgent." January 19, 2012. United States
ID. 20 White nationalist website/organization. February 4, 2012. United States
ID. 21 Non-profit philosophical, educational, and social organization. February 17, 2012. United States
ID. 22 Political party. February 22, 2012. United States
ID. 23 Ethno-political advocacy organization. May 11, 2012. United States
ID. 24 Organization "Nuove Destra Sociale." January 9, 2012. Italy
ID. 26 Organization "Movimento Nazional Popolare." April 16, 2012. Italy.
ID. 27 Organization "Patria Nostra." January 29, 2012. Italy.
ID. 31 Organization "Casapound." March 6, 2012. Italy.
ID. 33 Organization "UNT." February 2, 2012. Spain.
ID. 34 Political party "Falange de Las JONS." February 16, 2012. Spain.
ID. 35 Political party "España 2000." January 23, 2012. Spain.
ID. 36 Political party "Falange Autentica." April 11, 2012. Spain.
ID. 37 Organization "Bloc Identitaire." January 31, 2012. France.
ID. 38 Organization "Reflechir & Agir." February 14, 2012. France.
ID. 42 Organization "Front National de la Jeunesse." March 5, 2012. France.

10 Young Chinese Workers, Contentious Politics, and Cyberactivism in the Global Factory

Dorothy Kidd

THE EPICENTER OF GLOBAL LABOR UNREST

On May 8, 2012, a thousand workers, about a third of those employed at a shoe factory in Dongguan in the Pearl River Delta in China, walked out on strike over management's slashing of their performance bonus. Getting no response from the company, a young worker posted a photo to his *weibo* or microblogging page to generate public support and media attention.[1] Within an hour, the Hong Kong-based *China Labour Bulletin* posted the story, which was then picked up by local labor activists and reporters, and retweeted more than 50 times. By the next day, after local government mediation, management agreed to restore more than half the bonus.[2]

The Dongguan strikers are part of an emerging movement of young migrant workers whose protests in low- and high-end global factories number in the thousands per year.[3] Led by the very young, many still in their teens, their action repertoires combine on- and offline communications practices on the shop floor, in company-run dormitories, urban public space and cyberspace. Marginalized for their rural origins, with little representation in government or the dominant media, they represent themselves through their own do-it-yourself (DIY) media, poetry and song, and factory-level organization. Net-savvy, they organize and mobilize support through social media, the preexisting kin and friendship social networks of their rural home regions, and a growing labor solidarity network.

The protests of this movement of more than 250 million young workers occurs so routinely, so massively, and so effectively that China labor researcher Eli Friedman has called it the "epicenter of global labor unrest."[4] Almost all are "wildcats," outside of formal labor-management contracts, or the sanction of the Communist party-led All China Federation of Trade Unions (ACFTU). Nevertheless, since a strike wave begun at the Honda plants in 2010, their aims have gone beyond defensive attempts to get wages paid to win significant wage increases above and beyond legal requirements.

Using the leverage of a labor shortage, the young workers have already made a considerable impact with global repercussions. They have been able to disrupt the supply chain of Honda, Apple, Walmart, and other profitable global capitalist corporations. Together with other movements against the injustices taking place behind China's capitalist development, the young workers are a worrisome preoccupation of the Chinese party-state. The government has not only spent considerable resources on policing protests, taking measures against independent nongovernmental organizations, and monitoring the web, but has also increased minimum wages, enacted new labor legislation, and revitalized labor unions. The young workers are also central to the government plan to pump up the domestic consumer market and transfer technology, manufacturing, and jobs to the rural homelands of the migrant workers. Although this young workers' movement is rhizomatic—with sporadic and localized protests and no clear leadership or unified political direction—the scale of the movement and centrality to the circuits of Chinese and global capitalism means that the contagion will not go away soon.

Nevertheless, unlike the enthusiasms given to the various Twitter, Facebook, and YouTube "revolutions" of the "Arab spring" and other mass demonstrations, the reportage of the Chinese migrant workers' protests took a very different character. *Time* magazine being a case in point: In 2009, China's workers were the runners-up for the 2009 Person of the Year, who are "leading the world to economic recovery."[5] In stark contrast, in 2011, when *Time* named the "Protester" Person of the Year, citing the suicide of Tunisian Mohamed Bouazizi as the spark for the Arab spring and subsequent protests, there was absolutely no mention of the young Chinese workers and their cyberactivism.

The suicides of more than 17 young people at Foxconn in 2010 certainly garnered a lot of media attention from U.S. and UK business, tech industry, legacy news, and alternative media sources.[6] Foxconn is the giant Taiwanese-owned subcontractor that employs 1.4 million Chinese workers who produce electronic products and services for Apple, Hewlett Packard, Samsung, HP, Sony, Toshiba, Nokia, and Hitachi. Impossible to fully comprehend their motivation, interviews and blog posts suggest that the young workers were each protesting specific grievances, assaults on their dignity, and untenable working conditions.[7] Together with other forms of protest aimed at challenging the low wages, oppressive overtime, military-like supervision, and toxic conditions, the suicides sparked widespread discussions and mobilizations in the Chinese blogosphere and other forums, and offline among labor NGOs and activist networks. When activists in cities around the world[8] mourned the loss of life and explicitly linked the suicides to a critique of corporate sweatshops, some commentators wondered if this was the electronic industry's "Nike moment."[9]

Both the initial stumbling of Foxconn and Apple, and the global protests spotlighting them, were reminiscent of the anti-sweatshop campaigns targeting Nike and other multinational clothing brands in the 1990s. In well-reported gaffes, Foxconn CEO Terry Gou Tai Ming said that workers committed suicide to gain company compensation, and asked workers to sign "no-suicide" contracts;[10] Apple CEO Steve Jobs argued that Fox-conn was "not a sweatshop" because the suicide rate was well below the Chinese average.[11] A transnational coalition of students, faculty, and labor groups, with their hub in Hong Kong, and with DNA in the earlier anti-sweatshop movement, kept up the pressure with a repertoire of street protests, counter-evidence from academics, transnational petitions, and strategic media planning.

Then, in 2012, Apple and Foxconn adopted the more sophisticated apps of corporate social responsibility, much upgraded since the Nike crisis, and a new global industry in itself, worth $U.S. 31.7 billion in 2007.[12] Foxconn made more wage and shop floor concessions. Apple contracted the Fair Labor Association and mounted a public relations strategy that almost com-pletely erased the protagonism of the young workers and their allies from the news frame. As Guo and colleagues report, activists were almost invisi-ble in both the state-run Chinese media and *The New York Times*. Mirror-ing Foxconn's own press releases, the state-run media "attributed the cause of suicides to psychological vulnerability among the Chinese younger gen-eration."[13] *The New York Times* provided quotes from individual workers, and discussed human rights abuses.[14] However, their stories were framed as a domestic problem of China, with the Chinese government as the principal culprit; the international context in which Chinese workers and a global network of Chinese and international activists were challenging the global sweatshops, was missing.

The news frame of the dominant U.S. media, which treats everything "China" as foreign, exceptional, and in constant conflict with U.S. standards of human rights, is perhaps unsurprising. It has been variously explained as a function of U.S. foreign policy,[15] the trade imbalance between the United States and China,[16] the continuance of anti-Communist ideology,[17] or of persistent anti-Chinese racism.[18] Yet, the agency of the young workers at Foxconn, and their connections to global protest movements, was seldom the narrative even within the alternative and progressive media. Instead, as Cornell China labor scholar Eli Friedman argues, "Chinese workers are depicted . . . as the pitiable victims of globalization . . . who suffer stoically for our iPhones and bath towels. And only we can save them, by absorb-ing their torrent of exports, or campaigning benevolently for their humane treatment at the hands of 'our' multinationals."[19]

A WORKER-CENTERED INQUIRY

During communications conferences in Shanghai in 2002 and 2012, I wit-nessed the jaw-dropping pace and scale of redevelopment of that global city. I took a series of long walks through low-rise tenements where res-idents sat outside on the stoops, as huge cranes knocked down blocks of housing behind them; passed by new gated enclaves, and weaved through crowded brand store shopping streets, as spectacular towers were being thrown up into the sky. I reflected on Jack Qiu's comment that "the real source for China's success in the world economy, including the recent rise of its communication industry, is its enormous labor power in production processes."[20] However, there is still very little research, as he and Yeran Kim note, that "foregrounds grassroots politics among labor and youth as an essential source of communicative power against the established order of global capitalism."[21]

This chapter responds to those concerns and addresses the contentious use of communications by young Chinese workers. Limited, as I am not based within these movements, do not read Chinese, and have not conducted first-hand research in China, I instead draw from the growing grey and academic English-language literatures of labor, sociology, political economy, and communications scholars and activist researchers.[22] Much of their analytical frame parallels the autonomist Marxist workers' inquiry of the *Zerowork* collective, which I use.[23] In different social and cultural contexts, and political state formations, Zerowork and the China researchers share a common focus on the practices, self-activity and developing class identity of workers, in contention with the increasingly uniform contexts of global capitalist production of the neoliberal period.

A common concept is *class composition*, used to analyze the changing dynamics between capital and labor by Zerowork in the 1970s, and in the decades since by the China researchers.[24] Composition measures two antagonistic forces: *technical composition* or the shaping of the working class by the demands of capital, including restructuring and management discipline, and *political* composition, or the changing forms of everyday challenge and resistance, from work-refusal to organization. Importantly, "composition combines" Foucault's twinned concepts of "subjection" and "subjectification—labouring participation in the making of one's identity and social relations."[25] Decomposition, or "un-making," is part and parcel of both dynamics, and often underestimated; and although the dominant "decompositionary" force is capital, the complex divisions resulting from sectoral and segmented struggles are a necessary part of the analysis.

Dyer-Witheford has proposed a revival of Zerowork's inquiry that addresses communications for the enlarged horizon of struggles of movements beyond industrial workers, in and against global capitalism.[26] I draw from this protocol, and in very broad strokes, address how Chinese workers use communications, media, and mediated spaces, first as part of everyday challenges to material and immaterial forces of capitalism, and secondly in the making of new social, cultural, and political relations, and collective identities.[27] My questions include: What form, content, direction, and circulation are the struggles taking? How do they represent a process of becoming new kinds of subjects? What is their relationship to the official party-state institutions, the labor unions and media, and their social and political networks of support inside and outside China? How do all of these aspects relate to political and economic changes in China, and within transnational capitalism? Finally, what is the significance of young Chinese workers' contention for an understanding of cyberactivism?

THE UN-MAKING OF THE CHINESE WORKING CLASSES

In 1979, Deng Xiaoping began to completely restructure the Chinese economy and merge it with the global capitalist world. The radical surgery required massive investments in state planning, design, and development in the four sectors of agriculture, industry, national defense, and technology. The national plan was called the "Four Modernizations," and technology or more precisely, informatization, as Yuezhi Zhao has pointed out, was soon elevated "into the mother of all modernizations."[28] Unlike Japan and South Korea, China opened up to extraordinarily high amounts of foreign direct investment (FDI), and allowed foreign firms to develop new markets for goods and services. Most of the current "owners" of "Chinese" manufacturing—especially in the case of high-tech commodities—are American, European, and Japanese.[29]

Informatization, comprising computerization and telecommunications, allows global conglomerates to command and control entire commodity chains, from the initial exploitation of natural resources, to just-in-time assembly, marketing, and consumer distribution in centers around the world. The first two phases of telecommunications development involved huge injections of foreign direct investment (FDI) and privileged China's special economic zones (SEZ) on the southern coast, where the factories and the wealthier urban populations were located, whereas the hinterland and rural areas were initially ignored.[30]

If in the beginning, Chinese labor produced low-end products, the Chinese party leadership in the last 15 years has itself invested, and recruited FDI, in high technology in order to produce high-end products and move up the global value chain. In 2006, China overtook Japan as the largest national investor in technology, establishing a super ministry to coordinate the information industries, including the cultural industries, as engines of economic growth, and key components in the maintenance of political hegemony and social cohesion. They have developed a tightly controlled web of digital networks and fast-tracked the development of web connections to coordinate production in urban and rural centers. The electronic networks enhance labor mobility, crucially important for both conglomerates and workers, and by 2011, over 750 million Chinese had basic, affordable mobile phones, one of the primary modes of Internet access.[31]

Although the initial telecommunications lines and information and communication technologies (ICTs) privileged export-based production, the current goal is to expand ICT production to integrate the national consumer market, pumping up domestic demand as a new form of Fordism with Chinese characteristics, and a partial alternative to the problematic reliance on exports.[32] Jack Qiu describes this dual-purposed plan as "the wireless leash" embedding political and economic control.[33] Reluctant to sacrifice "economic gains to blunt methods of control" there has been a gradual move from hard to soft controls of the Internet, in which officials handle online dissent better, generate "positive" public opinion on official sites, and infiltrate online spaces and activist networks.[34] Nevertheless, if Chinese information capitalism has facilitated the assembly of a new mobile just-in-time labor force and consumer base, it has also provided opportunities for opening up new horizons of information, new social networks and identities, and new forms of labor contention.

DECOMPOSITION OF THE URBAN WORKING CLASS

China's turn to global capitalism took place on a scale and at a pace that was historically unprecedented. It was violent, with deep and long-lasting economic, social, and cultural imprints on millions of people. The opening to financial markets and foreign capital, and the rapid development of urban infrastructure, was comparatively easy. At the core of these processes was the "un-making" of two classes, the urban industrial working class, the bedrock of Mao's state socialism, and the rural farming class, through two decades of accumulation by dispossession, privatization, and deregulation, and austerity—or slashing of almost all of the social services and wages that Chinese workers had gained.[35]

First, the power of the urban industrial class was *decomposed*. Once heralded by Mao as the "masters of the country," their social contract, the "iron rice bowl," had included guaranteed employment, housing, educational and recreational opportunities, and the possibility of social and political advancement via party membership.[36] They had enjoyed a better ratio of social equality than in most other countries, including the United States and the U.S.S.R.[37] Within the constraints of party-state control, urban industrial workers had contributed to technical innovations and product improvements, with formal protocols helping to resolve workplace disputes.[38]

After the 1979 reforms, state-owned enterprises (SOEs) began to be privatized, bankrupted, or restructured. Inequality was increased as many party cadre were enriched by the sales. At the same time, more than 50 million people were laid off,[39] and left without full-time employment, housing, health, education, and recreation. A three-year package of compensation and benefits promised to many was never implemented at the local level, and millions of people never found secure well-paying jobs again. Although China ostensibly became the global factory, Chinese jobs in manufacturing dropped from 53.9 million to 37.3 million from 1990 to 2002, and wages dropped from approximately 63% of GDP in 1992 to less than 40% in 2006.[40]

The urban workers, in what is similarly called the "rust belt" as in the United States, lost much more than their jobs and paychecks. They lost their social security, medical insurance, and subsidized housing; the system of collective labor relations was privatized, and individual market-based contracts were introduced.[41] Many opposed the lay-offs, and claw-backs of their social wage, and especially the accumulation of state assets by former bosses; they saw privatization as a betrayal of socialist values of workers' control over the public means of production. In reaction, they began to resort to strikes and mass protests. The first notable high point of organizing took place in Tiananmen Square in Beijing in 1989, when student activists famously reached out to the international media. Unacknowledged by most foreign commentators, the majority of protesters were workers, with autonomous labor unions appearing throughout China, often partnering with student unions.[42]

During that period, workers' organizations utilized a variety of communication repertoires.[43] The Beijing Autonomous Workers Federation (BAWF), founded after the establishment of martial law on May 19, started with poetry, wall-posters, and handbills—practices derived from the Cultural Revolution and the Democracy Wall Movement. By the end of May 1989, they had separate propaganda and logistics departments, an office for communications between factories, campuses, and other groups, and a print shop. The BAWF broadcast news to listeners during working hours, dedicating the evening schedule to public readings of messages (including political statements and satire) from its audience.

In the wake of the state repression, many of the activists went into voluntary or compulsory exile, forming the basis of some of the transnational networks that still exist today. The working class leaders, who represented a potential connection across classes and social groups, were often the primary targets of state repression, as the Communist Party well knew the power of labor organizing from their own history. For example, Han Dongfang, a Beijing railway worker who cofounded the BAWF, was expelled to Hong Kong in 1993, where he soon set up the China Labour Bulletin. Despite repression, the number of workers' protests only increased, rising from 10,000 in 1993, to 60,000 in 2003.[44] Whereas petitions to local governments were the most common form, some former SOE workers used wider-reaching tactics to gain media attention, such as a collective march along a major highway to Beijing.[45]

Few of the protests, with the exception of the iron and steel industries, grew beyond local, cellular forms. Most took place after the massive layoffs so that workers' could not leverage their control of production. They were unable to overcome the inertia of state bureaucracies and the repression of the police and judiciary; and the commercialization of the media reduced possibilities for circulating working class struggles. However, although much of the restructuring of state-owned enterprises was completed by

2006, many rust-belt workers continue to lobby their former employers or local governments for justice.[46] Those remaining in finance, energy, and communications, where wages and skilled labor tend to be higher, maintain a strong sense of collective identity, and continue to wage struggles.[47]

REMAKING THE MEDIA

Both the Tiananmen protests and the cataclysmic break-up of the Soviet Union marked a renewed interest by the party-state in controlling media and information. Although much of the government was downsized, in line with neo-liberal orthodoxy, the number of government departments and bureaus tasked with the development and regulation of communications increased.[48] Before opening the Internet in 1994, the state set up a system of controls for network security, and policing of content; initially nine types of content were prohibited, with two more added in 2005 that explicitly restricted disseminating information about public protests or "illegal" civic associations.[49] The entire news propaganda apparatus was fortified under the direction of the party, with Xinhua as the only authoritative reporting agent. However, as Zhao notes, contradictions in daily practice mean that the "party line is not a straight line, but an ever-changing and hard-to-grasp-curve."[50]

In addition to the tightening of political control, the commercialization of media had direct consequences for workers' struggles. The party and government media had their funding slashed, and were expected to commercialize and compete with the growing private media sector. The economic imperative to target affluent urban consumers influenced the editorial line. For example, whereas the urban wealthy were celebrated, and their lifestyles profiled in admiring language, layoffs at SOEs were presented as "painful but unavoidable by-products of economic 'progress.'"[51] Workers were instead encouraged to adopt the virtues of market competition, and acquire a "sense of urgency, a sense of crisis" of learning skills and making endless efforts at self-improvement.[52]

During the 1990s, the "media opportunity structures" for reporting about struggles, and working class lives and experiences, shrunk even further.[53] Independent publications, from workers' organizations, and left-wing critics of the reforms, were censored or treated harshly.[54] Sympathetic journalists provided some investigative reports for official trade union and government labor departments but usually presented the protests as localized problems best remedied through official trade union or party mediation.[55] Then, in the late 1990s, the growing tensions between different nodes of power, the rise of popular commercial dailies, and the upswing in online activism by rural, urban, and working class citizens, resulted in complex fissures, which as we see below, opened the media opportunity structures for a newly forming class of workers.

THE MAKING OF THE *NONMINGONG*

Whereas the power of the rust-belt workers was being un-made, the farmers in rural areas were also suffering massive and violent social change. The privatization of collective farmland involved a massive transfer of land rights, and the dismantling of health and educational services.[56] Tens of millions were displaced, and rural livelihoods decimated. Still ongoing, farmers have launched 100,000 protests, riots, and other mass actions in reaction to land loss in 2004, 2005, and 2006 alone.[57] As a result, echoing the enclosure process in Europe, 250 million rural people from the underdeveloped western and central provinces of Sichuan, Anhui, Henan, and Gansu were forced to move to the cities and export zones: for many this was their first experience working as waged laborers in the capitalist system. Rural migrant workers now provide the backbone of the skilled and malleable labor force for the world's largest production center, with nearly 80% of the construction, mining, and quarrying workforce, 68% of manufacturing, and over 50% in service sectors.[58] Much like migrant workers in the United States, Europe, and elsewhere, they have no job security, and suffer from excessive overtime and unpaid wages and benefits as well as a lack of effective labor union representation.[59]

Their mass migration into the urban centers has involved a long process of re-making themselves, adapting to a new urban life of precarious industrial jobs, and consumerism. Most migrants are also treated as second-class citizens. The urban household registration (*hukou*) system has been relaxed but still presents restrictions for permanent settlement, and thus from establishing families, enjoying proper education, and receiving medical care or other social welfare services. Many workers must share accommodation in massive high-rise dormitory complexes, which are free-standing all-encompassing industrial cities; their close proximity to the factory means that they can easily be recruited to work overtime to meet the just-in-time delivery demands for the new iPhone or other brand product. After sending remittances home, they spend some of their low wages on the global brands and knock-offs that they are manufacturing, including the cell phones and apps that allow them to stay connected with their rural kin and navigate city life.

YOUNG MIGRANT WORKERS

The second and third generation of migrant workers, born in the 1980s and 1990s, is at the vanguard of the current cycle of labor organizing. Like the Dreamers, the younger generation of immigrants without formal citizenship papers in the United States, many Chinese migrant youth have lived all their lives in the industrial cities, have more formal schooling than their parents, and have greater access to the growing counter-public spheres of information. They are especially conscious and resistant to their unequal treatment as second-class citizens, who face growing income inequality and social exclusion.[60] There is a huge discrepancy between their expectations and the reality, and their wages and benefits, and those of better-paid urban workers, professionals, and government employees.[61] Their daily exclusion as *nongmingong*, between an identity as *nongmin* (peasant) and *gongren* (worker), leaves them feeling frustrated and angry, and more willing to contest their oppression and exploitation.[62]

At the same time, they have grown up as digital natives, with cell phones, the Internet, and other social media part of conflicting processes of enculturation as modern consumers and proletarians. The rapid expansion of the mobile phone network introduced a whole new class of people into the webs of the consumer market, providing constant opportunities to buy goods and services, part of the state's plan to increase domestic consumption. The costly mobile phones are a "symbol of social identity, and a marker of the keenly desired urban cosmopolitan life."[63] Mobile phones, as Qiu points out, are integral to the electronic assembly line, part of the surveillance apparatus used to monitor all classes of workers.[64] However, the digital-scape also provides an affective space separate from work, more private than the public TV rooms in the dormitories, and with less restrictive rules.[65]

Young migrant workers routinely use these tools to access new information, develop new literacies, reinforce residual networks, and experiment with new forms of individual and collective identity. Mobile phones and online chats connect them with their home communities, and sustain existing social networks that they can draw on for support.[66] Young women especially have used the mobile phones to negotiate new relationships with their families, developing a "greater degree of freedom from parental control without having to explicitly challenge the importance of parental authority."[67] In their urban environs, the youth have formed new friendships and collective bonds, not dependent on kinship, or native place ties, which can provide protection in social conflicts and help with finding jobs and navigating urban life.[68] They regularly use the web to chat about life experiences and publish poetry in their own online forums.

TACTICAL REPERTOIRES

One female migrant worker in Shenzhen told labor researchers Pun and Li the following:

> In junior high school we read quite a bit about Marxist theory. When the teachers explained the contradiction between productive forces and relations of production in capitalist society they also mentioned the inhuman exploitation of workers. At the time we did not understand. But since I came to Shenzhen for work I have started to figure out how capitalists oppress and exploit workers.[69]

By 2003, manufacturers in coastal provinces such as Guangdong, Zheji-ang, and Jiangsu were unable to attract and retain sufficient numbers of workers.[70] Young workers began to use their digital connections to share information about job opportunities and conditions, and move from job to job, beginning a massive it "silent protest against the hitherto poor working conditions, long hours of overtime work and low wages."[71] They seldom stay long in any one job. On the job they use mobiles to avoid the boredom and "overbearing demands of work supervisors." Some have even been able to physically leave, achieving a "feigned presence," as in the case of the Beijing security guards who covered for one another and took turns to go to the disco.[72]

The young migrant workers' recognition of their strategic value, their appropriation of organizing savvy, and use of cell phones and other ICTs, has improved their capacity to initiate, organize, and sustain protests. Since 2010, and the strike wave set off by vocational college interns at a Honda plant,[73] migrant workers have gone on the offensive in work-related pro-tests. They have demanded higher wages, and their own representatives in labor negotiations.[74] As documented on Chinastrikes, the crowd-sourced map, the number of participants can range from a few dozen to tens of thousands, although most range from several hundred to a few thousand.[75] Usually it is the line-workers, although skilled workers and supervisory staff have sometimes participated as well.

The form of the protests is often similar. Workers almost always first approach management to try and resolve the disputes. Then, if that's inef-fective, they set up inside or at the gates of the factory, to block the trans-port of goods and materials. On a number of occasions, protesters have moved out to occupy public space to alert government authorities, media, and other publics; they have blocked nearby roads and disrupted traffic, mounting demonstrations, processions, and sit-ins in central city plazas. Sometimes, as at Foxconn, the protests have escalated to riot-like dimen-sions, with physical destruction of the dormitories and the plants, and open confrontation with security or the police; and on a few occasions, managers have been attacked and killed.[76]

Mobile phones and the Internet have been important tools in these actions. In the strikes at Honda, in May and June of 2010, they used mobile phones to video events and update workers, reporters, labor activists, lawyers, and media. One of the workers told *The New York Times* that he had created a chat room the night of the strike where they discussed tactics.[77] At other protests, they have used cameras to photograph police beating workers.[78]

The youth have also drawn on the opportunities presented by their shared dormitory living experience to organize their daily lives, and to resist. The dormitories are noisy places, segregated by gender, in which everyone lives with strangers in crowded multi-bunk rooms. However, as Pun and Chan document from two years of fieldwork at Foxconn, the extended time and space has provided opportunities to share knowledge, and develop new collective understandings. They reported meeting young women who discussed the environmental problems, recognizing that the toxicity was not an individual problem but a "workplace-based systemic issue."[79] They also saw slogans that mocked Foxconn, turning "humane management" (*renxinghua guanli)* into "human subordination" (*renxunhua guanli).*[80] During Apple CEO Tim Cook's tour of the factory on March 28, 2012, workers sent out messages through mobile phones and microblogs to vent their anger toward both Foxconn and Apple: "It's just for show."[81]

On other occasions, the youth have decided to take direct action. They organized a series of sporadic actions, culminating, for example, in an incident on March 2, 2011, when hundreds of workers at Foxconn's Chengdu plant blocked a main entrance in protests against "working thirteen twelve-hour days in a row, including four hours of illegal overtime."[82] In October 2012, 3–4,000 employees at the Zhengzhou factory compound struck in protest over overtime and stringent quality control measures. Afterwards, one of the inspectors said: "Today was like a dream that will later become a memory!"[83]

SINGING ON THE CENTRAL STAGE BUILT BY OURSELVES

The making of the new Chinese working class is not only occurring in response to their subjection to industrial exploitation. There is also a parallel process of migrant workers remaking their own subjectivity, and identity. Painstaking, the process involves self-discovery, the acquisition of technical, cultural, and political literacies,[84] and the navigation of a complexity of new social relationships amidst very small cracks in the dominant society. Of course, many young workers aspire to the middle class housing, wages, and status that they witness around them, and to the western brands that they themselves produce.[85] Nevertheless, others are creatively challenging the neo-liberal era's "Chinese dream," forging a new working class identity.

Zheng Xiaoqiong is originally from Sichuan, and began to write poetry while coping with a series of precarious industrial jobs. Challenging the stereotypes about migrant workers, and distinguishing her work from the classical Chinese genres, she credits her sources to rock and roll and the rhythm of her heart. Her aim is to impart the "quality of iron," and the "sense of shrillness and toughness," she found working with machines.[86] In 2007, Zheng won China's prestigious People's Literature Award for "thought-provoking insights into the unhealthiness and inhumanity of the industrial system."[87] The dominant literati and state officials have attempted to coopt Zheng and other individual migrant workers with awards and jobs; nevertheless, she and many others refuse to be typecast, and continue to present their very different standpoints and perspectives.[88]

They are beginning to fashion a new language and collective identity. Groups, such as the Workers' Poetry Alliance in the Pearl River Delta, use the Internet to present poetry, literature, and articles written by migrant workers, and more classical poetry from labor movements in China and elsewhere.[89] In 2009, the First Culture and Art Festival for and by Chinese migrant workers was organized by the New Workers' Theater, part of the Home for Migrant Workers near Beijing. They used a combination of on and off-line networks to bring together more than 1,000 people, including performers of folk music, drama, and poetry, from over 20 workers' NGOs from Chongqing, Shenzhen and Xiamen.[90] The slogan "Singing on the central stage built by our-selves" underscored their refusal to be marginalized; instead, they asserted their own laboring participation as communicative subjects in the making and the projection of their own cultural representations.

REACTING TO THE MIGRANT WORKERS

Since 2007, partly in response to the labor struggles, the official Chinese media has increased the coverage of workers' grievances and demands. This shift is also in response to the growing power of the citizen blogosphere and social media sites. Over 500 million Chinese use these social networking sites as their primary source of news; workers, labor scholars, rights advocates, journalists, and trade union officials use them as relatively free platforms to interact and exchange information.[91] Citizens' organizations have also put much more pressure on government institutions for greater transparency and public participation.[92] Trying to keep ahead of this public sphere where news breaks in real time, the government must relax its restrictions on official media reporting and "try to direct the story from within."[93] The circulation of news about strikes and protests has emboldened workers, and provided practical lessons about how to proceed. Conscious of their workplace power, and less intimidated by threats from management, they are more willing to "put themselves forward as representatives in negotiations."[94]

The Chinese government has also enacted new legislation in response to the growing labor unrest.[95] During an unprecedented period of public debate, workers, NGOs, international trade union and business organizations submitted commentaries. Although the European and American Chambers of Commerce threatened that the laws would drive out foreign capital, many of the 200,000 plus domestic responses were from workers supporting greater protection.[96] At the local level, more than 20 provinces have raised the minimum wage at least 20% and have tried to get management and workers to negotiate.[97] Although enforcement of the laws is rudimentary, workers and their allies have used them to resolve individual cases and enforce contracts.[98] Collectively, the laws have emboldened workers to pursue more effective forms of representation and negotiation, developing an embryonic system of collective bargaining.[99]

In addition, central and provincial governments have put more pressure on the ACFTU, the official union federation, to manage workers' struggles. The ACFTU has considerably increased its membership, and regained a seat on the Worker's Group of the International Labor Organization (ILO). Although the national body continues to operate primarily as a company union, some of the local staff support workers in negotiations with corporate management. At the same time, the new ACFTU image provides a platform and a target for change, as in the case of the wildcat strike at Walmart in July 2012, where the ACFTU had famously set up union branches.[100]

If in the short term, the Chinese party state is trying to staunch the protests with a higher minimum wage, and more intervention from the ACFTU, in the long run, they are moving industrial development and the contagion to the interior provinces. Foreign export-oriented companies have already reaped tremendous benefits. Foxconn, for example, has been awarded much cheaper land, improved infrastructure, and lower tax rates, plus lower wages and social insurance costs as well as having been provided with free interns by the local colleges and universities.[101] However, as Eli Friedman argues, finding jobs in their own regions may change the dynamics and lead to a greater level of organizing, as the smaller cities have lower bars for residency, and workers may be able to establish themselves more easily, and begin to grow deeper bonds with the surrounding communities.[102]

ALLIED ORGANIZATIONS INSIDE MAINLAND CHINA

Starting in the 1990s, among the fast growing numbers of domestic citizens' groups and transnational NGOs operating in China, a small number of labor organizations sprang up to support the migrant workers.[103] For example, the Shenzhen Internet community, honghuacao.com, is a grassroots operation, named after a medicinal herb similar to vetch. Honghuacao.com supports workers attempting to receive secure employment, affordable medical care, accessible housing, children's education, and decent life after retirement—with economic and social rights as their long-term goals.[104] "The Workers' portal, *chuisi.net*, meaning hammer," provides domestic and international news of workers' struggles and facilitates 36 bulletin boards for workers across China to report and discuss ongoing struggles and conditions.[105] Offline, they provide legal consultation, and maintain a library and sports and entertainment facilities.

For the last decade, a number of NGOs in Hong Kong, Taiwan, and the diaspora have provided more direct support of organizing, campaigning, and advocacy.[106] Groups such as the China Labour Bulletin, whose founder, Han Dongfang, was exiled to Hong Kong because of his involvement in the Beijing Autonomous Workers Federation in 1989, help train workers, provide legal and paralegal assistance, and broadcast coverage of their struggles. These groups operate as part of a transnational movement that is building alliances with labor and civil society organizations in Hong Kong, and throughout Asian and western capitals, and advocating for legislative changes to labor law, pensions, and social security.[107]

LABOR ACTIVISTS AND NGOS OUTSIDE CHINA

Many of these organizations are part of the transnational network that led the earlier global mobilization against sweatshops in the toy and textile industry. In 2010, several groups joined with Students and Scholars Against Corporate Misbehavior (SACOM), a core member of GoodElectronics, a global network on human rights and sustainable production in the electronics industry. Coordinated on the web, they targeted Foxconn and Apple in a series of street-level protests in Hong Kong and other global cities, and kept up the pressure with a repertoire that includes documentation and exposure of the sweatshop conditions, domestic and transnational petitions, and a strategic media campaign.

Each time Foxconn and Apple have tried to minimize the damage and announced concessions, the watchdog network has quickly countered with well-documented accounts. When, for example, Foxconn claimed they had raised wages, they countered that the increase was only in line with Chinese legal minimums.[108] Foxconn, they argued, was actually reducing their overall wage bill by shifting their workforce to lower-waged zones in China's interior, hiring student interns with no remuneration,[109] and installing robots.[110] The watchdog network underscored Apple's complicity: Contractors were pressured to comply with short product delivery deadlines by imposing arduous overtime hours,[111] and to keep wages low in order to secure Apple's gross margins on the iPhone which are about 59%, compared to only 1.8% for labour compared to 20% for competitor products.[112] The watchdog groups continue to closely monitor and publicize problems, and protest the lack of any deep change to the operations.[113]

The labor solidarity groups challenge the complicity of Chinese authorities, and link the protests of Chinese workers to the larger context of globally networked capitalism. Their responses to each new corporate initiative come with more than two decades of transnational organizing, and research. Fahmi Panimbang, from the Asia Monitor Resource Centre (AMRC) writes that monitoring and "codes of conduct" can appease shareholders and consumers, but take the pressure off local authorities to enforce labor regulations, and in effect privatize labor law and increase corporate power. More broadly, she notes, the turn to these and other measures of corporate social responsibility (CSR) had led to some environmental and health and safety-related victories, but has "taken people in the wrong direction."[114] SACOM and the Hong Kong Labour Bulletin both say that it has failed to lead to any long-lasting change for Chinese workers.[115]

Instead, active, reciprocal solidarity with western movements is important, if, as Chung of Labour Action China Bulletin says, it is based on the self-organizing of workers.[116] There are some signs that other workers' groups have taken up the call. In 2011, there was a strike in Italy at Apple's launch of the iPhone 4 and an abortive attempt of employees in the United States to organize.[117] In the spring of 2013, a German-based labor organization sponsored a series of meetings to discuss solidarity with workers at Foxconn plants in China and Eastern Europe.[118]

CYBER-BOOMERANGS

Seldom cited for their contribution to contentious politics or cyberactivism, the content and form of the Chinese migrant workers' struggles parallels those of other contemporary contentious social movements. They are protesting much the same brutalizing competitive pressures and growing inequality of neo-liberal capitalism as young workers elsewhere. Their cyberactivism counters the very specific material grievances of high-tech capitalism, and they have won some wages concessions, and changes in the everyday conditions of work. They are also creatively and inventively using on- and offline networks as spaces for individual and collective expression, exchange of information and life experiences, and the development of new analyses and collective knowledge, not unlike those mobilizing in the public squares of Cairo, Istanbul, or Oakland Occupy.

The migrant workers face continuing domestic constraints. Although the party-state is taking a more soft-power approach to the Internet, state censorship of worker websites remains especially tight.[119] The migrant workers still remain largely separate from the rust-belt workers, as well as the environmentalists, dissidents, and consumer activists who make up China's field of civil society and Internet activism.[120] The independent labor movement is still tiny and vulnerable to state repression; much of its base is outside the mainland in Hong Kong.

In the long run, the greater barriers to the success of migrant workers' struggles are not within China, but in the corporate, government, and media headquarters of the United States and richer nations. Apple has certainly gone under the limelight, in all sectors of the media, from the corporate news services, to the tech industry, and alternative media, and even a congressional investigation for their off-shoring of tax responsibilities. However, lauded by President Obama and Congress as exemplary U.S. corporate citizens, Apple as of yet faces very little pressure to comply with existing labor laws in China, pay the workers in line with their huge profits, nor use their considerable resources to fundamentally change the shaky consumer-driven global commodity system.

The continuing geopolitical dominance of the global corporate media, and their news norms, pose an additional set of barriers. Operating in the home country of many of the global brands that manufacture in China, and with a much reduced labor news beat, the U.S. corporate media continue to frame the Chinese party-state as solely responsible, and the workers as powerless victims. In order for Chinese workers to effectively confront the corporate brands, and improve their work-life and living conditions, they will need to break through those media blind-spots and norms. For, as we have seen in recent uprisings in Egypt, and other regions, however much activists have utilized social media, they have required the reporting and circulation by the dominant corporate satellite news services to get global reach. It remains to be seen how the young Chinese workers will use their cyber-boomerangs to effect change in the heart of the electronic industry and icapitalism in Silicon Valley.[121]

NOTES

1. In comparison to Twitter, Weibo functions more as a blog site as it can accommodate many more words, allow more comments, and display up to 50 retweets. Weibo means scarf, which denotes warmth and intimacy. Subject to censorship, weibo sites produce volumes of contentious discourse (Yang, 2011: 232).
2. J. Cheung, 2012.
3. Manfred Elfstrom, *China Strikes* [Computer file], available at: https://chinas trikes.crowdmap.com.
4. Eli Friedman, 2012.
5. A. Ramzy, 2009.
6. For a list of most of the names, see SACOM 2010: 2. Three more suicides took place in May 2013. Kitchen (2013). As of May 24, 2013, the Wikipedia entry on Foxconn listed 75 news entries. Wikipedia (2013).
7. See among other statements, the translation by Chan and Pun of a worker's blog after the 12th jump at Foxconn (2010). J. Chan, J., and N. Pun, 2010.

   To die is the only way to testify that we ever lived
   Perhaps for the Foxconn employees and employees like us
   -we who are called *nongmingong*, rural migrant workers, in China—
   -the use of death is simply to testify that we were ever alive at all,
   -and that while we lived, we had only despair.

8. Condolences and protests took place in Shenzhen, Beijing, Hong Kong, Taipei, New York, Washington D.C., San Francisco, Boston, Canada, Mexico, the Czech Republic, Berlin, Amsterdam, Switzerland, France, Australia, South Korea, India, and other places around the world. J. Chan and N. Pun, 2010.
9. G. Brown (2009); M. Maisto (2012).
10. Jenny Chan and Ngai Pun (2010).
11. F. Viticci (June1, 2010).
12. F. Panimbang (2011).
13. Guo et al. (2012): 494.
14. Guo et al. (2012): 494.
15. Pan (2008).
16. Ramirez and Rong (2012).
17. Guo et al. (2012):

18. Hanser (2013).
19. Friedman (2012).
20. Qiu (2010).
21. Qiu and Kim (2010): 631.
22. Lee (2005); Zhao and Duffy (2007); Law and Peng (2008); Lin and Tong (2008), Nang and Ngai (2009); Chan and Pun (2009, 2010); Nang and Pun (2009); Chan and Peng (2011); China Labour Bulletin (2009, 2011, 2012); Chung (2010); Crothall (2012); Friedman (2009, 2013); Li (2011); Ngai and Huilin (2010); Qiu and Kim (2010); Pun and Chan (2013); Xing (2011, 2012); China Labor Watch (2011), SACOM (2011, 2012, 2012a); Van Regenmortel (2010); Xing (2011); Xing (2012).
23. ZeroWork (1975).
24. Dyer-Witheford has described composition in this way: "If workers resisting capital compose themselves as a collectivity, capital must strive to *decompose* or break up this threatening cohesion. It does this by constant revolutionising of the means of production—by recurrent restructurings, involving organisational changes and technological innovations that divide, deskill or eliminate dangerous groups of workers. But since capital is a system that depends on its power to organise labour . . . it cannot entirely destroy its antagonist. Each capitalist restructuring must recruit new and different types of labour, and thus yield the possibility of working class *re-composition* involving different strata of workers with fresh capacities of resistance and counter-initiative" (1999): 66.
25. Grindon (2012): 85.
26. Dyer-Witheford (2008).
27. Among those using autonomist protocols to research struggles in the cultural domain, see Zhao and Duffy, 2007; Grindon (2012); Dyer-Witheford (1999, 2008); Kidd (2009); Wright (2004); and Xing (2011).
28. Zhao (2007).
29. D. Schiller (2008): 112.
30. Steinbock (2003).
31. J. Liu (2011).
32. D. Schiller (2008): 113.
33. Qiu (2007).
34. Yang (2011): 222 and 235.
35. Lee (2005).
36. See Xing for a discussion of workers' communications practices and autonomous organization in foreign-invested ventures, in Shanghai in the earlier part of the 20th century (Xing: 80).
37. The ratio between shop floor wages and upper manager's income was less than two to one, compared to nine to one in Soviet factories, and even greater in the U.S. Richman, cited in Xing: 149.
38. Xing (2011), 63.
39. Chan and Peng, 426.
40. Asia Monitor Research Centre (2010): 3.
41. Pringle (2013): 193.
42. Cunningham and Wasserstrom, 13–18.
43. Zhao and Duffy (2007).
44. Chan and Peng (2001).
45. China Labour Bulletin (2012): 15.
46. China Labour Bulletin (2011): 30.
47. Li (2011): 44.
48. Zhao (2008): 22.
49. Yang (2011): 50–51.

50. Zhao (2008): 25.
51. Ibid.
52. Zhao (2003): 46.
53. See Costanza-Chock (2013) for a discussion of "media opportunity structures."
54. In 1999, for example, several laid off workers in Northwest China were jailed for publishing the *Chinese Workers' Monitor,* which reported on the official corruption and misconduct in managing their SOE. Zhao (2008): 202.
55. Chan (2001): 4–5.
56. Han (2009).
57. Han (2009): 36.
58. Nang and Pun (2009).
59. E. Friedman (2009): 224.
60. Pun and Lu (2011): 495.
61. Pun and Chan (2010).
62. Pun and Lu (2010): 498.
63. Lin and Tong (2008): 74.
64. Qiu (2007): 85.
65. Peng (2008).
66. Ibid.
67. K. Yang (2008): 70.
68. K. Yang (2008).
69. Pun and Li (2006).
70. Friedman (2012).
71. Ngan and Ma (2008): 62.
72. K. Yang (2008): 68.
73. Pringle (2013): 197.
74. China Labour Bulletin (2012): 16.
75. Elfstrom (2012): 12.
76. Friedman (2012).
77. Barboza and Bradsher (2010).
78. Chan and Pun (2009): 296.
79. Pun and Chan (2013): 186.
80. Pun and Chan (2013): 184.
81. Pun and Chan (2013): 186.
82. Ibid.
83. Jing and Rui (2012).
84. Zhao (2012): 18.
85. Boudreau (2013).
86. Xing (2011): 201.
87. Xing (2011): 204.
88. Xing (2011): 205.
89. Xing (2012): 79.
90. Xing (2011): 201.
91. Cheung, China Labour Bulletin (May 2012).
92. Yang (2011): 221.
93. China Labour Bulletin, March 2012.
94. China Labour Bulletin: 24.
95. The Employment Promotion Law (2007), Labour Contract Law (2007), and Labour Dispute Arbitration Law (2008).
96. Friedman (2009): 225.
97. Dreyfuss (2010): 18.
98. Friedman (2009): 226.
99. China Labour Bulletin (2012): 2.

100. Chen (2013).
101. One-hundred-fifty-thousand interns worked at Foxconn alone (15% Foxconn's workforce) in the summer of 2010. Chakraborrty (2013): 184.
102. Friedman (2012).
103. Friedman (2009): 229
104. Xing (2012): 75–76.
105. Xing (2012): 76.
106. Chung (2010).
107. Ibid.
108. Twenty provinces, including the Shenzhen local authority, where one of the largest Foxconn factories is located, raised their minimum wage in 2009 and 2011. Crothall (2012).
109. Pun and Chan (2011): 14.
110. SACOM (2011).
111. Chan, Pun and Selden (2013): 111.
112. Chan, Pun and Selden (2013): 106.
113. In 2013, as of this writing, SACOM and their allies are challenging Foxconn's statements that they are supporting union democratization and shortening overtime hours. During the Foxconn Annual General Meeting in Hong Kong on May 30, 2013, SACOM reported that 90% of the Foxconn workers knew nothing about the new union, and that overtime is "still severe."
114. Panimbang (2011).
115. SACOM (2012); China Labour Bulletin (August 2008).
116. Chung (2010).
117. Gupta (2011).
118. Gongchao (2013).
119. Yang (2011): 230.
120. Yang (2011): 240.
121. Keck and Sikkink first used the concept of boomerang, to describe domestic activists using an international boomerang to effect domestic change. Via Tarrow, Yang has applied the concept to China (2011): 198.

REFERENCES

Asia Monitor Resource Centre. "Position Statement on Corporate Social Responsibility." 2011. www.amrc.org.hk/node/1061 (accessed April 12, 2012).
Barboza, D., and K. Bradsher "A Labor Movement Enabled by Technology." *The New York Times*. June 17, 2010.
Boudreau, J. "Apple, Foxconn Open Up about China Factories." *Mercury News.* May 5, 2013.
Brown, G. "Global Electronics Industry: Poster Child of 21st Century Sweatshops and Despoiler of the Environment?" *EHS Today.* September 1, 2009. http://ehstoday.com/safety/news/global-electronics-industry-sweatshops-environment-1063 (accessed June 22, 2013).
Chakrabortty, A. "Forced student labour is central to the Chinese economic miracle. The Guardian, 14 October 2013. www.theguardian.com/commentisfree/2013/oct/14/forced-student-labour-china-apple (accessed March 3, 2004).
Chan, A. *Chinese Workers under Assault: The Exploitation of Labor in a Globalising Economy.* Amonk, NY: M.E. Sharpe, 2001.
Chan, C.K., and Z. Peng. "From Iron Rice Bowl to the World's Biggest Sweatshop: Globalization, Institutional Constraints, and the Rights of Chinese Workers." *Social Service Review* 85, no.3 (September 2011): 426.

Chan, J. "Labor Notes: Who Speaks for China's Workers?" *SACOM*. May 29, 2013. http://sacom.hk/archives/1619 (accessed June 30, 2013).

Chan, J., and N. Pun "The Making of a New Working Class?" A Study of Collective Actions of Migrant Workers in South China." *The China Quarterly*, 198 (June 2009): 287–303.

Chan, J., and N. Pun, "Suicide as Protest for the New Generation of Chinese Migrant Workers: Foxconn, Global Capital, and the State," *The Asia-Pacific Journal* 37-2-10 (September 13, 2010). http://japanfocus.org/-jenny-chan/3408 (accessed February 12, 2014).

Chan, J., N. Pun and M. Selden. (2013) "The politics of global production: Apple, Foxconn and China's new working class." New Technology, Work and Employment 28:2. ISSN 0268-1072.

Chen, M. "Walmart Empire Clashes with China." *The Progressive*. January, 8, 2013. http://progressive.org/walmart-empire-clashes-with-china (accessed June 15, 2013).

Cheung, J. "How Weibo Helped Dongguan Factory Workers Get Their Voices Heard." *China Labour Bulletin*. www.china-labour.org.hk/en/view-blogs-content/110058 (accessed May 14, 2012).

Cheung, J. "Pay Dispute and Factory Relocations the Focus of Strike Action in April." *China Labour Bulletin*. May 3, 2012. www.china-labour.org.hk/en/node/110050 (accessed May 9, 2012).

China Daily. "Migrant Workers Find the Pen Mightier than the Plow." February 7, 2006. http://french.china.org.cn/english/culture/157219.htm (accessed April 12, 2012).

China Labor Watch. "Tragedies of Globalization: The Truth Behind Electronics Sweatshops." 2011. www.chinalaborwatch.org/pro/proshow-149.html (accessed April 17, 2012).

China Labour Bulletin. "The Growth and Future Development of CSR in China: Bringing Workers into Play." *China Labour Bulletin*. August 5, 2008. www.china-labour.org.hk/en/node/100288 (accessed April 12, 2012).

China Labour Bulletin "Going it Alone?The Workers' Movement in China (2007–2008)." *China Labour Bulletin*. July 2009. www.clb.org.hk/en/content/going-it-alone-report-state-workers-movement-china. (accessed May 29, 2013).

China Labour Bulletin. "Unity is Strength: The Workers' Movement in China, 2009." *China Labour Bulletin*. 2011. www.clb.org.hk/en/node/100013 (accessed February 21, 2012).

China Labour Bulletin. "A Decade of Change: The Workers' Movement in China 2000–2010." *China Labour Bulletin*. March 28, 2012. www.china-labour.org.hk/en/node/110024 (accessed April 12, 2012).

Chung, S. "Hong Kong—China Solidarity: Reflections on the Past Ten Years of Supporting Worker Advocacy in China." *Asian Labour Update*. 75 (April-June 2010): 24–27. www.amrc.org.hk/node/998/print (accessed February 23, 2012).

Costanza-Chock, S. "Transmedia Mobilization in the Popular Association of the Oaxacan Peoples, Los Angeles." In *Mediation and Protest Movements*, edited by B. Cammaerts, A. Mattoni, and P. McCurdy (pp. 95–114). Bristol: Intellect Books, 2013.

Crothall, G. "The Real Reason Foxconn Raised Wages in Shenzhen." *China Labour Bulletin*. www.china-labour.org.hk/en/view-blogs-content/101252 (accessed April 15, 2012).

Cunningham, M. E. and J. Wasserstrom, "Interpreting Protest in Modern China." *Dissent*. (Winter 2011): 13–18.

Dreyfuss, R. "China in the Driver's Seat." *The Nation*. Sept. 20, 2010, 11–18.

Dyer-Witheford, N. *Cyber-Marx*. Urbana and Chicago: University of Illinois Press, 1999.

Dyer-Witheford, N. "For a Compositional Analysis of the Multitude." In *Subverting the Present, Imagining the Future: Class, Struggle, Commons*, edited by W. Bonefeld (pp. 247–266). New York: Autonomedia, 2008.

Elfstrom, Manfred. 2012. *China Strikes* [Computer File]. https://chinastrikes.crowd-map.com (accessed May 30, 2013).

Friedman, Eli. 2012. "China in Revolt." *Jacobin.* Issue 7–8: Emancipation. http://jacobinmag.com/2012/08/china-in-revolt/ (accessed May 20, 2013).

Friedman, Ellen. "U.S. and Chinese Labor at a Changing Moment in the Global Neoliberal Economy." *Working USA: The Journal of Labor and Society.* 12 (June 2009): 219–234.

Gongchao. "Incomplete List of Labor Unrest at Foxcon 2010–2013." www.gongchao.org/en/islaves-struggles/list-of-labor-unrest-at-foxconn (accessed May 25, 2013).

Grindon, G. "Surrealism, Dada, and the Refusal of Work: Autonomy, Activism, and Social Participation in the Radical Avant-Garde." *Oxford Art Journal* 34, no. 1 (2011): 79–96. doi:10.1093/oxartj/kcr003.

Guo, L., S. Hsu, A. Holton, and S. Jeong. "A Case Study of the Foxconn Suicides: An International Perspective to Framing the Sweatshop Issue." *International Communication Gazette* 74, no. 5 (2012): 484–503.

Gupta, P. Apple's iPhone 4S Greeted with a Strike in Italy? *Reuters.* October 28, 2011. http://blogs.reuters.com/mediafile/2011/10/28/apples-iphone-4s-greeted-with-a-strike-in-italy/ (accessed June 28, 2013).

Han, D. "Farmers, Mao, and Discontent in China." *Monthly Review* 61, no. 7 (2009): 20–36.

Hanser, A. "A Yellow Peril Consumerism: China, North America and an Era of Global Trade." *Ethnic and Racial Studies* 36, no. 4 (2013) 632–650. http://dx.doi.org/10.1080/01419870.2011.631559 (accessed February 12, 2014).

Jing W., and L. Rui "Sequel of Foxconn's Inland Movement: Some Workers' Life Too Monotonous." *Economic Observer.* October 13, 2012. Translated by China Labor Watch. http://tech.sina.com.cn/it/2012-10-13/00217697628.shtml (accessed June 1, 2013)

Kidd, D., and C. Fugazzola. "Contentious Politics and Workers' Communication: A Comparison of China and South Korea." In *Global Media Worlds and China,* edited by Luo Qing, Göran Svensson, and Lena Rydholm. Tsinghua University Press, 2013.

Kitchen, M. "New Suicides Reported at Foxconn China Factory." *Market Pulse Archives.* www.marketwatch.com/story/new-suicides-reported-at-foxconn-china-factories-2013-05-20 (accessed May 31, 2013).

Law, P., and Y. Peng, "Mobile Networks: Migrant Workers in Southern China." In *Handbook of Mobile Communication Studies,* edited by J. Katz (pp. 55–64). Cambridge: The MIT Press, 2008.

Lee, C.K. "Livelihood Struggles and Market Reform: Unmaking Chinese Labour after State Socialism." United Nations Research Institute for Social Development (UNRISD) *Occasional Paper* 2 (2005).

Li, M. "The Rise of the Working Class in China." *Monthly Review* 63, no. 2 (2011): 38–51.

Lin, A., and A. Tong. "Mobile Cultures of Migrant Workers in Southern China: Informal Literacies in the Negotiation of (New) Social Relations of the New Working Women." *Knowledge, Technology & Policy* 21 (2008): 73–81.

Liu, J. "Mobile Activism and Contentious Politics in Contemporary China." April 30, 2013. http://ssrn.com/abstract=2258519 or http://dx.doi.org/10.2139/ssrn.2258519 (accessed May 30, 2013).

Maisto, M. "Apple, Foxconn Controversy Gives Tech Industry its 'Nike Moment.'" *E-Week.com.* April 11, 2012. www.eweek.com/c/a/Mobile-and-Wireless/Apple-Foxconn-Controversy-Gives-Tech-Industry-Its-Nike-Moment-641049/ (accessed May 9, 2012).

Nang, L., and N. Pun. "The Radicalisation of the New Chinese Working Class: a case study of collective action in the gemstone industry." *Third World Quarterly* 30, no. 3 (2009): 551–565.

Ngan, R., and S. Ma. "The Relationship of Mobile Telephony to Job Mobility in China's Pearl River Delta." *Knowledge Technology Policy* (2008): 55–63.

Pan, P. "U.S. News Coverage of New Leaders in China." *China Media Research* 4, no. 1 (2008), 29–35.

Panimbang, F. "The Reality of Corporate Social Responsibility: Experiences from China, South Korea, India and Indonesia." *Asia Monitor Resource Center*. 2011. www.amrc.org.hk/node/1220 (accessed April 12, 2012).

Peng, Y. "Internet Use of Migrant Workers in the Pearl River Delta." *Knowledge, Technology & Policy* 21 (2008): 47–54.

Pun, N., and J. Chan. "Global Capital, the State, and Chinese Workers: The Foxconn Experience." The Foxconn Research Group. 2011. rdln.files.wordpress.com/2012/01/pun-ngai_chan-jenny_on-foxconn.pdf (accessed June 24, 2013).

Pun, N., and J. Chan. "The Spatial Politics of Labor in China: Life, Labor, and a New Generation?of Migrant Workers." *The South Atlantic Quarterly* 112, no.1 (Winter 2013): 179–190. doi:10.1215/00382876–1891332.

Pun N. and C. K. Lee. (2006) "China's Migrant Workers." Gongchao. www.gong-chao.org/www.prol-position.net/nl/2008/10/chinas%20migrant%20workers (accessed November).

Pun, N., and H. Lu. "Unfinished Proletarianization: Self, Anger, and Class Action among the Second Generation of Peasant-Workers in Present-Day China." *Modern China* 36, no. 5 (2010): 493–519.

Pringle, T. "Reflections on Labor in China: From a Moment to a Movement." *The South Atlantic Quarterly* 112, no.1 (Winter 2013): 179–190. doi:10.1215/00382876–1891332.

Qiu, J. "The Wireless Leash: Mobile Message Service as a Means of Control." *International Journal of Communication* 1 (2007): 74–91.

Qiu, J., and Y. Kim. "Recession and Progression? Notes on Media, Labor, and Youth from East Asia. "*International Journal of Communication* 4 (2010): 630–648.

Qi, L. Heavy metal poet. (2008) China Daily, March 3, p. 18. www.chinadaily.com.cn/cndy/2008-03/13/content_6531572.htm (accessed May 15, 2013).

Ramirez, C., and R. Rong. "China Bashing: Does Trade Drive the 'Bad' News about China in the USA?" *Review of International Economics* 20, no. 2 (2012): 350–363.

Ramzy, A. "Runners Up: The Chinese Worker." *Time Magazine*. Wednesday, December 16, 2009 (accessed January 14, 2014).

Schiller, D. "An update on China in the Political Economy of Information and Communications." *Chinese Journal of Communication* 1, no. 1 (April 2008) 109–116.

Steinbock, D. Wireless Horizon: Strategy and Competition in the Worldwide Mobile Marketplace. Amacom, 172, 2003.

Students and Scholars Against Corporate Misbehaviour. (SACOM). "Workers as Machines: Military Management in Foxconn." October 12, 2010. http://sacom.hk/archives/738 (accessed June 2, 2013).

Students and Scholars Against Corporate Misbehaviour. (SACOM). "iSlave Behind the iPhone Foxconn Workers in Central China." September 24, 2011. http://sacom.hk/archives/898 (accessed June 1, 2012).

Students and Scholars Against Corporate Misbehaviour. (SACOM). "Give Apple Workers a Voice in Their Future." 2012. http://sacom.hk/archives/944 (accessed March 23, 2012).

Students and Scholars Against Corporate Misbehaviour. (SACOM). "Apple Concedes Problems in Supply Chain at Last: FLA Report Omits Work Stress and Forced Internship." 2012a. http://sacom.hk/archives/946 (accessed April 17, 2012).

Van Regenmortel, H. "Corporate Social Responsibility (CSR): a Vehicle for International Solidarity?" Asia Monitor Resource Centre. 2010. www.amrc.org.hk/node/1022 (accessed April 12, 2012).

Viticci F. Steve Jobs Email Conversation about Foxconn Suicides. *Macstories*, June1, 2010. www.macstories.net/stories/steve-jobs-email-conversation-about-foxconn-suicides/ (accessed May 31, 2013).

Wikipedia. "Foxconn Suicides." http://en.wikipedia.org/wiki/Foxconn_suicides (Accessed May 31, 2013).

Wright, S. (2004) "Informing, Communicating and ICTs in contemporary anti-capitalist movements." In *Cyberprotest: New media, Citizens and Social Movements*, edited by W. van de Donk et al. (pp. 77–94). New York: Routledge.

Xing, G. *Living with the Revolutionary Legacy: Communication, Culture and Workers' Radicalism in Post-Mao China*. Ph.D. dissertation, Simon Fraser University, 2011.

Xing, G. "Online Activism and Counter-Public Spheres: A Case study of Migrant Labour Resistance." *Javnost-The Public* 19, no. 2 (2012): 63–82.

Yang, G. *The Power of the Internet in China: Citizen Activism Online*. New York: Columbia University Press, 2011.

Yang, K. "A Preliminary Study on the Use of Mobile Phones among Migrant Workers in Beijing." *Knowledge, Technology & Policy* 21 (2008): 65–72.

ZeroWork Editorial Collective. *ZeroWork: Political Materials 1*. New York and Toronto: Zerowork, 1975.

Zhao, Y. Enter the World': Neo-liberalism, the Dream for a Strong Nation, and Chinese Press Discourse on the WTO, in Chinese Media, Global Contexts, edited by Chin- Chuan Lee. London; New York: Routledge, 2003.

Zhao, Y. "The Rich, the Laid-off and the Criminal in Tabloid Tales: Read All about It!" in Perry Link, Richard Madsen and Paul Pickowicz (eds.), Popular China: Unofficial Culture in A Globalising Society. (pp. 111–135). Lanham: Rowman and Littlefield, 2002.

Zhao, Y. "Marketizing the 'Information Revolution' in China." In *Media in the Age of Marketization*, edited by. G. Murdoch and J. Wasko. Cresskill, NJ: Hampton Press, 2007.

Zhao, Y. *Communication in China: Political Economy, Power and Conflict*. Lanham, Maryland: Rowman & Littlefield, 2008.

Zhao, Y. "Introduction to Communication and Class Divide in China." *Javnost* 19, no. 2 (2012): 5–22.

Zhao, Y., and R. Duffy. "Short-Circuited: Communication and Working Class Struggle in China." In *Knowledge Workers in the Information Society*, edited by Catherine McKercher and Vincent Mosco (pp. 229–248). Lanham, MD: Lexington Books, 2007.

11 Women Activists of Occupy Wall Street

Consciousness-Raising and Connective Action in Hybrid Social Movements

Megan Boler and Christina Nitsou

REDEFINING SOCIAL MOVEMENT "SUCCESS"

On the Second Anniversary of Occupy Wall Street, September 17, 2013, political commentator Robert Reich dismissed the movement as having failed, in part due to its "lack of a clear leadership."[1] Such judgments persistently accusing Occupy Wall Street (OWS) of having "no clear goals or aims"—widely held misrepresentations of OWS which began almost as soon as media began reporting—reflect a fundamental misunderstanding and misrecognition of the particular commitments, aims, and visions of OWS as well as how contemporary "hybrid social movements" function, mobilized by a new generation of young, often first-time activists. In particular, the horizontal (nonhierarchical) organizational structure can appear to those unfamiliar with horizontalism as a lack of clear goals. Such accusations fail to recognize a key feature of contemporary social movements: the increasingly important commitment to a process of liberation as part and parcel of any end goals or singular aims. OWS is known as a leaderless movement for this reason, including features such as consensus-based decisions and radical inclusivity.

Horizontalism creates a nonhierarchical space which invites women to thrive and find spaces and places to assume "leadership." A key participant from Occupy Santa Cruz tells us,

> . . . since we were in a horizontal structure, and in a vertical structure women are often put at the lower rung of the ladder, it was a way for women to be heard. So that did happen and . . . the leaders of the group, quote unquote, even though we weren't supposed to have leaders, were mostly all women, so that was kind of fascinating. But . . . the horizontal structure of Occupy is essential in kind of giving women the power to discuss and to even set agendas . . . (Leanne, Occupy Santa Cruz; news radio activist, mid-30s)

The comparison of OWS with the 1970s women's liberation movement (also called second-wave feminism) thus turns out to be highly significant to the evaluation of OWS, as we will show through our analysis of interviews with 23 women participants from nine Occupy sites across North America.[2] The practices of General Assemblies (GAs), people's mic(rophone), working groups, and "progressive stack" in OWS, all engaged consciousness-raising (CR) components originating in second-wave feminism. Without question, differences of racialized, ethnic, and class identities played out throughout the OWS movement; these fraught and nuanced dimensions are explored in Boler (2012).

However, because these components have morphed to hybrid spaces (online and offline), classic face-to-face (F2F) CR dialogues now include significant other modalities that require significant labor, much of which was conducted by women in OWS including information sharing, serving as FB administrator (adminning) for local Occupy Facebook (FB) sites, and conducting working groups. In all of these activities, significant components of CR include engaging in in-depth dialogues about the personal and political to move forward with consensus. The widespread massive shift to uses of social media for information sharing, organizing, dialogue, strategizing, documenting, and connecting is recognized most insightfully in the work of Maria Bakardjieva. As she notes, "The Internet transforms the process of identification by exploding the number of discourses and subject positions to which the individual becomes exposed, as well as by multiplying the participation forms available at that individual's fingertips."[3] For horizontally-structured, consensus-based movements, measures of success formerly applied within social movement theory (SMT) and political theory are no longer sufficient.

Before illustrating how CR was taken up and how hybrid forms of CR developed through the integration of social media platforms such as Facebook, it is helpful to clarify how the principle of horizontalism redefines the contemporary landscape of social movements. The structure itself is key to the aims of such movements and this principle must be understood in order to fully appreciate the politicization of the new generation of young activists around the globe.

THE AIMS OF OWS: HORIZONTALISM AS PROCESS AND AIM

In the December 2011 issue of Ms. Magazine, blogger and film critic Stephanie Rogers wrote one of the first "mainstream" news pieces on the overlap of OWS and the reemergence of feminism, particularly practices from second-wave feminism such as CR and horizontalism.[4] The essay is titled "What Occupy Wall Street Owes to Feminist Consciousness-Raising," and notes:

> On November 17th, the national day of action for the Occupy Wall Street movement, I was interviewed by a man from a Swedish newspaper who wanted to know why I was there. I smiled and said, "That's

the question, isn't it?" Everyone wants to know, still, even after the two-month anniversary of a movement that's only continued to grow stronger and gain more momentum, why people are occupying, who and what they're protesting, and what they hope to change. I regurgitated what has effectively become The Message, "We want the power back in the hands of the people."[5]

Those presuming that a social movement must have a single or at least bounded legislative or policy change goal should account for the fact that myriad social movements since the 1960s have not embraced the single-demand formula.

In her recent article "Horizontal Democracy Now: From Alterglobalization to Occupation,"[6] Marianne Maeckelbergh draws on years of participatory research to define horizontalism and provide its historical contexts and development. Two key practices that define the current historical moment have a long history: (1) the refusal of singular demands, ideologies, or programs for social change (linked to the movement terms "diversity" and "horizontality"), and (2) the idea that the political practices the movement itself develops are part and parcel of the movement's aims (prefiguration).[7]

Maeckelbergh traces multi-issue movements through contemporary history "from the New Left in the 1960s to feminist movements, anti-nuclear and peace movements in the 1970s and 1980s, to environmental and do-it-yourself (DIY) movements in the 1980s and 1990s all the way through to the alterglobalization movement at the turn of the century."[8] Maeckelbergh emphasizes the recognition of inequalities ingrained in social interactions, which makes horizontalism effective in contemporary times:

> . . . horizontality refers to the active creation of nonhierarchical relations through decision-making processes. Horizontality is both a value and a practice. Rather than assuming that equality can be declared or created through a centralized authority that is legitimated to rule by "the people," movement practices of horizontality rest on the assumption that inequality will always permeate every social interaction. This shift in assumptions results in an acknowledgement that these inequalities always exist and that each person is responsible for continuously challenging these inequalities at every step of a decision-making process.[9]

Thus, in counter to the all-too-frequent accusation of lacking clear aims and goals, what critics fail to recognize is the radical commitment built into the histories and principles of horizontalism as an organizational structure for social movements, highlighting the concept of "economic injustice" which, for some time, replaced terms like "class warfare,"[10] and the long-haul consciousness raising commitment of participants. Many of those interviewed expressed their commitment to OWS in these terms:

Well, of course with any social movement you learn right from the beginning, you start learning about social movements in general, and it is not something that is taken care of in a day, or a week, or a year. People who, most people I believe who are involved with Occupy are in it for the long haul . . . (Deena, Occupy Santa Ana, female, mid-60s, some experience with activism)

As Samuel Farber notes, recognition of activists' "long haul commitment" defines such communities as the "conscious minority," characterized by "an ebb and flow with the inevitable loss of people and cadre in the downswing of the socio-economic and political cycles . . . referring not primarily to the leaders but to the long-term, politically conscious activists who are involved for the long haul and who constitute the heart of movements."[11]

Journalists also noted this long-term commitment as essential to the Occupy Movement:

"What's change?" said Rob, a protester who said he has worked in minimum wage jobs all his life and asked not to be identified by his full name. "What isn't change? We're here. That's change." "We're here for the long haul," said Patrick Bruner, a protester and student at Skidmore College in upstate New York, who is among those camped out in a private park near One World Trade Center.[12]

In a blog marking the one-year anniversary of OWS, Rogers calls for recognizing the feminist organizing legacies behind OWS: "We owe it to the women within the movement—and our feminist foremothers—to acknowledge women's work, and to understand that a movement claiming to fight for the disenfranchised can't afford to erase the contributions of women."[13]

Heather Gautney reinforces these key points about the misreading of "demands" and the unique spaces occupied by women thanks to the horizontal structure of OWS by the wider public and media:

This is a leaderless movement without an official set of demands. There are no projected outcomes, no bottom lines and no talking heads. In the Occupy movement, we are all leaders. This is not just a charming mess. We are all leaders represents a real praxis, and it has a real history. In the 1960s and 70s, feminists convened consciousness-raising meetings aimed at politicizing the various forms of women's oppression that were occurring in private. . . . feminist consciousness-raising eschewed formal leadership because each woman's experience and opinion had to be valued equally. The personal was the political.[14]

For those we interviewed, the "personal is political" awakening occurred not only through traditional F2F CR and long haul commitment, but "hybrid" CR. Social technologies, participatory democracy, and CR are radically enhanced by uses of a hybrid form of personal interaction.

OWS'S DEBT TO SECOND-WAVE FEMINISM: PERSONAL IS POLITICAL, CR, PROCESS

Early in our research, the resonance between OWS and feminist organizing practices began to emerge with increasing clarity and certainty. By the spring of 2012, some seven months after the camps had been closed, sites we were following like Occupy Patriarchy and Women Occupying Wall Street (WOW) announced that a Feminist General Assembly (FemGA) would be held in NYC. It would turn out to be one of five FemGAs held that summer. Stephanie Rogers writes in her blog Bitch Flicks,

> . . . Like consciousness-raising, Occupy Wall Street started with small groups of oppressed people who spoke to one another about their personal struggles, and in doing so, learned they weren't alone or insane or weak or lazy, the way Those In Charge suggested. That discovery gave them the strength to channel the individual anger and suffering they experienced into a larger collective call to action.[15]

Sidney Tarrow, renowned political scientist of Cornell University, noted in an October 2011 Foreign Affairs article that OWS most closely resembles the second-wave of feminism:

> If Occupy Wall Street resembles any movement in recent American history, it would actually be the so-called new women's movement of the 1970s. When that struggle emerged in the wake of the civil rights movement, it shocked conservatives and befuddled liberals. The first saw the activists as a bunch of bra-burning anarchists; the second considered them unladylike, or, well-meaning liberals gone off the reservation. Although the leaders of the new women's movement had policies they wanted on the agenda, their foremost demand was for recognition of, and credit for, the gendered reality of everyday life. Likewise, when the Occupy Wall Street activists attack Wall Street, it is not capitalism as such they are targeting, but a system of economic relations that has lost its way and failed to serve the public.[16]

Activist and writer David Graeber also points out the key role of feminism as a precursor to direct democracy.

> The direct democratic process adopted by Occupy Wall Street has deep roots in American radical history. It was widely employed in the civil

rights movement and by the Students for a Democratic Society. But its current form has developed from within movements like feminism and even spiritual traditions (both Quaker and Native American) as much as from within anarchism itself.[17]

This recognition of the influence of second-wave feminism on OWS affirms what we have observed in our research interviews[18] that "There's a 'manarchist' problem in a lot of left-wing spaces," and "a strong current of actively saying 'no' to that" and "a lot of people doing work around safer spaces and speaking out against sexual assault. And while women are leading, there are also other men involved."[19] In the summer of 2012, five Fem-GAs were held, four in New York City and one at the National Occupy Gathering held on the July 4th weekend in Philadelphia. Announced via Facebook and other social media, the events were F2F like all GA meetings and were livestreamed. The format and focus of the FemGAs reflected classic practices of CR; and the format reflected commonly used practices from all GAs—namely, the use of human mic, collective agenda setting, small breakout groups asked to discuss particular topics, report-backs to the larger group, etc. To a great extent, the FemGAs were able to engage traditional F2F CR practices given that these were real-time events held in open public outdoor spaces.

Intrinsic to this aspect of OWS, consciousness-raising is understood as "a personal face-to-face interaction which appears to create new psychological orientations for those involved in the process . . . the face-to-face interaction technique is selected because it is consistent with the radical revolutionary's belief that shared personal experience should generate political theory and action."[20] The CR processes used in the women's liberation movement allowed "validity of personal experience, of the necessity for self-exposure and self-criticism, of the value of dialogue and of the goal of autonomous, individual decision making."[21]

A new evolution of "personal is political" is visible throughout OWS, reflected in both the process and aims of OWS as well as in the intentional and conscious decisions of using consensus groups and assemblies. Graeber notes that OWS was unique amongst this recent spate of global social revolutions in its commitment to consensus-based decision-making (initially defined as 100%, later shifted to 90% agreement for many sites). This use of consensus was the first time it has been adopted for such a large-scale grassroots movement.

Our research also focused on the internal dynamics within OWS that required elements of CR in order to address such matters as unconscious and internalized sexism or racism, for example. A common refrain in Occupy was "Check your privilege!," a direct request to participants to examine their own entitlement and lack of awareness of inequalities. A great deal of this CR work took place F2F. For example, we researched when and how different Occupy sites engaged "progressive stack," which involves a facilitator of the GA creating a list of those who want to speak and ensuring that those who historically have been marginalized from speaking in public (people of color and women, for example) get the opportunity to speak. We studied the development of working groups, which tended to be people of color or queer folks organizing to raise issues important to them. In Oakland, the very word "occupy" was deeply contested, resulting in the split of a group calling themselves "Decolonize" rather than "Occupy" Oakland.[22]

Here, a participant describes the kind of active listening and dialogue central both to OWS and to CR and group settings:

> . . . Hopefully we want to try to understand each other, and if we're working together as a group I think there was that need to kind of reflect. . . . M. was leading us in Council. . . . We would sit around in a group and pass a . . . stone or petrified wood. And whenever it was your turn you would speak freely on the topic that had been chosen and everyone else was just to listen, and then each of us would have our chance . . . it just developed intimacy. It also did develop open lines of communication. (Bria, Occupy Santa Ana, female, late 20s, late December, educational experience in activism, expert in General Assembly)

REVOLUTION GOES VIRAL: SITUATING OCCUPY WALL STREET WITHIN HYBRID GLOBAL LANDSCAPES

The OWS movement emerged amidst multiple uprisings, protests, and grassroots revolutions taking place around the globe. A hybrid movement combines web-based interactions with more traditional F2F meetings, encampments, and crowds-in-the-streets. Chadwick provides us with a definition for hybrid social movements that embraces two key concepts. One is organizational hybridity, built by "creating appealing and increasingly convergent forms of online citizen action, fostering distributed trust across horizontally linked citizen groups, promoting the fusion of sub-cultural and political discourses, and creating and building upon sedimentary networks." Two, Chadwick defines a "hybrid mobilization movement" as one where "organization types move in and out of their traditional identities of a social movement."[23]

In many ways, OWS's call to action was a materialized meme: a demonstration of "We are the 99%." Richard Dawkins in 1989 defined a meme as "a symbolic packet that travels easily across large and diverse populations because it is easy to imitate, adapt personally, and share broadly with others."[24] Dawkins also noted that, "Memes are network building and bridging units of social information transmission."[25] Social media networks and widely accessible information-communication technologies (ICTs) including one-to-many live streams, tweets, posts, pages, cloud- and web-based video and photos (YouTube), and short message service (SMS) enable global connectivity, allowing large-scale organization, circulation of information, alternative and citizen journalistic coverage of events, and public dialogue and self-expression in pluralistic spaces unique to participatory media. The shared global sensibility of the 99%, the sense of "revolution in the air,"[26] is a zeitgeist, a spirit of these times, largely due to the affordance of the internet and social media practices, referred to by one participant as "hive mind." Her description explicitly references the key role played by mediated connectivity:

> I'm like—"This is strange . . . our ideas are on everybody's minds." It was this weird feeling of "hive mind" where you felt like you were— and I'm not a spiritual person at all—but you actually felt like you were in touch with the population at a speed that was quicker than the media because you could . . . you got echoes of things before they would happen and they would become these great sort of media spectacles . . . all of those emotions really stirred up in me a sense that you could possibly accomplish anything through Occupy. You could Occupy anything. (Deena, Occupy LA)

Within mediated publics and networked spaces, such shared sensibilities as "hive mind" travel like/as viral information, or memes:

> One of the things I've been trying to track is how conversations developed without any central means of communication. Because they don't just happen in one space. They travel amongst many spaces, so I've been taking sort of the big conversation about violence and non-violence and trying to track where it flowed. You can't tell where it started of course. It's completely rhizomatic. (Alice, Occupy LA, female, late 50s, December 2012, longtime activist)

This interviewee calls the spread of decentralized shared networked information and conversation "rhizomatic," a form of dissemination that complements the concept of virality to describe how information can travel within our mediascapes.[27] The issue of speed—"you actually felt like you were in touch with the population at a speed that was quicker than the media"—echoes Virilio's theorizations in Pure War.[28]

These connections between individuals and between movements are afforded by social technologies like Facebook, as described by this participant who moves from being a technophobe to immersing herself in FB communities and international news via Google Translate:

> I never would have jumped into it if the Occupy movement hadn't suddenly catalyzed that. I was totally technophobic . . . but when the movement started I just started adding people and within, I remember, in nine days I had like 900 new friends . . . and it's people from all over the world. What I saw in terms of the mobilization over the Internet was

fascinating and how everybody started sharing what was really going on in places, and how it has Google Translate right there, and I could read articles from everywhere in the world. People were sending stuff about what was happening in their city . . . and what's happening in some city, in Hamburg, Germany, and what's happening . . . in Algeria . . . I never would have jumped into it if the Occupy movement hadn't suddenly catalyzed that . . . (Hattie, female, late 20s, December 21, 2012, first time activist)

The shift from social movements to hybrid social movements helps to create diverse points of entry into spaces for dialogue, connection, and community and action. As Chadwick notes, "Such organizational types could not work without the Internet because the technologies set up complex interactions between the online and offline environment and the organizational flexibility required for fast 'repertoire switching' within a single campaign or from one campaign to the next."[29]

HORIZONTAL SOCIAL MOVEMENT STRUCTURES AND HYBRID CONSCIOUSNESS-RAISING

What is unique to contemporary horizontal social movements is how CR is morphing into modalities that combine F2F with online or occur solely through online communication platforms.

Of course, a large part of consciousness-raising exists on the internet, and I've heard people refer to Occupy Wall Street as the first-ever internet revolution. Suffice it to say, Occupy Wall Street wouldn't exist without the fast-as-hell sharing of information over Twitter, personal e-mail exchanges among both participants and skeptics, blogs such as We Are the 99% (a site that showcases photos of people from all over the world sharing personal stories of economic struggle), Facebook (where pages for new feminist groups devoted to Occupy camps crop up daily), and YouTube footage that captures precisely how personal struggle translates into collective political action.[30]

Stephanie Rogers describes how CR begins to take off virally through instances like the "We Are the 99 Percent" Tumblr site:

The "We Are the 99 Percent? blog on Tumblr also represents a viral version of consciousness-raising, where a diverse group of individuals impacted most by the Economy Tankers take to the blog and share their personal experiences in order to raise consciousness about the tangible consequences of the rising economic inequalities.[31]

The hybridity of contemporary social movements is further reflected in contested nicknames such as the "Twitter revolution" (the populist opposition during the 2009 Iranian election protests) and the "Facebook revolution" (another term used for the Egyptian revolution). The networked interconnectivity of the global uprisings is apparent in the accessible web-based public spaces for dialogue, ICTs for ongoing communication, and social media platforms for information sharing, connecting, organizing, mobilizing, and documenting. The capacity to broadcast events—whether marches, protests, incidents of police brutality, inspiring speeches, etc.—through handheld, personalized digital mobile devices and web-based platforms reflects the global reach and nearly real-time facets of hybrid social movements.

It is thanks to such web-based connectivity that events in Tahrir Square as well as in Spain inspired OWS. In the late spring prior to OWS, the movement of Los Indignados in Spain—"organized entirely over the internet by DRY (Democracia Real Ya—Real Democracy Now)"—established a permanent encampment as of May 15, 2011, to protest the effects of the economic crisis in Spain.[32] This directly inspired and catalyzed Adbuster's call to America to occupy Wall Street.

When our research team interviewed participants at the Occupy Toronto public encampment in November 2011, we learned that everyone—from the most radical anarchist to those who did not own any mobile device—engaged Facebook (FB) for all communications related to Occupy and as their primary filter and news source. This primary use of FB was reiterated by every interviewee in the subsequent 23 interviews we conducted with female OWS activists from nine different Occupy cities in the United States; 100% of those we spoke to use FB for most aspects of their political and social organizing, and identified links with their own CR. On occasion, a news article will capture this link between Occupy participants' demands and the role of CR:

> Demands can act as a form of consciousness-raising, helping to develop a sense of entitlement that may exist only in a latent form among large number of people. The Occupy movement has shown its enormous capacity to affect the popular consciousness as witness the rapid popularization of the ideas about the 1 and 99 percent. When raised by a mass movement, demands can bring to the surface ideas that have a latent support in the moral economy of the 99 percent of Americans but have not yet been articulated as expectations that people think are legitimate and possible.[33]

Dismissals such as Reich's are especially disappointing, because for those who paid attention, OWS clearly expressed their goals and aims; and because of the intentional inclusivity of the principles of horizontalism and its leaderless organization, the breadth and diversity of aims were upheld and respected. Finally, for this movement, the means were conscientiously tied to the ends—i.e., the process of communication, conversation, and decision making was as important as any particular goal. "The Arab Spring and Occupy movements have brought the idea of leaderless social movement organizing to the attention of the mass media. Although perhaps too diffuse to meet common definitions of an 'organization,' they have nevertheless challenged the orthodoxy that social action needs clearly identifiable, hierarchically positioned leaders."[34]

Highlighting process as both an aim and representative of a radical shift in Social Media Organizations (SMO), Sutherland et al. cite activist and scholar David Graeber's key point that "'we don't want leaders'. . . What is needed therefore, is not an all-out rejection, but a different conceptualization, of leadership defined as a process."[35] Providing a description of the characteristics of horizontal SMO, Sutherland et al. state:

> . . . attention must be paid to the ways in which organizational members collectively construct shared meanings through interaction processes (Coburn, 2001; Ganz, 2000). Although specific actors may take the lead in meaning-management, these meanings must be shared, common and valued by all in the organization before collective action can occur. The key move here is away from an individual perspective of leadership towards a conception that emphasizes relationality and the construction of social meaning.[36]

CONSCIOUSNESS-RAISING VIA SOCIAL MEDIA

So how are CR practices originally designed for F2F settings being adapted for networked environments? Rogers describes various other web-based forums and sites in which CR is taking place including:

> . . . the Divine Feminine, a group in which female-bodied or female-identified women talk about the oppressions they experience; Ambiguous UpSparkles, started by Eve Ensler, where people come together and share their personal stories of oppression using the people's mic; and similar groups, like POCcupy (People of Color), a group for people of color to talk about oppression, WOW (Women Occupying Wall Street) and Safer Spaces, two groups that focus on the presence and safety of women in the movement.[37]

Processes like CR are, in a sense, organic opportunities to educate oneself and others, to develop reflective skills for collective discussion, active listening, and critical and reflexive awareness. Here one participant describes how social media tools opened her eyes to new imaginings of communication and connections, resonating with the CR aim of opening new ways of seeing oneself and one's agency in the world:

> One of the most important experiences for me was reaching out and learning how to use the internet and not just consuming things but being

a productive agent in learning how to broadcast and learning how to leverage all of these different spaces of communication. Becoming part of inter-Occupy and then learning that even things that I had believed were wild in the beginning, almost nearly impossible, are now coming to fruition and we're just learning the possibilities of building out this network, just leveraging the tools that we have while also building new ones. And these new ones are really only limited by our capacity to imagine what communication should look like. (Alice, Occupy LA)

Her experience reflects a common theme of empowerment through a kind of DIY/DIT (do-it-yourself/together) ethos,[38] providing her with a sense of agency as a result of active peer-to-peer broadcasting versus passive consuming. This young woman echoes the CR aim of the importance of "validating" experience, that through the strength of numbers one no longer feels like a "crazy person," reinforcing the experience of the personal as political:

But I was trying to fight some of the media narrative because we have so much paid advertisement, paid media coming at us that I really wanted to educate people. And really connect with people too that were of the same mind because I can shout all I want as one person and you look maybe kind of like a crazy person, but if you have 100 people shouting about what they want then you're a force to be reckoned with, so it's a little different. (Leanne, Occupy Santa Cruz, news radio activist, mid-30s)

She spoke of her commitment to using radio and social media for education. In her awakening to the "personal is political" via a Facebook virtual art installation, she like many others mentions blogs and video-logs, ("vlogs") as sparking new consciousness and unification of women:

I saw this thing on Facebook yesterday . . . The Wall of Vagina. And it's this art project that is a cast, plaster cast of hundreds of women's vaginas. That has been shown, I think it's in the UK, and it's across the entire wall and I was just like wow that's crazy, but I would never know about that if it wasn't for Facebook. And I'm like, "that is really interesting" and it's just another way to communicate, to expose ourselves to different ideas. So I think it's been incredibly helpful. (Bria, female, late 20s, educational experience in activism, Occupy Santa Ana)

She describes her growing awareness of the significant gaps between what was reported in traditional media vs. media produced from the front lines of the movement. Key to this was Facebook in various uses and re-purposing:

So, I followed all the traditional media attention but then I got very invested in understanding what was happening with the difference between my Facebook account before Occupy and afterwards. (Alice, Occupy LA)

A final frequent topic for CR dialogue and discussion both online and off was what was most frequently referred to by Occupy members as "Check Your Privilege." When asked what language was used in OWS to address issues of feminism or oppression, this woman mentioned "check your privilege" first and then described other features designed for equity ranging from "progressive stack" to "safe space":

> So definitely check your privilege. Step up, step back, like the philosophy I mentioned before. We had a progressive stack at all the meetings, which was basically . . . it's similar to the step up step back, if you're taking a stack of people and there's four white men that are first in line, you might put a woman ahead of them to speak . . . to try to get more diverse voices having a say in the meeting. . . . I know we used . . . "safe space" a lot. Which can mean a variety of things but I think it meant like a safe space for people to feel comfortable speaking up without being attacked or judged. (Sabrina, female, early 30s, April 10, 2013, previous activist experience, Occupy New York)

"Safe space" is a hallmark of CR,[39] and each of the above terms were extensively discussed and debated via online platforms (FB, comments on You-Tube videos, blog posts, Twitter, and listservs). Another activist describes intervening in the Occupy Los Angeles FB page to make it more queer-friendly, an effort to create more 'safe space' for queer members of OWS.

> When we organized the queer affinity group, first thing I did was create a Facebook page for it. Because that is how you legitimize yourself as an entity in existence . . . I spent a lot of time on the queering OWS, their Facebook page and their group as well in terms of cross fertilization of ideas and interests. (Craig, male, late 50s, December 2012, longtime activist, Occupy Los Angeles)

He then concludes,

> The tools that we have, the online tools for organizing are so incredibly powerful and different from anything that has existed previous to the Internet that I really do think it's gonna change incredibly how political movements function and are able to operate. (Craig, Occupy Los Angeles)

THE PERSONALIZATION OF POLITICS AND THE SHIFT FROM COLLECTIVE TO CONNECTIVE ACTION

A number of recent scholarly contributions highlight new ways of thinking about the individual in relation to networks and mediated publics. Bennett and Segerberg note that conventional social movement theory no longer accounts for the individual, and focus on the personalization of politics and how connective action is replacing collective action within the context of what Barry Wellman refers to as "networked individualism."[40]

> These easily personalized frames contrast with more conventional collective action frames (e.g., "eat the rich") that may require more socialization and brokerage to propagate in large numbers. Participation is importantly channeled through often dense social networks over which people can share their own stories and concerns—the pervasive use of social technology enables individuals to become important catalysts of collective action processes as they activate their own social networks.[41]

Each of these features is recognizable throughout our research into OWS practices. The concept of "personalized politics" or what is termed "connective" (as contrasted with "collective") action, illustrates how social networking involves "co-production and co-distribution revealing a different economic and psychological logic: co-production and sharing based on personalized expression."[42]

The logic of connective action illuminates the high value placed on dialogue, awakening, and working to align the OWS movement's process with the utopian values and ethos being called for that has been a hallmark of OWS. "When people who seek more personalized paths to concerted action are familiar with practices of social networking in everyday life, and when they have access to technologies from mobile phones to computers, they are already familiar with a different logic of organization: the logic of connective action."[43]

Personalized action frames and the "logic of connective action" help explain the phenomenon of hundreds of thousands of relatively isolated or privatized individuals sharing in the "connective" (as opposed to "collective") zeitgeist of demands for economic justice expressed by participants in diverse social uprisings around the world. The new theorizations that emphasize the individualized experience of politics within networked, connected spaces and relations take us closer toward understanding citizens engaged in connective action around the globe. Bruce Bimber et al. note that "[a]mong scholars, one important strand of thought about digital media and collective action has emphasized the point that formal organizations with structures and incentives are no longer critical for accomplishing things collectively,"[44] which in turn raises questions about what constitutes these selves, these individuals, who enact agency within political participation.

Neither political philosophy nor sociology considers the subject or the individual when theorizing about social movements and both ignore an individual's motivations to participate. Bimber et al. state that the recent global uprisings no longer reflect shared identities or ideologies but rather shared "diverse [individual] frustrations."[45] This "enhanced connectivity" in a hybrid online and offline movement ties directly to Bennett and Seger-berg's "logic of connective action."[46] Bakardjieva similarly addresses the importance of the internet helping to make visible "facets of democracy located outside of the visible arena of politics":[47]

> I would like to propose a perspective on the democratic potential of the Internet that casts light on facets of democracy located outside of the visible arena of politics, typically occupied by campaigning, voting, assemblies, and organized action in the street or the media. I would like to divert attention from the structural, institutional, and proce-dural effects of the Internet on democracy and direct it toward changes unfolding at the level of meaning and individual agency. My main pre-occupation will be to inquire into the capacity of the Internet to enhance democracy through the multiplication and enrichment of the everyday practices of citizenship.[48]

POLITICS AND SUBPOLITICS: NEW FORMS NEED A NEW LANGUAGE OF CONNECTIVE ACTION

The uses of social technologies by participants around the world are rede-fining the modalities, forms and potential capacities of social movements. Our research reveals that social movements like OWS reflect in its articula-tions and diverse expressions the second sense of revolution, "a fundamen-tal change in the way of thinking about or visualizing something: a change of paradigm."[49]

> At the turn of the 19th century Kant posed the question, How is knowl-edge possible? Today, two centuries later, the parallel question is, How is political design possible? It is no coincidence that this raises an over-arching question that ties together art and politics. Beyond nature, God, altars, truth, causality, ego, id, and superego begins the "art of living," as the late Foucault called it, or the art of the self-design or renaissance of politics as a fundamental universal condition of human existence. Without a doubt, no age of hope or paradise is dawning. Reflexive modernization is the age of uncertainty and ambivalence, which com-bines the constant threat of disasters on an entirely new scale with the possibility and necessity to reinvent our political institutions and invent new ways of conducting politics at social "sites" that we previously considered unpolitical.[50]

Not only are we at a key historical moment faced with this "necessity to reinvent" our understanding of politics, but indeed "Some of the necessary conditions for a functioning democracy exist at the level of lived experi-ence, resources, and subjective dispositions" which may mark a significant " 'cultural turn' in the study of democracy and political communication."[51]

Next we outline several key insights and concepts provided by recent media and social movement scholars that amplify the significance of the return of feminist organizing practices, and may clarify the nature of this cultural turn.

In the context of scholarly "dismissal" or "de-valuation" of OWS as a "social outcry and 'merely' a fledgling version of a social movement," our research suggests the critical importance of reevaluating the criteria of "success" of contemporary social movements, closely related to the often-debated characteristics of a clear demand or goal, the importance of the individual, and participants' sense of connectivity within subpolitics.

Information and communication technologies provide multiple entry points through which an individual can connect with political activity. Subpolitics, as defined presciently by Ulrich Beck in 1997, reflects the blurring of categories including social and political, private and public, personal and political:

> But why can or should the political be at home or take place only in the political system? Who says that politics are possible only in the forms and terms of governmental, parliamentary, and party politics? Perhaps the truly political disappears in and from the political system and reappears, changed and generalized, in a form that remains to be comprehended and developed, as sub(system) politics (Beck, 1992) in all the other fields of society.[52]

Between 1997 and today, subpolitics (elaborated aptly by Bakardjieva's notion of subactivism[53]) has come to describe networked communities that reflect individuals, publics, audiences, and virtual publics actively engaged in developing critical awareness of systemic social structures. Specifically in the case of OWS, this subpolitical realm captures how Occupy participants share informal education to understand and analyze how power functions in corporate oligarchies to better comprehend the breakdown of capitalism.

Henry Jenkins and Nico Carpentier address this overlap of the political and cultural within contemporary media practices:

> Ethan Zuckerman . . . has proposed the "cute cat picture theory of revolution": young people around the world have developed "latent capacities" (in terms of their access and understanding of technologies for working around hierarchical control, of their ability to form and navigate through social networks, to create and circulate images), which may be deployed toward more explicitly political ends under the right circumstances. So, it is not simply that the cultural constitutes a distinctive sphere or register of politics, but that what happens in the realm of cultural politics may have a direct impact on institutional politics.[54]

In her 2010 book *A Private Sphere: Democracy in a Digital Age*, Zizi Papacharissi provides a compelling case for redefining digital democracy with a much deeper understanding of the blurring of private, public, personal, and political spheres, informing and redefining how individuals are engaging in contemporary politics.[55] In the 2011 conclusion to her edited collection *A Networked Self: Identity, Community and Culture on Networked Sites*, she further describes "convergence" as it applies to the kinds of identities expressed by our interviewees—a hybrid sense of self and community constituted by very fluid, overlapping, and porous boundaries between the spheres noted above.[56] Specifically addressing the "inner workings" of what Bennett and Segerberg refer as "Personal Action Frames, (PAFs)"[57] we point out the background concept of convergence as it is key to understanding hybrid CR.

Convergence is a useful concept for analyzing the forms and modalities of the sense of self or subjectivity that we must account for in studying how individuals make their way in mediated and hybrid networks. Papacharissi's description is thus worth quoting at length to outline the complex layers that we note constitute connective action and PAFs:

> The architecture of the technology that belies these networked platforms of interaction rests upon principles of convergence, which enable multiple and overlapping connections between varieties of distinct social spheres. The social platforms or spaces sustained by convergent technologies accentuate confluence, flexibility, and reflexivity of media content. Jenkins (2006) has broadly defined convergence as "a word that describes technological, industrial, cultural and social changes in the ways media circulates within our culture . . . a situation in which multiple media systems coexist and where media content flows fluidly across them." Jenkins emphasizes that convergence references several common ideas, including the flow of content across media platforms, overlap between media industries, financing that serves the interest of combined processes of media production, migratory behavior on the part of audiences that virally follow content, and of course, the ability for audiences to interact with content as both consumers and producers. The convergent properties of media render them both remixed and remixable; the product of institutions and independent socio-cultural agents. It is helpful to understand social network platforms as hosting social resources that are both remixed and remixable, in the sense that they actively combine all aspects of our social identity into a singular sphere, which then further evolves as these distinct parts converge and evolve.[58]

Our research bears out Papacharissi's description that social network platforms "actively combine all aspects of our social identity into a singular sphere, which then further evolves as these distinct parts converge and evolve."[59] Media scholar Mark Deuze (2007) further suggests that convergence "is not just a technological process" and must therefore also be recognized as "having a cultural logic of its own, blurring the lines between production and consumption, between making media and using media, and between active or passive spectatorship of mediated culture."[60]

Bennett and Segerberg's theory on PAFs and connective logic[61] resonates as descriptors for what is a morphed form of traditional CR, for which we transpose Beck's subpolitical. This contemporary modality of using social media for the simultaneous counter-public sphere and space for subpolitical behaviors (critical awakening) forms a conceptual framework for digitally networked action (DNA) to be legitimately examined.[62] This theory of connective action allows a reevaluation of the way in which social movement theory understands the individual and their motivations for participation when attempting to define collective action.

CONCLUSION: "WE'RE STILL HERE: 99%"

Our chapter has sought to show how this subpolitical awakening results in significant part from the easy "opt-in" provided by mediated platforms and information-communication technologies (ICTs), social networks which then bleed into political networks. Such subpolitical constituencies include unprecedented millions of first-time activists who may not even call themselves such but who are taking part in the streets and within mediated publics.[63]

Such spaces for "dreaming in public," as some reference OWS—engaged through both F2F and web-based communications, particularly FB and Twitter—allow participants to develop increased critical awareness, growth, and transformed social relations to help create a culture and ethos for the aspired-towards "new world." Our research affirms how OWS and numerous other contemporary social movements reflect the complex, rapidly changing face of participatory democracy and subpolitics. The prefigurative nature of the movement is crucial to 21st-century transformations of participatory democracy. We have shown the overlap of OWS and second-wave feminism, highlighting key strands of attention within social movement theory and political theory. In particular, the renewal of the "personal is political" adds significantly to new conceptions for thinking about the 21st-century subject and the renewed importance of not only the individual but such eschewed concerns as "consciousness," "awakening," and "dialogue" as centrally important to adequate theorization of hybrid social movements.

We suggest that the understandings of social movements—like much of the vocabulary used to describe this rapidly changing arena of grassroots and participatory democracy—require radical redefinition. The blurring of public and private, social and political, requires rethinking traditional and binaristic vocabulary, discourses, and assumptions in order to best understand the changing modalities of participatory democracy, organizational structures and practices of contemporary hybrid social movements. Further, our research confirms the nascent recognition of social movements in a digital media environment that the roles played by individuals require much greater attention than political theories have previously acknowledged.

We have argued that it is precisely the hybrid (offline and online) nature of Occupy that allowed for a new hybrid CR, a generational wake-up call. We further showed how these new hybrid CR practices represent a radical tool for critical consciousness by virtue of the multiple entry points afforded by social media platforms such as FB (the media most widely used by OWS participants), horizontal structures, and with the "logic of connective action" explaining such networked spaces.

Given the predominant discourses of the last 30 years lamenting young people's disaffection from "civic participation," OWS marks the radical revolutionizing of a generation of consciousness, part of a "global awakening." Within the context of hybridized lives in which "real life" and "cyber-life" overlap and mutually shape one another, as scholars we must account for the "cultural turn" in political theory—the complexity of digitally mediated landscapes, communications, and connective action.

NOTES

1. Robert Reich, "Happy Birthday Occupy," *The Huffington Post,* last modified Sept. 15, 2013, www.huffingtonpost.com/robert-reich/happy-birthday-occupy_b_3931978.html?utm_source=Alert-blogger&utm_medium=email&utm_campaign=Email+Notifications.
2. During 2012–2013, our research team conducted, transcribed, coded, and analyzed the interviews from the 23 participants. Most of the interviewees were female, offering a unique perspective in the leaderless movement of Occupy, with a wide range of political activist experience. An outline of questions was provided in a semi-structured fashion and concerned their motivations for participating in Occupy, hopes for the Occupy movement, social media participation throughout encampment and post-encampment stages, cross-generational dialogues, shared texts and philosophies within the movement, and exploration of the consciousness-raising practices witnessed throughout their involvement of Occupy. The 23 interviewees selected for this study were individuals who we actively sought out via Facebook and Twitter accounts who held a consistent presence online and created a large volume of online content. We were particularly interested in interviewing women who had been involved with the social media aspect of the OWS movement. We were also able to interview two men who were present for a two-person interview. Our research team then continued to analyze the interviews through a grounded theory approach, generating three layers of code lists to use in the analysis of our findings, a driving force of content in this chapter.
3. Maria Bakardjieva, "Subactivism: Lifeworld and Politics in the Age of the Internet," *The Information Society* 25, no. 2 (2009): 91–104.
4. Stephanie Rogers, "What Occupy Wall Street Owes to Feminist Consciousness-Raising," *Ms. Magazine Blog,* (December 13, 2011), last modified January 18, 2014, http://msmagazine.com/blog/2011/12/13/what-occupy-wall-street-owes-to-feminist-consciousness-raising/ (accessed October 6, 2013).
5. Ibid.

6. "The assumption underlying this article is that the more we know about the history of these processes of horizontal decision making, the better equipped we will be to improve them. In this way we can, when appropriate, draw on lessons learned in the past and come to understand horizontal decision making today not as an entirely new invention, but as part of a much longer political process that is continuously evolving. The current historical juncture has brought about unprecedented opportunities for experimentation with horizontal decision making and decentralized forms of democratic governance, and as such it seems an apt moment to reflect on the politics of these procedures as part of an attempt to remain open to the new lessons as we learn them." Marianne Maeckelbergh, "Horizontal Democracy Now: From Alterglobalization to Occupation," *Interface: a journal for and about social movements* 4, no. 1 (2012): 207–234.
7. Marianne Maeckelbergh, "Horizontal Democracy Now: From Alterglobalization to Occupation." *Interface: a journal for and about social movements* 4, no. 1 (2012): 207–234.
8. Marianne Maeckelbergh, "Horizontal Democracy Now," 211.
9. Ibid.
10. Occupy changed the national dialogue, in the sense that it branded itself to take on many different aid missions, i.e., Occupy Sandy, Fort Hernandez, and Fort Luciero (foreclosure) and Occupy Eugene Medical and their work to overturn Citizens United. Occupy became a brand where it was possible to Occupy anything.
11. Samuel Farber, "The Art of Demanding." *Jacobin: A magazine of culture and polemic,* last modified Sept. 7, 2012, last modified January 19, 2014, http://jacobinmag.com/2012/09/the-art-of-demanding/.
12. Alexander Eichler, "Wall Street Occupiers in for the Long Haul," *Common Dreams,* last modified Sept. 29, 2011, last modified January 19, 2014, www.commondreams.org/headline/2011/09/29-7.
13. S. Rogers, "Happy Birthday OWS."
14. H. Gautney, "What is Occupy Wall Street?"
15. Stephanie Rogers, "Occupy Wall Street and Feminism and Misogyny," Bitch Flicks, last modified Oct. 17, 2011, last modified January 19, 2014, www.btchflcks.com/2011/10/occupy-wall-street-and-feminism-and-misogyny-oh-my.html.
16. Sidney Tarrow, (2011) "Why Occupy Wall Street Is Not the Tea Party of the Left," Council on Foreign Relations, last modified January 18, 2014, www.foreignaffairs.com/print/98544.
17. David Graeber, *The Democracy Project* (New York: The Random House Publishing Group, 2013), 23.
18. Megan Boler, "Occupy Women: Will Feminism's Fourth Wave Be a Swell or a Ripple?," Truthout.org, last modified January 18, 2014, http://truth-out.org/news/item/9188-occupy-women-will-fourth-wave-feminism-be-a-wave-or-a-ripple.
19. Sarah Seltzer, "Where are the Women at Occupy Wall Street," Truthout.org, last modified January 18, 2014, www.truth-out.org/news/item/4419:where-are-the-women-at-occupy-wall-street.
20. Karlyn Kohrs Campbell, "The Rhetoric of Women's Liberation: An Oxymoron," *Quarterly Journal of Speech* 59, no. 1 (1973): 74–86.
21. Challenging public/private ties to earlier debates between Marxists and feminists, in 1989 Jaggar follows MacKinnon's 1981 assertion "Consciousness raising is to feminism what labor is to Marxism" when she develops a significant epistemological intervention on "Love and Knowledge": "Critical reflection on emotion is not a self-indulgent substitute for political analysis

and political action. It is itself a kind of political theory and political practice, indispensable for an adequate social theory and social transformation"
(Jaggar 1989, 64), which countered the Marxist critique that reflecting on
subjective experience is a bourgeois, cultural endeavor not appropriate to or
necessary for political revolution.

22. The extensive accounts and analyses regarding these issues include the following: John Paul Montano, "Open Letter to the Occupy Wall Street Activists," (September 24, 2011), last modified January 18, 2014, www.zashnain.
com/2011/09/open-letter-to-occupy-wallstreet.html. For more information,
see "Open Letter to the 'Occupy' Movement: The Decolonization Proposal,"
last modified January 18, 2014, www.youtube.com/watch?v=r_s3X0u
W9Ec; Robert Desjarlait, "Decolonization and Occupy Wall Street," guest
blog post (October 11, 2011), last modified January 18, 2014; and Miranda
J. Brady and Derek Antoine, "Decolonize Wall Street! Situating Indigenous
Critiques of the Occupy Wall Street Movement," *American Communication
Journal* 15, no. 1 (2013), last modified January 18, 2014, www.racialicious.
com/2011/10/11/decolonization-and-occupy-wall-street/.

23. Andrew Chadwick, "Digital Network Repertoires and Organizational
Hybridity." *Political Communication*, (2007): 283–301. doi:10.1080/10584
600701471666.

24. Richard Dawkins, *The Selfish Gene* (Oxford: Oxford University Press, 1989).
Quoted in W. Lance Bennett and Alexandra Segerberg, "The Logic of Connective Action: Digital Media and the Personalization of Contentious Politics," *Information, Communication and Society* 15, no. 5 (2012): 739–768.

25. Richard Dawkins, *The Selfish Gene.*

26. Bob Dylan, "Tangled Up in Blue," CBS (1975).

27. McKenzie Wark, *Celebrities, Culture and Cyberspace: The Light on the Hill
in a Postmodern World* (Australia: Pluto Press, 1999); see McKenzie Wark
for more on virality, a feature of 21st-century media, including Richard
Dawkin's definition of a meme.

28. Paul Virilio and Sylvere Lotringer. "Pure War," *Semiotext* (1997).

29. Andrew Chadwick, "Digital Network Repertoires," 284.

30. Stephanie Rogers, "Happy Birthday, Occupy Wall Street!" Bitch Flicks, last
modified Sept. 17, 2012, www.btchflcks.com/2012/09/happy-birthday-occu
py-wall-street.html.

31. Stephanie Rogers, "Occupy Wall Street and Feminism and Misogyny," Bitch
Flicks, last modified Oct. 17, 2011, www.btchflcks.com/2011/10/occupy-
wall-street-and-feminism-and-misogyny-oh-my.html.

32. Georgina Blakeley, "Los Indignados: A Movement that Is Here to Stay,"
Open Democracy, last modified January 18, 2014, www.opendemocracy.net/
georgina-blakeley/los-indignados-movement-that-is-here-to-stay. "The
arrest of 24 demonstrators at the end of the march in Madrid led to a spontaneous sit-down on the evening of the May 15 in Madrid's main square, the
Plaza del Sol . . . Facebook, Twitter and other social media called for a mass
sit-down that same evening which then became a more permanent camp. This
was the start of the 15-M—los indignados movement—although it had roots
in other movements such as VdeVivienda which began in 2006 in support of
the right to affordable housing, Precarios en movimiento, a loose network of
groups struggling against the lack of certainty (precariedad) in employment,
housing, pensions, health and education and Juventud Sin Futuro (Youth
without a Future) which coalesced in Madrid's universities in April 2011
around the slogan 'no house, no job, no pension, no fear.' " Georgina Blakeley, "Los Indignados: A Movement that is Here to Stay," Open Democracy,

last modified October 5, 2012, www.opendemocracy.net/georgina-blakeley/
los-indignados-movement-that-is-here-to-stay www.opendemocracy.net/geo
rgina-blakeley/los-indignados-movement-that-is-here-to-stay.

33. Samuel Farber, "The Art of Demanding," *Jacobin: A magazine of culture
and polemic*, last modified Sept. 7, 2012, last modified January 18, 2014,
http://jacobinmag.com/2012/09/the-art-of-demanding/.

34. Neil Sutherland, Christopher Land, and Steffen Böhm, "Anti-leaders (Hip)
in Social Movement Organizations: The Case of Autonomous Grassroots
Groups," *Organization* (2013).

35. Neil Sutherland, Christopher Land, and Steffen Böhm. "Anti-leaders (hip)
in Social Movement Organizations: The Case of Autonomous Grassroots
Groups." *Organization* (2013), 5.

36. Sutherland et al, 5.

37. S. Rogers, "What Occupy Wall Street Owes to Feminist Consciousness-Raising."

38. See Matt Ratto and Megan Boler, eds. *DIY Citizenship: Critical Making and
Social Media* (Cambridge: MIT Press, 2014).

39. See for example Berenice Fisher, 2001.

40. Lance W. Bennett and Alexandra Segerberg, "The Logic of Connective
Action."

41. W. Lance Bennett, "The Personalization of Politics Political Identity, Social
Media, and Changing Patterns of Participation," *The Annals of the American Academy of Political and Social Science* 644, no. 1 (2012): 20–39.

42. L. Bennett, "Personalization of Politics."

43. Ibid.

44. Bruce Bimber, Andrew Flanagin, and Cynthia Stohl, "Reconceptualizing
Collective Action in the Contemporary Media Environment," *Communication Theory* no. 4 (2005): 365–388.

45. Lance W. Bennett and Alexandra Segerberg, "The Logic of Connective
Action."

46. Ibid., 739–768.

47. M. Bakardjieva, "Subactivism."

48. Ibid., 91–92.

49. Merriam Webster Dictionary.

50. Ulrich Beck, "Subpolitics Ecology and the Disintegration of Institutional
Power," *Organization & Environment* 10, no. 1 (1997): 52–65, 53.

51. M. Bakardjieva, "Subactivism," 92.

52. U. Beck, "Subpolitics Ecology," 1.

53. "We attempt to connect the problematic of citizenship with that of everyday life through the concept of subactivism. Subactivism in my definition
is a kind of politics that unfolds at the level of subjective experience and is
submerged in the flow of everyday life. It is constituted by small-scale, often
individual, decisions and actions that have either a political or ethical frame
of reference (or both) and are difficult to capture using the traditional tools
with which political participation is measured. Subactivism is a refraction
of the public political arena in the private and personal world." M. Bakardjieva, "Subactivism," 92.

54. Jenkins, Henry. "Rethinking 'Rethinking Convergence/Culture.'" *Cultural
Studies Ahead-of-Print* (2013): 1–31.

55. Zizi Papacharissi, *A Private Sphere: Democracy in a Digital Age* (Polity,
2010).

56. Zizi Papacharissi, ed. *A Networked Self: Identity, Community, and Culture
on Social Network Sites* (Routledge, 2010).

57. Lance W. Bennett and Alexandra Segerberg, "The Logic of Connective Action."

58. Zizi Papacharissi, ed., *A Networked Self*, 282.
59. Ibid., 305.
60. Mark Deuze, *Media Work* (Polity, 2007), 74.
61. Lance W. Bennett and Alexandra Segerberg, "A Logic of Connective Action," 22.
62. Ibid., 742.
63. For more on first time activists see: Ian Reilly and Megan Boler, "Satire and Social Change: "The Rally to Restore Sanity, Pre-politicization, and the Future of Politics," *Communication, Culture and Critique* 7 (forthcoming).

REFERENCES

Bakardjieva, Maria. "Subactivism: Lifeworld and Politics in the Age of the Internet." *The Information Society* 25, no. 2 (2009): 91–104.
Beck, Ulrich. "Subpolitics Ecology and the Disintegration of Institutional Power." *Organization & Environment* 10, no. 1 (1997): 52–65.
Bennett, W. Lance. "The Personalization of Politics Political Identity, Social Media, and Changing Patterns of Participation." *The Annals of the American Academy of Political and Social Science* 644, no. 1 (2012): 20–39.
Bennett, Lance W. and Alexandra Segerberg. "The Logic of Connective Action: Digital Media and the Personalization of Contentious Politics." *Information, Communication and Society* 15, no. 5 (2012): 739–768.
Bimber, Bruce, Andrew J. Flanagin, and Cynthia Stohl. "Reconceptualizing Collective Action in the Contemporary Media Environment." *Communication Theory* no. 4 (2005): 365–388.
Blakeley, Georgina. Open Democracy, "Los Indignados: A Movement that is Here to Stay." www.opendemocracy.net/georgina-blakeley/los-indignados-movement-that-is-here-to-stay (accessed September 1, 2013).
Boler, Megan. "Occupy Women: Will Feminism's Fourth Wave Be a Swell or a Ripple?" May 16 2012. Truthout.org. http://truth-out.org/news/item/9188-occupy-women-will-fourth-wave-feminism-be-a-wave-or-a-ripple (accessed January 18, 2014).
Brady, Miranda J. and Derek Antoine. "Decolonize Wall Street! Situating Indigenous Critiques of the Occupy Wall Street Movement," *American Communication Journal* 15, no. 1 (2013). www.racialicious.com/2011/10/11/decolonization-and-occupy-wall-street/ (accessed February 16, 2014).
Campbell, Karlyn Kohrs. "The Rhetoric of Women's Liberation: An Oxymoron." *Quarterly Journal of Speech* 59, no. 1 (1973): 74–86.
Chadwick, Andrew. "Digital Network Repertoires and Organizational Hybridity." *Political Communication* (2007): 283–301. doi:10.1080/10584600701471666 (accessed June 21, 2013).
Dawkins, R. *The Selfish Gene.* Oxford: Oxford University Press, 1989. Quoted in Bennett, W. Lance, and Segerberg Alexandra. "The Logic of Connective Action: Digital Media and the Personalization of Contentious Politics." *Information, Communication and Society* no. 5 (2012): 739–768.
Desjarlait, Robert. "Decolonization and Occupy Wall Street." guest blog post (October 11, 2011). http://indiancountrytodaymedianetwork.com/2011/10/23/decolonization-and-occupy-wall-street (accessed January 18, 2014).
Deuze, Mark. *Media Work.* Polity, 2007, 74.
Dylan, Bob. Tangled Up in Blue. CBS, 1975.
Eichler, Alexander. Common Dreams, "Wall Street Occupiers in for the Long Haul." www.commondreams.org/headline/2011/09/29-7 (accessed October 6, 2013).

Farber, Samuel. "The Art of Demanding." Jacobin/ a magazine of culture and polemic, http://jacobinmag.com/2012/09/the-art-of-demanding/ (accessed October 6, 2013).

Fisher, Berenice. *No Angel in the Classroom: Teaching Through Feminist Discourse.* NY: Rowman & Littlefield, 2001.

Gautney, Heather. "What is Occupy Wall Street? The History of Leaderless Movements." *The Washington Post.* October 10, 2011. http://articles.washingtonpost.com/2011–10–10/national/35277702_1_heather-gautney-movement-gay-rights (accessed October 6, 2013).

Graeber, David. *The Democracy Project.* New York: The Random House Publishing Group, 2013.

Jaggar, Alison. "Love And Knowledge: Emotion In Feminist Epistemology." *Inquiry* 32, no. 2 (1989): 151–176.

Jenkins, Henry. "Rethinking 'Rethinking Convergence/Culture.'" *Cultural Studies ahead-of-print* (2013): 1–31.

Lorde, Audre. "The Master's Tools Will Never Dismantle the Master's House," *Feminist Postcolonial Theory: A Reader* (2003): 23–28.

Maeckelbergh, Marianne. "Horizontal Democracy Now: From Alterglobalization to Occupation." *Interface: a journal for and about social movements* 4, no. 1 (2012): 207–34.

Montano, John Paul. "Open Letter to the Occupy Wall Street Activists." September 24, 2011. www.zashnain.com/2011/09/open-letter-to-occupy-wallstreet.html (accessed January 18, 2014).

Papacharissi, Zizi, ed. *A Networked Self: Identity, Community, and Culture on Social Network Sites.* Routledge, 2010.

Papacharissi, Zizi. *A Private Sphere: Democracy in a Digital Age.* Polity, 2010.

Rebeccista. "Open Letter to the 'Occupy' Movement: The Decolonization Proposal." December 7, 2011. www.youtube.com/watch?v=r_s3X0uW9Ec (accessed January 18, 2014).

Reich, Robert. "Happy Birthday Occupy." *The Huffington Post.* September 15, 2013. www.huffingtonpost.com/robert-reich/happy-birthday-occupy_b_3931978.html?utm_source=Alert-blogger&utm_medium=email&utm_campaign=Email+Notifications (accessed October 7, 2013).

Reilly, Ian and Megan Boler. "Satire and Social Change: The Rally to Restore Sanity and the Future of Politics," *Communication, Culture and Critique* 7, no. 3 (forthcoming June 2014).

Rogers, Stephanie. "Occupy Wall Street and Feminism and Misogyny." Bitch Flicks. www.btchflcks.com/2011/10/occupy-wall-street-and-feminism-and-misogyny-oh-my.html (accessed October 6, 2013).

Rogers, Stephanie. "What Occupy Wall Street Owes to Feminist Consciousness-Raising." *Ms. Magazine Blog* (blog). December 13, 2011. http://msmagazine.com/blog/2011/12/13/what-occupy-wall-street-owes-to-feminist-consciousness-raising/ (accessed October 6, 2013).

Rogers, Stephanie. "Happy Birthday, Occupy Wall Street!" Bitch Flicks. www.btchflcks.com/2012/09/happy-birthday-occupy-wall-street.html (accessed October 7, 2013).

Seltzer, Sarah. "Where are the Women at Occupy Wall Street." Truthout.org. www.truth-out.org/news/item/4419:where-are-the-women-at-occupy-wall-street (accessed October 6, 2013).

Sutherland, Neil, Christopher Land, and Steffen Böhm. "Anti-leaders (hip) in Social Movement Organizations: The Case of Autonomous Grassroots Groups." *Organization* (2013).

Tarrow, Sidney. "Why Occupy Wall Street Is Not the Tea Party of the Left." Council on Foreign Relations. 2011. www.foreignaffairs.com/print/98544 (accessed June 21, 2013).

Virilio, Paul, and Sylvere Lotringer. *Pure War.* Los Angeles, CA: Semiotext, 1997.

Wark, McKenzie. *Celebrities, Culture and Cyberspace: The Light on the Hill in a Postmodern World.* Australia: Pluto Press, 1999, 29.

Williams, Raymond. *The Long Revolution.* Broadview Press, 1965.

12 Emergent Social Movements in Online Media and States of Crisis

Analyzing the Potential for Resistance and Repression Online

Lee Salter

ONLINE ACTIVISM, SURVEILLANCE, AND SOUSVEILLANCE

The promise of the Internet for activists has been well documented. At the same time, its shortcomings have been less central to academic discourses. In this chapter, I outline the transition of one of the most important media activist projects, Indymedia, in the context of political economy in the first instance, and then consider its replacement by much championed social media activism. Social media have gained massive plaudits for their transformational roles, especially in the "Arab Spring." However, their use in protests in liberal states has been less well received by the corporate media and political authorities, leading to serious questions about the dangers of social media for activists. The chapter will compare the corporate media coverage of the protests in the Arab world with those in the liberal Western states, especially the UK, and highlight how not only how social media have become key instruments of surveillance for the state[1] and its repressive aspects but also how their use by different protesters is still mediated by the ever-powerful corporate media.

POLITICAL ECONOMY AND THE MARGINALIZATION OF ACTIVISM ONLINE

The potential of the Internet to facilitate radical movements was clear over a decade ago. The Seattle protests of 1999 tested this potential and the results were impressive. Across the world, Independent Media Centers (IMCs) were created by activists with interests in the environmental movement, trade justice and workers' rights activists, anarchists, socialists, and refugee rights activists among many others. A host of studies pointed to the value of these spaces as well as to their shortcomings.[2] A number of works looked initially at the potential of the Internet for activism[3] but also at the difficulties faced by them, such as resourcing and legal issues.[4]

Jones and Martin[5] found that despite the worthy intention to create a network of networks that was organizationally horizontal, non-repressive, open, and fair, the reality was quite different—the "iron law of oligarchy" constrained this intent. However, we can see least from Bristol (UK) and UK Indymedia—that the intent was never totalizing horizontality but rather a hierarchy of activity where those who held greater sway did so because of their overall contribution to the project, through their knowledge and activity. Thus the "hierarchies" evident in IMCs differed from those in bureaucratic organizations as they were hierarchies of action rather than of office.

In some instances, arguments in IMCs did result in splits and people leaving, but then that is the point of their fluid organization. More pressing, however, was the ability to fund and sustain IMCs. Whereas many IMCs felt they needed little in the way of resources, it is likely that this reflects perhaps the most problematic blind spot of many studies of the cyber-world and digital technology—political economy.

Human labor is more often than not omitted from considerations of "resources," not in terms of getting participants to do things, but in the sense that the vast majority of people around the globe have to labor for their means of sustenance. This means that activists participating in grass roots projects such as Indymedia always have to balance remunerative labor against volunteering. The necessity of the means of sustenance often means that those with more time had more influence, but more pressingly that disposable time would fluctuate and therefore so would activity in any given IMC. The impact of the scarcity of labor is that many of the sites that retained an open newswire couldn't clear of spam and nonsense quickly enough to maintain an adequately usable service. Moreover, if the local community didn't contribute regularly with interesting quality reports, the sites would dry up.

In some instances, it was clear that local communities and activists within them had found new outlets for their news, and in some instances chose not to use IMCs for personal-political reasons. Blogs, Twitter, Facebook, and other social media began to challenge Indymedia on the activist scene. Social media proved more direct, more responsive, more communicative, and more networked than many IMCs.

Whatever the other reasons for the decline of IMCs, the facts of political economy remain—IMCs had to struggle in a commercial online environment. In most of the world it is clear to see how what has been referred to as the "colonization" of cyberspace[6] and online attention[7] have developed. Despite the initial promise of communicative freedom, most credible studies show how corporate media either retains its dominant position or has established new ones.

According to the Project for Excellence in Journalism,[8] in 2008 two of the five most popular websites in the United States—CNN and AOL News—were both owned by the largest media company in the world, Time Warner. The others were owned by Yahoo, NBC Universal, and *The New York Times*. Overall, the 10 richest companies owned 28% of the most popular news sites. In 2010, the Project listed the most popular news websites in the United States and their owners. The list showed clear corporate domination with Yahoo, MSNBC, CNN, USA Today, AOL, Fox News, New York Times, LA Times, Google, and National Public Radio dominating the top 10 places.[9] By 2012, the top 10 news websites in the United States were Yahoo, MSNBC, CNN, USA Today, AOL, Fox News, The New York Times, LA Times, Google, National Public Radio. In the U.K., the Internet has done little to diminish the power of the old media giants. Newman shows that the old media giants dominate online news audiences—the access rates for the major newspaper and television news websites were very much higher in the U.K. compared to blogs and social media, although the difference was less significant in the United States (Denmark and France were similar to the U.K.). According to Newman's research, 66% of the U.K. population access television news, 56% the websites of those organizations, 50% printed newspapers, 29% ISPs or aggregators, and only 18% social media and blogs as for news. Of the means of sharing news, Facebook, e-mail, Twitter, and Google+ dominated.[10]

The particular configurations have shifted over the past 10 years, but large corporations, whether MSN and Yahoo in the past or Google and Facebook today, direct the vast majority of traffic to news websites. Hitwise's analysis of Google News U.K. showed that 68% of its traffic is generated by searches for "celebrity" (24%), "sport" (18%), "film and television" (15%), and "music" (11%).[11] Traffic from "UK news" and "world news" accounted for just 5.6% of overall visits. In 2005, the Project for Excellence in Journalism found that 60% of the most popular news websites were owned by just 20 media companies. It concluded that "in short, despite the attention paid to blogs and the openness of the Internet, when it comes to sheer numbers, online news appears dominated by a handful of traditional big media sites, and for now that domination appears to be increasing."[12] There has been little change on this front. In fact, despite the possibilities, by 2012 the top referrals to news web sites from Facebook in the United States were to the Huffington Post, the Daily Mail, Yahoo, BBC, New York Times, Guardian, CNN, ABC, BuzzFeed, and Fox.[13]

Thus Robert McChesney's suggestion that the corporate giants would roll on seems to be the case.[14] Indeed it is important to note that this is a systemic relation rather than the intention of a single "bad" corporation. These systemic relations come to affect the very technological base itself.[15] Indeed, 10 years ago Rogers analyzed the impact of search engine algorithms on results, expressing concern about the varieties of commercial impact on search results.[16] Although the players have changed, the systemic inequities remain. By 2009, Google had taken over as the biggest search engine, accounting for roughly 73% of searches. Between Google and Yahoo, Indymedia had been all but hidden in searches for "news," appearing at position 115 on Google but not at all within the top 300 results on Yahoo, despite having more than 900,000 links to the global site. Today, Newman shows that beyond direct access, search engines such as Google or Bing are the second most popular means of finding news, followed by portals such as MSN and Yahoo.[17]

Together these statistics are not reassuring for those who'd hoped that the Internet would challenge the material and ideological hegemony of the big media corporations, providing a new deal for activists. Yet the general tendency to use the Internet for activism is also still rather slight. Of those interviewed in Newman's research, 44% had signed an online petition, 15% had posted on social media, 11% had joined a campaign via social media, 6% had made a donation, and only 4% had used the Internet to organize or find a meeting.[18]

However, there are some celebrated cases of online activism around the world. Although in once sense indicative of the corporate colonization of cyberspace, the likes of YouTube, Facebook, and Twitter have been employed by activists on a number of fronts. Perhaps the most celebrated examples of this use relates to the so-called "Arab Spring."

The "Arab Spring" of 2011, which saw revolutions take place in Tunisia, Egypt, Libya, and Syria, was welcomed by Western corporate media. The revolutions were said to have witnessed the power of media activists to carve out spaces in even the most authoritarian regimes. Activists used blogs, alternative news websites, Facebook, Twitter, mobile phones, and a whole array of online tools to report their struggles and the responses of the state. Of note, the protesters were celebrated across the Western corporate media, or at least some of them were. Reuters, the Washington Post, the BBC, the New York Times, Current TV, in fact almost the entire corporate media celebrated these rebellions, and especially their use of online social media.[19] Regarding Libya, the New York Times told of "Colonel Qaddafi's supporters, who were using the state-run news media, and Libyan protesters, who were turning to social media and the foreign news media, to win over hearts and minds, inside and outside Libya."[20] In relation to Egypt, the BBC noted that "Social media has played a crucial role in the unrest in Egypt, with many of the protests organised through Facebook. The Egyptian government reacted quickly by blocking social media sites but this act of censorship was spectacularly unsuccessful."[21]

In contrast to corporate coverage, in many of the online spaces great attention was given to the less "favorable" (to Western interests—particularly Yemen, Bahrain, and Saudi Arabia) protests and rebellions. Whereas Bahrain, Saudi Arabia, and Yemen were less visible in corporate news reporting, they were celebrated causes among Western activists, who distributed images of repression, police brutality, army intervention, and eye witness reports from mobile phones, cameras, and camcorders via social media, blogs, and websites.

Against corporate coverage, one of the key messages on blogs and some of the more radical online publications was that much of the power of the protests in places like Egypt came from trade unions and socialist activists who had been agitating for years. Despite involvement of workers in strikes, occupations, and demonstrations, their role was largely ignored in corporate news, leaving it for the websites of the Coalition of Resistance, Counterfire, Socialist Workers' Party, and innumerable blogs to carry for example the February 19th Statement of Independent Trade Unionists in Egypt. Indeed, the main information on the enormous involvement of the workers' movement came from blogs such as arabawy.org, egyptworkersolidarity.org, and The Arabist. Alternative news reports erased the picture of peaceful liberal protesters gathering in city squares to ask for subtle changes, replacing it with one of protesters storming and raiding police barracks and using the guns against the police in an armed revolution. The violent aspects of revolution were naturally downplayed when the Libyan army's (or "Gadaffi's army" as the BBC called it) attacks on rebels were described as attacks on "civilian areas," but in contrast the rebels seemed to target only military targets. Given the intensity of the challenge to "public order" presented by the protesters around the Arab world, it is perhaps unsurprising that one of the strategies used by those states was to disrupt the online communication flows (usually with little effect given the international solidarity).

Thorsen's account of the role of Twitter in the so-called "Arab Spring"— in the revolutions that were underway from 2010 in Egypt, Tunisia, and Libya—can perhaps provide an insight into why certain aspects of the Arab Spring were reported in the corporate media and others weren't. Thorsen cites the celebrated case of NPR's Andy Carvin's Tweeting of the uprising as a paradigm example of how to use social media for reporting. However, Benjamin Doherty notes that it would be "difficult to imagine anyone from NPR engaging in similar—apparently symbiotic—interactions with, say, Palestinians organizing protests against Israel and surviving in their job."[22] There's a clear delineation of the acceptable forms and topics of protest.

In this sense, we might question the ability to use social media to challenge the hegemonic conceptualization of protest. Where routinized corporate journalism tends to reproduce the dominant narratives of domestic state institutions, activists *can* challenge this. However, whether such challenges are amplified through corporate media is another matter—political economy seems to hold sway.

Indeed, study after study seems to indicate that new social media has become dominated by institutionalized power. Burgess and Bruns[23] showed how Twitter failed to effectively challenge the dominant media ecology during the 2010 Australian election. Andrew Chadwick's research[24] seems to indicate that although there may be significant disruptions to the old news agenda, institutions seem to be reconfiguring themselves to meet these challenges and retain control. Similarly Lasorsa et al. talk of Twitter use among journalists becoming "normalised."[25] Poell and Borra's large-scale analysis of the use of social media in the G20 protests in Toronto, 10 years on from Seattle, found that its use tended to mirror the mainstream's and to be dominated by a small number of users. They also found that Twitter was used effectively (although by a small number), whereas YouTube and Flikr failed to gain any purchase among activists.[26]

SURVEYING OURSELVES TO DEATH?

One of the most significant innovations for activists over the past 20 years has been the development of video and photographic technologies to the point of near ubiquity. Video activism has its roots in the very first days of cinema but came into its own with the development of Hi8 and VCR technologies in the 1980s and 1990s. But digitalization led to an era of pervasive media. The growth of closed-circuit television (CCTV) across liberal democracies in the 1990s led to concerns about permanent surveillance, which are no doubt well founded as the concept of the surveillance society was realized. However, ubiquitous surveillance does not mean continual surveillance—indeed, the distribution of CCTV surveillance had an analogue, hierarchical, and centralized character.

Whereas the technologies of surveillance developed, we saw at the turn of the century the development of what Steve Mann referred to as "sousveillance."[27] For Mann, the term "surveillance" referred to a centralized age where people were watched from above by authorities, wherein "the capture of multimedia content (audio, video, or the like), by a higher entity that is not a peer of, or a party to, the activity being recorded." On the other hand, for Mann digital technologies enable "sousveillance," surveillance from below, enabling ordinary citizens to survey police, shops, and other authorities. Mann was particularly interested in its capacity to bring "cameras from the lamp posts and ceilings, down to eye-level, for human-centered recording of personal experience."[28]

Jean-Gabriel Ganascia developed this idea by contrasting the Panopticon with the Catopticon, which reveals a total transparency of society: "fundamental equality, which gives everybody the ability to watch—and consequently to control—everybody else . . . total communication, which enables everyone to exchange with everyone else."[29] For Ganascia, "In the logic of surveillance that was introduced by Jeremy Bentham, some supervisors had to control the whole society. Here is a totally different logic, where everybody is watching everybody."[30] As an example of the virtues of this arrangement, Ganascia offers,

> On 20 June 2009, during the demonstrations against the results of the Iranian presidential elections, a young woman, Neda Agha-Soltan, was shot. Immediately, her tragic death was video-captured and broadcast over the Internet, which drew immediate international attention; in old totalitarian countries, such information would have been totally ignored.[31]

Very well. Yet there are plenty of examples of state brutality and violence that get passed by or lack amplification by the corporate media. It has been a preoccupation for corporate media ever since its inception to promote and amplify certain voices at the expense of others, and some rebellions but not others. Whereas there is much complexity to this process, decades of research have made it an indisputable fact that, within hegemonic confines, the voices that get amplified tend to be those that accord with a given hegemony. The dominant ideas are best understood as those associated with the interests of a dominant class under a given system.[32]

CRISIS, SOUSVEILLANCE, AND REPRESSION

Although under relatively stable conditions a liberal state may allow more or less sousveillance and its media more or less plurality, it is also the case that when threatened a liberal state is disposed to quelling opposition, although it remains less obvious than in authoritarian states. This is to say that power in liberal states is decentralized and distributed, and therefore less recognizable. This power works in two ways.

In the first instance, censorship through omission takes place, in which key stories are ignored by the corporate media, as we've seen with the rebellions in the Arab Spring. Moreover, radical protests and activism in liberal states are often excluded or at least that they have to pass a much greater threshold to be deemed newsworthy. Cats stuck up trees, on the other hand, have no such problems.

When they do manage to get onto the agenda—usually as a result of violence—such movements tend to be framed as curiosities, exceptions and problems, and are "othered." This is to say they and, crucially, the interests they represent, are marginalized and abstracted from their context in the ordinary interests of ordinary people.[33]

In the second instance, there are some important examples of sousveillance gaining purchase. The raid on the media center of the Genoa Social Forum in 2001 was observed and recorded by many participants, with Indymedia taking a key role in getting footage of the brutal near massacre out to the corporate media and around the world. Ian Tomlinson's killing at the hands of the police in the 2009 anti-G20 demonstration in London was also captured on film by citizens and amplified by the corporate media. Both of these examples of sousveillance had significant implications, and in both cases resulted in the assailants facing trial—although none facing significant charges. Other cases can be brought to light—images of the brutal repression of Occupy Wall Street at Zuccotti Park spread rapidly around social media, as did the swathes of occupations and protests in Spain in 2012, student demonstrations in the U.K. in 2010, and the 2013 protests Portugal.

However, despite the occasional successes of sousveillance, and despite the occasional amplification by mainstream media, it must be understood that these are exceptions. More often than not the very sousveillance that may be championed by activists can also contribute to their repression, especially when conditions of crisis pertain.

The German jurisprudentialist Carl Schmitt famously suggested that in modern states the "*Sovereign* is he who decides on the *exception.*" It is this concept of the exception that ought to be at the forefront of understanding the limitations to online activism. Liberal, undialectical enquiries into activism and political radicalism sometimes suggest that activist strategies can move the state and the political hegemony in which it is situated as a result of pressure from the street.

Such one-dimensionality hardly does justice to our investigations. Protest—serious protest—takes places amidst a range of countervailing powers. Indeed, the state as one of these powers may allow greater or lesser dissent depending on its own sense of security. The circumstances under which the state gives way are also important to consider. Whether in regard to slavery, working class enfranchisement, women's rights, or the civil rights movement, in many respects the victories of these movements were contingent on their co-option by the state. Habermas explains this very clearly in reference to the welfare state compromise that quelled the workers' uprisings in the first half of the 20th century.[34] This is to say that a racist, sexist, and classist state can be rather flexible when those prejudices threaten to undermine its fundamental interests.

When a state cannot co-opt or incorporate demands, it may turn to evoke "emergency laws," such as those enacted in South Africa in the 1980s and in Egypt from the 1950s onwards, but also in liberal states, such as in France in the 1960s and in 2005, in Ireland from the 1970s until 1994, and in the U.K., where they were last used in 1974. Faced with both natural disaster and political challenge, only the state can declare a state of emergency that suspends normal constitutional limits, civil liberties, and the like. It is in such times that state power can be seen in its rawest form. We have seen an increasing use of emergency laws in everyday life over the past quarter of a century, and in policing what McPhail and McCarthy call the "militarization of policing."[35] In Italy, the Berlusconi administration notoriously extended emergency laws including the suspension of political and civil rights and the extension of the power of the state to "grandi eventi" (great events), which include political summits and conferences. The use of emergency powers in the United States has been even more worrying.

Writing some 80 years after Schmitt, Agamben argues that the "exception" became frequent throughout the 20th century, with increases in surveillance, military, and domestic and foreign "intelligence" expenditure, alongside increasingly flagrant human rights abuses, whether in Northern Ireland, Guantanamo Bay, Abu Ghraib, Belmarsh prison, or the "black sites" where kidnapped "suspects" are transported outside liberal jurisdictions to be tortured. Indeed, for him the anomie in which the state operates during the exception has become the norm. For Agamben,

The state of exception has today reached its maximum worldwide deployment. The normative aspect of law can thus be obliterated and contradicted with impunity by a governmental violence that—while ignoring international law externally and producing a permanent state of exception internally—nevertheless still claims to be applying the law.[36]

If one considers Jurgen Habermas's charge that Western liberal states have been facing "legitimation crises" since at least the 1960s, the notion of exceptionalism-as-normal comes into starker perspective. For Habermas, a legitimation crisis exists when states still have the *power* to rule but are unable to boast active support from populations, resulting in dwindling consent. The crises take place in three realms—the economic, the political, and the sociocultural. The capitalist economic system has an inbuilt tendency towards a declining rate of profit, which results in periodic crises. The political system faces crises as its inability to control the economic system and the contradictions between labor and capital are exposed, resulting in the withdrawal of mass loyalty. Faced with these inadequacies, sociocultural crises emerge when faith in the economic and political systems is not maintained, thus resulting in motivational crises among workers and citizens.[37]

Together, these crises generate significant challenges to the economic and political order, resulting in the development of complex systems to manage the public, most notably in the form of public relations, a critique of which forms the foundations of *The Structural Transformation of the Public Sphere* and *The Theory of Communicative Action*. It is also, contrary to so many interpretations of Habermas's work, during crises that public spheres are most effective. And it is *radical* public spheres that can act as a motor for political change,[38] especially in an online environment.[39]

Unable to rely on whole-hearted consent of the people, governments perceive a permanent underlying threat to their legitimacy and their authority. This threat is manifested, or at least becomes most notable, in times of explicit crisis, such as during war, recession, constitutional crisis, major scandal, and so on, especially when met with disruptive protests. Furthermore, it is during such crises that systemic contradiction and political hypocrisy becomes most evident, further undermining the legitimacy of the political order. As we shall see below, on one hand the Internet and digital technologies offer great potential to facilitate protest, but on the other hand the potential is also afforded to states and security forces to stymie protest.

The economic crisis that began in 2007 had the potential to prompt serious political upheaval, as it did in Greece most notably. The task states faced in retaining if not mass loyalty then at least apathy was enormous. Despite the blame for the crisis initially being laid at the feet of the banking sector (and some rumbles about broader economic problems), it was soon turned to "public debt" alone. Citizens were told by politicians, economists, journalists, and other "experts," that the crisis was not the fault of an economic system facing a crisis of profitability, exposed through increasingly risky investment decisions made by banks. Neither, apparently, was the problem that of an impotent political system unable to manage international capitalism without deepening the crisis. Rather, the problem was that governments had spent "too much" on the people who allow them to govern (rather than even the multi-trillion dollar invasions the West had embarked upon in the early 21st century). Thus, beyond the economic and political crises, there was the risk of a huge sociocultural crisis, necessitating careful management.

The delegitimation of the economic system had been an undercurrent for many years, manifesting itself in protests against G8, World Bank, and World Trade Organization meetings, which Indymedia centers played a key role in mediating.[40] The realization of the undemocratic nature of such organizations, and their clear objectives of broadening and deepening capitalism, meant that the 2007 collapse of the economic system had the potential to strip the last vestiges of legitimacy from capitalism.

The banking and finance sector in London and New York diverted enormous resources to defend its interests through lobbying and PR,[41] governments around the world rallied to punish the poor for the failure of the rich, and state security forces manned positions to defend capital. Against this we see a range of movements, which indicates a number of problems being faced by media activists in these times of crisis.

STUDENT DEMOS, RIOTS, AND SOCIAL MEDIA DRAGNETS

In the midst of the Arab Spring, the U.K. saw massive student protests against the government's desire, against half a century of progressive social policy, to subject education to the whimsical will of the "market"—by charging young people £9000 ($14,000) per year to be educated.

Students organized demonstrations, direct actions, and occupations throughout the country, during which social media played an enormously important role. Spontaneous demonstrations were organized via Facebook, which was also used to arrange and publicize occupations via occupation "pages." Twitter was also useful for those seeking to quickly publicize actions, and activists communicated via video chat technologies as well as secure email lists on Rise Up.[42]

Crucially, the student movement was based on a broad range of connections with other nodes in movement networks, such as anti-cuts activists, socialist parties, and trade unions. Many of these connections were facilitated by publicity via social networking alongside more traditional activist links. The organization of protests was curious, from an analogue perspective. In Bristol, activists would set up several pages advertising protests and demonstration, the timing and location of which would often conflict with each other. There was often a lack of communication between activists as groups would arise and actions be arranged spontaneously. This mode seemed rather indicative of the digital mind-set, of those raised in a virtual world where the supposed concreteness of the world is shattered, of a population habituated to simulacra. Given the flexibility of this mind-set, the apparent lack of organization and coordination seemed to work in favor of the protestors. Students would arrive at the several declared starting points but via Twitter, Facebook, and especially phone text messages would eventually congregate. The routes of the marches would be decided spontaneously, simply by going where the protesters wanted to go. At the same time, actions would take place spontaneously—the passing of a college building by students who studied there may result in a temporary occupation of the space.

This form of "wildcat" protest was in marked contrast to "analogue" protest. In the U.K., the tradition in policing has been for the police to dissipate the power of political action by the facilitation of protest rather than direct repression and confrontation.[43] One method of so doing was for the police to work with protest organizers to coordinate timing, assembly points, and routes, effectively allowing police to assemble their forces and strategize to control protest. Without this collaboration, the ability of police to control the students was markedly lost. Police liaison officers would contact those on Facebook who were marked as administrators of action pages, or those who simply appeared to be more active posting on protest pages to ask for details of actions. Of course the young activists, some of whom had been on few if any actions previously, were oblivious to such "requirements," leaving the police on the back heel.

A change occurred in the first student mass demonstration in November 2010 when a curiously low level of policing meant they were unable to prevent protesters raiding the Conservative Party Headquarters at Millbank Tower in London. Whereas corporate media coverage was not wholly opposed to the student protests, their framing followed a predictable pattern—a focus on violence, that was initiated by students, the principle of opposing fee rises imposed by a government coalition that included a party that had a manifesto commitment to eradicate fees was understood as long as it would take nonviolent and ineffective form. The focus then turned to giving space to calls by the ineffective student union leadership for ineffective "lobbying" whilst marginalizing the more effective forms of direct action.

As the university occupations went on, the police were moved in to clear some, whereas others petered out. The mass demonstration on the day of the vote on fees in Parliament on December 9, 2010, saw the state turn to repressive techniques. Over the previous 10 years, in order to "contain" anti-capitalist protesters, the police had developed a method of "kettling." Kettling is a strategy of "allowing" a protest to take place but entirely surrounding it by police, thus completely controlling its movements.

Although many activists were aware of the illegality of this method of repression, naturally the corporate media was unwilling to describe it as the outrageous human rights abuse it was—effectively preventing freedom of association. In the December 2010 protest, the police kettled thousands of students, many of whom were only children, for up to seven hours. Early on in the kettle the police launched a cavalry charge against the children, and at least one protester—Alfie Meadows—was beaten almost to death.[44]

All of these repressive instances were photographed, filmed, written about, and distributed through YouTube, Twitter, Flikr, and Facebook. Whereas perhaps many lacked the vocabulary and legal knowledge to understand the police repression as human rights abuses, at least a light was shone on it. However, none of this was reported as repression in the corporate media. Moreover, the increase in fees was never articulated as a human rights abuse, in breach, as it was, of Article 13/2/c of the International Covenant on Economic, Social and Cultural Rights. Rather, the usual process was explicated by the corporate media—a group of violent thugs, egged on by an "anarchist minority" and "professional troublemakers" decided to attack the police for no reason! For example, the *Daily Mail* reported "Defacing the Cenotaph, urinating on Churchill . . . how young thugs at student protest broke every taboo,"[45] while the *Telegraph*[46] explained (after children had been cavalry-charged, beaten, and held en mass) "Gangs of anarchists joined student protests against tuition fees that turned into violent attacks on police and systematic vandalism of property, the Cenotaph and even Trafalgar Square's Christmas tree."

A year later, in 2011, on the back of growing youth unemployment and impoverishment, educational policies that manifestly excluded the poorer sections of society, cuts to public investment, almost total political and economic exclusion, and after a local suspected drug dealer was executed by police in the street, the London borough of Tottenham rioted. The riots spread around London and then to other cities around the U.K., including Manchester, Birmingham, Bristol, Liverpool, and most of the major cities.

Within hours of the riots starting, the elite explanatory framework was set. The Prime Minister, Home Secretary, and much of the corporate media had realized: lazy but greedy young people with bad parents had spontaneously decided to go stealing because they were bad people. This was made possible by Facebook, Twitter, and Blackberry Messaging. As a consequence, Prime Minister David Cameron announced on August 11, 2011,

> Everyone watching these horrific actions will be struck by how they were organized via social media. Free flow of information can be used for good. But it can also be used for ill . . .
>
> And when people are using social media for violence we need to stop them. So we are working with the police, the intelligence services and industry to look at whether it would be right to stop people communicating via these websites and services when we know they are plotting violence, disorder and criminality.

Perhaps unsurprisingly, given their history of selective coverage,[47] this latter suggestion of shutting down social media was almost completely ignored by media rights organizations.

In both the student demonstrations and the 2011 riots, social media were clearly useful for organizing and for reporting on the actions. Particularly in relation to the student demonstrations as well as the anti-cuts movement, tax justice movement, and of course the global Occupy movement, social media filled a gap for publicizing and arranging actions, reporting on them, and communicating internally and externally.

The use of social media became part of the corporate media discourse on protest. At home it could now rail against the "violent minority" and these dangerous new media. Abroad, the Arab Spring protesters were celebrated, their actions championed, and any problematic elements obscured by the dominant rhetoric about the core and shared motivation for the revolution being a commitment to liberal democracy. In one indicative piece, a BBC reporter reports with great enthusiasm (and positioned among the protesters) that Egyptian protesters were throwing rocks and collecting Molotov cocktails to throw at police. The protesters who'd been attacked were treated sympathetically, almost as home soldiers returning from a tour of duty. In contrast, not a single violent act in the U.K. was explained or understood, and certainly not championed, and those who were beaten, assaulted, locked up, and falsely imprisoned in kettles were roundly ignored.[48]

SOCIAL MEDIA AS PANOPTICON: PROTEST AND THE FREEDOM TO BE WATCHED

Whereas social media may well be useful for activists, it is also perhaps the greatest surveillance opportunity offered to the police and security services. In the first instance, the police have become significant users of social media. Gorringe and his colleagues[49] and Waddington[50] have shown how social media can be used to gently influence, manage, and direct protesters (in keeping with the British tradition of policing)[51] and Denef and his colleagues[52] compare effective strategies of "consensual" policing using Twitter during the 2011 U.K. riots.

More crucially, the police began to monitor social media. As mentioned, during the student protests, police liaison officers were monitoring Facebook and other sources to find contacts with whom they could liaise. The visibility of certain activists would prove costly—they became targets of police repression. In Bristol, a number of activists were arrested and held, in many cases identified through their social media interaction, resulting in dawn raids, arrests, and confiscation of equipment. Such surveillance was not new, with IMCs having been subject to such repression for many years.[53] However, the difference was that raids and arrests at IMCs saw a significant reaction from journalist and media rights groups. In contrast, as many individual activists were acting precisely as individuals, there was far less recognition of their plight.

The selective recognition of repression in liberal states comes into the starkest relief when compared with coverage of repression elsewhere. The behavior of "official enemies" towards online activists is well documented. In 2005, Reporters Without Frontiers listed some 15 states it considered to be "enemies-of-the-Internet" and 70 "cyberdissidents" imprisoned by oppressive regimes, although dissidents repressed in "non-oppressive" regimes, such as those in the table below, seem not to register. Raids on IMCs in London in 2004 and Bristol 2005, were hardly on the radar of international "media rights" organizations, even though we can see in Table 12.1 such actions are not rare.

Table 12.1.   Police actions against Independent Media Centers

Seattle, U.S., May 2001	FBI demand IMC logs and impose gag order on IMC
Ohio, U.S., May 2001	IMC domain owner served subpoena to appear before Ohio grand jury and release IP logs
Genoa, Italy, August 2001	Raid of IMC centre & hospitalization of journalist at anti-G8 protests
Ottawa, Canada, November 2001	IMC camera operator arrested at anti-IMF/World Bank demonstration
Georgia, U.S., November 2001	Arrest of IMC journalist at demo against School of the Americas
Copenhagen, January 2002	IMC journalist arrested at EU Summit demonstration
Italy, March 2002	Police raids on "IMC offices" in Bologna, Florence, Turin, Taranto
Israel, May 2002	Investigation into IMC Israel after publication of 'Factories of Death' article
South Africa, September 2002	Arrest of IMC journalist, dispute over accreditation
Washington D.C., U.S., September 2002	Two IMC journalists arrested in anti-WTO/World Bank demonstration
Argentina, October, 2002	Two IMC journalists shot with rubber bullets while covering arrest of environmental activists
Sydney, Australia, November 2002	Arrest of IMC journalist in anti-WTO demonstration
Urbana, U.S., May 2003	Urbana-Champaign Independent Media Center closed down for fire code violations
St. Louis, U.S., May 2003	Police search IMC St. Louis offices
Argentina, June 2003	IMC participant beaten covering demonstration outside textile factory
Evian, June 2003	Raid of IMC offices, IMC journalist shot in leg at anti-G8 demonstration
Dublin, July 2003	IMC journalist arrested at EU Summit demonstration

Seattle, U.S., May 2001	FBI demand IMC logs and impose gag order on IMC
Miami, U.S., November 2003	Assault and arrest of 4 IMC journalists during demonstrations against the Free Trade Area of the Americas
Miami, U.S., November 2003	Arrest of IMC journalist covering a jail solidarity rally
Israel, December 2003	Investigation of IMC Israel for "incitement"
Thailand, April 2004	Arrest of IMC journalist
Cyprus, July 2004	CIA ask U.S. embassy to instruct Cyprus Criminal Investigation Division of police to investigate IMC participant for posting information to website
New York, U.S., August 2004	5–7 Indymedia participants arrested at Republican National Convention
New York, U.S., August 2004	U.S. Justice Department subpoena ISP Calyx for the IP address of a post on the New York IMC Website
New York, U.S., September 2004	NYPD subpoena NYC IMC for an IP address relating to the posting of a purported internal NYPD memorandum during the Republican Convention
New York, U.S., November 2004	New York City subpoena NYC IMC list of information relating to a civil suit related to suppression of Animal and Earth Liberation March.
Trafalgar Square, London, October 2004	Arrest of IMC participant at European Social Forum
London, October 2004	IMC server seized
San Diego, U.S., January 2005.	IMC journalistarrested during "Reclaim the Streets" action
Goiania, Brazil, February 2005	Arrest of two IMC journalists during eviction
Warsaw, Poland, May 2005	Arrest of IMC journalist after filming anti-war demonstration
Bristol, England, June 2005	Seizure of IMC server and arrest of journalist
Tomball, Texas, U.S., June 2005	Arrest of IMC journalist at anti-KKK rally
California, U.S., July 2005	Arrest of IMC participant for littering.
Manila, Philippines, July 2005	IMC journalist arrested during protest at U.S. Embassy
Arizona, U.S., July 2005	IMC journalist arrested for trespass
Paris, August 2005	IMC journalist summoned to court over publication of anti-Jewish spam & republication of revolutionary leaflet
London, October 2005	IMC journalistarrested at anarchist book fair
Oaxaca, Mexico, October 2006	IMC reporter shot and killed filming armed assault on a Popular Assembly

Although many of the actions against IMC participants resulted from their dual role as protesters and media activists, the raids on IMCs certainly serve to mark out a key difference between them and social media—the raids took place precisely because IMCs consciously protect activists and their online interactions. Both the London and Bristol raids were preceded by requests from security forces to disclose IP addresses, something that IMCs fought against on principle. In contrast, commercial social media have no such scruples.

That social media content may be under surveillance is sometimes recognized by activists. Certainly during the occupations many activists would have a public profile while using "safe" discussion groups and email accounts as well as private Facebook pages. Indeed it was telling that Cameron's assertion that the 2011 riots were organized via social media was found by researchers not only to be false, but it also presumed the rioters and other activists weren't aware of police surveillance. Indeed, the research into the riots conducted by *The Guardian* and the London School of Economics found that

> while politicians, journalists and police were constantly tweeting about the disorder, rioters were not. Perhaps unsurprisingly, those taking part in the looting and violence were mostly avoiding communicating on public forums. . . .
>
> "The Internet and that is a bit too bait, so no one really broadcasts it on the Internet," said one Hackney rioter. "Like in Twitter there's like a hashtag innit, like if someone hashtags riots you can go to that certain page and see what everyone has been saying about the riots. Police could easily go to that page there and see who's been setting up or organising groups to come."[54]

The concerns expressed here were not without foundation. After the riots, the state clampdown was swift, broad, and disproportionate. The corporate media celebrated with relish that more than 3000 people were swept up in a post-riot dragnet. They enthused about the lack of judicial process and cheered the fact that poor inner-city youth would be sent to prison without the "privilege" of adequate legal representation. International media rights groups were silent when one youth received three years in prison for posting on Facebook whereas four others received four years in prison for "incitement" on Facebook (when no riots actually resulted from their comments). Indeed police engagement with social media that had preceded the riots enabled them to sharpen their surveillance skills, which could now be turned to repressive means.

In fact, Cameron's suggestion that social media should be shut down in response to the riots ran counter to the very British method of permissive policing. Permissive policing acts in one sense to dissipate power but in another sense to give protesters enough confidence to show themselves for identification. This is to say that shutting down social media would have disabled the police more than anyone else. Moreover it would also have shut down two aspects of civilian social media use—to assist police in their surveillance and to maintain hegemonic understandings of the riots.

In both instances, sousveillance played a crucial role. Social media provided a wealth of information for police forces—in the main through people innocently uploading photographs and videos, sometimes in attempts to publicize the struggles, but with the unintended consequence of drawing police attention to participants. Moreover, social media were used to "name and shame" protestors and rioters. Denef et al.[55] found that the police in the U.K. made significant use of social media to "crowd source" surveillance during the riots.

> [Greater Manchester Police] further promoted their crowd sourcing efforts and launched a campaign entitled 'shop a looter'. Large posters in the city showed the faces of suspects and asked people to help with their identification. Twitter was used to announce the campaign and also to introduce the hashtag #shopalooter

In addition to this use of social media by state security services, less formal means were used to maintain hegemonic understandings of the riots. As with other forms of protest that turn violent, the overwhelming preoccupation with corporate media is to prevent any attempt to explain or understand what happened at home, encouraging the mythical understanding of violence as caused by pathological individuals bent on violence. This understanding pervaded social media, the most common use of it was to condemn the rioters and forbid understanding and explanation. Indeed, Procter and his colleagues found a constant repression of such attempts to understand. They point to a Tweet that tried to explain,

> This is what happens when you consistently opress [sic] the youth, have some of your own medicine #londonriots' but suggested this reflected a "tiny fraction of tweeters? and those who did to explain, understand or support "were typically swamped with a deluge of overwhelmingly negative responses . . . The broader reaction was simpler still: such messages were overwhelmingly ignored.?[56]

At the same time, although, Procter explains, "we do find strong evidence that Twitter was a valuable tool for mobilising support for the post-riot clean-up and for organising specific clean-up activities." Indeed in their analysis of riot Tweets, they found that of the 10 most retweeted messages, three were from Piers Morgan (living in the United States and with no knowledge of the riots whatsoever), one was a campaign to get Blackberry to shut down, two were links to sites to identify rioters, three were imploring people to help "tidy up" after the riots and one was a corporate news report. All were intensely negative toward the rioters, amplifying the notion that they were simply "yobs," not protesters, "scummy wankers," and so on.[57]

Since the riots, police in the U.K. and elsewhere have continued to sharpen social media surveillance. In the run up to the funeral of former British Prime Minister Margaret Thatcher, parties were held across the country to celebrate her death. In the first instance, social media was again used to attack those in attendance. The right wing press did its best to "name and shame" those in attendance—especially those organizing the parties and administering the Facebook pages, as a form of social tyranny that J.S. Mill had pointed to a century and a half before. Given the levels of animosity toward Thatcher held by vast sections of the population, the corporate media attempt to stimulate hostility toward the parties failed. On the other hand, the parties saw the policing of social media return. One person in Bristol was arrested and held without charge for 23 hours for posting onto his Facebook wall that he was attending the party. Moreover, the police were monitoring social media sites for details on arrangements.

From all this came the call for a professionalization of social media surveillance, with the "liberal left" think tank *Demos* calling for the establishment of

> one central command for monitoring social media intelligence and encouraging local constabularies use social media to work with law-abiding members of the community would go a long way to ensure officers are better equipped to meet the challenges of 21st century policing.[58]

Whereas the presumption is that social media simply provide yet another space for surveillance, activists in liberal states ought to take note of their own security. Whereas the "old" new media, such as Indymedia, were in every way activist media, and the participants upheld a strong commitment to protecting the identity of other activists and protesters, the newer social media have no such commitments—a judgment recently confirmed in the Edward Snowden case.

NOTES

1. This chapter was written before the spy controversy in which former NSA employee Edward Snowden released details of the U.S. and U.K. governments' massive spy operations in which it was shown how Microsoft, Facebook, and Google were cooperating with governments in universal surveillance.
2. Janet Jones and Royston Martin, "Crypto-hierarchy and its Discontents: Indymedia UK," in *Making Our Media, Global Initiatives Toward a Democratic Public Sphere*: Vol. 1, eds. Clemencia Rodriguez et al. (New Jersey: Hampton Press, 2010).
3. Lisa Brooten, "Digital Deconstruction: The Independent Media Center as a Process of Collective Critique" in *Global Media Goes to War*, ed. Ralph

Berenger (Spokane: Marquette Books, 2004); Victor Pickard, "United Yet Autonomous: Indymedia and the Struggle to Sustain a Radical Democratic Network," *Media, Culture and Society* 28, no. 3 (2006): 315–336; Jenny Pickerill, "'Autonomy Online': Indymedia and Practices Of Alter-Globalisation," *Environment and Planning* 39 (2007): 2668–2684; Lee Salter, "Democracy & Online News: Indymedia and the Limits of Participatory Media," [online] *Scan: Journal of Media, Arts, Culture* 3, no. 1 (2006); Lee Salter, *Conflicting Forms of Use: The Potential of and Limits to the Use of the Internet as a Public Sphere* (Saarbrücken: VDM Verlag, 2010).

4. Lee Salter, *Conflicting Forms of Use*.
5. Jones and Martin, "Crypto-hierarchy."
6. Lee Salter, "New Social Movements and the Internet: A Habermasian Analysis," in *Cyberactivism: Online Activism in Theory and Practice*, Martha McCaughey and Michael D. Ayers (New York: Routledge, 2003), 117–144; Lee Salter, *Conflicting Forms of Use*.
7. Lincoln Dahlberg, "The Corporate Colonization of Online Attention and the Marginalization of Critical Communication?" *The Journal of Communication Inquiry* 29, no. 2 (2004): 160–180.
8. Project for Excellence in Journalism, *State of the News Media 2008*, last modified July 16, 2013, http://stateofthemedia.org/2008/overview/ownership/.
9. Project for Excellence in Journalism, *State of the News Media 2010*, last modified July 16, 2013, http://stateofthemedia.org/2010/online-summary-essay/ownership/.
10. Nic Newman, *Reuters Institute Digital News Report 2012: Tracking the Future of the News* (Oxford: Reuters, 2012).
11. Hitwise, *Celeb and Entertainment Searches Dominate Google News*, last modified June 13, 2011, http://weblogs.hitwise.com/robin-goad/2009/03/celeb_and_entertainment_searches_google_news_uk.html 2009.
12. Project for Excellence in Journalism, *State of the News Media 2005*, last modified July 16, 2013, http://stateofthemedia.org/2005/online-intro/ownership/.
13. Project for Excellence in Journalism, "Digital: As Mobile Grows Rapidly, the Pressures on News Intensify," last modified May 2013, http://stateofthemedia.org/2013/digital-as-mobile-grows-rapidly-the-pressures-on-news-intensify/.
14. Robert McChesney, "The Titanic Sails On: Why the Internet Won't Sink the Media Giants," in *Gender, Race and Class in Media*, Gail Dines and Jean Humez (London: Sage, 2002).
15. Lee Salter, "Structure and Forms of Use: A Contribution to Understanding the Role of the Internet in Deliberative Democracy," *Information, Communication and Society* 7, no. 2 (2004): 185–206.
16. Richard Rogers, ed., *Preferred Placement* (Maastricht: Jan van Eyek Akademie, 2000).
17. Nic Newman, *Reuters Institute Digital News Report 2012*, 46.
18. Nic Newman, *Reuters Institute Digital News Report 2012*, 34.
19. Lee Salter, "Crises, Radical Online Journalism and the State," in *The Handbook of Global Online Journalism*, E. Siapera and A. Veglis (London: Wiley Blackwell, 2012).
20. Emad Mekay, "One Libyan Battle is Fought in Social and News Media" *New York Times*, (February 23, 2011), last modified April 2011, www.nytimes.com/2011/02/24/world/middleeast/24iht-m24libya.html.
21. "Did social media create Egypt's revolution?" BBC, (February 11, 2011), last modified April 2011, www.bbc.co.uk/news/world-middle-east-12435550.
22. Einar Thorsen, "Live Blogging and Social Media Curation: Challenges and Opportunities for Journalism" in *Journalism: New Challenges*, eds. Karen Fowler-Watt and Stuart Allan (London: Pearson 2013, forthcoming).

23. Jean Burgess and Axel Bruns, "(NOT) The Twitter Election: The Dynamics of the #ausvotes Conversation in Relation to the Australian Media Ecology," *Journalism Practice* 6, no. 3 (2012): 384–402.
24. Andrew Chadwick, "The Political Information Cycle in a Hybrid News System: The British Prime Minister and the 'Bullygate' Affair," *The International Journal of Press/Politics* 16, no. 3 (2011): 3–29.
25. Dominic Lasorsa, Seth Lewis, and Avery Holton, "Normalizing Twitter," *Journalism Studies* 13, no. 1 (2012): 19–36.
26. Thomas Poell and Erik Borra, "Twitter, YouTube, and Flickr as Platforms of Alternative Journalism: The Social Media Account of the 2010 Toronto G20 Protests," *Journalism* 13, no. 6 (2012): 695–713.
27. Steve Mann, "Sousveillance," (2002), last modified May 21, 2012, http://wearcam.org/sousveillance.htm.
28. Steve Mann, "Sousveillance: Inverse surveillance in multimedia imaging," *International Multimedia Conference: Proceedings of the 12th ACM International Conference,* New York, October 10–16, 2004, p.620.
29. Jean-Gabriel Ganascia, "The Great Catopticon," (2010), last modified May 23, 2013, www-poleia.lip6.fr/˜ganascia/Catopticon.
30. Jean-Gabriel Ganascia, "The Generalized Sousveillance Society," *Social Science Information* 49, no. 3 (2010): 498.
31. Jean-Gabriel Ganascia, "The Generalized Sousveillance Society," 494.
32. See Stuart Hall et al., *Policing the Crisis* (London: Palgrave, 1978); Edward Herman and Noam Chomsky, *Manufacturing Consent: The Political Economy of the Mass Media* (London: Vintage, 1994); Graham Murdoch, "Large Corporations and the Control of the Communications Industries," in *Culture, Society and the Media,* Michael Gurrevitch et al. (London: Routledge, 1982); Peter Golding and Graham Murdoch, "Culture, Communications and Political Economy," in *Mass Media and Society*, J. James Curran and Michael Gurevitch (London: Arnold, 2000); Deepa Kumar " 'What's Good for UPS Is Good for America': Nation and Class in Network Television News Coverage of the UPS Strike," *Television and New Media* 6, no. 2 (2005): 131–52.
33. Jilly Finola and Lee Salter, "Framing the Cuts. An Analysis of the BBC's Discursive Framing of the Condem Cuts Agenda," *Journalism: Theory, Practice, Criticism* (forthcoming).
34. Jurgen Habermas, *The Theory of Communicative Action: The Critique of Functionalist Reason*, trans. Thomas McCarthy (Cambridge: Polity Press, 1987).
35. Clark McPhail and John McCarthy, "Protest Mobilization, Repression and Their Interaction," in *Repression and Mobilization (Social Movements, Protest, and Contention)*, Christian Davenport et al. (Minnesota: University of Minnesota Press, 2005).
36. Giorgio Agamben, *State of Exception* (Chicago: University of Chicago Press, 2005), 87.
37. Jurgen Habermas, *Legitimation Crisis* (London: Heinemann, 1976).
38. Oskar Negt and Alexander Kluge, *The Public Sphere and Experience: An Analysis of the Bourgeois and Proletarian Public Sphere*, trans. Peter Labanyi, Jamie Daniel, and Assenka Oksiloff (Minnesota: University of Minnesota Press, 1993).
39. Lee Salter, *Conflicting Forms of Use.*
40. Dorothy Kidd, "Carnival to Commons," in *Confronting Capitalism: Dispatches from a Global Movement*, eds. Daniel Rose, Eddie Yuen, and George Katsiaficas (New York: Soft Skull Press, 2004); Sasha Costanza-Chock, "The Globalization of Resistance to Capitalist Communication," in *Media in the*

Age of Marketization, eds. Graham Murdock and Janet Wasko (Creskill, NJ: Hampton Press, 2007).

41. Michael Chanan and Lee Salter, *Secret City* (London, E2Films, 2013).
42. The following account is based on three months of observation of in par-ticular the occupation at the University of the West of England and student demonstrations and actions in Bristol and London, U.K. See Lee Salter and Jilly Finola "The UWE Occupation," *Social Movement Studies* 10, no. 4 (2011): 423–429.
43. Lee Salter, "Crises, Radical Online Journalism and the State."
44. Michael Mansfield, "A Dangerous Use of Police Force to Quell Protest," last modified July 3, 2013, www.guardian.co.uk/commentisfree/2013/mar/10/dangerous-police-protest-alfie-meadows.
45. "Defacing the Cenotaph, rinating on Churchill . . . How Young Thugs at Student Protest Broke Every Taboo," *Daily Mail,* last modified July 4, 2013, www.dailymail.co.uk/news/article-1337315/TUITION-FEES-VOTE-PRO TEST-Thugs-deface-Cenotaph-urinate-Churchill.html.
46. "Tuition Fees Protesters Attack Police and Vandalise Buildings," *Telegraph,* last modified July 4, 2013, www.telegraph.co.uk/news/uknews/theroyalfam ily/8193376/Tuition-fees-protesters-attack-police-and-vandalise-buildings. html.
47. Noam Chomsky and Edward Herman, *The Political Economy of Human Rights Volume II After The Cataclysm* (Nottingham: Spokesman, 1979); Connor Foley "Beware Human Rights Imperialism," *The Guardian,* last modified July 4, 2013, www.guardian.co.uk/commentisfree/2009/jun/23/human-rights-imperialism-western-values; Silvio Waisbord, "Can NGOs Change the News?" *International Journal of Communication* no. 5 (2011): 142–165.
48. I've provided a link to a collection of indicative news clips here: Egypt: http://youtu.be/_ON4F_jjGrQ UK student protests http://youtu.be/FPGLrFLdxNc.
49. Hugo Gorringe, Clifford Stott, and Michael Rosie, "Dialogue Police, Deci-sion Making, and the Management of Public Order during Protest Crowd Events," *Journal of Investigative Psychology and Offender Profiling* no. 9 (2012): 111–125.
50. David Waddington, "A 'Kinder Blue': Analysing the Police Management of the Sheffield Anti-'Lib Dem' Protest of March 2011," *Policing and Society: An International Journal of Research and Policy* 23, no. 1 (2013): 46–64.
51. Lee Salter, "Crises, Radical Online Journalism and the State."
52. Sebastian Denef, Petra Bayerl, and Nico Kaptein, "Social Media and the Police—Tweeting Practices of British Police Forces during the August 2011 Riots," *CHI 2013,* (April 27–May 2, 2013), Paris, France.
53. Lee Salter, "Independent Media Centres and the Law: Some Problems for Citizen Journalism," in *Citizen Journalism: Global Perspectives*, eds. Stuart Allan and Einar Thorsen (New York: Peter Lang, 2009).
54. James Ball and Paul Lewis, "Twitter and the Riots: How the News Spread," *The Guardian,* (December 11, 2011), last modified July 17, 2013, www. theguardian.com/uk/2011/dec/07/twitter-riots-how-news-spread.
55. Sebastian Denef et al., "Social Media and the Police."
56. James Ball and Paul Lewis, "Twitter and the Riots."
57. James Ball and Paul Lewis, "Twitter and the Riots."
58. "Hire Social Media Chiefs to Put 'Twitter Snooping' on a Legal Footing, Think-Tank Tells Police," Demos, last modified July 17, 2013, www.demos. co.uk/press_releases/hiresocialmediachiefstoputtwittersnoopingonalegalfoo tingthinktanktellspolice.

REFERENCES

Agamben, Giorgio. *State of Exception.* Chicago: University of Chicago Press, 2005.

Ball, James and Paul Lewis. "Twitter and the Riots: How the News Spread." *The Guardian.* December 11, 2011. www.theguardian.com/uk/2011/dec/07/twitter-riots-how-news-spread (accessed July 17, 2013).

BBC. "Did Social Media Create Egypt's Revolution?" February 11, 2011. www.bbc.co.uk/news/world-middle-east-12435550 (accessed April 2011).

Brooten, Lisa. "Digital Deconstruction: The Independent Media Center as a Process of Collective Critique." In *Global Media Goes to War,* edited by Ralph Berenger. Spokane: Marquette Books, 2004.

Burgess, Jean, and Axel Bruns. "(NOT) The Twitter Election: The Dynamics of the #ausvotes Conversation in Relation to the Australian Media Ecology." *Journalism Practice* 6, no. 3 (2012):.384–402.

Chadwick, Andrew. "The Political Information Cycle in a Hybrid News System: The British Prime Minister and the 'Bullygate' Affair." *The International Journal of Press/Politics* 16, no. 3 (2011): 3–29.

Chanan, Michael, and Lee Salter. *Secret City.* London: E2Films, 2013.

Chomsky, Noam, and Edward Herman. *The Political Economy of Human Rights Volume II after the Cataclysm.* Nottingham: Spokesman, 1979.

Costanza-Chock, Sasha. "The Globalization of Resistance to Capitalist Communication." In *Media in the Age of Marketization*, edited by Graham Murdock and Janet Wasko. Creskill, NJ: Hampton Press, 2007.

Dahlberg, Lincoln. "The Corporate Colonization of Online Attention and the Marginalization of Critical Communication?" *The Journal of Communication Inquiry* 29, no. 2 (2004): 160–180.

Daily Mail "Defacing the Cenotaph, Urinating on Churchill . . . How Young Thugs at Student Protest Broke Every Taboo." www.dailymail.co.uk/news/article-1337315/TUITION-FEES-VOTE-PROTEST-Thugs-deface-Cenotaph-urinate-Churchill.html (accessed July 4, 2013).

Demos. "Policing in an Information Age." 2013. www.demos.co.uk/publications/policinginaninformationage (accessed May 4, 2013).

Denef, Sebastian, Petra Bayerl, and Nico Kaptein. "Social Media and the Police—Tweeting Practices of British Police Forces during the August 2011 Riots" *CHI 2013*, April 27–May 2, 2013, Paris, France.

Finola, Jilly, and Lee Salter. "Framing the Cuts. An Analysis of the BBC's Discursive Framing of the Condem Cuts Agenda." *Journalism: Theory, Practice, Criticism* (forthcoming).

Foley, Connor. "Beware Human Rights Imperialism." *The Guardian.* June 23, 2009. www.guardian.co.uk/commentisfree/2009/jun/23/human-rights-imperialism-western-values (accessed July 4, 2013).

Ganascia, Jean-Gabriel. "The Generalized Sousveillance Society." *Social Science Information* 49, no. 3 (2010): 489–507.

Ganascia, Jean-Gabriel. "The Great Catopticon." 2010. www-poleia.lip6.fr/ˉganascia/Catopticon (accessed May 23 2013).

Golding, Peter, and Graham Murdoch. "Culture, Communications and Political Economy." In *Mass Media and Society*, J. James Curran and Michael Gurevitch. London: Arnold, 2000.

Gorringe, Hugo, Clifford Stott, and Michael Rosie. "Dialogue Police, Decision Making, and the Management of Public Order During Protest Crowd Events." *Journal of Investigative Psychology and Offender Profiling* no. 9 (2012): 111–125.

Habermas, Jurgen. *Legitimation Crisis.* London: Heinemann, 1976.

Habermas, Jurgen. *The Theory of Communicative Action: The Critique of Functionalist Reason.* Translated by Thomas McCarthy. Cambridge: Polity Press, 1987.

Hall, Stuart et al. *Policing the Crisis.* London: Palgrave, 1978.

Herman, Edward, and Noam Chomsky. *Manufacturing Consent: The Political Economy of the Mass Media.* London: Vintage, 1994.

Hitwise. "Celeb and Entertainment Searches Dominate Google News." http://weblogs.hitwise.com/robin-goad/2009/03/celeb_and_entertainment_searches_google_news_uk.html 2009 (accessed June 13, 2011).

Jones, Janet, and Royston Martin. "Crypto-hierarchy and its Discontents: Indymedia UK." In *Making Our Media, Global Initiatives Toward a Democratic Public Sphere*: Vol. 1, edited by Clemencia Rodriguez et al. New Jersey: Hampton Press, 2010.

Kidd, Dorothy. "Carnival to Commons." In *Confronting Capitalism: Dispatches from a Global Movement*, edited by Daniel Rose, Eddie Yuen, and George Katsiaficas. New York: Softskull Press, 2004.

Kumar, Deepa. " 'What's good for UPS is good for America': Nation and Class in Network Television News Coverage of the UPS Strike." *Television and New Media* 6, no. 2 (2005): 131–52.

Lasorsa, Dominic, Seth Lewis and Avery Holton. "Normalizing Twitter." *Journalism Studies* 13, no. 1 (2013): 19–36.

Mann, Steve. "Sousveillance." 2002. http://wearcam.org/sousveillance.htm (accessed May 21, 2012).

Mann, Steve. "Sousveillance: Inverse Surveillance in Multimedia Imaging." *International Multimedia Conference: Proceedings of the 12th ACM International Conference*, New York, October 10–16, 2004, 620.

Mansfield, Michael. "A Dangerous Use of Police Force to Quell Protest." www.guardian.co.uk/commentisfree/2013/mar/10/dangerous-police-protest-alfie-meadows (accessed March 7, 2013).

McChesney, Robert. "The Titanic Sails On: Why the Internet Won't Sink the Media Giants." In *Gender, Race and Class in Media*, Gail Dines and Jean Humez. London: Sage, 2002.

McPhail, Clark, and John McCarthy. "Protest Mobilization, Repression and Their Interaction." In *Repression and Mobilization (Social Movements, Protest, and Contention)*, Christian Davenport et al. Minnesota: University of Minnesota Press, 2005.

Mekay, Emad. "One Libyan Battle Is Fought in Social and News Media." *New York Times.* February 23, 2011. www.nytimes.com/2011/02/24/world/middleeast/24iht-m24libya.html (accessed April 19, 2011).

Murdoch, Graham. "Large Corporations and the Control of the Communications Industries." In *Culture, Society and the Media*, Michael Gurrevitch et al. London: Routledge, 1982.

Negt, Oskar, and Alexander Kluge. *The Public Sphere and Experience: An Analysis of the Bourgeois and Proletarian Public Sphere,* translated by Peter Labanyi, Jamie Daniel, and Assenka Oksiloff. Minnesota: University of Minnesota Press, 1993.

Newman, Nic. *Reuters Institute Digital News Report 2012: Tracking the Future of the News.* Oxford: Reuters, 2012.

Pickard, Victor. "United Yet Autonomous: Indymedia and the Struggle to Sustain a Radical Democratic Network." In *Media, Culture and Society* 28, no. 3 (2006): 315–336.

Pickerill, Jenny. " 'Autonomy Online': Indymedia and Practices of Alter-globalisation." *Environment and Planning* no. 39 (2007): 2668.

Poell, Thomas, and Erik Borra. "Twitter, YouTube, and Flickr as Platforms of Alternative Journalism: The Social Media Account of the 2010 Toronto G20 Protests." *Journalism* 13, no. 6 (2012): 695–713.

Project for Excellence in Journalism. *State of the News Media 2005.* http://stateoft hemedia.org/2005/online-intro/ownership/ (accessed July 16, 2013).

Project for Excellence in Journalism. *State of the News Media 2008.* http://stateoft hemedia.org/2008/overview/ownership/ (accessed July 16, 2013).

Project for Excellence in Journalism. *State of the News Media 2012* http://stateoft hemedia.org/files/2012/08/2012_sotm_annual_report.pdf (accessed April 19, 2012).

Project for Excellence in Journalism. "Digital: As Mobile Grows Rapidly, the Pressures on News Intensify." 2013. http://stateofthemedia.org/2013/digital-as-mo bile-grows-rapidly-the-pressures-on-news-intensify/ (accessed May 4, 2013).

Rogers, Richard (ed.). *Preferred Placement*. Maastricht: Jan van Eyek Akademie, 2000.

Salter, Lee. "New Social Movements and the Internet: A Habermasian Analysis." In *Cyberactivism: Online Activism in Theory and Practice*, Michael Ayers and Martha McCaughey (pp.117–144). New York: Routledge 2003.

Salter, Lee. "Structure and Forms of Use: A Contribution to Understanding the Role of the Internet in Deliberative Democracy." *Information, Communication and Society* 7, no. 2 (2004): 185–206.

Salter, Lee. "Democracy & Online News: Indymedia and the Limits of Participatory Media." [online] *Scan: Journal of Media, Arts, Culture* 3, no. 1 (2006).

Salter, Lee. "Independent Media Centres and the Law: Some Problems for Citizen Journalism." In *Citizen Journalism: Global Perspectives*, Stuart Allan and Einar Thorsen. New York: Peter Lang, 2009.

Salter, Lee. *Conflicting Forms of Use: The Potential of and Limits to the Use of the Internet as a Public Sphere*. Saarbrücken VDM Verlag, 2010.

Salter, Lee. "Crises, Radical Online Journalism and the State." In *The Handbook of Global Online Journalism*, E. Siapera and A. Veglis. London: Wiley Blackwell, 2012.

Salter, Lee, and Jilly Finola "The UWE Occupation." *Social Movement Studies* 10, no. 4 (2011): 423–429.

Telegraph "Tuition Fees Protesters Attack Police and Vandalise Building." www.tele graph.co.uk/news/uknews/theroyalfamily/8193376/Tuition-fees-protesters-attack-police-and-vandalise-buildings.html (accessed July 4, 2013).

Thorsen, Einar. "Live Blogging and Social Media Curation: Challenges and Opportunities for Journalism." In *Journalism: New Challenges*, edited by Karen Fowler-Watt and Stuart Allan. London: Pearson 2013, forthcoming.

Waddington, David. "A 'Kinder Blue': Analysing the Police Management of the Sheffield Anti-'Lib Dem' Protest of March 2011." *Policing and Society: An International Journal of Research and Policy* 23, no. 1 (2013): 46–64.

Waisbord, Silvio. "Can NGOs Change the News?" *International Journal of Communication* no. 5 (2011): 142–165.

List of Contributors

Megan Boler is a professor of media and education at the University of Toronto. Her books include *Digital Media and Democracy: Tactics in Hard Times* (2008, MIT Press) and *DIY Citizenship: Critical Making and Social Media* (eds. Ratto and Boler, forthcoming January 2014, MIT Press). Funded by SSHRC for the last 10 years, her previous research, "Rethinking Media Democracy and Citizenship," examined the motivations of producers of web-based challenges to MSM. Her web-based productions include a study guide to the documentary *The Corporation* (dirs. Achbar and Abbott 2003), and the multimedia website Critical Media Literacy in Times of War.

Rossella Borri is a PhD candidate at the University of Siena, Centre for the Study of Political Change (CIRCaP), where she also obtained a Master's degree in comparative European politics in 2008. She is working on her doctoral project, a comparative work on right-wing radicalism, with a focus on radical right-wing movement organizations in Italy and Spain. In 2012 she collaborated on a project directed by Manuela Caiani on right-wing extremist organizations and the Internet. Her main research interests include political participation, social movements, collective action, right-wing radicalism, and party politics.

Axel Bruns is an associate professor in the Creative Industries Faculty at Queensland University of Technology in Brisbane, Australia, and a Chief Investigator in the ARC Centre of Excellence for Creative Industries and Innovation. He is the author of *Blogs, Wikipedia, Second Life and Beyond: From Production to Produsage* (2008) and *Gatewatching: Collaborative Online News Production* (2005), and a co-editor of *Twitter and Society* (2013), *A Companion to New Media Dynamics* (2012), and *Uses of Blogs* (2006). His research blog is at http://snurb.info/, and he tweets at @snurb_dot_info. See http://mappingonlinepublics.net/ for more details on his current social media research.

Jean Burgess is Deputy Director of the ARC Centre of Excellence for Creative Industries & Innovation and Associate Professor, Digital Media in the Creative Industries Faculty at Queensland University of Technology. Her books include *YouTube: Online Video and Participatory Culture* (2009), *Studying Mobile Media: Cultural Technologies, Mobile Communication, and the iPhone* (2012), and *A Companion to New Media Dynamics* (2013).

Manuela Caiani is an assistant professor at the Institute for Advanced Studies (IHS) in Vienna (on leave) and a Marie Curie fellow at the University Rey Juan Carlos of Madrid for a project on "Disengagement from Terrorism." She has worked on several comparative projects on collective action and Europeanization and on right-wing extremism. Her main research interests concern social movements and collective action, right-wing extremism in Europe and the United States, Europeanization and the public sphere, and political participation and the Internet. Among her publications are: *L'Europeizzazione degli attori domestici: policy networks, mobilitazione e frames sull'Europa* (Bonanno Editore, Roma, 2011); *Mobilizing on the Extreme Right* (with Donatella della Porta and Claudius Wagemann, Oxford University Press, Oxford, 2012); *European and American Extreme Right Groups and the Internet* (with Linda Parenti, Ashgate, 2013); and *Il Web Nero* (Il Mulino, Bologna, 2013).

Jessie Daniels (PhD, UT-Austin) is a professor of public health, sociology and critical psychology at the Graduate Center and Hunter College-CUNY. Daniels is the author of *Cyber Racism* (Rowman & Littlefield, 2009), as well as dozens of peer-reviewed articles in journals such as *New Media & Society, Gender & Society, American Journal of Public Health*, and *Women's Studies Quarterly*.

Maria Garrido is a research assistant professor at the University of Washington's Information School. Her research explores how people, in communities facing social and economic challenges, use information and communication technologies to promote social change. Much of her work focuses on technology appropriation in the context of social movements and in international migration. Maria holds a PhD in Communications from the University of Washington and a master's degree in International Relations from the University of Chicago.

Laura J. Gurak is a professor and founding chair of the Department of Writing Studies in the College of Liberal Arts at the University of Minnesota. She holds an MS in technical communication and a PhD in communication and rhetoric from Rensselaer Polytechnic Institute. Gurak takes a rhetorical approach to her work, investigating the ways in which language both shapes and reflects our uses and perceptions of digital technologies. She is author of *Cyberliteracy: Navigating the Internet with Awareness* (Yale University Press, 2001) and *Persuasion and Privacy in*

Cyberspace: The Online Protests over Lotus MarketPlace and the Clipper Chip (Yale University Press, 1997). *Persuasion and Privacy* was the first book-length work to study the nature of online communities and Internet-based social actions. Current research expands on this work, addressing the nature of trust in all human communication, with an emphasis on virtual and digital settings.

Alexander Halavais is an associate professor in the School of Social and Behavioral Sciences at Arizona State University, where he researches ways in which social media change the nature of scholarship and learning and allow for new forms of collaboration and self-government. He serves as the president of the Association of Internet Researchers, and is affiliated with the Digital Media and Learning Hub at the University of California and the Learning Sciences Institute at ASU. His most recent book was *Search Engine Society* (Polity, 2008).

Tim Highfield is a research fellow in the ARC Centre of Excellence for Creative Industries and Innovation at Queensland University of Technology. He was awarded his PhD in 2011 from Queensland University of Technology for research into political blogging in Australia and France.

Constance Kampf is an associate professor in the Department of Business Communication, Business and Social Sciences at Aarhus University, Denmark, and a member of the Corporate Communication and Knowledge Communication Research Groups.

Dorothy Kidd teaches media studies at the University of San Francisco. After many years as a media producer and activist in community radio, video, and web-based efforts, she is documenting contentious communications practices by social justice movements around the world. Her work has been published in several academic and movement book collections. dorothykidd@academia.org.

John Logie is an associate professor of rhetoric in the Department of Writing Studies at the University of Minnesota-Twin Cities. His work addresses Internet rhetorics, rhetorical invention, authorship, copyright, and visual rhetoric. His 2006 book *Peers, Pirates, and Persuasion* addressed the flawed rhetoric surrounding debates over peer-to-peer downloading. He is currently working on a book titled *Writing in the Cloud* addressing the implications of cloud-based computing for writing, composing, and creative practices.

Martha McCaughey is a professor of sociology at Appalachian State University. Her research examines the convergence of gender, violence, technology, and privacy, with a current project on cyberrape. She is the editor (with Michael D. Ayers) of *Cyberactivism: Online Activism in Theory and Practice* (2003).

Christina Nitsou is a Masters of Arts part-time graduate student in OISE's Humanities, Social Sciences and Social Justice Education program. She currently heads the Student Success Department in a Toronto high school. Most of her time at work is spent connecting with community agencies on programs for disengaged students and creating school-wide initiatives that focus on student participation. This work has given Christina a keen interest in social movements in the online era, and specifically in how these movements play out in the high school environment.

Lee Salter is a lecturer in news media at the School of Media Film and Music at the University of Sussex, UK. His research spans a range of areas, focusing largely on dissent and its representations in corporate and radical media. His recent work on digital media has focused on the uses of social media and protest during the crisis, especially the repressive functions of the state under such circumstances. His work has been published in a range of international journals and edited volumes. His co-authored book, *Digital Journalism,* was published by Sage in 2011. His recent projects include writing and producing the award-winning documentary film *Secret City* with Michael Chanan.

Jennifer Terrell is a doctoral candidate studying social informatics in the School of Informatics and Computing at Indiana University. Building on her background in cultural anthropology, her research explores the ethnographic study of digitally mediated sociality. Her work focuses specifically on participatory culture through the study of Harry Potter fans.

Richard Widick is Co-Director of the International Institute of Climate Action Theory, a visiting scholar at the Orfalea Center for Global and International Studies, and an assistant project scientist in sociology at the University of California, Santa Barbara. He is the author of *Trouble in the Forest: California's Redwood Timber Wars* (University of Minnesota Press, 2009).

Index

Printed and bound by CPI Group (UK) Ltd, Croydon, CR0 4YY

01/11/2024

01782639-0001